Office for Disarmament Affairs
New York, 2019

The United Nations
DISARMAMENT YEARBOOK

Volume 43 (Part I): 2018

Disarmament Resolutions and Decisions
of the Seventy-third Session
of the United Nations General Assembly

Guide to the user

To facilitate early analysis of the resolutions and decisions on disarmament adopted at the seventy-third session of the General Assembly, the United Nations Office for Disarmament Affairs offers Part I of the Yearbook as a handy, concise reference tool, containing the full texts of all the resolutions and decisions, the date of adoption by the Assembly and the First Committee, the agenda item number, the symbol number of the Report of the Rapporteur, the main sponsors and the voting patterns in the Assembly. For a snapshot of this information in a convenient chart, see "Quick view of votes by cluster". For a list of agenda items and their corresponding reports, see the Annex.

Bold type in the list of sponsors indicates the State(s) that submitted the draft resolution or decision.

Voting statistics in this publication are presented as three sets of numbers separated by two dashes, where the first figure represents the total of votes in favour, followed by votes against and abstentions.

Electronically available in PDF or database format at
www.un.org/disarmament

UNITED NATIONS PUBLICATION
Sales No. E.19.IX.3

ISBN 978-92-1-139167-1
eISBN 978-92-1-004074-7
Print ISSN 0252-5607
Online ISSN 2412-1193

Contents

Decisions

Annex

Preface

The *United Nations Disarmament Yearbook* is now in its forty-third year of publication. Part I presents the official texts of the 63 resolutions and 5 decisions related to disarmament, arms control and international security that were debated in the First Committee and forwarded to the General Assembly for adoption at its seventy-third session.

Part I is issued as a separate publication to provide early access to the resolutions and decisions, each presented with key information: relevant agenda items, main sponsors and co-sponsors, vote counts, including voting patterns in the First Committee and the General Assembly, adoption and meeting number dates and draft resolution numbers.

A *Quick view by cluster* gives the reader an easy handle (using the First Committee's "cluster" arrangement of agenda items) on resolution numbers, titles and votes in the First Committee and in the Assembly.

We hope that Part I furnishes the reader with a handy, consolidated reference book on multilateral disarmament, in print and electronic form.

Part II of the Yearbook will contain main multilateral issues under consideration, including their trends, summaries of First Committee and General Assembly actions taken on resolutions and a convenient issue-oriented timeline. Part II is forthcoming in October 2019.

Quick view of votes by cluster (63 resolutions and 5 decisions)*

No.	Title	GA action, 5 Dec. (vote)	First Cttee action (vote, date)
Cluster 1: Nuclear weapons			
73/26	African Nuclear-Weapon-Free Zone Treaty	w/o vote	w/o vote 1 Nov.
73/28	Establishment of a nuclear-weapon-free zone in the region of the Middle East	171-2-5	174-2-5 1 Nov.
73/29	Conclusion of effective international arrangements to assure non-nuclear-weapon States against the use or threat of use of nuclear weapons	125-0-58	122-0-65 1 Nov.
73/40	Follow-up to the 2013 high-level meeting of the General Assembly on nuclear disarmament	143-27-14 129-19-23, p.p. 12	143-27-14 129-20-22, p.p. 12 1 Nov.
73/44	Mongolia's international security and nuclear-weapon-free status	w/o vote	w/o vote 1 Nov.
73/47	Humanitarian consequences of nuclear weapons	142-15-26	143-15-26 1 Nov.
73/48	Treaty on the Prohibition of Nuclear Weapons	126-41-16	122-41-16 1 Nov.
73/49	The Hague Code of Conduct against Ballistic Missile Proliferation	171-1-12	171-1-12 1 Nov.
73/50	Nuclear disarmament	125-40-18 116-38-15, p.p. 32 167-2-6, o.p. 16	120-41-21 117-37-19, p.p. 32 168-2-8, o.p. 16 1 Nov.
73/56	Reducing nuclear danger	126-49-11	127-49-10 1 Nov.
73/57	Universal Declaration on the Achievement of a Nuclear-Weapon-Free-World	138-21-26 128-20-25, p.p. 7 136-3-35, p.p. 9	135-21-27 126-21-26, p.p. 7 137-3-36, p.p. 9 1 Nov.
73/58	Treaty on a Nuclear-Weapon-Free Zone in Central Asia	w/o vote	w/o vote 1 Nov.

---

* Abbreviations: o.p. = operative paragraph; p.p. = preambular paragraph.

No.	Title	GA action, 5 Dec. (vote)	First Cttee action (vote, date)
73/60	Decreasing the operational readiness of nuclear weapons systems	175-5-5 164-2-7, p.p. 8	173-4-7 166-2-10, p.p. 8 1 Nov.
73/62	United action with renewed determination towards the total elimination of nuclear weapons	162-4-23 167-3-10, p.p. 19 168-2-6, p.p. 20 150-5-21, o.p. 2 147-8-22, o.p. 3 175-3-2, o.p. 5 162-3-10, o.p. 7 152-1-26, o.p. 10 148-2-27, o.p. 12 170-3-4, o.p. 13 159-2-20, o.p. 18 174-1-5, o.p. 20 173-2-4, o.p. 21 172-0-8, o.p. 31	160-4-24 164-3-12, p.p. 19 170-2-7, p.p. 20 145-5-23, o.p. 2 139-8-29, o.p. 3 173-3-5, o.p. 5 165-4-11, o.p. 7 152-1-23, o.p. 10 147-2-26, o.p. 12 170-3-6, o.p. 13 158-2-19, o.p. 18 172-2-5, o.p. 20 172-2-5, o.p. 21 170-0-9, o.p. 31 1 Nov.
73/64	Follow-up to the advisory opinion of the International Court of Justice on the legality of the threat or use of nuclear weapons	138-32-17 138-2-31, p.p. 9 118-35-20, p.p. 17 121-35-18, o.p. 2	131-31-19 137-1-35, p.p. 9 118-34-23, p.p. 17 120-34-22, o.p. 2 1 Nov.
73/65	Treaty banning the production of fissile material for nuclear weapons or other nuclear explosive devices	182-1-5	180-1-5 1 Nov.
73/68	Ethical imperatives for a nuclear-weapon-free world	136-36-14 122-29-18, p.p. 11	130-34-18 121-29-22, p.p. 11 1 Nov.
73/70	Towards a nuclear-weapon-free world: accelerating the implementation of nuclear disarmament commitments	139-32-17 139-1-33, p.p. 4 122-35-17, p.p. 12 132-2-41, o.p. 13 162-4-8, o.p. 15 122-36-15, o.p. 24	134-31-18 134-1-36, p.p. 4 120-35-18, p.p. 12 131-2-41, o.p. 13 160-5-9, o.p. 15 122-35-17, o.p. 24 1 Nov.
73/71	Fourth Conference of Nuclear-Weapon-Free Zones and Mongolia, 2020	179-0-5	171-0-6 8 Nov.

No.	Title	GA action, 5 Dec. (vote)	First Cttee action (vote, date)
73/74	Convention on the Prohibition of the Use of Nuclear Weapons	124-50-13	120-50-15 1 Nov.
73/83	The risk of nuclear proliferation in the Middle East	158-6-21 168-3-4, p.p. 5 167-3-4, p.p. 6	158-5-21 170-4-4, p.p. 5 171-3-5, p.p. 6 1 Nov.
73/86	Comprehensive Nuclear-Test-Ban Treaty	183-1-4 167-0-11, p.p. 4 172-0-7, p.p. 7	181-1-4 169-0-13, p.p. 4 170-0-9, p.p. 7 1 Nov.
73/513	Missiles (decision)	174-2-7	166-2-9 1 Nov.
73/514	Nuclear disarmament verification (decision)	181-0-2	177-0-3 1 Nov.
73/546	Convening a conference on the establishment of a Middle East zone free of nuclear weapons and other weapons of mass destruction (decision)	88-4-75 22 Dec.	103-3-71 1 Nov.

Cluster 2: Other weapons of mass destruction

No.	Title	GA action, 5 Dec. (vote)	First Cttee action (vote, date)
73/43	Measures to uphold the authority of the 1925 Geneva Protocol	181-0-2	178-0-2 5 Nov.
73/45	Implementation of the Convention on the Prohibition of the Development, Production, Stockpiling and Use of Chemical Weapons and on Their Destruction	152-7-22 134-7-25, p.p. 4 122-13-26, o.p. 2 122-13-30, o.p. 3 112-18-35, o.p. 4 110-15-38, o.p. 16	148-7-23 128-7-30, p.p. 4 120-14-32, o.p. 2 123-13-33, o.p. 3 113-19-34, o.p. 4 112-15-39, o.p. 16 5 Nov.
73/55	Measures to prevent terrorists from acquiring weapons of mass destruction	w/o vote	w/o vote 5 Nov.
73/66	Preventing the acquisition by terrorists of radioactive sources	w/o vote	w/o vote 5 Nov.
73/87	Convention on the Prohibition of the Development, Production and Stockpiling of Bacteriological (Biological) and Toxin Weapons and on Their Destruction	w/o vote	w/o vote 5 Nov.

No.	Title	GA action, 5 Dec. (vote)	First Cttee action (vote, date)
Cluster 3: Outer space (disarmament aspects)			
73/30	Prevention of an arms race in outer space	178-2-0	181-2-1 5 Nov.
73/31	No first placement of weapons in outer space	128-12-40	129-12-40 5 Nov.
73/72	Transparency and confidence-building measures in outer space activities	180-2-1	176-2-2 5 Nov.
73/512	Further practical measures for the prevention of an arms race in outer space (decision)	128-3-48	127-3-49 5 Nov.
Cluster 4: Conventional weapons			
73/36	The Arms Trade Treaty	151-0-29 158-0-16. p.p. 8 138-0-33, o.p. 4 134-2-35, o.p. 9	151-0-30 153-0-18, p.p. 8 138-0-35, o.p. 4 136-2-35. o.p. 9 6 Nov.
73/51	Information on confidence-building measures in the field of conventional arms	w/o vote	w/o vote 6 Nov.
73/52	Assistance to States for curbing the illicit traffic in small arms and light weapons and collecting them	w/o vote	w/o vote 6 Nov.
73/54	Implementation of the Convention on Cluster Munitions	144-1-38 153-0-18, p.p. 14	139-1-39 152-0-17, p.p. 14 6 Nov.
73/61	Implementation of the Convention on the Prohibition of the Use, Stockpiling, Production and Transfer of Anti-personnel Mines and on Their Destruction	169-0-16	154-0-17 8 Nov.
73/63	Preventing and combating illicit brokering activities	185-1-2 157-0-19, p.p. 9	177-1-2 149-0-20, p.p. 9 6 Nov.
73/67	Countering the threat posed by improvised explosive devices	w/o vote	w/o vote 6 Nov.

No.	Title	GA action, 5 Dec. (vote)	First Cttee action (vote, date)
73/69	The illicit trade in small arms and light weapons in all its aspects	w/o vote 176-2-1, p.p. 7 176-2-0, o.p. 6	w/o vote 173-2-1, p.p. 7 174-2-1, o.p. 6 6 Nov.
73/84	Convention on Prohibitions or Restrictions on the Use of Certain Conventional Weapons Which May Be Deemed to Be Excessively Injurious or to Have Indiscriminate Effects	w/o vote	w/o vote 6 Nov.

Cluster 5: Other disarmament measures and international security

No.	Title	GA action, 5 Dec. (vote)	First Cttee action (vote, date)
73/27	Developments in the field of information and telecommunications in the context of international security	119-46-14	109-45-16 8 Nov.
73/32	Role of science and technology in the context of international security and disarmament	w/o vote	w/o vote 8 Nov.
73/37	Relationship between disarmament and development	w/o vote	w/o vote 8 Nov.
73/38	Effects of the use of armaments and ammunitions containing depleted uranium	151-4-25	140-4-26 8 Nov.
73/39	Observance of environmental norms in the drafting and implementation of agreements on disarmament and arms control	w/o vote	w/o vote 8 Nov.
73/41	Promotion of multilateralism in the area of disarmament and non-proliferation	128-4-52	121-4-51 8 Nov.
73/46	Women, disarmament, non-proliferation and arms control	w/o vote 149-0-23, p.p. 10	w/o vote 149-0-23, p.p. 10 8 Nov.
73/53	Consolidation of peace through practical disarmament measures	w/o vote 168-2-7, p.p. 9	w/o vote 162-2-8, p.p. 9 8 Nov.
73/59	Disarmament and non-proliferation education	w/o vote 171-0-3, o.p. 3	w/o vote 166-0-4, o.p. 3 8 Nov.
73/73	United Nations disarmament fellowship, training and advisory services	w/o vote	w/o vote 8 Nov.

No.	Title	GA action, 5 Dec. (vote)	First Cttee action (vote, date)
73/78	Regional confidence-building measures: activities of the United Nations Standing Advisory Committee on Security Questions in Central Africa	w/o vote	w/o vote 8 Nov.
73/80	United Nations regional centres for peace and disarmament	w/o vote	w/o vote 8 Nov.
73/81	Report of the Conference on Disarmament	w/o vote	w/o vote 8 Nov.
73/82	Report of the Disarmament Commission	w/o vote	w/o vote 8 Nov.

Agenda item 94

73/26   African Nuclear-Weapon-Free Zone Treaty

Text

The General Assembly,

Recalling its resolutions 51/53 of 10 December 1996 and 56/17 of 29 November 2001 and all its other relevant resolutions, as well as those of the Organization of African Unity and of the African Union,

Recalling also the signing of the African Nuclear-Weapon-Free Zone Treaty (Treaty of Pelindaba) in Cairo on 11 April 1996,[1]

Recalling further the Cairo Declaration adopted on that occasion,[2] in which it was emphasized that nuclear-weapon-free zones, especially in regions of tension, such as the Middle East, enhance global and regional peace and security,

Recalling the statement made by the President of the Security Council on behalf of the members of the Council on 12 April 1996,[3] in which the Council affirmed that the signature of the Treaty constituted an important contribution by the African countries to the maintenance of international peace and security,

Considering that the establishment of nuclear-weapon-free zones, especially in the Middle East, would enhance the security of Africa and the viability of the African nuclear-weapon-free zone,

1.   *Recalls with satisfaction* the entry into force of the African Nuclear-Weapon-Free Zone Treaty (Treaty of Pelindaba)[1] on 15 July 2009;

2.   *Calls upon* African States that have not yet done so to sign and ratify the Treaty as soon as possible;

3.   *Recalls* the convening of the first Conference of States Parties to the African Nuclear-Weapon-Free Zone Treaty (Treaty of Pelindaba), on 4 November 2010, the second Conference of States Parties, on 12 and 13 November 2012, the third Conference of States Parties, on 29 and 30 May

---

[1] A/50/426, annex.
[2] A/51/113-S/1996/276, annex.
[3] S/PRST/1996/17; see *Resolutions and Decisions of the Security Council, 1996* (S/INF/52).

2014, and the fourth Conference of States Parties, on 14 and 15 March 2018, all held in Addis Ababa;

4. *Expresses its appreciation* to the nuclear-weapon States that have signed the Protocols to the Treaty[1] that concern them, and calls upon those that have not yet ratified the Protocols that concern them to do so as soon as possible;

5. *Calls upon* the States contemplated in Protocol III to the Treaty that have not yet done so to take all measures necessary to ensure the speedy application of the Treaty to territories for which they are, de jure or de facto, internationally responsible and which lie within the limits of the geographical zone established in the Treaty;

6. *Calls upon* the African States parties to the Treaty on the Non-Proliferation of Nuclear Weapons[4] that have not yet done so to conclude comprehensive safeguards agreements with the International Atomic Energy Agency pursuant to the Treaty, thereby satisfying the requirements of article 9 (b) and annex II to the Treaty of Pelindaba, and encourages them to conclude additional protocols to their safeguards agreements on the basis of the model protocol approved by the Board of Governors of the Agency on 15 May 1997;

7. *Expresses its gratitude* to the Secretary-General of the United Nations, the Chairperson of the African Union Commission and the Director General of the International Atomic Energy Agency for the diligence with which they have rendered effective assistance to the signatories to the Treaty;

8. *Decides* to include in the provisional agenda of its seventy-fourth session the item entitled "African Nuclear-Weapon-Free Zone Treaty".

Action by the General Assembly

Date: 5 December 2018   Meeting: 45th plenary meeting
Vote: Adopted without a vote   Report: A/73/503

Sponsors

Australia, Austria, Georgia, Haiti, Kazakhstan, **Nigeria** (on behalf of the States Members of the United Nations that are members of the Group of African States), Portugal, Trinidad and Tobago

Co-sponsors

Canada, Mexico, Republic of Moldova, Turkey

Action by the First Committee

Date: 1 November 2018   Meeting: 26th meeting
Vote: Adopted without a vote   Draft resolution: A/C.1/73/L.33

---

[4] United Nations, *Treaty Series*, vol. 729, No. 10485.

Agenda item 96

73/27 Developments in the field of information and telecommunications in the context of international security

Text

The General Assembly,

Recalling its resolutions 36/103 of 9 December 1981, 43/78 H of 7 December 1988, 53/70 of 4 December 1998, 54/49 of 1 December 1999, 55/28 of 20 November 2000, 56/19 of 29 November 2001, 57/53 of 22 November 2002, 58/32 of 8 December 2003, 59/61 of 3 December 2004, 60/45 of 8 December 2005, 61/54 of 6 December 2006, 62/17 of 5 December 2007, 63/37 of 2 December 2008, 64/25 of 2 December 2009, 65/41 of 8 December 2010, 66/24 of 2 December 2011, 67/27 of 3 December 2012, 68/243 of 27 December 2013, 69/28 of 2 December 2014, 70/237 of 23 December 2015 and 71/28 of 5 December 2016,

Noting that considerable progress has been achieved in developing and applying the latest information technologies and means of telecommunication,

Underscoring the aspirations of the international community to the peaceful use of information and communications technologies (ICTs) for the common good of humankind and to further the sustainable development of all countries, irrespective of their scientific and technological development,

Noting that capacity-building is essential for cooperation of States and confidence-building in the field of ICT security,

Recognizing that some States may require assistance in their efforts to bridge the divide in the security of ICTs and their use,

Noting that providing assistance, upon request, to build capacity in the area of ICT security is essential for international security,

Affirming that capacity-building measures should seek to promote the use of ICTs for peaceful purposes,

Confirming that ICTs are dual-use technologies and can be used for both legitimate and malicious purposes,

Expressing concern that a number of States are developing ICT capabilities for military purposes and that the use of ICTs in future conflicts between States is becoming more likely,

Stressing that it is in the interest of all States to promote the use of ICTs for peaceful purposes, with the objective of shaping a community of shared future for humankind in cyberspace, and that States also have an interest in preventing conflict arising from the use of ICTs,

Noting that the United Nations should play a leading role in promoting dialogue among Member States to develop common understandings on the security of and the use of ICTs, as well as in developing common understandings on the application of international law and norms, rules and principles for responsible State behaviour in this sphere, encourage regional efforts, promote confidence-building and transparency measures and support capacity-building and the dissemination of best practices,

Expressing concern that embedding harmful hidden functions in ICTs could be used in ways that would affect secure and reliable ICT use and the ICT supply chain for products and services, erode trust in commerce and damage national security,

Considering that it is necessary to prevent the use of information resources or technologies for criminal or terrorist purposes,

Underlining the importance of respect for human rights and fundamental freedoms in the use of ICTs,

Welcoming the effective work of the Group of Governmental Experts on Developments in the Field of Information and Telecommunications in the Context of International Security and the relevant outcome reports transmitted by the Secretary-General,[1]

Welcoming also that, in considering the application of international law to State use of ICTs, the Group of Governmental Experts, in its 2015 report,[2] identified as of central importance the commitments of States to the following principles of the Charter of the United Nations and other international law: sovereign equality; the settlement of international disputes by peaceful means in such a manner that international peace and security and justice are not endangered; refraining in their international relations from the threat or use of force against the territorial integrity or political independence of any State, or in any other manner inconsistent with the purposes of the United Nations; respect for human rights and fundamental freedoms; and non-intervention in the internal affairs of other States,

Confirming the conclusions of the Group of Governmental Experts, in its 2013[3] and 2015[2] reports, that international law, and in particular the Charter of the United Nations, is applicable and essential to maintaining peace and stability and promoting an open, secure, stable, accessible and peaceful ICT environment, that voluntary and non-binding norms, rules and principles of responsible behaviour of States in the use of ICTs can reduce risks to international peace, security and stability, and that, given the unique attributes of such technologies, additional norms can be developed over time,

---

[1] A/65/201, A/68/98 and A/70/174.

[2] A/70/174.

[3] A/68/98.

Confirming also that State sovereignty and international norms and principles that flow from sovereignty apply to State conduct of ICT-related activities and to their jurisdiction over ICT infrastructure within their territory,

Reaffirming the right and duty of States to combat, within their constitutional prerogatives, the dissemination of false or distorted news, which can be interpreted as interference in the internal affairs of other States or as being harmful to the promotion of peace, cooperation and friendly relations among States and nations,

Recognizing the duty of a State to abstain from any defamatory campaign, vilification or hostile propaganda for the purpose of intervening or interfering in the internal affairs of other States,

Stressing that, while States have a primary responsibility for maintaining a secure and peaceful ICT environment, effective international cooperation would benefit from identifying mechanisms for the participation, as appropriate, of the private sector, academia and civil society organizations,

1.   *Welcomes* the following set of international rules, norms and principles of responsible behaviour of States, enshrined in the reports of the Group of Governmental Experts on Developments in the Field of Information and Telecommunications in the Context of International Security of 2013[3] and 2015[2] adopted by consensus and recommended in resolution 71/28 entitled "Developments in the field of information and telecommunications in the context of international security", adopted by the General Assembly on 5 December 2016:

1.1. Consistent with the purposes of the United Nations, including to maintain international peace and security, States should cooperate in developing and applying measures to increase stability and security in the use of ICTs and to prevent ICT practices that are acknowledged to be harmful or that may pose threats to international peace and security.

1.2. States must meet their international obligations regarding internationally wrongful acts attributable to them under international law. However, the indication that an ICT activity was launched or otherwise originates from the territory or objects of the ICT infrastructure of a State may be insufficient in itself to attribute the activity to that State. Accusations of organizing and implementing wrongful acts brought against States should be substantiated. In case of ICT incidents, States should consider all relevant information, including the larger context of the event, the challenges of attribution in the ICT environment and the nature and extent of the consequences.

1.3. States should not knowingly allow their territory to be used for internationally wrongful acts using ICTs. States must not use proxies to commit internationally wrongful acts using ICTs and should seek to ensure that their territory is not used by non-State actors to commit such acts.

1.4. States should consider how best to cooperate to exchange information, assist each other, prosecute terrorist and criminal use of ICTs and implement other cooperative measures to address such threats. States may need to consider whether new measures need to be developed in this respect.

1.5. States, in ensuring the secure use of ICTs, should respect Human Rights Council resolutions 20/8 of 5 July 2012[4] and 26/13 of 26 June 2014[5] on the promotion, protection and enjoyment of human rights on the Internet, as well as General Assembly resolutions 68/167 of 18 December 2013 and 69/166 of 18 December 2014 on the right to privacy in the digital age, to guarantee full respect for human rights, including the right to freedom of expression.

1.6. A State should not conduct or knowingly support ICT activity contrary to its obligations under international law that intentionally damages critical infrastructure or otherwise impairs the use and operation of critical infrastructure to provide services to the public.

1.7. States should take appropriate measures to protect their critical infrastructure from ICT threats, taking into account General Assembly resolution 58/199 of 23 December 2003 on the creation of a global culture of cybersecurity and the protection of critical information infrastructures, and other relevant resolutions.

1.8. States should respond to appropriate requests for assistance by another State whose critical infrastructure is subject to malicious ICT acts. States should also respond to appropriate requests to mitigate malicious ICT activity aimed at the critical infrastructure of another State emanating from their territory, taking into account due regard for sovereignty.

1.9. States should take reasonable steps to ensure the integrity of the supply chain so that end users can have confidence in the security of ICT products.

1.10. States should seek to prevent the proliferation of malicious ICT tools and techniques and the use of harmful hidden functions.

1.11. States should encourage responsible reporting of ICT vulnerabilities and share associated information on available remedies for such vulnerabilities to limit and possibly eliminate potential threats to ICTs and ICT-dependent infrastructure.

1.12. States should not conduct or knowingly support activity to harm the information systems of the authorized emergency response

---

[4] See *Official Records of the General Assembly, Sixty-seventh Session, Supplement No. 53* and corrigendum (A/67/53 and A/67/53/Corr.1), chap. IV, sect. A.
[5] Ibid., *Sixty-ninth Session, Supplement No. 53* (A/69/53), chap. V, sect. A.

teams (sometimes known as computer emergency response teams or cybersecurity incident response teams) of another State. A State should not use authorized emergency response teams to engage in malicious international activity.

1.13. States should encourage the private sector and civil society to play an appropriate role to improve security of and in the use of ICTs, including supply chain security for ICT products and services. States should cooperate with the private sector and the organizations of civil society in the sphere of implementation of rules of responsible behaviour in information space with regard to their potential role;

2.   *Calls upon* Member States to promote further, at multilateral levels, the consideration of existing and potential threats in the field of information security, as well as possible strategies to address the threats emerging in this field, consistent with the need to preserve the free flow of information;

3.   *Considers* that the purpose of such measures could be served through further examination of relevant international concepts aimed at strengthening the security of global information and telecommunications systems;

4.   *Invites* all Member States, taking into account the assessments and recommendations contained in the reports of the Group of Governmental Experts on Developments in the Field of Information and Telecommunications in the Context of International Security,[1] to continue to inform the Secretary-General of their views and assessments on the following questions:

(a)   General appreciation of the issues of information security;

(b)   Efforts taken at the national level to strengthen information security and promote international cooperation in this field;

(c)   The content of the concepts mentioned in paragraph 3 above;

(d)   Possible measures that could be taken by the international community to strengthen information security at the global level;

5.   *Decides* to convene, beginning in 2019, with a view to making the United Nations negotiation process on security in the use of information and communications technologies more democratic, inclusive and transparent, an open-ended working group acting on a consensus basis, to continue, as a priority, to further develop the rules, norms and principles of responsible behaviour of States listed in paragraph 1 above, and the ways for their implementation; if necessary, to introduce changes to them or elaborate additional rules of behaviour; to study the possibility of establishing regular institutional dialogue with broad participation under the auspices of the United Nations; and to continue to study, with a view to promoting common understandings, existing and potential threats in the sphere of information security and possible cooperative measures to address them and

how international law applies to the use of information and communications technologies by States, as well as confidence-building measures and capacity-building and the concepts referred to in paragraph 3 above, and to submit a report on the results of the study to the General Assembly at its seventy-fifth session, and to provide the possibility of holding, from within voluntary contributions, intersessional consultative meetings with the interested parties, namely business, non-governmental organizations and academia, to share views on the issues within the group's mandate;

6.   *Also decides* that the open-ended working group shall hold its organizational session in June 2019 in order to agree on the organizational arrangements connected with the group;

7.   *Further decides* to include in the provisional agenda of its seventy-fourth session the item entitled "Developments in the field of information and telecommunications in the context of international security".

Action by the General Assembly

Date: 5 December 2018   Meeting: 45th plenary meeting
Vote: 119-46-14   Report: A/73/505

Sponsors

Algeria, Angola, Azerbaijan, Belarus, Bolivia (Plurinational State of), Burundi, Cambodia, China, Cuba, Democratic People's Republic of Korea, Democratic Republic of the Congo, Eritrea, Iran (Islamic Republic of), Kazakhstan, Lao People's Democratic Republic, Madagascar, Malawi, Namibia, Nepal, Nicaragua, Pakistan, **Russian Federation**, Samoa, Sierra Leone, Suriname, Syrian Arab Republic, Tajikistan, Turkmenistan, Uzbekistan, Venezuela (Bolivarian Republic of), Zimbabwe

Co-sponsors

Guinea, Kyrgyzstan, Myanmar

*Recorded vote**

In favour:

Afghanistan, Algeria, Angola, Argentina, Armenia, Azerbaijan, Bahrain, Bangladesh, Barbados, Belarus, Belize, Bhutan, Bolivia (Plurinational State of), Bosnia and Herzegovina, Brunei Darussalam, Burkina Faso, Burundi, Cabo Verde, Cambodia, Central African Republic, China, Colombia, Comoros, Congo, Costa Rica, Côte d'Ivoire, Cuba, Democratic People's Republic of Korea, Democratic Republic of the

---

*   Subsequently, the delegation of Benin informed the Secretariat that it had intended to vote in favour; Côte d'Ivoire had intended to abstain. The voting tally above does not reflect this information.

Congo, Djibouti, Dominican Republic, Ecuador, Egypt, El Salvador, Equatorial Guinea, Eritrea, Ethiopia, Gambia, Ghana, Grenada, Guatemala, Guinea, Guinea-Bissau, Guyana, Honduras, India, Indonesia, Iran (Islamic Republic of), Iraq, Jamaica, Jordan, Kazakhstan, Kenya, Kuwait, Kyrgyzstan, Lao People's Democratic Republic, Lebanon, Lesotho, Liberia, Libya, Madagascar, Malawi, Malaysia, Maldives, Mali, Mauritania, Mauritius, Mexico, Mongolia, Morocco, Mozambique, Myanmar, Namibia, Nepal, Nicaragua, Niger, Nigeria, Oman, Pakistan, Palau, Panama, Paraguay, Peru, Philippines, Qatar, Russian Federation, Saint Lucia, Saint Vincent and the Grenadines, Samoa, Sao Tome and Principe, Saudi Arabia, Serbia, Seychelles, Sierra Leone, Singapore, South Africa, South Sudan, Sri Lanka, Sudan, Suriname, Syrian Arab Republic, Tajikistan, Thailand, Timor-Leste, Togo, Trinidad and Tobago, Tunisia, Turkmenistan, Tuvalu, Uganda, United Arab Emirates, United Republic of Tanzania, Uruguay, Vanuatu, Venezuela (Bolivarian Republic of), Viet Nam, Yemen, Zambia, Zimbabwe

Against:

Albania, Andorra, Australia, Austria, Belgium, Bulgaria, Canada, Croatia, Cyprus, Czechia, Denmark, Estonia, Finland, France, Georgia, Germany, Greece, Hungary, Iceland, Ireland, Israel, Italy, Japan, Latvia, Liechtenstein, Lithuania, Luxembourg, Malta, Marshall Islands, Monaco, Montenegro, Netherlands, New Zealand, Norway, Poland, Portugal, Romania, San Marino, Slovakia, Slovenia, Spain, Sweden, the former Yugoslav Republic of Macedonia, Ukraine, United Kingdom, United States

Abstaining:

Antigua and Barbuda, Bahamas, Botswana, Brazil, Chile, Eswatini, Fiji, Haiti, Papua New Guinea, Republic of Korea, Republic of Moldova, Rwanda, Switzerland, Turkey

Action by the First Committee

Date: 8 November 2018	Meeting: 31st meeting
Vote: 109-45-16	Draft resolution: A/C.1/73/L.27/Rev.1

Agenda item 97

73/28   Establishment of a nuclear-weapon-free zone in the region of the Middle East

Text

The General Assembly,

Recalling its resolutions 3263 (XXIX) of 9 December 1974, 3474 (XXX) of 11 December 1975, 31/71 of 10 December 1976, 32/82 of 12 December 1977, 33/64 of 14 December 1978, 34/77 of 11 December 1979, 35/147 of 12 December 1980, 36/87 A and B of 9 December 1981, 37/75 of 9 December 1982, 38/64 of 15 December 1983, 39/54 of 12 December 1984, 40/82 of 12 December 1985, 41/48 of 3 December 1986, 42/28 of 30 November 1987, 43/65 of 7 December 1988, 44/108 of 15 December 1989, 45/52 of 4 December 1990, 46/30 of 6 December 1991, 47/48 of 9 December 1992, 48/71 of 16 December 1993, 49/71 of 15 December 1994, 50/66 of 12 December 1995, 51/41 of 10 December 1996, 52/34 of 9 December 1997, 53/74 of 4 December 1998, 54/51 of 1 December 1999, 55/30 of 20 November 2000, 56/21 of 29 November 2001, 57/55 of 22 November 2002, 58/34 of 8 December 2003, 59/63 of 3 December 2004, 60/52 of 8 December 2005, 61/56 of 6 December 2006, 62/18 of 5 December 2007, 63/38 of 2 December 2008, 64/26 of 2 December 2009, 65/42 of 8 December 2010, 66/25 of 2 December 2011, 67/28 of 3 December 2012, 68/27 of 5 December 2013, 69/29 of 2 December 2014, 70/24 of 7 December 2015, 71/29 of 5 December 2016 and 72/24 of 4 December 2017 on the establishment of a nuclear-weapon-free zone in the region of the Middle East,

Recalling also the recommendations for the establishment of a nuclear-weapon-free zone in the region of the Middle East consistent with paragraphs 60 to 63, and in particular paragraph 63 (d), of the Final Document of the Tenth Special Session of the General Assembly,[1]

Emphasizing the basic provisions of the above-mentioned resolutions, in which all parties directly concerned are called upon to consider taking the practical and urgent steps required for the implementation of the proposal to establish a nuclear-weapon-free zone in the region of the Middle East and, pending and during the establishment of such a zone, to declare solemnly that they will refrain, on a reciprocal basis, from producing, acquiring or in any other way possessing nuclear weapons and nuclear explosive devices and from permitting the stationing of nuclear weapons on their territory by any third party, to agree to place their nuclear facilities under International Atomic Energy Agency safeguards and to declare their support for the establishment of the zone and to deposit such declarations with the Security Council for consideration, as appropriate,

---

[1] Resolution S-10/2.

Reaffirming the inalienable right of all States to acquire and develop nuclear energy for peaceful purposes,

Emphasizing the need for appropriate measures on the question of the prohibition of military attacks on nuclear facilities,

Bearing in mind the consensus reached by the General Assembly since its thirty-fifth session that the establishment of a nuclear-weapon-free zone in the region of the Middle East would greatly enhance international peace and security,

Desirous of building on that consensus so that substantial progress can be made towards establishing a nuclear-weapon-free zone in the region of the Middle East,

Welcoming all initiatives leading to general and complete disarmament, including in the region of the Middle East, and in particular on the establishment therein of a zone free of weapons of mass destruction, including nuclear weapons,

Noting the peace negotiations in the Middle East, which should be of a comprehensive nature and represent an appropriate framework for the peaceful settlement of contentious issues in the region,

Recognizing the importance of credible regional security, including the establishment of a mutually verifiable nuclear-weapon-free zone,

Emphasizing the essential role of the United Nations in the establishment of a mutually verifiable nuclear-weapon-free zone,

Having examined the report of the Secretary-General on the implementation of resolution 72/24,[2]

1. *Urges* all parties directly concerned seriously to consider taking the practical and urgent steps required for the implementation of the proposal to establish a nuclear-weapon-free zone in the region of the Middle East in accordance with the relevant resolutions of the General Assembly, and, as a means of promoting this objective, invites the countries concerned to adhere to the Treaty on the Non-Proliferation of Nuclear Weapons;[3]

2. *Calls upon* all countries of the region that have not yet done so, pending the establishment of the zone, to agree to place all their nuclear activities under International Atomic Energy Agency safeguards;

3. *Takes note* of resolution GC(62)/RES/12, adopted on 20 September 2018 by the General Conference of the International Atomic Energy Agency at its sixty-second regular session, concerning the application of Agency safeguards in the Middle East;

---

[2] A/73/182 (Part I).
[3] United Nations, *Treaty Series*, vol. 729, No. 10485.

4.   *Notes* the importance of the ongoing bilateral Middle East peace negotiations and the activities of the multilateral Working Group on Arms Control and Regional Security in promoting mutual confidence and security in the Middle East, including the establishment of a nuclear-weapon-free zone;

5.   *Invites* all countries of the region, pending the establishment of a nuclear-weapon-free zone in the region of the Middle East, to declare their support for establishing such a zone, consistent with paragraph 63 (d) of the Final Document of the Tenth Special Session of the General Assembly,[1] and to deposit those declarations with the Security Council;

6.   *Also invites* those countries, pending the establishment of the zone, not to develop, produce, test or otherwise acquire nuclear weapons or permit the stationing on their territories, or territories under their control, of nuclear weapons or nuclear explosive devices;

7.   *Invites* the nuclear-weapon States and all other States to render their assistance in the establishment of the zone and at the same time to refrain from any action that runs counter to both the letter and the spirit of the present resolution;

8.   *Takes note* of the report of the Secretary-General on the implementation of resolution 72/24;[2]

9.   *Invites* all parties to consider the appropriate means that may contribute towards the goal of general and complete disarmament and the establishment of a zone free of weapons of mass destruction in the region of the Middle East;

10.   *Requests* the Secretary-General to continue to pursue consultations with the States of the region and other concerned States, in accordance with paragraph 7 of resolution 46/30 and taking into account the evolving situation in the region, and to seek from those States their views on the measures outlined in chapters III and IV of the study annexed to the report of the Secretary-General of 10 October 1990[4] or other relevant measures, in order to move towards the establishment of a nuclear-weapon-free zone in the region of the Middle East;

11.   *Also requests* the Secretary-General to submit to the General Assembly at its seventy-fourth session a report on the implementation of the present resolution;

12.   *Decides* to include in the provisional agenda of its seventy-fourth session the item entitled "Establishment of a nuclear-weapon-free zone in the region of the Middle East".

Action by the General Assembly

Date: 5 December 2018   Meeting: 45th plenary meeting
Vote: 171-2-5   Report: A/73/506

---

[4] A/45/435.

Sponsors

Egypt

Recorded vote

In favour:

Afghanistan, Albania, Algeria, Andorra, Angola, Antigua and Barbuda, Argentina, Armenia, Australia, Austria, Azerbaijan, Bahamas, Bahrain, Bangladesh, Barbados, Belarus, Belgium, Belize, Benin, Bhutan, Bolivia (Plurinational State of), Bosnia and Herzegovina, Botswana, Brazil, Brunei Darussalam, Bulgaria, Burkina Faso, Burundi, Cabo Verde, Cambodia, Canada, Central African Republic, Chile, China, Colombia, Comoros, Congo, Costa Rica, Côte d'Ivoire, Croatia, Cuba, Cyprus, Czechia, Democratic People's Republic of Korea, Democratic Republic of the Congo, Denmark, Djibouti, Dominican Republic, Ecuador, Egypt, El Salvador, Eritrea, Estonia, Eswatini, Ethiopia, Finland, France, Gambia, Georgia, Germany, Ghana, Greece, Grenada, Guatemala, Guinea, Guinea-Bissau, Guyana, Honduras, Hungary, Iceland, India, Indonesia, Iran (Islamic Republic of), Iraq, Ireland, Italy, Jamaica, Japan, Jordan, Kazakhstan, Kenya, Kuwait, Kyrgyzstan, Lao People's Democratic Republic, Latvia, Lebanon, Lesotho, Liberia, Libya, Liechtenstein, Lithuania, Luxembourg, Madagascar, Malawi, Malaysia, Maldives, Mali, Malta, Mauritania, Mauritius, Mexico, Monaco, Mongolia, Montenegro, Morocco, Mozambique, Myanmar, Namibia, Nepal, Netherlands, New Zealand, Nicaragua, Niger, Nigeria, Norway, Oman, Pakistan, Panama, Paraguay, Peru, Philippines, Poland, Portugal, Qatar, Republic of Korea, Republic of Moldova, Romania, Russian Federation, Rwanda, Saint Lucia, Saint Vincent and the Grenadines, Samoa, San Marino, Sao Tome and Principe, Saudi Arabia, Senegal, Serbia, Seychelles, Sierra Leone, Singapore, Slovakia, Slovenia, South Africa, South Sudan, Spain, Sri Lanka, Sudan, Suriname, Sweden, Switzerland, Syrian Arab Republic, Tajikistan, Thailand, the former Yugoslav Republic of Macedonia, Timor-Leste, Togo, Trinidad and Tobago, Tunisia, Turkey, Turkmenistan, Uganda, Ukraine, United Arab Emirates, United Republic of Tanzania, Uruguay, Vanuatu, Venezuela (Bolivarian Republic of), Viet Nam, Yemen, Zambia, Zimbabwe

Against:

Israel, United States

Abstaining:

Cameroon, Fiji, Papua New Guinea, Tuvalu, United Kingdom

Action by the First Committee

Date: 1 November 2018	Meeting:	26th meeting
Vote: 174-2-5	Draft resolution:	A/C.1/73/L.1

Agenda item 98

73/29 Conclusion of effective international arrangements to assure non-nuclear-weapon States against the use or threat of use of nuclear weapons

Text

The General Assembly,

Bearing in mind the need to allay the legitimate concern of the States of the world with regard to ensuring lasting security for their peoples,

Convinced that nuclear weapons pose the greatest threat to humankind and to the survival of civilization,

Noting that the renewed interest in nuclear disarmament should be translated into concrete actions for the achievement of general and complete disarmament under effective international control,

Convinced that nuclear disarmament and the complete elimination of nuclear weapons are essential to remove the danger of nuclear war,

Determined to abide strictly by the relevant provisions of the Charter of the United Nations on the non-use of force or threat of force,

Recognizing that the independence, territorial integrity and sovereignty of nonnuclear-weapon States need to be safeguarded against the use or threat of use of force, including the use or threat of use of nuclear weapons,

Considering that, until nuclear disarmament is achieved on a universal basis, it is imperative for the international community to develop effective measures and arrangements to ensure the security of non-nuclear-weapon States against the use or threat of use of nuclear weapons from any quarter,

Recognizing that effective measures and arrangements to assure non-nuclear-weapon States against the use or threat of use of nuclear weapons can contribute positively to the prevention of the spread of nuclear weapons,

Bearing in mind paragraph 59 of the Final Document of the Tenth Special Session of the General Assembly, the first special session devoted to disarmament,[1] in which it urged the nuclear-weapon States to pursue efforts to conclude, as appropriate, effective arrangements to assure non-nuclear-weapon States against the use or threat of use of nuclear weapons, and desirous of promoting the implementation of the relevant provisions of the Final Document,

---

[1] Resolution S-10/2.

Recalling the relevant parts of the special report of the Committee on Disarmament[2] submitted to the General Assembly at its twelfth special session, the second special session devoted to disarmament,[3] and of the special report of the Conference on Disarmament submitted to the Assembly at its fifteenth special session, the third special session devoted to disarmament,[4] as well as the report of the Conference on its 1992 session,[5]

Recalling also paragraph 12 of the Declaration of the 1980s as the Second Disarmament Decade, contained in the annex to its resolution 35/46 of 3 December 1980, in which it is stated, inter alia, that all efforts should be exerted by the Committee on Disarmament urgently to negotiate with a view to reaching agreement on effective international arrangements to assure non-nuclear-weapon States against the use or threat of use of nuclear weapons,

Noting the in-depth negotiations undertaken in the Conference on Disarmament and its Ad Hoc Committee on Effective International Arrangements to Assure Non-Nuclear-Weapon States against the Use or Threat of Use of Nuclear Weapons,[6] with a view to reaching agreement on this question,

Taking note of the proposals submitted under the item in the Conference on Disarmament, including the drafts of an international convention,

Taking note also of the relevant decision of the Thirteenth Conference of Heads of State or Government of Non-Aligned Countries, held in Kuala Lumpur on 24 and 25 February 2003,[7] which was reiterated at the Seventeenth Conference of Heads of State or Government of Non-Aligned Countries, held on Margarita Island, Bolivarian Republic of Venezuela, from 13 to 18 September 2016, as well as the relevant recommendations of the Organization of Islamic Cooperation,

Taking note further of the unilateral declarations made by all the nuclear-weapon States on their policies of non-use or non-threat of use of nuclear weapons against the non-nuclear-weapon States,

Noting the support expressed in the Conference on Disarmament and in the General Assembly for the elaboration of an international convention to assure nonnuclear-weapon States against the use or threat of use of nuclear weapons, as well as the difficulties pointed out in evolving a common approach acceptable to all,

---

[2] The Committee on Disarmament was redesignated the Conference on Disarmament as from 7 February 1984.

[3] *Official Records of the General Assembly, Twelfth Special Session, Supplement No. 2* (A/S-12/2), sect. III.C.

[4] Ibid., *Fifteenth Special Session*, Supplement No. 2 (A/S-15/2), sect. III.F.

[5] Ibid., *Forty-seventh Session*, Supplement No. 27 (A/47/27), sect. III.F.

[6] Ibid., *Forty-eighth Session*, Supplement No. 27 (A/48/27), sect. III.E.

[7] See A/57/759-S/2003/332, annex I.

Taking note of Security Council resolution 984 (1995) of 11 April 1995 and the views expressed on it,

Recalling its relevant resolutions adopted in previous years, in particular resolutions 45/54 of 4 December 1990, 46/32 of 6 December 1991, 47/50 of 9 December 1992, 48/73 of 16 December 1993, 49/73 of 15 December 1994, 50/68 of 12 December 1995, 51/43 of 10 December 1996, 52/36 of 9 December 1997, 53/75 of 4 December 1998, 54/52 of 1 December 1999, 55/31 of 20 November 2000, 56/22 of 29 November 2001, 57/56 of 22 November 2002, 58/35 of 8 December 2003, 59/64 of 3 December 2004, 60/53 of 8 December 2005, 61/57 of 6 December 2006, 62/19 of 5 December 2007, 63/39 of 2 December 2008, 64/27 of 2 December 2009, 65/43 of 8 December 2010, 66/26 of 2 December 2011, 67/29 of 3 December 2012, 68/28 of 5 December 2013, 69/30 of 2 December 2014, 70/25 of 7 December 2015, 71/30 of 5 December 2016 and 72/25 of 4 December 2017,

1. *Reaffirms* the urgent need to reach an early agreement on effective international arrangements to assure non-nuclear-weapon States against the use or threat of use of nuclear weapons;

2. *Notes with satisfaction* that in the Conference on Disarmament there is no objection, in principle, to the idea of an international convention to assure nonnuclear-weapon States against the use or threat of use of nuclear weapons, although the difficulties with regard to evolving a common approach acceptable to all have also been pointed out;

3. *Appeals* to all States, especially the nuclear-weapon States, to work actively towards an early agreement on a common approach and, in particular, on a common formula that could be included in an international instrument of a legally binding character;

4. *Recommends* that further intensive efforts be devoted to the search for such a common approach or common formula and that the various alternative approaches, including, in particular, those considered in the Conference on Disarmament, be further explored in order to overcome the difficulties;

5. *Also recommends* that the Conference on Disarmament actively continue intensive negotiations with a view to reaching early agreement and concluding effective international agreements to assure the non-nuclear-weapon States against the use or threat of use of nuclear weapons, taking into account the widespread support for the conclusion of an international convention and giving consideration to any other proposals designed to secure the same objective;

6. *Decides* to include in the provisional agenda of its seventy-fourth session the item entitled "Conclusion of effective international arrangements to assure nonnuclear-weapon States against the use or threat of use of nuclear weapons".

Action by the General Assembly

Date: 5 December 2018   Meeting: 45th plenary meeting
Vote: 125-0-58   Report: A/73/507

Sponsors

Algeria, Bolivia (Plurinational State of), Cuba, Egypt, Ghana, Honduras, Iran (Islamic Republic of), Kazakhstan, Libya, Namibia, Nicaragua, **Pakistan**, Paraguay, Peru, Saudi Arabia, Syrian Arab Republic, Venezuela (Bolivarian Republic of

Co-sponsors

Bangladesh, Colombia, Iraq, Kuwait, Sri Lanka, Uzbekistan

Recorded vote

In favour:

Afghanistan, Algeria, Angola, Antigua and Barbuda, Azerbaijan, Bahamas, Bahrain, Bangladesh, Barbados, Belarus, Belize, Benin, Bhutan, Bolivia (Plurinational State of), Botswana, Brazil, Brunei Darussalam, Burkina Faso, Burundi, Cabo Verde, Cambodia, Cameroon, Central African Republic, Chile, China, Colombia, Comoros, Congo, Costa Rica, Côte d'Ivoire, Cuba, Democratic People's Republic of Korea, Democratic Republic of the Congo, Djibouti, Dominican Republic, Ecuador, Egypt, El Salvador, Equatorial Guinea, Eritrea, Eswatini, Ethiopia, Gambia, Ghana, Grenada, Guatemala, Guinea, Guinea-Bissau, Guyana, Honduras, India, Indonesia, Iran (Islamic Republic of), Iraq, Jamaica, Japan, Jordan, Kazakhstan, Kenya, Kuwait, Kyrgyzstan, Lao People's Democratic Republic, Lebanon, Lesotho, Liberia, Libya, Madagascar, Malawi, Malaysia, Maldives, Mali, Mauritania, Mauritius, Mexico, Mongolia, Morocco, Mozambique, Myanmar, Namibia, Nauru, Nepal, Nicaragua, Niger, Nigeria, Oman, Pakistan, Panama, Papua New Guinea, Paraguay, Peru, Philippines, Qatar, Rwanda, Saint Lucia, Saint Vincent and the Grenadines, Samoa, Sao Tome and Principe, Saudi Arabia, Senegal, Seychelles, Sierra Leone, Singapore, Sri Lanka, Sudan, Suriname, Syrian Arab Republic, Tajikistan, Thailand, Timor-Leste, Togo, Tonga, Trinidad and Tobago, Tunisia, Turkmenistan, Tuvalu, Uganda, United Arab Emirates, United Republic of Tanzania, Uruguay, Vanuatu, Venezuela (Bolivarian Republic of), Viet Nam, Yemen, Zambia, Zimbabwe

Against:
None

Abstaining:
Albania, Andorra, Argentina, Armenia, Australia, Austria, Belgium, Bosnia and Herzegovina, Bulgaria, Canada, Croatia, Cyprus, Czechia,

Denmark, Estonia, Fiji, Finland, France, Georgia, Germany, Greece, Haiti, Hungary, Iceland, Ireland, Israel, Italy, Latvia, Liechtenstein, Lithuania, Luxembourg, Malta, Marshall Islands, Micronesia (Federated States of), Monaco, Montenegro, Netherlands, New Zealand, Norway, Poland, Portugal, Republic of Korea, Republic of Moldova, Romania, Russian Federation, San Marino, Serbia, Slovakia, Slovenia, South Africa, Spain, Sweden, Switzerland, the former Yugoslav Republic of Macedonia, Turkey, Ukraine, United Kingdom, United States

Action by the First Committee

Date:	1 November 2018	Meeting:	26th meeting
Vote:	122-0-65	Draft resolution:	A/C.1/73/L.4

Agenda item 99 (a)

73/30   Prevention of an arms race in outer space

Text

The General Assembly,

Recognizing the common interest of all humankind in the exploration and use of outer space for peaceful purposes,

Reaffirming the will of all States that the exploration and use of outer space, including the Moon and other celestial bodies, shall be for peaceful purposes and shall be carried out for the benefit and in the interest of all countries, irrespective of their degree of economic or scientific development,

Reaffirming also the provisions of articles III and IV of the Treaty on Principles Governing the Activities of States in the Exploration and Use of Outer Space, including the Moon and Other Celestial Bodies,[1]

Recalling the obligation of all States to observe the provisions of the Charter of the United Nations regarding the use or threat of use of force in their international relations, including in their space activities,

Reaffirming paragraph 80 of the Final Document of the Tenth Special Session of the General Assembly,[2] in which it is stated that, in order to prevent an arms race in outer space, further measures should be taken and appropriate international negotiations held in accordance with the spirit of the Treaty,

Recalling its previous resolutions on this issue, the most recent of which is resolution 72/26 of 4 December 2017, and taking note of the proposals submitted to the General Assembly at its tenth special session and at its regular sessions and of the recommendations made to the competent organs of the United Nations and to the Conference on Disarmament,

Recognizing that the prevention of an arms race in outer space would avert a grave danger for international peace and security,

Emphasizing the paramount importance of strict compliance with existing arms limitation and disarmament agreements relevant to outer space, including bilateral agreements, and with the existing legal regime concerning the use of outer space,

Considering that wide participation in the legal regime applicable to outer space could contribute to enhancing its effectiveness,

Noting that the Ad Hoc Committee on the Prevention of an Arms Race in Outer Space, taking into account its previous efforts since its establishment in 1985 and seeking to enhance its functioning in qualitative terms, continued

---

[1] United Nations, *Treaty Series*, vol. 610, No. 8843.
[2] Resolution S-10/2.

the examination and identification of various issues, existing agreements and existing proposals, as well as future initiatives relevant to the prevention of an arms race in outer space, and that this contributed to a better understanding of a number of problems and to a clearer perception of the various positions,

Noting also that there were no objections in principle in the Conference on Disarmament to the re-establishment of the Ad Hoc Committee, subject to reexamination of the mandate contained in the decision of the Conference on Disarmament of 13 February 1992,[3]

Emphasizing the mutually complementary nature of bilateral and multilateral efforts for the prevention of an arms race in outer space, and hoping that concrete results will emerge from those efforts as soon as possible,

Convinced that further measures should be examined in the search for effective and verifiable bilateral and multilateral agreements in order to prevent an arms race in outer space, including the weaponization of outer space,

Stressing that the growing use of outer space increases the need for greater transparency and better information on the part of the international community,

Recalling, in this context, its previous resolutions, in particular resolutions 45/55 B of 4 December 1990, 47/51 of 9 December 1992 and 48/74 A of 16 December 1993, in which, inter alia, it reaffirmed the importance of confidence-building measures as a means conducive to ensuring the attainment of the objective of the prevention of an arms race in outer space,

Conscious of the benefits of confidence- and security-building measures in the military field,

Recognizing that negotiations for the conclusion of an international agreement or agreements to prevent an arms race in outer space remain a priority task of the Conference on Disarmament and that the concrete proposals on confidence-building measures could form an integral part of such agreements,

Noting with satisfaction the constructive, structured and focused debate on the prevention of an arms race in outer space at the Conference on Disarmament each year from 2009 to 2018,

Noting the introduction by China and the Russian Federation at the Conference on Disarmament of the draft treaty on the prevention of the placement of weapons in outer space and of the threat or use of force against outer space objects in 2008 and the submission of its updated version in 2014,[4]

---

[3] See *Official Records of the General Assembly, Forty-seventh Session, Supplement No. 27* (A/47/27), para. 76.

[4] See CD/1839 and CD/1985.

Taking note of the decision of the Conference on Disarmament to establish for its 2009 session a working group to discuss, substantially, without limitation, all issues related to the prevention of an arms race in outer space, and the decision to establish for its 2018 session a subsidiary body on the prevention of an arms race in outer space,

1. *Reaffirms* the importance and urgency of preventing an arms race in outer space and the readiness of all States to contribute to that common objective, in conformity with the provisions of the Treaty on Principles Governing the Activities of States in the Exploration and Use of Outer Space, including the Moon and Other Celestial Bodies;[1]

2. *Reaffirms* its recognition, as stated in the report of the Ad Hoc Committee on the Prevention of an Arms Race in Outer Space, that the legal regime applicable to outer space by itself does not guarantee the prevention of an arms race in outer space, that the regime plays a significant role in the prevention of an arms race in that environment, that there is a need to consolidate and reinforce that regime and enhance its effectiveness and that it is important to comply strictly with existing agreements, both bilateral and multilateral;

3. *Emphasizes* the necessity of further measures with appropriate and effective provisions for verification to prevent an arms race in outer space;

4. *Calls upon* all States, in particular those with major space capabilities, to contribute actively to the objective of the peaceful use of outer space and of the prevention of an arms race in outer space and to refrain from actions contrary to that objective and to the relevant existing treaties in the interest of maintaining international peace and security and promoting international cooperation;

5. *Reiterates* that the Conference on Disarmament, as the sole multilateral disarmament negotiating forum, has the primary role in the negotiation of a multilateral agreement or agreements, as appropriate, on the prevention of an arms race in outer space in all its aspects;

6. *Invites* the Conference on Disarmament to establish a working group under its agenda item entitled "Prevention of an arms race in outer space" as early as possible;

7. *Recognizes*, in this respect, the growing convergence of views on the elaboration of measures designed to strengthen transparency, confidence and security in the peaceful uses of outer space;

8. *Urges* States conducting activities in outer space, as well as States interested in conducting such activities, to keep the Conference on Disarmament informed of the progress of bilateral and multilateral negotiations on the matter, if any, so as to facilitate its work;

9. *Decides* to include in the provisional agenda of its seventy-fourth session the item entitled "Prevention of an arms race in outer space".

Action by the General Assembly

Date: 5 December 2018   Meeting: 45th plenary meeting
Vote: 178-2-0   Report: A/73/508

Sponsors

Algeria, Bolivia (Plurinational State of), China, Cuba, **Egypt**, Eswatini, Honduras, Kazakhstan, Lesotho, Libya, Malawi, Mongolia, Myanmar, Namibia, Nepal, Nicaragua, Nigeria, Pakistan, Russian Federation, Senegal, **Sri Lanka**, Suriname, Syrian Arab Republic, Thailand, Venezuela (Bolivarian Republic of)

Co-sponsors

Armenia, Bangladesh, Belarus, Brazil, Burkina Faso, Ecuador, India, Indonesia, Iraq, Kuwait, Kyrgyzstan, Malaysia, Samoa, Uruguay, Uzbekistan

Recorded vote*

In favour:

Afghanistan, Albania, Algeria, Andorra, Angola, Antigua and Barbuda, Argentina, Armenia, Australia, Austria, Azerbaijan, Bahamas, Bahrain, Bangladesh, Barbados, Belarus, Belgium, Belize, Benin, Bhutan, Bolivia (Plurinational State of), Bosnia and Herzegovina, Botswana, Brazil, Brunei Darussalam, Bulgaria, Burkina Faso, Burundi, Cabo Verde, Cambodia, Cameroon, Canada, Central African Republic, Chile, China, Colombia, Comoros, Congo, Costa Rica, Côte d'Ivoire, Croatia, Cuba, Cyprus, Czechia, Democratic People's Republic of Korea, Democratic Republic of the Congo, Denmark, Djibouti, Dominican Republic, Ecuador, Egypt, El Salvador, Eritrea, Estonia, Eswatini, Ethiopia, Fiji, Finland, France, Gambia, Georgia, Germany, Ghana, Greece, Grenada, Guatemala, Guinea, Guinea-Bissau, Guyana, Honduras, Hungary, Iceland, India, Indonesia, Iran (Islamic Republic of), Iraq, Ireland, Italy, Jamaica, Japan, Jordan, Kazakhstan, Kenya, Kuwait, Kyrgyzstan, Lao People's Democratic Republic, Latvia, Lebanon, Lesotho, Liberia, Libya, Liechtenstein, Lithuania, Luxembourg, Madagascar, Malawi, Malaysia, Maldives, Mali, Malta, Mauritania, Mauritius, Mexico, Micronesia (Federated States of), Monaco, Mongolia, Montenegro, Morocco, Mozambique, Myanmar, Namibia, Nauru, Nepal, Netherlands, New Zealand, Nicaragua, Niger, Norway, Oman, Pakistan, Panama,

---

* Subsequently, the delegation of Nigeria informed the Secretariat that it had intended to vote in favour. The voting tally above does not reflect this information.

Papua New Guinea, Paraguay, Peru, Philippines, Poland, Portugal, Qatar, Republic of Korea, Republic of Moldova, Romania, Russian Federation, Rwanda, Saint Lucia, Saint Vincent and the Grenadines, Samoa, San Marino, Sao Tome and Principe, Saudi Arabia, Senegal, Serbia, Seychelles, Sierra Leone, Singapore, Slovakia, Slovenia, South Africa, South Sudan, Spain, Sri Lanka, Sudan, Suriname, Sweden, Switzerland, Syrian Arab Republic, Tajikistan, Thailand, the former Yugoslav Republic of Macedonia, Timor-Leste, Togo, Tonga, Trinidad and Tobago, Tunisia, Turkey, Turkmenistan, Tuvalu, Uganda, Ukraine, United Arab Emirates, United Kingdom, United Republic of Tanzania, Uruguay, Vanuatu, Venezuela (Bolivarian Republic of), Viet Nam, Yemen, Zambia, Zimbabwe

Against:
Israel, United States

Abstaining:
None

Action by the First Committee

Date: 5 November 2018   Meeting: 28th meeting
Vote: 181-2-1   Draft resolution: A/C.1/73/L.3

Agenda item 99 (b)

73/31   No first placement of weapons in outer space

Text

The General Assembly,

Recognizing the common interest of all humankind in the exploration and use of outer space for peaceful purposes,

Seriously concerned about the possibility of an arms race in outer space and of outer space turning into an arena for military confrontation, and bearing in mind the importance of articles III and IV of the Treaty on Principles Governing the Activities of States in the Exploration and Use of Outer Space, including the Moon and Other Celestial Bodies,[1]

Conscious that the prevention of an arms race in outer space would avert a grave danger to international peace and security,

Reaffirming that practical measures should be examined and taken in the search for agreements to prevent an arms race in outer space in a common effort towards a community of shared future for humankind,

Emphasizing the paramount importance of strict compliance with the existing legal regime providing for the peaceful use of outer space,

Reaffirming its recognition that the legal regime applicable to outer space by itself does not guarantee prevention of an arms race in outer space and that there is a need to consolidate and reinforce that regime,

Convinced that such measures could critically improve conditions for efficiently addressing the threat of an arms race in outer space, including the placement of weapons in outer space,

Welcoming, in this regard, the draft treaty on the prevention of the placement of weapons in outer space and of the threat or use of force against outer space objects, introduced by China and the Russian Federation at the Conference on Disarmament in 2008,[2] and the submission of its updated version in 2014,[3]

Considering that transparency and confidence-building measures in outer space activities are an integral part of the draft treaty referred to above,

Recalling its resolutions 69/32 of 2 December 2014, 70/27 of 7 December 2015, 71/32 of 5 December 2016 and 72/27 of 4 December 2017, and its resolutions 45/55 B of 4 December 1990 and 48/74 B of 16 December 1993, which, inter alia, confirm the importance of transparency and confidence-

---

[1] United Nations, *Treaty Series*, vol. 610, No. 8843.

[2] See CD/1839.

[3] See CD/1985.

building measures as a means conducive to ensuring the attainment of the objective of preventing an arms race in outer space,

Noting the importance of the political statements made by a number of States[4] that they would not be the first to place weapons in outer space,

1.   *Reaffirms* the importance and urgency of the objective of preventing an arms race in outer space and the willingness of States to contribute to reaching this common goal;

2.   *Reiterates* that the Conference on Disarmament, as the single multilateral negotiating forum on this subject,[5] has the primary role in the negotiation of a multilateral agreement, or agreements, as appropriate, on the prevention of an arms race in outer space in all its aspects;

3.   *Urges* an early commencement of substantive work based on the updated draft treaty on the prevention of the placement of weapons in outer space and of the threat or use of force against outer space objects,[3] introduced by China and the Russian Federation at the Conference on Disarmament in 2008,[2] under the agenda item entitled "Prevention of an arms race in outer space";

4.   *Stresses* that, while such an agreement is not yet concluded, other measures may contribute to ensuring that weapons are not placed in outer space;

5.   *Encourages* all States, especially spacefaring nations, to consider the possibility of upholding, as appropriate, a political commitment not to be the first to place weapons in outer space;

6.   *Decides* to include in the provisional agenda of its seventy-fourth session, under the item entitled "Prevention of an arms race in outer space", the sub-item entitled "No first placement of weapons in outer space".

Action by the General Assembly

Date: 5 December 2018   Meeting: 45th plenary meeting
Vote: 128-12-40   Report: A/73/508

Sponsors

Algeria, Angola, Argentina, Armenia, Belarus, Bolivia (Plurinational State of), Brazil, Burundi, Chad, China, Cuba, Democratic People's Republic of Korea, Egypt, El Salvador, Eswatini, Guinea, Honduras, Kazakhstan, Lao People's Democratic Republic, Madagascar, Malawi,

---

[4] Argentina, Armenia, Belarus, Bolivia (Plurinational State of), Brazil, Cuba, Ecuador, Guatemala, Indonesia, Kazakhstan, Kyrgyzstan, Nicaragua, Russian Federation, Sri Lanka, Suriname, Tajikistan, Uruguay, Venezuela (Bolivarian Republic of) and Viet Nam.
[5] See resolution S-10/2.

Mali, Myanmar, Namibia, Nicaragua, Pakistan, **Russian Federation**, Senegal, Sierra Leone, Suriname, Syrian Arab Republic, Tajikistan, Thailand, Uganda, Venezuela (Bolivarian Republic of), Viet Nam, Zimbabwe

Co-sponsors

Bangladesh, Cambodia, Equatorial Guinea, Eritrea, Guinea-Bissau, Indonesia, Kyrgyzstan, Morocco, Sri Lanka, Sudan, Turkmenistan, Uzbekistan, Zambia

Recorded vote

In favour:

Afghanistan, Algeria, Angola, Antigua and Barbuda, Argentina, Armenia, Azerbaijan, Bahamas, Bahrain, Bangladesh, Barbados, Belarus, Belize, Benin, Bhutan, Bolivia (Plurinational State of), Botswana, Brazil, Brunei Darussalam, Burkina Faso, Burundi, Cabo Verde, Cambodia, Cameroon, Central African Republic, Chile, China, Colombia, Comoros, Congo, Costa Rica, Côte d'Ivoire, Cuba, Democratic People's Republic of Korea, Democratic Republic of the Congo, Djibouti, Dominican Republic, Ecuador, Egypt, El Salvador, Equatorial Guinea, Eritrea, Ethiopia, Fiji, Gambia, Ghana, Grenada, Guatemala, Guinea, Guinea-Bissau, Guyana, Honduras, India, Indonesia, Iran (Islamic Republic of), Iraq, Jamaica, Jordan, Kazakhstan, Kenya, Kuwait, Kyrgyzstan, Lao People's Democratic Republic, Lebanon, Lesotho, Liberia, Libya, Madagascar, Malawi, Malaysia, Maldives, Mali, Mauritania, Mauritius, Mexico, Mongolia, Morocco, Mozambique, Myanmar, Namibia, Nauru, Nepal, Nicaragua, Niger, Nigeria, Oman, Pakistan, Panama, Papua New Guinea, Paraguay, Peru, Philippines, Qatar, Russian Federation, Rwanda, Saint Lucia, Saint Vincent and the Grenadines, Samoa, Sao Tome and Principe, Saudi Arabia, Senegal, Serbia, Seychelles, Sierra Leone, Singapore, South Africa, South Sudan, Sri Lanka, Sudan, Suriname, Syrian Arab Republic, Tajikistan, Thailand, Timor-Leste, Togo, Trinidad and Tobago, Tunisia, Turkmenistan, Uganda, United Arab Emirates, United Republic of Tanzania, Uruguay, Vanuatu, Venezuela (Bolivarian Republic of), Viet Nam, Yemen, Zambia, Zimbabwe

Against:

Australia, Estonia, France, Georgia, Hungary, Israel, Latvia, Lithuania, Poland, Ukraine, United Kingdom, United States

Abstaining:

Albania, Andorra, Austria, Belgium, Bosnia and Herzegovina, Bulgaria, Canada, Croatia, Cyprus, Czechia, Denmark, Eswatini, Finland, Germany, Greece, Iceland, Ireland, Italy, Japan, Liechtenstein, Luxembourg, Malta, Monaco, Montenegro, Netherlands, New Zealand,

Norway, Portugal, Republic of Korea, Republic of Moldova, Romania, San Marino, Slovakia, Slovenia, Spain, Sweden, Switzerland, the former Yugoslav Republic of Macedonia, Turkey, Tuvalu

Action by the First Committee

Date: 5 November 2018   Meeting: 28th meeting
Vote: 129-12-40   Draft resolution: A/C.1/73/L.51

Agenda item 100

73/32 Role of science and technology in the context of international security and disarmament

Text

The General Assembly,

Recognizing that scientific and technological developments can have both civilian and military applications and that progress in science and technology for civilian applications needs to be maintained and encouraged,

Underlining the keen interest of the international community to keep abreast of the latest developments in science and technology of relevance to international security and disarmament and to channel scientific and technological developments for beneficial purposes,

Mindful of the need to regulate the transfer of technologies for peaceful uses, in accordance with relevant international obligations, to address the risk of proliferation by States or non-State actors,

Acknowledging the need to continue the exchange of technologies for peaceful uses, including in accordance with relevant international obligations,

Mindful of the rights of States, reflected in relevant international agreements, regarding the development, production, transfer and use of technologies for peaceful purposes, in accordance with relevant international obligations, as well as the need for all Member States to fulfil their obligations in relation to arms control and disarmament and to prevent proliferation in all its aspects of all weapons of mass destruction and their means of delivery,

Cognizant of the discussions on developments in science and technology at the International Atomic Energy Agency and the Organisation for the Prohibition of Chemical Weapons and within the meetings of experts on science and technology under the 2018–2020 intersessional programme established by the 2017 Meeting of the States Parties to the Convention on the Prohibition of the Development, Production and Stockpiling of Bacteriological (Biological) and Toxin Weapons and on Their Destruction,

Cognizant also of the discussions in the Conference on Disarmament in 2018 under its subsidiary body 5,

Mindful of the discussions in other forums, such as the Committee on the Peaceful Uses of Outer Space, on the long-term sustainability of outer space activities and on the prevention of an arms race in outer space in the United Nations disarmament machinery,

Noting the discussions on various dimensions of emerging technologies under the framework of the Convention on Prohibitions or Restrictions on the Use of Certain Conventional Weapons Which May Be Deemed to Be

Excessively Injurious or to Have Indiscriminate Effects,[1] and welcoming the adoption of the report of the 2018 session of the Group of Governmental Experts on lethal autonomous weapons systems, including the section on emerging commonalities, conclusions and recommendations,

Noting also the discussions within the United Nations and the specialized agencies on developments in the field of information and communications technologies, including in the context of international security,

Acknowledging that the accelerating pace of technological change necessitates a system-wide assessment of the potential impact of developments in science and technology on international security and disarmament, with due regard to avoiding duplication and complementing efforts already under way in United Nations entities and in the framework of the relevant international conventions,

Noting the discussions on current developments in science and technology and their potential impact on international security and disarmament efforts in the Advisory Board on Disarmament Matters during its sixty-ninth and seventieth sessions, in 2018,

1.   *Invites* Member States to continue efforts to apply developments in science and technology for disarmament-related purposes, including the verification of disarmament, arms control and non-proliferation instruments, and to make disarmament-related technologies available to interested States;

2.   *Calls upon* Member States to remain vigilant in understanding new and emerging developments in science and technology that could imperil international security, and underlines the importance of Member States engaging with experts from industry, the research community and civil society in addressing this challenge;

3.   *Welcomes* the report of the Secretary-General on current developments in science and technology and their potential impact on international security and disarmament efforts,[2] in which he highlights recent developments in science and technology, including in artificial intelligence and autonomous systems, biology and chemistry, advanced missile and missile-defence technologies, space-based technologies, electromagnetic technologies and materials technologies, and takes note of the section containing submissions from Member States giving their views on the matter;

4.   *Requests* the Secretary-General to submit to the General Assembly at its seventy-fourth session an updated report on recent developments in science and technology and their potential impact on international security and disarmament efforts, with an annex containing submissions from Member States giving their views on the matter;

---

[1] United Nations, *Treaty Series*, vol. 1342, No. 22495.
[2] A/73/177.

5.   *Encourages* the Advisory Board on Disarmament Matters to continue its discussions on current developments in science and technology and their potential impact on international security and disarmament efforts;

6.   *Requests* the United Nations Institute for Disarmament Research to convene, from voluntary contributions, a one-day focused informal seminar in Geneva in 2019 on the role of science and technology in the context of international security and disarmament, in order to facilitate dialogue among relevant stakeholders on current developments in science and technology and their potential impact on international security and disarmament efforts;

7.   *Decides* to include in the provisional agenda of its seventy-fourth session the item entitled "Role of science and technology in the context of international security and disarmament".

Action by the General Assembly

Date: 5 December 2018   Meeting: 45th plenary meeting
Vote: Adopted without a vote   Report: A/73/509

Sponsors

Austria, Bhutan, Central African Republic, Croatia, Germany, **India**, Italy, Netherlands, Spain, Sweden

Co-sponsors

Bangladesh, Canada, Finland, Guinea, Japan, Kazakhstan, Mauritius, Montenegro, Singapore, Slovenia, Switzerland

Action by the First Committee

Date: 8 November 2018   Meeting: 30th meeting
Vote: Adopted without a vote Draft resolution: A/C.1/73/L.65/Rev.1

Agenda item 101 (e)

73/33 Regional disarmament

Text

The General Assembly,

Recalling its resolutions 45/58 P of 4 December 1990, 46/36 I of 6 December 1991, 47/52 J of 9 December 1992, 48/75 I of 16 December 1993, 49/75 N of 15 December 1994, 50/70 K of 12 December 1995, 51/45 K of 10 December 1996, 52/38 P of 9 December 1997, 53/77 O of 4 December 1998, 54/54 N of 1 December 1999, 55/33 O of 20 November 2000, 56/24 H of 29 November 2001, 57/76 of 22 November 2002, 58/38 of 8 December 2003, 59/89 of 3 December 2004, 60/63 of 8 December 2005, 61/80 of 6 December 2006, 62/38 of 5 December 2007, 63/43 of 2 December 2008, 64/41 of 2 December 2009, 65/45 of 8 December 2010, 66/36 of 2 December 2011, 67/57 of 3 December 2012, 68/54 of 5 December 2013, 69/45 of 2 December 2014, 70/43 of 7 December 2015, 71/40 of 5 December 2016 and 72/34 of 4 December 2017 on regional disarmament,

Believing that the efforts of the international community to move towards the ideal of general and complete disarmament are guided by the inherent human desire for genuine peace and security, the elimination of the danger of war and the release of economic, intellectual and other resources for peaceful pursuits,

Affirming the abiding commitment of all States to the purposes and principles enshrined in the Charter of the United Nations in the conduct of their international relations,

Noting that essential guidelines for progress towards general and complete disarmament were adopted at the tenth special session of the General Assembly,[1]

Taking note of the guidelines and recommendations for regional approaches to disarmament within the context of global security adopted by the Disarmament Commission at its 1993 substantive session,[2]

Welcoming the prospects of genuine progress in the field of disarmament engendered in recent years as a result of negotiations between the two super-Powers,

Taking note of the recent proposals for disarmament at the regional and subregional levels,

---

[1] Resolution S-10/2.

[2] *Official Records of the General Assembly, Forty-eighth Session, Supplement No. 42* (A/48/42), annex II.

Recognizing the importance of confidence-building measures for regional and international peace and security,

Convinced that endeavours by countries to promote regional disarmament, taking into account the specific characteristics of each region and in accordance with the principle of undiminished security at the lowest level of armaments, would enhance the security of all States and would thus contribute to international peace and security by reducing the risk of regional conflicts,

1.　*Stresses* that sustained efforts are needed, within the framework of the Conference on Disarmament and under the umbrella of the United Nations, to make progress on the entire range of disarmament issues;

2.　*Affirms* that global and regional approaches to disarmament complement each other and should therefore be pursued simultaneously to promote regional and international peace and security;

3.　*Calls upon* States to conclude agreements, wherever possible, for nuclear non-proliferation, disarmament and confidence-building measures at the regional and subregional levels;

4.　*Welcomes* the initiatives towards disarmament, nuclear non-proliferation and security undertaken by some countries at the regional and subregional levels;

5.　*Supports and encourages* efforts aimed at promoting confidence-building measures at the regional and subregional levels to ease regional tensions and to further disarmament and nuclear non-proliferation measures at the regional and subregional levels;

6.　*Decides* to include in the provisional agenda of its seventy-fourth session, under the item entitled "General and complete disarmament", the sub-item entitled "Regional disarmament".

Action by the General Assembly

Date: 5 December 2018　　Meeting: 45th plenary meeting
Vote: Adopted without a vote　Report: A/73/510

Sponsors

Ecuador, Egypt, Nepal, Nigeria, **Pakistan**, Peru, Saudi Arabia

Co-sponsors

Bangladesh, Iraq, Kuwait, Sri Lanka, Turkey

Action by the First Committee

Date: 8 November 2018　　Meeting:　　30th meeting
Vote: Adopted without a vote　Draft resolution: A/C.1/73/L.5

Agenda item 101 (f)

73/34　Conventional arms control at the regional and subregional levels

Text

The General Assembly,

Recalling its resolutions 48/75 J of 16 December 1993, 49/75 O of 15 December 1994, 50/70 L of 12 December 1995, 51/45 Q of 10 December 1996, 52/38 Q of 9 December 1997, 53/77 P of 4 December 1998, 54/54 M of 1 December 1999, 55/33 P of 20 November 2000, 56/24 I of 29 November 2001, 57/77 of 22 November 2002, 58/39 of 8 December 2003, 59/88 of 3 December 2004, 60/75 of 8 December 2005, 61/82 of 6 December 2006, 62/44 of 5 December 2007, 63/44 of 2 December 2008, 64/42 of 2 December 2009, 65/46 of 8 December 2010, 66/37 of 2 December 2011, 67/62 of 3 December 2012, 68/56 of 5 December 2013, 69/47 of 2 December 2014, 70/44 of 7 December 2015, 71/41 of 5 December 2016 and 72/35 of 4 December 2017,

Recognizing the crucial role of conventional arms control in promoting regional and international peace and security,

Recognizing also the importance of equitable representation of women in arms control discussions and negotiations,

Convinced that conventional arms control needs to be pursued primarily in the regional and subregional contexts since most threats to peace and security in the post-cold-war era arise mainly among States located in the same region or subregion,

Aware that the preservation of a balance in the defence capabilities of States at the lowest level of armaments would contribute to peace and stability and should be a prime objective of conventional arms control,

Desirous of promoting agreements to strengthen regional peace and security at the lowest possible level of armaments and military forces,

Noting with particular interest the initiatives taken in this regard in different regions of the world, in particular the commencement of consultations among a number of Latin American countries and the proposals for conventional arms control made in the context of South Asia, and recognizing, in the context of this subject, the relevance and value of the Treaty on Conventional Armed Forces in Europe,[1] which is a cornerstone of European security,

---

[1]　See CD/1064.

Believing that militarily significant States and States with larger military capabilities have a special responsibility in promoting such agreements for regional security,

Believing also that an important objective of conventional arms control in regions of tension should be to prevent the possibility of military attack launched by surprise and to avoid aggression,

1. *Decides* to give urgent consideration to the issues involved in conventional arms control at the regional and subregional levels;

2. *Requests* the Conference on Disarmament to consider the formulation of principles that can serve as a framework for regional agreements on conventional arms control, and looks forward to a report of the Conference on this subject;

3. *Requests* the Secretary-General, in the meantime, to seek the views of Member States on the subject and to submit a report to the General Assembly at its seventy-fourth session;

4. *Decides* to include in the provisional agenda of its seventy-fourth session, under the item entitled "General and complete disarmament", the sub-item entitled "Conventional arms control at the regional and subregional levels".

Action by the General Assembly

Date: 5 December 2018   Meeting: 45th plenary meeting
Vote: 179-1-3   Report: A/73/510
      128-2-43, o.p. 2*

Sponsors

Ecuador, **Pakistan**, Peru, Syrian Arab Republic, Zambia

Co-sponsors

Bangladesh, Belarus, Italy, Ukraine

Recorded vote

As a whole

In favour:

Afghanistan, Albania, Algeria, Andorra, Angola, Antigua and Barbuda, Argentina, Armenia, Australia, Austria, Azerbaijan, Bahamas, Bahrain, Bangladesh, Barbados, Belarus, Belgium, Belize, Benin, Bolivia (Plurinational State of), Bosnia and Herzegovina, Botswana, Brazil, Brunei Darussalam, Bulgaria, Burkina Faso, Burundi, Cabo Verde, Cambodia, Cameroon, Canada, Central African Republic, Chile, China,

---

* Abbreviations: o.p. = operative paragraph; p.p. = preambular paragraph.

Colombia, Comoros, Congo, Costa Rica, Côte d'Ivoire, Croatia, Cuba, Cyprus, Czechia, Democratic People's Republic of Korea, Democratic Republic of the Congo, Denmark, Djibouti, Dominican Republic, Ecuador, Egypt, El Salvador, Equatorial Guinea, Eritrea, Estonia, Eswatini, Ethiopia, Fiji, Finland, France, Gambia, Georgia, Germany, Ghana, Greece, Grenada, Guatemala, Guinea, Guinea-Bissau, Guyana, Haiti, Honduras, Hungary, Iceland, Indonesia, Iran (Islamic Republic of), Iraq, Ireland, Israel, Italy, Jamaica, Japan, Jordan, Kazakhstan, Kenya, Kuwait, Kyrgyzstan, Lao People's Democratic Republic, Latvia, Lebanon, Lesotho, Liberia, Libya, Liechtenstein, Lithuania, Luxembourg, Madagascar, Malawi, Malaysia, Maldives, Mali, Malta, Marshall Islands, Mauritania, Mauritius, Mexico, Micronesia (Federated States of), Monaco, Mongolia, Montenegro, Morocco, Mozambique, Myanmar, Namibia, Nauru, Nepal, Netherlands, New Zealand, Nicaragua, Niger, Nigeria, Norway, Oman, Pakistan, Panama, Papua New Guinea, Paraguay, Peru, Philippines, Poland, Portugal, Qatar, Republic of Korea, Republic of Moldova, Romania, Saint Lucia, Saint Vincent and the Grenadines, Samoa, San Marino, Sao Tome and Principe, Saudi Arabia, Senegal, Serbia, Seychelles, Sierra Leone, Singapore, Slovakia, Slovenia, South Africa, Spain, Sri Lanka, Sudan, Suriname, Sweden, Switzerland, Syrian Arab Republic, Tajikistan, Thailand, the former Yugoslav Republic of Macedonia, Timor-Leste, Togo, Tonga, Trinidad and Tobago, Tunisia, Turkey, Turkmenistan, Tuvalu, Uganda, Ukraine, United Arab Emirates, United Kingdom, United Republic of Tanzania, United States, Uruguay, Vanuatu, Venezuela (Bolivarian Republic of), Viet Nam, Yemen, Zambia, Zimbabwe

Against:
India

Abstaining:
Bhutan, Russian Federation, Rwanda

Operative paragraph 2

In favour:
Afghanistan, Algeria, Angola, Antigua and Barbuda, Argentina, Azerbaijan, Bahamas, Bahrain, Bangladesh, Barbados, Belarus, Belize, Benin, Bolivia (Plurinational State of), Botswana, Brazil, Brunei Darussalam, Bulgaria, Burkina Faso, Burundi, Cabo Verde, Cambodia, Canada, Chile, China, Colombia, Comoros, Congo, Costa Rica, Côte d'Ivoire, Cuba, Democratic People's Republic of Korea, Democratic Republic of the Congo, Djibouti, Dominican Republic, Ecuador, Egypt, El Salvador, Equatorial Guinea, Eritrea, Eswatini, Ethiopia, Fiji, Gambia, Georgia, Ghana, Guatemala, Guinea, Guinea-Bissau, Guyana, Haiti, Honduras, Hungary, Iran (Islamic Republic of), Iraq,

Italy, Jamaica, Japan, Jordan, Kazakhstan, Kenya, Kuwait, Kyrgyzstan, Lao People's Democratic Republic, Lebanon, Lesotho, Liberia, Libya, Madagascar, Malawi, Malaysia, Maldives, Mali, Marshall Islands, Mauritania, Mongolia, Morocco, Mozambique, Myanmar, Namibia, Nepal, Nicaragua, Niger, Nigeria, Oman, Pakistan, Panama, Papua New Guinea, Paraguay, Peru, Philippines, Portugal, Qatar, Republic of Korea, Republic of Moldova, Saint Lucia, Saint Vincent and the Grenadines, Samoa, Sao Tome and Principe, Saudi Arabia, Senegal, Sierra Leone, Singapore, Sri Lanka, Sudan, Suriname, Syrian Arab Republic, Tajikistan, Thailand, Timor-Leste, Togo, Trinidad and Tobago, Tunisia, Turkey, Turkmenistan, Tuvalu, Uganda, Ukraine, United Arab Emirates, United Republic of Tanzania, United States, Uruguay, Vanuatu, Venezuela (Bolivarian Republic of), Viet Nam, Yemen, Zambia, Zimbabwe

Against:

India, Russian Federation

Abstaining:

Albania, Andorra, Australia, Austria, Belgium, Bhutan, Bosnia and Herzegovina, Croatia, Cyprus, Czechia, Denmark, Estonia, Finland, France, Germany, Greece, Iceland, Indonesia, Ireland, Israel, Latvia, Liechtenstein, Lithuania, Luxembourg, Malta, Mexico, Monaco, Montenegro, Netherlands, New Zealand, Norway, Poland, Romania, San Marino, Serbia, Slovakia, Slovenia, South Africa, Spain, Sweden, Switzerland, the former Yugoslav Republic of Macedonia, United Kingdom

Action by the First Committee

Date:	8 November 2018	Meeting:	30th meeting
Vote:	179-1-2	Draft resolution:	A/C.1/73/L.6
	127-2-45, o.p. 2		

Agenda item 101 (x)

73/35   Confidence-building measures in the regional and subregional context

Text

The General Assembly,

Guided by the purposes and principles enshrined in the Charter of the United Nations,

Recalling its resolutions 58/43 of 8 December 2003, 59/87 of 3 December 2004, 60/64 of 8 December 2005, 61/81 of 6 December 2006, 62/45 of 5 December 2007, 63/45 of 2 December 2008, 64/43 of 2 December 2009, 65/47 of 8 December 2010, 66/38 of 2 December 2011, 67/61 of 3 December 2012, 68/55 of 5 December 2013, 69/46 of 2 December 2014, 70/42 of 7 December 2015, 71/39 of 5 December 2016 and 72/33 of 4 December 2017 on confidence-building measures in the regional and subregional context,

Recalling also its resolution 57/337 of 3 July 2003 on the prevention of armed conflict, in which the General Assembly calls upon Member States to settle their disputes by peaceful means, as set out in Chapter VI of the Charter, inter alia, by any procedures adopted by the parties,

Recalling further the resolutions and guidelines adopted by consensus by the General Assembly and the Disarmament Commission relating to confidence-building measures and their implementation at the global, regional and subregional levels,

Considering the importance and effectiveness of confidence-building measures taken at the initiative and with the agreement of all States concerned, and taking into account the specific characteristics of each region, since such measures can contribute to regional stability,

Convinced that resources released by disarmament, including regional disarmament, can be devoted to economic and social development and to the protection of the environment for the benefit of all peoples, in particular those of the developing countries,

Recognizing the need for meaningful dialogue among States concerned to avert conflict,

Welcoming the peace processes already initiated by States concerned to resolve their disputes through peaceful means bilaterally or through mediation, inter alia, by third parties, regional organizations or the United Nations,

Recognizing that States in some regions have already taken steps towards confidence-building measures at the bilateral, subregional and regional levels in the political and military fields, including arms control and disarmament, and noting that such confidence-building measures have improved peace and security in those regions and contributed to progress in the socioeconomic conditions of their people,

Concerned that the continuation of disputes among States, particularly in the absence of an effective mechanism to resolve them through peaceful means, may contribute to the arms race and endanger the maintenance of international peace and security and the efforts of the international community to promote arms control and disarmament,

1. *Calls upon* Member States to refrain from the use or threat of use of force in accordance with the purposes and principles of the Charter of the United Nations;

2. *Reaffirms its commitment* to the peaceful settlement of disputes under Chapter VI of the Charter, in particular Article 33, which provides for a solution by negotiation, enquiry, mediation, conciliation, arbitration, judicial settlement, resort to regional agencies or arrangements or other peaceful means chosen by the parties;

3. *Reaffirms* the ways and means regarding confidence- and security-building measures set out in the report of the Disarmament Commission on its 1993 session;[1]

4. *Calls upon* Member States to pursue these ways and means through sustained consultations and dialogue, while at the same time avoiding actions that may hinder or impair such a dialogue;

5. *Urges* States to comply strictly with all bilateral, regional and international agreements, including arms control and disarmament agreements, to which they are party;

6. *Emphasizes* that the objective of confidence-building measures should be to help to strengthen international peace and security and to be consistent with the principle of undiminished security at the lowest level of armaments;

7. *Encourages* the promotion of bilateral and regional confidence-building measures, with the consent and participation of the parties concerned, to avoid conflict and prevent the unintended and accidental outbreak of hostilities;

8. *Requests* the Secretary-General to submit a report to the General Assembly at its seventy-fourth session containing the views of Member States on confidence-building measures in the regional and subregional context;

9. *Decides* to include in the provisional agenda of its seventy-fourth session, under the item entitled "General and complete disarmament",

---

[1] *Official Records of the General Assembly, Forty-eighth Session, Supplement No. 42* (A/48/42), annex II, sect. III.A.

the sub-item entitled "Confidence-building measures in the regional and subregional context".

Action by the General Assembly

Date: 5 December 2018   Meeting: 45th plenary meeting
Vote: Adopted without a vote   Report: A/73/510

Sponsors

Pakistan, Syrian Arab Republic

Co-sponsors

Bangladesh, Ukraine, Zambia

Action by the First Committee

Date: 8 November 2018   Meeting: 30th meeting
Vote: Adopted without a vote   Draft resolution: A/C.1/73/L.7

Agenda item 101 (bb)

73/36   The Arms Trade Treaty

Text

The General Assembly,

Recalling its resolutions 61/89 of 6 December 2006, 63/240 of 24 December 2008, 64/48 of 2 December 2009, 67/234 A of 24 December 2012, 67/234 B of 2 April 2013, 68/31 of 5 December 2013, 69/49 of 2 December 2014, 70/58 of 7 December 2015, 71/50 of 5 December 2016 and 72/44 of 4 December 2017 and its decision 66/518 of 2 December 2011,

Recognizing that disarmament, arms control and non-proliferation are essential for the maintenance of international peace and security,

Recognizing also the security, social, economic and humanitarian consequences of the illicit and unregulated trade in conventional arms,

Recognizing further the legitimate political, security, economic and commercial interests of States in the international trade in conventional arms,

Underlining the need to prevent and eradicate the illicit trade in conventional arms and to prevent their diversion to the illicit market, or for unauthorized end use and end users, including the commission of terrorist acts,

Recalling the contribution made by the Programme of Action to Prevent, Combat and Eradicate the Illicit Trade in Small Arms and Light Weapons in All Its Aspects,[1] as well as the Protocol against the Illicit Manufacturing of and Trafficking in Firearms, Their Parts and Components and Ammunition, supplementing the United Nations Convention against Transnational Organized Crime,[2] and the International Instrument to Enable States to Identify and Trace, in a Timely and Reliable Manner, Illicit Small Arms and Light Weapons,[3]

Highlighting the links and synergies between the Arms Trade Treaty[4] and the 2030 Agenda for Sustainable Development,[5] including Sustainable Development Goal 16 and target 16.4, which aims at significantly reducing illicit arms flows by 2030,

---

[1] *Report of the United Nations Conference on the Illicit Trade in Small Arms and Light Weapons in All Its Aspects, New York, 9–20 July 2001* (A/CONF.192/15), chap. IV, para. 24.

[2] United Nations, *Treaty Series*, vol. 2326, No. 39574.

[3] See decision 60/519 and A/60/88 and A/60/88/Corr.2, annex.

[4] See resolution 67/234 B.

[5] Resolution 70/1.

Taking note of the Secretary-General's disarmament agenda, *Securing Our Common Future: An Agenda for Disarmament*, in particular the section of the agenda entitled "Disarmament that saves lives",

Recognizing the negative impact of the illicit and unregulated trade in conventional arms and related ammunition on the lives of women, men, girls and boys, and that the Arms Trade Treaty was the first international agreement to identify and call upon States to address the link between conventional arms transfers and the risk of serious acts of gender-based violence and serious acts of violence against women and children,

Recognizing also the important role that civil society organizations, including non-governmental organizations, and industry play, by raising awareness, in efforts to prevent and eradicate the unregulated and illicit trade in conventional arms and prevent their diversion and in supporting the implementation of the Arms Trade Treaty,

Recalling the adoption by the General Assembly and the entry into force of the Treaty on 2 April 2013 and 24 December 2014, respectively, and noting that the Treaty remains open for accession by any State that has not signed it,

Welcoming the latest ratifications of the Treaty, bearing in mind that universalization of the Treaty is essential to achieving its object and purpose,

Noting the efforts by the States parties to the Treaty to continue exploring ways and means to enhance national implementation of the Treaty through the working group on effective treaty implementation and the voluntary trust fund for the implementation of the Arms Trade Treaty,

1. *Welcomes* the decisions taken at the Fourth Conference of States Parties to the Arms Trade Treaty, held in Tokyo from 20 to 24 August 2018, and notes that the Fifth Conference of States Parties will be held in Geneva from 26 to 30 August 2019;

2. *Also welcomes* the progress made by the standing working groups on effective treaty implementation, on transparency and reporting, and on universalization in advancing the object and purpose of the Arms Trade Treaty;[4]

3. *Recognizes* that the consolidation of the institutional structure of the Treaty provides a framework for supporting further work under the Treaty, in particular its effective implementation, and in this regard expresses concern about the unpaid assessed contributions of States and the potential adverse implications this has for the Treaty processes, and calls upon States that have not yet done so to address their financial obligations under the Treaty in a prompt and timely manner;

4. *Calls upon* all States that have not yet done so to ratify, accept, approve or accede to the Treaty, according to their respective constitutional processes, in order to achieve its universalization;

5. *Calls upon* those States parties in a position to do so to provide assistance, including legal or legislative assistance, institutional capacity-building and technical, material or financial assistance, to requesting States in order to promote the implementation and universalization of the Treaty;

6. *Stresses* the vital importance of the full and effective implementation of and compliance with all provisions of the Treaty by States parties, and urges the States parties to meet their obligations under the Treaty, thereby contributing to international and regional peace, security and stability, to the reduction of human suffering and to the promotion of cooperation, transparency and responsible action;

7. *Recognizes* the complementarity among all relevant international instruments on conventional arms and the Treaty, and to this end urges all States to implement effective national measures to prevent, combat and eradicate the illicit and unregulated trade in conventional arms and ammunition in fulfilment of their respective international obligations and commitments;

8. *Encourages* further steps to enable States to increasingly prevent and tackle diversion of conventional arms and ammunition to unauthorized end uses and end users;

9. *Recognizes* the added value of the adoption in June 2018 of the report of the third United Nations Conference to Review Progress Made in the Implementation of the Programme of Action to Prevent, Combat and Eradicate the Illicit Trade in Small Arms and Light Weapons in All Its Aspects,[6] including the outcome document annexed thereto, and acknowledges synergies between the Programme of Action and the Arms Trade Treaty;

10. *Encourages* all States parties to make available, in a timely manner, and to update, as appropriate, their initial report, as well as their annual report for the preceding calendar year, as required under article 13 of the Treaty, thereby enhancing confidence, transparency, trust and accountability, and notes the endorsement by the Second Conference of States Parties of templates that may facilitate the reporting task;

11. *Encourages* States parties and signatory States to ensure the full and equal participation of women and men in pursuing the object and purpose of the Treaty and its implementation;

12. *Welcomes* the successful operationalization of the voluntary trust fund for the implementation of the Arms Trade Treaty, encourages eligible States to make best use of the voluntary trust fund, and encourages all States parties in a position to do so to contribute to the voluntary trust fund;

---

[6] A/CONF.192/2018/RC/3.

13. *Encourages* States parties and signatory States in a position to do so to provide financial assistance, through a voluntary sponsorship fund, that could contribute to meeting the costs of participation in meetings under the Treaty for those States that would otherwise be unable to attend;

14. *Encourages* States parties to strengthen their cooperation with civil society, including non-governmental organizations, industry and relevant international organizations and to work with other States parties at the national and regional levels, and invites those stakeholders, in particular those that are underrepresented in Arms Trade Treaty processes, to engage further with States parties with the aim of ensuring the effective implementation and universalization of the Treaty;

15. *Decides* to include in the provisional agenda of its seventy-fourth session, under the item entitled "General and complete disarmament", the sub-item entitled "The Arms Trade Treaty", and to review the implementation of the present resolution at that session.

Action by the General Assembly

Date: 5 December 2018   Meeting: 45th plenary meeting
Vote: 151-0-29   Report: A/73/510
        158-0-16. p.p. 8
        138-0-33, o.p. 4
        134-2-35, o.p. 9

Sponsors

Afghanistan, Albania, Antigua and Barbuda, Argentina, Australia, Austria, Bahamas, Belgium, Belize, Bosnia and Herzegovina, Bulgaria, Canada, Central African Republic, Chile, Costa Rica, Croatia, Cyprus, Czechia, Denmark, Dominican Republic, El Salvador, Estonia, Finland, France, Georgia, Germany, Ghana, Greece, Guatemala, Guyana, Haiti, Honduras, Hungary, Iceland, Ireland, Italy, Jamaica, Japan, Kazakhstan, **Latvia**, Lesotho, Liechtenstein, Lithuania, Luxembourg, Madagascar, Malawi, Malta, Mexico, Monaco, Mongolia, Montenegro, Namibia, Netherlands, New Zealand, Norway, Panama, Paraguay, Peru, Poland, Portugal, Republic of Korea, Republic of Moldova, Romania, Saint Lucia, Saint Vincent and the Grenadines, Samoa, San Marino, Senegal, Serbia, Seychelles, Slovakia, Slovenia, South Africa, Spain, Suriname, Sweden, Switzerland, the former Yugoslav Republic of Macedonia, Togo, Trinidad and Tobago, Tuvalu, Ukraine, United Kingdom, Uruguay, Zambia

Co-sponsors

Andorra, Benin, Burkina Faso, Chad, Grenada, Guinea, Guinea-Bissau, Liberia, Maldives, Nigeria, Palau, Philippines, Saint Kitts and Nevis, Thailand, Turkey

Recorded vote

As a whole

In favour:

Afghanistan, Albania, Algeria, Andorra, Angola, Antigua and Barbuda, Argentina, Australia, Austria, Bahamas, Bahrain, Bangladesh, Barbados, Belgium, Belize, Benin, Bhutan, Bosnia and Herzegovina, Botswana, Brazil, Brunei Darussalam, Bulgaria, Burkina Faso, Burundi, Cabo Verde, Cambodia, Cameroon, Canada, Central African Republic, Chile, China, Colombia, Comoros, Congo, Costa Rica, Côte d'Ivoire, Croatia, Cyprus, Czechia, Democratic Republic of the Congo, Denmark, Djibouti, Dominican Republic, El Salvador, Equatorial Guinea, Eritrea, Estonia, Ethiopia, Fiji, Finland, France, Gabon, Gambia, Georgia, Germany, Ghana, Greece, Grenada, Guatemala, Guinea, Guinea-Bissau, Guyana, Haiti, Honduras, Hungary, Iceland, Iraq, Ireland, Israel, Italy, Jamaica, Japan, Jordan, Kazakhstan, Kenya, Latvia, Lebanon, Lesotho, Liberia, Libya, Liechtenstein, Lithuania, Luxembourg, Madagascar, Malawi, Malaysia, Maldives, Mali, Malta, Marshall Islands, Mauritania, Mauritius, Mexico, Micronesia (Federated States of), Monaco, Mongolia, Montenegro, Morocco, Mozambique, Namibia, Nepal, Netherlands, New Zealand, Niger, Nigeria, Norway, Pakistan, Panama, Papua New Guinea, Paraguay, Peru, Philippines, Poland, Portugal, Republic of Korea, Republic of Moldova, Romania, Saint Lucia, Saint Vincent and the Grenadines, Samoa, San Marino, Sao Tome and Principe, Senegal, Serbia, Seychelles, Sierra Leone, Singapore, Slovakia, Slovenia, South Africa, Spain, Suriname, Sweden, Switzerland, Thailand, the former Yugoslav Republic of Macedonia, Timor-Leste, Togo, Tonga, Trinidad and Tobago, Tunisia, Turkey, Turkmenistan, Tuvalu, Ukraine, United Arab Emirates, United Kingdom, United Republic of Tanzania, Uruguay, Vanuatu, Zambia

Against:

None

Abstaining:

Armenia, Azerbaijan, Belarus, Bolivia (Plurinational State of), Cuba, Democratic People's Republic of Korea, Ecuador, Egypt, India, Indonesia, Iran (Islamic Republic of), Kuwait, Lao People's Democratic Republic, Myanmar, Nicaragua, Oman, Qatar, Russian Federation, Rwanda, Saudi Arabia, Sri Lanka, Sudan, Syrian Arab Republic,

Tajikistan, Uganda, United States, Venezuela (Bolivarian Republic of), Yemen, Zimbabwe

Eighth preambular paragraph

In favour:

Afghanistan, Albania, Algeria, Andorra, Angola, Antigua and Barbuda, Argentina, Australia, Austria, Bahamas, Bahrain, Bangladesh, Barbados, Belarus, Belgium, Belize, Benin, Bhutan, Bolivia (Plurinational State of), Bosnia and Herzegovina, Botswana, Brazil, Brunei Darussalam, Bulgaria, Burkina Faso, Burundi, Cabo Verde, Cambodia, Canada, Chile, China, Colombia, Comoros, Congo, Costa Rica, Côte d'Ivoire, Croatia, Cuba, Cyprus, Czechia, Democratic People's Republic of Korea, Democratic Republic of the Congo, Denmark, Djibouti, Dominican Republic, Ecuador, El Salvador, Equatorial Guinea, Eritrea, Estonia, Ethiopia, Finland, France, Gabon, Gambia, Georgia, Germany, Ghana, Greece, Guatemala, Guinea, Guinea-Bissau, Guyana, Haiti, Honduras, Hungary, Iceland, India, Indonesia, Iraq, Ireland, Italy, Jamaica, Japan, Jordan, Kazakhstan, Kenya, Lao People's Democratic Republic, Latvia, Lebanon, Lesotho, Liberia, Libya, Liechtenstein, Lithuania, Luxembourg, Madagascar, Malawi, Malaysia, Maldives, Mali, Malta, Marshall Islands, Mauritania, Mauritius, Mexico, Micronesia (Federated States of), Monaco, Mongolia, Montenegro, Morocco, Mozambique, Myanmar, Namibia, Nepal, Netherlands, New Zealand, Nicaragua, Niger, Nigeria, Norway, Pakistan, Panama, Papua New Guinea, Paraguay, Peru, Philippines, Poland, Portugal, Republic of Korea, Republic of Moldova, Romania, Rwanda, Saint Lucia, Saint Vincent and the Grenadines, Samoa, San Marino, Sao Tome and Principe, Senegal, Serbia, Seychelles, Sierra Leone, Singapore, Slovakia, Slovenia, South Africa, Spain, Suriname, Sweden, Switzerland, Thailand, the former Yugoslav Republic of Macedonia, Timor-Leste, Togo, Trinidad and Tobago, Tunisia, Turkey, Turkmenistan, Tuvalu, Uganda, Ukraine, United Arab Emirates, United Kingdom, United Republic of Tanzania, Uruguay, Vanuatu, Venezuela (Bolivarian Republic of), Zambia

Against:

None

Abstaining:

Armenia, Azerbaijan, Egypt, Fiji, Israel, Kuwait, Oman, Qatar, Russian Federation, Saudi Arabia, Sri Lanka, Sudan, Syrian Arab Republic, United States, Yemen, Zimbabwe

Operative paragraph 4*

In favour:

Afghanistan, Albania, Andorra, Angola, Antigua and Barbuda, Argentina, Australia, Austria, Bahamas, Bahrain, Bangladesh, Barbados, Belgium, Belize, Benin, Bosnia and Herzegovina, Botswana, Brazil, Brunei Darussalam, Bulgaria, Burkina Faso, Burundi, Cabo Verde, Canada, Chile, China, Colombia, Comoros, Congo, Costa Rica, Côte d'Ivoire, Croatia, Cyprus, Czechia, Democratic Republic of the Congo, Denmark, Djibouti, Dominican Republic, El Salvador, Equatorial Guinea, Eritrea, Estonia, Ethiopia, Finland, France, Gambia, Georgia, Germany, Ghana, Greece, Guatemala, Guinea, Guinea-Bissau, Guyana, Haiti, Honduras, Hungary, Iceland, Iraq, Ireland, Italy, Jamaica, Japan, Kazakhstan, Kenya, Latvia, Lebanon, Lesotho, Liberia, Libya, Liechtenstein, Lithuania, Luxembourg, Madagascar, Malawi, Malaysia, Maldives, Mali, Malta, Marshall Islands, Mauritania, Mexico, Micronesia (Federated States of), Monaco, Mongolia, Montenegro, Mozambique, Namibia, Nepal, Netherlands, New Zealand, Niger, Nigeria, Norway, Pakistan, Panama, Papua New Guinea, Paraguay, Peru, Philippines, Poland, Portugal, Republic of Korea, Republic of Moldova, Romania, Saint Lucia, Saint Vincent and the Grenadines, Samoa, San Marino, Sao Tome and Principe, Senegal, Serbia, Seychelles, Sierra Leone, Singapore, Slovakia, Slovenia, South Africa, Spain, Suriname, Sweden, Switzerland, Thailand, the former Yugoslav Republic of Macedonia, Timor-Leste, Togo, Trinidad and Tobago, Tunisia, Turkey, Turkmenistan, Tuvalu, Ukraine, United Arab Emirates, United Kingdom, United Republic of Tanzania, Uruguay, Vanuatu, Zambia

Against:

None

Abstaining:

Algeria, Armenia, Azerbaijan, Belarus, Bhutan, Bolivia (Plurinational State of), Cambodia, Cuba, Democratic People's Republic of Korea, Ecuador, Egypt, Fiji, India, Indonesia, Iran (Islamic Republic of), Israel, Jordan, Kuwait, Lao People's Democratic Republic, Myanmar, Nicaragua, Oman, Qatar, Russian Federation, Saudi Arabia, Sri Lanka, Sudan, Syrian Arab Republic, Uganda, United States, Venezuela (Bolivarian Republic of), Yemen, Zimbabwe

---

* Subsequently, the delegation of Iraq informed the Secretariat that it had intended to abstain. The voting tally above does not reflect this information.

Operative paragraph 9

In favour:

Afghanistan, Albania, Andorra, Angola, Antigua and Barbuda, Argentina, Australia, Austria, Bahamas, Bangladesh, Barbados, Belgium, Belize, Benin, Bhutan, Bosnia and Herzegovina, Botswana, Brunei Darussalam, Bulgaria, Burkina Faso, Burundi, Cabo Verde, Canada, Chile, China, Colombia, Comoros, Congo, Costa Rica, Côte d'Ivoire, Croatia, Cyprus, Czechia, Democratic Republic of the Congo, Denmark, Djibouti, Dominican Republic, El Salvador, Equatorial Guinea, Eritrea, Estonia, Ethiopia, Fiji, Finland, France, Gambia, Georgia, Germany, Ghana, Greece, Guatemala, Guinea, Guinea-Bissau, Guyana, Honduras, Hungary, Iceland, Ireland, Italy, Jamaica, Japan, Kazakhstan, Kenya, Latvia, Lesotho, Liberia, Liechtenstein, Lithuania, Luxembourg, Madagascar, Malaysia, Maldives, Mali, Malta, Marshall Islands, Mauritania, Mexico, Micronesia (Federated States of), Monaco, Mongolia, Montenegro, Morocco, Mozambique, Myanmar, Namibia, Nepal, Netherlands, New Zealand, Niger, Nigeria, Norway, Pakistan, Panama, Papua New Guinea, Paraguay, Peru, Philippines, Poland, Portugal, Republic of Korea, Republic of Moldova, Romania, Rwanda, Saint Lucia, Saint Vincent and the Grenadines, Samoa, San Marino, Sao Tome and Principe, Senegal, Serbia, Seychelles, Sierra Leone, Singapore, Slovakia, Slovenia, South Africa, Spain, Suriname, Sweden, Switzerland, Thailand, the former Yugoslav Republic of Macedonia, Timor-Leste, Togo, Trinidad and Tobago, Tunisia, Turkey, Turkmenistan, Tuvalu, Ukraine, United Kingdom, Uruguay, Vanuatu, Zambia

Against:

Israel, United States

Abstaining:

Algeria, Armenia, Azerbaijan, Bahrain, Belarus, Bolivia (Plurinational State of), Brazil, Cambodia, Cuba, Democratic People's Republic of Korea, Ecuador, Egypt, Haiti, India, Indonesia, Iran (Islamic Republic of), Iraq, Jordan, Kuwait, Lebanon, Libya, Nicaragua, Oman, Qatar, Russian Federation, Saudi Arabia, Sri Lanka, Sudan, Syrian Arab Republic, Uganda, United Arab Emirates, United Republic of Tanzania, Venezuela (Bolivarian Republic of), Yemen, Zimbabwe

Action by the First Committee

Date: 6 November 2018
Vote: 151-0-30
153-0-18, p.p. 8
138-0-35, o.p. 4
136-2-35. o.p. 9

Meeting: 29th meeting
Draft resolution: A/C.1/73/L.8/Rev.1

Agenda item 101 (d)

73/37   Relationship between disarmament and development

Text

The General Assembly,

Recalling that the Charter of the United Nations envisages the establishment and maintenance of international peace and security with the least diversion for armaments of the world's human and economic resources,

Recalling also the provisions of the Final Document of the Tenth Special Session of the General Assembly concerning the relationship between disarmament and development,[1] as well as the adoption on 11 September 1987 of the Final Document of the International Conference on the Relationship between Disarmament and Development,[2]

Recalling further its resolutions 49/75 J of 15 December 1994, 50/70 G of 12 December 1995, 51/45 D of 10 December 1996, 52/38 D of 9 December 1997, 53/77 K of 4 December 1998, 54/54 T of 1 December 1999, 55/33 L of 20 November 2000, 56/24 E of 29 November 2001, 57/65 of 22 November 2002, 59/78 of 3 December 2004, 60/61 of 8 December 2005, 61/64 of 6 December 2006, 62/48 of 5 December 2007, 63/52 of 2 December 2008, 64/32 of 2 December 2009, 65/52 of 8 December 2010, 66/30 of 2 December 2011, 67/40 of 3 December 2012, 68/37 of 5 December 2013, 69/56 of 2 December 2014, 70/32 of 7 December 2015, 71/62 of 5 December 2016 and 72/46 of 4 December 2017 and its decision 58/520 of 8 December 2003,

Bearing in mind the Final Document of the Eighteenth Midterm Ministerial Meeting of the Movement of Non-Aligned Countries, held in Baku from 3 to 6 April 2018,

Mindful of the changes in international relations that have taken place since the adoption in 1987 of the Final Document of the International Conference on the Relationship between Disarmament and Development, including the development agenda that has emerged over the past decade,

Bearing in mind the new challenges for the international community in the fields of development, poverty eradication and the elimination of the diseases that afflict humanity,

Stressing the importance of the symbiotic relationship between disarmament and development and the important role of security in this

---

[1] See resolution S-10/2.

[2] See *Report of the International Conference on the Relationship between Disarmament and Development, New York, 24 August–11 September 1987* (A/CONF.130/39).

connection, and concerned at increasing global military expenditure, which could otherwise be spent on development needs,

Recalling the report of the Group of Governmental Experts on the relationship between disarmament and development[3] and its reappraisal of this significant issue in the current international context,

Bearing in mind the importance of following up on the implementation of the action programme adopted at the 1987 International Conference on the Relationship between Disarmament and Development,[2]

Taking note of the report of the Secretary-General submitted pursuant to resolution 72/46,[4]

1. *Stresses* the central role of the United Nations in the relationship between disarmament and development, and requests the Secretary-General to strengthen further the role of the Organization in this field, in particular the high-level Steering Group on Disarmament and Development, in order to ensure continued and effective coordination and close cooperation between the relevant United Nations departments, agencies and subagencies;

2. *Requests* the Secretary-General to continue to take action, through appropriate organs and within available resources, for the implementation of the action programme adopted on 11 September 1987 at the International Conference on the Relationship between Disarmament and Development;[2]

3. *Urges* the international community to devote part of the resources made available by the implementation of disarmament and arms limitation agreements to economic and social development, with a view to reducing the ever-widening gap between developed and developing countries;

4. *Encourages* the international community to achieve the Sustainable Development Goals[5] and to make reference to the contribution that disarmament could provide in meeting them when it reviews its progress towards this purpose, as well as to make greater efforts to integrate disarmament, humanitarian and development activities;

5. *Encourages* the relevant regional and subregional organizations and institutions, non-governmental organizations and research institutes to incorporate issues related to the relationship between disarmament and development into their agendas and, in this regard, to take into account the report of the Group of Governmental Experts on the relationship between disarmament and development;[3]

6. *Reiterates its invitation* to Member States to provide the Secretary-General with information regarding measures and efforts to devote part of the

---

[3] See A/59/119.
[4] A/73/117.
[5] See resolution 70/1.

resources made available by the implementation of disarmament and arms limitation agreements to economic and social development, with a view to reducing the ever-widening gap between developed and developing countries;

7.   *Requests* the Secretary-General to report to the General Assembly at its seventy-fourth session on the implementation of the present resolution, including the information provided by Member States pursuant to paragraph 6 above;

8.   *Decides* to include in the provisional agenda of its seventy-fourth session, under the item entitled "General and complete disarmament", the sub-item entitled "Relationship between disarmament and development".

Action by the General Assembly

Date: 5 December 2018   Meeting: 45th plenary meeting
Vote: Adopted without a vote   Report: A/73/510

Sponsors

Indonesia (on behalf of the States Members of the United Nations that are members of the Movement of Non-Aligned Countries)

Action by the First Committee

Date: 8 November 2018   Meeting: 30th meeting
Vote: Adopted without a vote   Draft resolution: A/C.1/73/L.11

Agenda item 101 (cc)

73/38 Effects of the use of armaments and ammunitions containing depleted uranium

Text

The General Assembly,

Guided by the purposes and principles enshrined in the Charter of the United Nations and the rules of international humanitarian law,

Recalling its resolutions 62/30 of 5 December 2007, 63/54 of 2 December 2008, 65/55 of 8 December 2010, 67/36 of 3 December 2012, 69/57 of 2 December 2014 and 71/70 of 5 December 2016,

Determined to promote multilateralism as an essential means to carry forward negotiations on arms regulation and disarmament,

Taking note of the opinions expressed by Member States and relevant international organizations on the effects of the use of armaments and ammunitions containing depleted uranium, as reflected in the reports submitted by the Secretary-General pursuant to resolutions 62/30, 63/54, 65/55, 67/36, 69/57 and 71/70,[1]

Recognizing the importance of implementing, as appropriate, the recommendations of the International Atomic Energy Agency, the United Nations Environment Programme and the World Health Organization to mitigate potential hazards to human beings and the environment from the contamination of territories with depleted uranium residues,

Considering that studies conducted so far by relevant international organizations have not provided a detailed enough account of the magnitude of the potential long-term effects on human beings and the environment of the use of armaments and ammunitions containing depleted uranium,

Recalling that the United Nations Environment Programme, in its report to the Secretary-General on the subject,[2] affirms that major scientific uncertainties persist regarding the long-term environmental impacts of depleted uranium, particularly with respect to long-term groundwater contamination, and calls for a precautionary approach to the use of depleted uranium,

Convinced that, as humankind becomes more aware of the need to take immediate measures to protect the environment, any event that could jeopardize such efforts requires urgent attention to implement the required measures,

---

[1] A/63/170, A/63/170/Add.1, A/65/129, A/65/129/Add.1, A/67/177, A/67/177/Add.1, A/69/151, A/71/139 and A/73/99.

[2] A/65/129/Add.1, sect. III.

Noting that further research should be done to assess the health risks and environmental impact of the use of arms and ammunitions containing depleted uranium in conflict situations,

Noting also the technical and financial barriers faced by affected States seeking to implement post-conflict remedial measures that meet international standards for radioactive waste management for locations, infrastructure and materiel contaminated by arms and ammunitions containing depleted uranium,

Taking into consideration the potential harmful effects of the use of armaments and ammunitions containing depleted uranium on human health and the environment, and the ongoing concerns of affected States and communities, health experts and civil society about such effects,

1.   *Expresses its appreciation* to the Member States and international organizations that submitted their views to the Secretary-General pursuant to resolution 71/70 and previous resolutions on the subject;

2.   *Invites* Member States and relevant international organizations, particularly those that have not yet done so, to communicate to the Secretary-General their views on the effects of the use of armaments and ammunitions containing depleted uranium;

3.   *Requests* the Secretary-General to request relevant international organizations to update and complete, as appropriate, their studies and research on the effects of the use of armaments and ammunitions containing depleted uranium on human health and the environment;

4.   *Encourages* Member States, particularly the affected States, as necessary, to facilitate the studies and research referred to in paragraph 3 above;

5.   *Also encourages* Member States to follow closely the development of the studies and research referred to in paragraph 3 above;

6.   *Invites* Member States that have used armaments and ammunitions containing depleted uranium in armed conflicts to provide the relevant authorities of affected States, upon request, with information, as detailed as possible, about the location of the areas of use and the amounts used, with the objective of facilitating the assessment and clearance of such areas;

7.   *Encourages* Member States in a position to do so to provide assistance to States affected by the use of arms and ammunitions containing depleted uranium, in particular in identifying and managing contaminated sites and material;

8.   *Requests* the Secretary-General to submit an updated report on the subject to the General Assembly at its seventy-fifth session, reflecting the information submitted by Member States and relevant international organizations, including the information submitted pursuant to paragraphs 2 and 3 above;

9.   *Decides* to include in the provisional agenda of its seventy-fifth session, under the item entitled "General and complete disarmament", the sub-item entitled "Effects of the use of armaments and ammunitions containing depleted uranium".

Action by the General Assembly

Date: 5 December 2018   Meeting: 45th plenary meeting
Vote: 151-4-25   Report: A/73/510

Sponsors

Indonesia (on behalf of the States Members of the United Nations that are members of the Movement of Non-Aligned Countries)

Recorded vote

In favour:

Afghanistan, Algeria, Angola, Antigua and Barbuda, Argentina, Armenia, Austria, Azerbaijan, Bahamas, Bahrain, Bangladesh, Barbados, Belarus, Belgium, Belize, Benin, Bhutan, Bolivia (Plurinational State of), Bosnia and Herzegovina, Botswana, Brazil, Brunei Darussalam, Bulgaria, Burkina Faso, Burundi, Cabo Verde, Cambodia, Cameroon, Central African Republic, Chile, Colombia, Comoros, Congo, Costa Rica, Côte d'Ivoire, Cuba, Cyprus, Democratic People's Republic of Korea, Democratic Republic of the Congo, Djibouti, Dominican Republic, Ecuador, Egypt, El Salvador, Equatorial Guinea, Eritrea, Eswatini, Ethiopia, Fiji, Finland, Gabon, Gambia, Ghana, Greece, Grenada, Guatemala, Guinea, Guinea-Bissau, Guyana, Honduras, Iceland, India, Indonesia, Iran (Islamic Republic of), Iraq, Ireland, Italy, Jamaica, Japan, Jordan, Kenya, Kuwait, Kyrgyzstan, Lao People's Democratic Republic, Lebanon, Lesotho, Liberia, Libya, Liechtenstein, Luxembourg, Madagascar, Malawi, Malaysia, Maldives, Mali, Malta, Marshall Islands, Mauritania, Mauritius, Mexico, Mongolia, Montenegro, Morocco, Mozambique, Myanmar, Namibia, Nepal, Netherlands, New Zealand, Nicaragua, Niger, Nigeria, Norway, Oman, Pakistan, Panama, Papua New Guinea, Paraguay, Peru, Philippines, Qatar, Republic of Moldova, Saint Lucia, Saint Vincent and the Grenadines, Samoa, San Marino, Sao Tome and Principe, Saudi Arabia, Senegal, Serbia, Seychelles, Sierra Leone, Singapore, Slovenia, South Africa, Sri Lanka, Sudan, Suriname, Sweden, Switzerland, Syrian Arab Republic, Tajikistan, Thailand, the former Yugoslav Republic of Macedonia, Timor-Leste, Togo, Tonga, Trinidad and Tobago, Tunisia, Turkmenistan, Tuvalu, Uganda, United Arab Emirates, United Republic of Tanzania, Uruguay, Vanuatu, Venezuela (Bolivarian Republic of), Viet Nam, Yemen, Zambia, Zimbabwe

Against:
France, Israel, United Kingdom, United States

Abstaining:
Albania, Andorra, Australia, Canada, Croatia, Czechia, Denmark, Estonia, Georgia, Germany, Hungary, Kazakhstan, Latvia, Lithuania, Micronesia (Federated States of), Monaco, Poland, Portugal, Republic of Korea, Romania, Russian Federation, Slovakia, Spain, Turkey, Ukraine

Action by the First Committee

Date:	8 November 2018	Meeting:	30th meeting
Vote:	140-4-26	Draft resolution:	A/C.1/73/L.12

Agenda item 101 (h)

73/39 Observance of environmental norms in the drafting and implementation of agreements on disarmament and arms control

Text

The General Assembly,

Recalling its resolutions 50/70 M of 12 December 1995, 51/45 E of 10 December 1996, 52/38 E of 9 December 1997, 53/77 J of 4 December 1998, 54/54 S of 1 December 1999, 55/33 K of 20 November 2000, 56/24 F of 29 November 2001, 57/64 of 22 November 2002, 58/45 of 8 December 2003, 59/68 of 3 December 2004, 60/60 of 8 December 2005, 61/63 of 6 December 2006, 62/28 of 5 December 2007, 63/51 of 2 December 2008, 64/33 of 2 December 2009, 65/53 of 8 December 2010, 66/31 of 2 December 2011, 67/37 of 3 December 2012, 68/36 of 5 December 2013, 69/55 of 2 December 2014, 70/30 of 7 December 2015, 71/60 of 5 December 2016 and 72/47 of 4 December 2017,

Emphasizing the importance of the observance of environmental norms in the preparation and implementation of disarmament and arms limitation agreements,

Recognizing that it is necessary to take duly into account the agreements adopted at the United Nations Conference on Environment and Development, as well as prior relevant agreements, in the drafting and implementation of agreements on disarmament and arms limitation,

Taking note of the report of the Secretary-General submitted pursuant to resolution 72/47,[1]

Noting that the Eighteenth Midterm Ministerial Meeting of the Movement of Non-Aligned Countries, held in Baku from 3 to 6 April 2018, welcomed the adoption by the General Assembly, without a vote, of resolution 72/47 on the observance of environmental norms in the drafting and implementation of agreements on disarmament and arms control,

Mindful of the detrimental environmental effects of the use of nuclear weapons,

1.　*Reaffirms* that international disarmament forums should take fully into account the relevant environmental norms in negotiating treaties and agreements on disarmament and arms limitation and that all States, through their actions, should contribute fully to ensuring compliance with the aforementioned norms in the implementation of treaties and conventions to which they are parties;

---

[1]　A/73/92.

2.   *Calls upon* States to adopt unilateral, bilateral, regional and multilateral measures so as to contribute to ensuring the application of scientific and technological progress within the framework of international security, disarmament and other related spheres, without detriment to the environment or to its effective contribution to attaining sustainable development;

3.   *Welcomes* the information provided by Member States on the implementation of the measures that they have adopted to promote the objectives envisaged in the present resolution;[1]

4.   *Invites* all Member States to communicate to the Secretary-General information on the measures that they have adopted to promote the objectives envisaged in the present resolution, and requests the Secretary-General to submit a report containing that information to the General Assembly at its seventy-fourth session;

5.   *Decides* to include in the provisional agenda of its seventy-fourth session, under the item entitled "General and complete disarmament", the sub-item entitled "Observance of environmental norms in the drafting and implementation of agreements on disarmament and arms control".

Action by the General Assembly

Date: 5 December 2018   Meeting: 45th plenary meeting
Vote: Adopted without a vote   Report: A/73/510

Sponsors

Indonesia (on behalf of the States Members of the United Nations that are members of the Movement of Non-Aligned Countries)

Action by the First Committee

Date: 8 November 2018   Meeting: 30th meeting
Vote: Adopted without a vote   Draft resolution: A/C.1/73/L.13

Agenda item 101 (hh)

73/40   Follow-up to the 2013 high-level meeting of the General Assembly on nuclear disarmament

Text

The General Assembly,

Recalling its resolutions 67/39 of 3 December 2012, 68/32 of 5 December 2013, 69/58 of 2 December 2014, 70/34 of 7 December 2015, 71/71 of 5 December 2016 and 72/251 of 24 December 2017,

Welcoming the convening of the high-level meeting of the General Assembly on nuclear disarmament, on 26 September 2013, and recognizing its contribution to furthering the objective of the total elimination of nuclear weapons,

Emphasizing the importance of seeking a safer world for all and achieving peace and security in a world without nuclear weapons,

Reaffirming that effective measures of nuclear disarmament have the highest priority, as affirmed at the first special session of the General Assembly devoted to disarmament,

Convinced that nuclear disarmament and the total elimination of nuclear weapons are the only absolute guarantee against the use or threat of use of nuclear weapons,

Acknowledging the significant contribution made by a number of countries towards realizing the objective of nuclear disarmament by the establishment of nuclear-weapon-free zones, as well as by voluntary renunciation of nuclear weapon programmes or withdrawal of all nuclear weapons from their territories, and strongly supporting the speedy establishment of a nuclear-weapon-free zone in the Middle East,

Recalling the resolve of the Heads of State and Government, as contained in the United Nations Millennium Declaration,[1] to strive for the elimination of weapons of mass destruction, particularly nuclear weapons, and to keep all options open for achieving this aim, including the possibility of convening an international conference to identify ways of eliminating nuclear dangers,

Reaffirming the central role of the United Nations in the field of disarmament, and reaffirming also the continued importance and relevance of multilateral disarmament machinery as mandated by the General Assembly at its first special session devoted to disarmament,

---

[1] Resolution 55/2.

Acknowledging the important role of civil society, including non-governmental organizations, academia, parliamentarians and the mass media, in advancing the objective of nuclear disarmament,

Sharing the deep concern at the catastrophic humanitarian consequences of any use of nuclear weapons, and in this context reaffirming the need for all States at all times to comply with applicable international law, including international humanitarian law,

Taking note of the report of the Secretary-General submitted pursuant to resolution 72/251,[2] and welcoming the fact that a large number of Member States contributed their views to this report,

Noting the adoption, with a vote, of the Treaty on the Prohibition of Nuclear Weapons[3] on 7 July 2017 at the United Nations conference to negotiate a legally binding instrument to prohibit nuclear weapons, leading towards their total elimination,

Mindful of the solemn obligations of States parties, undertaken in article VI of the Treaty on the Non-Proliferation of Nuclear Weapons,[4] particularly to pursue negotiations in good faith on effective measures relating to the cessation of the nuclear arms race at an early date and to nuclear disarmament,

Expressing its deep concern that the negotiations in the Conference on Disarmament for the conclusion of a comprehensive convention on nuclear weapons have not yet commenced,

Determined to work collectively towards the realization of nuclear disarmament,

1.   *Underlines* the strong support, expressed at the high-level meeting of the General Assembly on nuclear disarmament, held on 26 September 2013, for taking urgent and effective measures to achieve the total elimination of nuclear weapons;

2.   *Calls for* urgent compliance with the legal obligations and the fulfilment of the commitments undertaken on nuclear disarmament;

3.   *Endorses* the wide support expressed at the high-level meeting for a comprehensive convention on nuclear weapons;

4.   *Calls for* the urgent commencement of negotiations in the Conference on Disarmament on effective nuclear disarmament measures to achieve the total elimination of nuclear weapons, including, in particular, on a comprehensive convention on nuclear weapons;

---

[2] A/73/122.

[3] A/CONF.229/2017/8.

[4] United Nations, *Treaty Series*, vol. 729, No. 10485.

5.   *Decides* to convene, in New York, on a date to be decided later, a United Nations high-level international conference on nuclear disarmament to review the progress made in this regard;

6.   *Takes note* of the views provided by Member States with regard to achieving the objective of the total elimination of nuclear weapons, in particular on the elements of a comprehensive convention on nuclear weapons, as reflected in the report submitted by the Secretary-General pursuant to resolution 72/251,[2] and requests the Secretary-General to forward this report to the Conference on Disarmament and the Disarmament Commission for their early consideration;

7.   *Welcomes* the commemoration and promotion of 26 September as the International Day for the Total Elimination of Nuclear Weapons devoted to furthering this objective;

8.   *Expresses its appreciation* to Member States, the United Nations system and civil society, including non-governmental organizations, academia, parliamentarians, the mass media and individuals that developed activities in promotion of the International Day for the Total Elimination of Nuclear Weapons;

9.   *Reiterates its request* to the President of the General Assembly to organize, on 26 September every year, a one-day high-level plenary meeting of the Assembly to commemorate and promote the International Day for the Total Elimination of Nuclear Weapons;

10. *Decides* that the aforementioned high-level plenary meeting shall be held with the participation of Member and observer States, represented at the highest possible level, as well as with the participation of the President of the General Assembly and the Secretary-General;

11. *Requests* the Secretary-General to undertake all arrangements necessary to commemorate and promote the International Day for the Total Elimination of Nuclear Weapons, including through the United Nations Offices at Geneva and Vienna, as well as the United Nations regional centres for peace and disarmament;

12. *Calls upon* Member States, the United Nations system and civil society, including non-governmental organizations, academia, parliamentarians, the mass media and individuals, to commemorate and promote the International Day for the Total Elimination of Nuclear Weapons through all means of educational and public awareness-raising activities about the threat posed to humanity by nuclear weapons and the necessity for their total elimination in order to mobilize international efforts towards achieving the common goal of a nuclear-weapon-free world;

13. *Requests* the Secretary-General to seek the views of Member States with regard to achieving the objective of the total elimination of nuclear

weapons, in particular on effective nuclear disarmament measures, including elements of a comprehensive convention on nuclear weapons, and to submit a report thereon to the General Assembly at its seventy-fourth session, and also to transmit the report to the Conference on Disarmament;

14. *Also requests* the Secretary-General to report on the implementation of the present resolution to the General Assembly at its seventy-fourth session;

15. *Decides* to include in the provisional agenda of its seventy-fourth session, under the item entitled "General and complete disarmament", the sub-item entitled "Follow-up to the 2013 high-level meeting of the General Assembly on nuclear disarmament".

Action by the General Assembly

Date: 5 December 2018 Meeting: 45th plenary meeting
Vote: 143-27-14   Report: A/73/510
129-19-23, p.p. 12

Sponsors

Indonesia (on behalf of the States Members of the United Nations that are members of the Movement of Non-Aligned Countries)

Recorded vote

As a whole

In favour:
Afghanistan, Algeria, Andorra, Angola, Antigua and Barbuda, Argentina, Armenia, Austria, Azerbaijan, Bahamas, Bahrain, Bangladesh, Barbados, Belarus, Belize, Benin, Bhutan, Bolivia (Plurinational State of), Botswana, Brazil, Brunei Darussalam, Burkina Faso, Burundi, Cabo Verde, Cambodia, Cameroon, Central African Republic, Chile, China, Colombia, Comoros, Congo, Costa Rica, Côte d'Ivoire, Cuba, Cyprus, Democratic People's Republic of Korea, Democratic Republic of the Congo, Djibouti, Dominican Republic, Ecuador, Egypt, El Salvador, Equatorial Guinea, Eritrea, Eswatini, Ethiopia, Fiji, Gabon, Gambia, Ghana, Grenada, Guatemala, Guinea, Guinea-Bissau, Guyana, Honduras, India, Indonesia, Iran (Islamic Republic of), Iraq, Ireland, Jamaica, Jordan, Kazakhstan, Kenya, Kuwait, Kyrgyzstan, Lao People's Democratic Republic, Lebanon, Lesotho, Liberia, Libya, Liechtenstein, Madagascar, Malawi, Malaysia, Maldives, Mali, Malta, Marshall Islands, Mauritania, Mauritius, Mexico, Mongolia, Morocco, Mozambique, Myanmar, Namibia, Nauru, Nepal, New Zealand, Nicaragua, Niger, Nigeria, Oman, Pakistan, Palau, Panama, Papua New Guinea, Paraguay, Peru, Philippines, Qatar, Republic of Moldova, Rwanda, Saint Lucia, Saint Vincent and the Grenadines, Samoa, San Marino, Sao Tome and Principe, Saudi Arabia, Senegal, Seychelles, Sierra Leone, Singapore,

South Africa, Sri Lanka, Sudan, Suriname, Sweden, Switzerland, Syrian Arab Republic, Tajikistan, Thailand, Timor-Leste, Togo, Tonga, Trinidad and Tobago, Tunisia, Turkmenistan, Tuvalu, Uganda, United Arab Emirates, United Republic of Tanzania, Uruguay, Uzbekistan, Vanuatu, Venezuela (Bolivarian Republic of), Viet Nam, Yemen, Zambia, Zimbabwe

Against:

Albania, Australia, Belgium, Croatia, Czechia, Denmark, Estonia, France, Germany, Hungary, Israel, Italy, Latvia, Lithuania, Luxembourg, Monaco, Montenegro, Netherlands, Poland, Republic of Korea, Romania, Russian Federation, Slovakia, Slovenia, Turkey, United Kingdom, United States

Abstaining:

Bosnia and Herzegovina, Bulgaria, Canada, Finland, Georgia, Greece, Iceland, Japan, Norway, Portugal, Serbia, Spain, the former Yugoslav Republic of Macedonia, Ukraine

Twelfth preambular paragraph

In favour:

Algeria, Andorra, Angola, Antigua and Barbuda, Argentina, Austria, Azerbaijan, Bahamas, Bahrain, Bangladesh, Barbados, Belarus, Belize, Benin, Bhutan, Bolivia (Plurinational State of), Botswana, Brazil, Brunei Darussalam, Burkina Faso, Burundi, Cabo Verde, Cambodia, Chile, Colombia, Comoros, Congo, Costa Rica, Côte d'Ivoire, Cuba, Cyprus, Democratic People's Republic of Korea, Democratic Republic of the Congo, Djibouti, Dominican Republic, Ecuador, Egypt, El Salvador, Equatorial Guinea, Eritrea, Eswatini, Ethiopia, Fiji, Gabon, Gambia, Ghana, Guatemala, Guinea, Guinea-Bissau, Guyana, Honduras, India, Indonesia, Iran (Islamic Republic of), Iraq, Ireland, Jamaica, Jordan, Kazakhstan, Kenya, Kuwait, Lao People's Democratic Republic, Lebanon, Lesotho, Libya, Liechtenstein, Madagascar, Malawi, Malaysia, Maldives, Mali, Malta, Mauritania, Mauritius, Mexico, Mongolia, Morocco, Mozambique, Myanmar, Namibia, Nepal, Netherlands, New Zealand, Nicaragua, Niger, Nigeria, Oman, Pakistan, Panama, Papua New Guinea, Paraguay, Peru, Philippines, Qatar, Republic of Moldova, Saint Lucia, Saint Vincent and the Grenadines, Samoa, San Marino, Sao Tome and Principe, Saudi Arabia, Senegal, Seychelles, Sierra Leone, Singapore, South Africa, Sri Lanka, Sudan, Suriname, Sweden, Switzerland, Syrian Arab Republic, Thailand, Timor-Leste, Togo, Trinidad and Tobago, Tunisia, Turkmenistan, Uganda, United Arab Emirates, United Republic of Tanzania, Uruguay, Uzbekistan, Vanuatu, Venezuela (Bolivarian Republic of), Viet Nam, Yemen, Zambia, Zimbabwe

Against:
> China, Croatia, Denmark, Estonia, France, Hungary, Israel, Italy, Latvia, Lithuania, Luxembourg, Monaco, Poland, Romania, Russian Federation, Slovakia, Slovenia, United Kingdom, United States

Abstaining:
> Albania, Armenia, Australia, Belgium, Bosnia and Herzegovina, Bulgaria, Canada, Czechia, Finland, Georgia, Germany, Greece, Iceland, Japan, Liberia, Montenegro, Norway, Portugal, Serbia, Spain, the former Yugoslav Republic of Macedonia, Turkey, Ukraine

Action by the First Committee

Date: 1 November 2018   Meeting: 26th meeting
Vote: 143-27-14   Draft resolution: A/C.1/73/L.14
      129-20-22, p.p. 12

Agenda item 101 (v)

73/41   Promotion of multilateralism in the area of disarmament and non-proliferation

Text

The General Assembly,

Determined to foster strict respect for the purposes and principles enshrined in the Charter of the United Nations,

Recalling its resolution 56/24 T of 29 November 2001 on multilateral cooperation in the area of disarmament and non-proliferation and global efforts against terrorism and other relevant resolutions, as well as its resolutions 57/63 of 22 November 2002, 58/44 of 8 December 2003, 59/69 of 3 December 2004, 60/59 of 8 December 2005, 61/62 of 6 December 2006, 62/27 of 5 December 2007, 63/50 of 2 December 2008, 64/34 of 2 December 2009, 65/54 of 8 December 2010, 66/32 of 2 December 2011, 67/38 of 3 December 2012, 68/38 of 5 December 2013, 69/54 of 2 December 2014, 70/31 of 7 December 2015, 71/61 of 5 December 2016 and 72/48 of 4 December 2017 on the promotion of multilateralism in the area of disarmament and non-proliferation,

Recalling also the purpose of the United Nations to maintain international peace and security and, to that end, to take effective collective measures for the prevention and removal of threats to the peace and for the suppression of acts of aggression or other breaches of the peace, and to bring about by peaceful means, and in conformity with the principles of justice and international law, adjustment or settlement of international disputes or situations which might lead to a breach of the peace, as enshrined in the Charter,

Recalling further the United Nations Millennium Declaration,[1] in which it is stated, inter alia, that the responsibility for managing worldwide economic and social development, as well as threats to international peace and security, must be shared among the nations of the world and should be exercised multilaterally and that, as the most universal and most representative organization in the world, the United Nations must play the central role,

Convinced that, in the globalization era and with the information revolution, arms regulation, non-proliferation and disarmament problems are more than ever the concern of all countries in the world, which are affected in one way or another by these problems and therefore should have the possibility to participate in the negotiations that arise to tackle them,

Bearing in mind the existence of a broad structure of disarmament and arms regulation agreements resulting from non-discriminatory and transparent

---

[1] Resolution 55/2.

multilateral negotiations with the participation of a large number of countries, regardless of their size and power,

Aware of the need to advance further in the field of arms regulation, nonproliferation and disarmament on the basis of universal, multilateral, nondiscriminatory and transparent negotiations with the goal of reaching general and complete disarmament under strict international control,

Recognizing the complementarity of bilateral, plurilateral and multilateral negotiations on disarmament,

Recognizing also that the proliferation and development of weapons of mass destruction, including nuclear weapons, are among the most immediate threats to international peace and security which need to be dealt with, with the highest priority,

Considering that the multilateral disarmament agreements provide the mechanism for States parties to consult one another and to cooperate in solving any problems which may arise in relation to the objective of, or in the application of, the provisions of the agreements and that such consultations and cooperation may also be undertaken through appropriate international procedures within the framework of the United Nations and in accordance with the Charter,

Stressing that international cooperation, the peaceful settlement of disputes, dialogue and confidence-building measures would make an essential contribution to the creation of multilateral and bilateral friendly relations among peoples and nations,

Being concerned at the continuous erosion of multilateralism in the field of arms regulation, non-proliferation and disarmament, and recognizing that a resort to unilateral actions by Member States in resolving their security concerns would jeopardize international peace and security and undermine confidence in the international security system as well as the foundations of the United Nations itself,

Noting that the Eighteenth Midterm Ministerial Meeting of the Movement of Non-Aligned Countries, held in Baku from 3 to 6 April 2018, welcomed the adoption of resolution 72/48 on the promotion of multilateralism in the area of disarmament and non-proliferation and underlined the fact that multilateralism and multilaterally agreed solutions, in accordance with the Charter, provide the only sustainable method of addressing disarmament and international security issues,

Reaffirming the absolute validity of multilateral diplomacy in the field of disarmament and non-proliferation, and determined to promote multilateralism as an essential way to develop arms regulation and disarmament negotiations,

1.   *Reaffirms* multilateralism as the core principle in negotiations in the area of disarmament and non-proliferation with a view to maintaining and strengthening universal norms and enlarging their scope;

2. *Also reaffirms* multilateralism as the core principle in resolving disarmament and non-proliferation concerns;

3. *Urges* the participation of all interested States in multilateral negotiations on arms regulation, non-proliferation and disarmament in a non-discriminatory and transparent manner;

4. *Underlines* the importance of preserving the existing agreements on arms regulation and disarmament, which constitute an expression of the results of international cooperation and multilateral negotiations in response to the challenges facing humankind;

5. *Calls once again upon* all Member States to renew and fulfil their individual and collective commitments to multilateral cooperation as an important means of pursuing and achieving their common objectives in the area of disarmament and non-proliferation;

6. *Requests* the States parties to the relevant instruments on weapons of mass destruction to consult and cooperate among themselves in resolving their concerns with regard to cases of non-compliance as well as on implementation, in accordance with the procedures defined in those instruments, and to refrain from resorting or threatening to resort to unilateral actions or directing unverified non-compliance accusations against one another to resolve their concerns;

7. *Takes note* of the report of the Secretary-General containing the replies of Member States on the promotion of multilateralism in the area of disarmament and non-proliferation, submitted pursuant to resolution 72/48;[2]

8. *Requests* the Secretary-General to seek the views of Member States on the issue of the promotion of multilateralism in the area of disarmament and nonproliferation and to submit a report thereon to the General Assembly at its seventy-fourth session;

9. *Decides* to include in the provisional agenda of its seventy-fourth session, under the item entitled "General and complete disarmament", the sub-item entitled "Promotion of multilateralism in the area of disarmament and non-proliferation".

Action by the General Assembly

Date: 5 December 2018   Meeting: 45th plenary meeting
Vote: 128-4-52   Report: A/73/510

Sponsors

Indonesia (on behalf of the States Members of the United Nations that are members of the Movement of Non-Aligned Countries)

---

[2] A/73/95.

Recorded vote

In favour:

Afghanistan, Algeria, Angola, Antigua and Barbuda, Argentina, Azerbaijan, Bahamas, Bahrain, Bangladesh, Barbados, Belarus, Belize, Benin, Bhutan, Bolivia (Plurinational State of), Botswana, Brazil, Brunei Darussalam, Burkina Faso, Burundi, Cabo Verde, Cambodia, Cameroon, Central African Republic, Chile, China, Colombia, Comoros, Congo, Costa Rica, Côte d'Ivoire, Cuba, Democratic People's Republic of Korea, Democratic Republic of the Congo, Djibouti, Dominican Republic, Ecuador, Egypt, El Salvador, Equatorial Guinea, Eritrea, Eswatini, Ethiopia, Fiji, Gabon, Gambia, Ghana, Grenada, Guatemala, Guinea, Guinea-Bissau, Guyana, Honduras, India, Indonesia, Iran (Islamic Republic of), Iraq, Jamaica, Jordan, Kazakhstan, Kenya, Kuwait, Kyrgyzstan, Lao People's Democratic Republic, Lebanon, Lesotho, Liberia, Libya, Madagascar, Malawi, Malaysia, Maldives, Mali, Marshall Islands, Mauritania, Mauritius, Mexico, Mongolia, Morocco, Mozambique, Myanmar, Namibia, Nepal, Nicaragua, Niger, Nigeria, Oman, Pakistan, Palau, Panama, Papua New Guinea, Paraguay, Peru, Philippines, Qatar, Russian Federation, Rwanda, Saint Lucia, Saint Vincent and the Grenadines, Sao Tome and Principe, Saudi Arabia, Senegal, Seychelles, Sierra Leone, Singapore, South Africa, Sri Lanka, Sudan, Suriname, Syrian Arab Republic, Tajikistan, Thailand, Timor-Leste, Togo, Trinidad and Tobago, Tunisia, Turkmenistan, Uganda, United Arab Emirates, United Republic of Tanzania, Uruguay, Uzbekistan, Vanuatu, Venezuela (Bolivarian Republic of), Viet Nam, Yemen, Zambia, Zimbabwe

Against:

Israel, Micronesia (Federated States of), United Kingdom, United States

Abstaining:

Albania, Andorra, Armenia, Australia, Austria, Belgium, Bosnia and Herzegovina, Bulgaria, Canada, Croatia, Cyprus, Czechia, Denmark, Estonia, Finland, France, Georgia, Germany, Greece, Hungary, Iceland, Ireland, Italy, Japan, Latvia, Liechtenstein, Lithuania, Luxembourg, Malta, Monaco, Montenegro, Netherlands, New Zealand, Norway, Poland, Portugal, Republic of Korea, Republic of Moldova, Romania, Samoa, San Marino, Serbia, Slovakia, Slovenia, Spain, Sweden, Switzerland, the former Yugoslav Republic of Macedonia, Tonga, Turkey, Tuvalu, Ukraine

Action by the First Committee

Date:	8 November 2018	Meeting:	30th meeting
Vote:	121-4-51	Draft resolution:	A/C.1/73/L.15

Agenda item 101 (g)

73/42 Convening of the fourth special session of the General Assembly devoted to disarmament

Text

The General Assembly,

Recalling its resolutions 49/75 I of 15 December 1994, 50/70 F of 12 December 1995, 51/45 C of 10 December 1996, 52/38 F of 9 December 1997, 53/77 AA of 4 December 1998, 54/54 U of 1 December 1999, 55/33 M of 20 November 2000, 56/24 D of 29 November 2001, 57/61 of 22 November 2002, 59/71 of 3 December 2004, 61/60 of 6 December 2006, 62/29 of 5 December 2007, 65/66 of 8 December 2010 and 72/49 of 4 December 2017, as well as its decisions 58/521 of 8 December 2003, 60/518 of 8 December 2005, 60/559 of 6 June 2006, 63/519 of 2 December 2008, 64/515 of 2 December 2009 and 70/551 of 23 December 2015,

Recalling also that, there being a consensus to do so in each case, three special sessions of the General Assembly devoted to disarmament were held in 1978, 1982 and 1988, respectively,

Bearing in mind the Final Document of the Tenth Special Session of the General Assembly, adopted by consensus at the first special session devoted to disarmament,[1]

Bearing in mind also the ultimate objective of general and complete disarmament under effective international control,

Reiterating its conviction that a special session of the General Assembly devoted to disarmament can set the future course of action in the fields of disarmament, arms control, non-proliferation and related international security matters,

Emphasizing the importance of multilateralism in the process of disarmament, arms control, non-proliferation and related international security matters,

Recalling the conclusion of the work of the Open-ended Working Group on the fourth special session of the General Assembly devoted to disarmament to consider the objectives and agenda of the fourth special session, and to adopt its report and substantive recommendations by consensus,[2]

Recalling also the report of the Open-ended Working Group and the recommendations contained therein,

---

[1] Resolution S-10/2.
[2] A/AC.268/2017/2.

1.   *Recalls* the adoption by consensus of the recommendations on the objectives and agenda of the fourth special session of the General Assembly devoted to disarmament by the Open-ended Working Group on the fourth special session of the General Assembly devoted to disarmament, which was established by the Assembly by its resolution 65/66 and its decision 70/551 and which met in New York in 2016 and 2017;

2.   *Also recalls* the report of the Open-ended Working Group and the substantive recommendations contained therein;[2]

3.   *Reiterates its appreciation* to the participants of the Open-ended Working Group for their constructive contribution to its work;

4.   *Encourages* Member States to continue consultations on the next steps for convening of the fourth special session of the General Assembly devoted to disarmament;

5.   *Decides* to include in the provisional agenda of its seventy-fourth session, under the item entitled "General and complete disarmament", the sub-item entitled "Convening of the fourth special session of the General Assembly devoted to disarmament".

Action by the General Assembly

Date: 5 December 2018   Meeting: 45th plenary meeting
Vote: 178-0-4   Report: A/73/510

Sponsors

Indonesia (on behalf of the States Members of the United Nations that are members of the Movement of Non-Aligned Countries)

Recorded vote

In favour:
Afghanistan, Albania, Algeria, Andorra, Angola, Antigua and Barbuda, Argentina, Armenia, Australia, Austria, Azerbaijan, Bahamas, Bahrain, Bangladesh, Barbados, Belarus, Belgium, Belize, Benin, Bhutan, Bolivia (Plurinational State of), Bosnia and Herzegovina, Botswana, Brazil, Brunei Darussalam, Bulgaria, Burkina Faso, Burundi, Cabo Verde, Cambodia, Cameroon, Canada, Central African Republic, Chile, China, Colombia, Comoros, Congo, Costa Rica, Côte d'Ivoire, Croatia, Cuba, Cyprus, Czechia, Democratic People's Republic of Korea, Democratic Republic of the Congo, Denmark, Djibouti, Dominican Republic, Ecuador, Egypt, El Salvador, Equatorial Guinea, Eritrea, Estonia, Eswatini, Ethiopia, Fiji, Finland, Gabon, Gambia, Georgia, Germany, Ghana, Greece, Grenada, Guatemala, Guinea, Guinea-Bissau, Guyana, Haiti, Honduras, Hungary, Iceland, India, Indonesia, Iran (Islamic Republic of), Iraq, Ireland, Italy, Jamaica, Japan, Jordan, Kazakhstan, Kenya, Kuwait, Kyrgyzstan, Lao People's Democratic Republic,

Latvia, Lebanon, Lesotho, Liberia, Libya, Liechtenstein, Lithuania, Luxembourg, Madagascar, Malawi, Malaysia, Maldives, Mali, Malta, Mauritania, Mauritius, Mexico, Monaco, Mongolia, Montenegro, Morocco, Mozambique, Myanmar, Namibia, Nepal, Netherlands, New Zealand, Nicaragua, Niger, Nigeria, Norway, Oman, Pakistan, Palau, Panama, Paraguay, Peru, Philippines, Poland, Portugal, Qatar, Republic of Korea, Republic of Moldova, Romania, Russian Federation, Rwanda, Saint Lucia, Saint Vincent and the Grenadines, Samoa, San Marino, Sao Tome and Principe, Saudi Arabia, Senegal, Serbia, Seychelles, Sierra Leone, Singapore, Slovakia, Slovenia, South Africa, Spain, Sri Lanka, Sudan, Suriname, Sweden, Switzerland, Syrian Arab Republic, Tajikistan, Thailand, the former Yugoslav Republic of Macedonia, Timor-Leste, Togo, Trinidad and Tobago, Tunisia, Turkey, Turkmenistan, Tuvalu, Uganda, Ukraine, United Arab Emirates, United Kingdom, United Republic of Tanzania, Uruguay, Uzbekistan, Vanuatu, Venezuela (Bolivarian Republic of), Viet Nam, Yemen, Zambia, Zimbabwe

Against:
    None

Abstaining:
    France, Israel, Papua New Guinea, United States

Action by the First Committee

Date: 8 November 2018   Meeting: 30th meeting
Vote: 174-0-3   Draft resolution: A/C.1/73/L.16

Agenda item 101 (l)

73/43　Measures to uphold the authority of the 1925 Geneva Protocol

Text

The General Assembly,

Recalling its previous resolutions on the subject, in particular resolution 71/59 of 5 December 2016,

Determined to act with a view to achieving effective progress towards general and complete disarmament under strict and effective international control,

Recalling the long-standing determination of the international community to achieve the effective prohibition of the development, production, stockpiling and use of chemical and biological weapons, as well as the continuing support for measures to uphold the authority of the Protocol for the Prohibition of the Use in War of Asphyxiating, Poisonous or Other Gases, and of Bacteriological Methods of Warfare, signed at Geneva on 17 June 1925,[1] as expressed by consensus in many previous resolutions,

Emphasizing the necessity of easing international tension and strengthening trust and confidence between States,

1.　*Takes note* of the note by the Secretary-General;[2]

2.　*Renews its previous call* to all States to observe strictly the principles and objectives of the Protocol for the Prohibition of the Use in War of Asphyxiating, Poisonous or Other Gases, and of Bacteriological Methods of Warfare,[1] and reaffirms the vital necessity of upholding its provisions;

3.　*Calls upon* those States that continue to maintain reservations to the 1925 Geneva Protocol to withdraw them;

4.　*Requests* the Secretary-General to submit to the General Assembly at its seventy-fifth session a report on the implementation of the present resolution.

Action by the General Assembly

Date:　5 December 2018　　Meeting:　45th plenary meeting
Vote:　181-0-2　　　　　　Report:　A/73/510

Sponsors

Indonesia (on behalf of the States Members of the United Nations that are members of the Movement of Non-Aligned Countries)

---

[1]　League of Nations, *Treaty Series*, vol. XCIV, No. 2138.

[2]　A/73/91.

Recorded vote

In favour:

Afghanistan, Albania, Algeria, Andorra, Angola, Antigua and Barbuda, Argentina, Armenia, Australia, Austria, Azerbaijan, Bahamas, Bahrain, Bangladesh, Barbados, Belarus, Belgium, Belize, Benin, Bhutan, Bolivia (Plurinational State of), Bosnia and Herzegovina, Botswana, Brazil, Brunei Darussalam, Bulgaria, Burkina Faso, Burundi, Cabo Verde, Cambodia, Cameroon, Canada, Central African Republic, Chile, China, Colombia, Comoros, Congo, Costa Rica, Côte d'Ivoire, Croatia, Cuba, Cyprus, Czechia, Democratic People's Republic of Korea, Democratic Republic of the Congo, Denmark, Djibouti, Dominican Republic, Ecuador, Egypt, El Salvador, Equatorial Guinea, Eritrea, Estonia, Eswatini, Ethiopia, Fiji, Finland, France, Gabon, Gambia, Georgia, Germany, Ghana, Greece, Grenada, Guatemala, Guinea, Guinea-Bissau, Guyana, Haiti, Honduras, Hungary, Iceland, India, Indonesia, Iran (Islamic Republic of), Iraq, Ireland, Italy, Jamaica, Japan, Jordan, Kazakhstan, Kenya, Kuwait, Kyrgyzstan, Lao People's Democratic Republic, Latvia, Lebanon, Lesotho, Liberia, Libya, Liechtenstein, Lithuania, Luxembourg, Madagascar, Malawi, Malaysia, Maldives, Mali, Malta, Mauritania, Mauritius, Mexico, Monaco, Mongolia, Montenegro, Morocco, Mozambique, Myanmar, Namibia, Nepal, Netherlands, New Zealand, Nicaragua, Niger, Nigeria, Norway, Oman, Pakistan, Palau, Panama, Papua New Guinea, Paraguay, Peru, Philippines, Poland, Portugal, Qatar, Republic of Korea, Republic of Moldova, Romania, Russian Federation, Rwanda, Saint Lucia, Saint Vincent and the Grenadines, Samoa, San Marino, Sao Tome and Principe, Saudi Arabia, Senegal, Serbia, Seychelles, Sierra Leone, Singapore, Slovakia, Slovenia, South Africa, Spain, Sri Lanka, Sudan, Suriname, Sweden, Switzerland, Syrian Arab Republic, Tajikistan, Thailand, the former Yugoslav Republic of Macedonia, Timor-Leste, Togo, Tonga, Trinidad and Tobago, Tunisia, Turkey, Turkmenistan, Tuvalu, Uganda, Ukraine, United Arab Emirates, United Kingdom, United Republic of Tanzania, Uruguay, Uzbekistan, Vanuatu, Venezuela (Bolivarian Republic of), Viet Nam, Yemen, Zambia, Zimbabwe

Against:

None

Abstaining:

Israel, United States

Action by the First Committee

Date: 5 November 2018   Meeting: 28th meeting
Vote: 178-0-2   Draft resolution: A/C.1/72/L.17

Agenda item 101 (s)

73/44 Mongolia's international security and nuclear-weapon-free status

Text

The General Assembly,

Recalling its resolutions 53/77 D of 4 December 1998, 55/33 S of 20 November 2000, 57/67 of 22 November 2002, 59/73 of 3 December 2004, 61/87 of 6 December 2006, 63/56 of 2 December 2008, 65/70 of 8 December 2010, 67/52 of 3 December 2012, 69/63 of 2 December 2014 and 71/43 of 5 December 2016,

Recalling also the purposes and principles of the Charter of the United Nations, as well as the Declaration on Principles of International Law concerning Friendly Relations and Cooperation among States in accordance with the Charter of the United Nations,[1]

Bearing in mind its resolution 49/31 of 9 December 1994 on the protection and security of small States,

Proceeding from the fact that nuclear-weapon-free status is one of the means of ensuring the national security of States,

Convinced that the internationally recognized status of Mongolia contributes to enhancing stability and confidence-building in the region and promotes Mongolia's security by strengthening its independence, sovereignty and territorial integrity, the inviolability of its borders and the preservation of its ecological balance,

Welcoming the declaration by Mongolia regarding its nuclear-weapon-free status of 17 September 2012,[2]

Welcoming also the joint declaration of the five nuclear-weapon States on Mongolia's nuclear-weapon-free status of 17 September 2012,[3]

Noting that the declarations referred to above have been transmitted to the Security Council,

Welcoming the adoption by the Mongolian parliament of legislation defining and regulating Mongolia's nuclear-weapon-free status[4] as a concrete step towards promoting the aims of nuclear non-proliferation,

Bearing in mind the joint statement of the five nuclear-weapon States on security assurances to Mongolia in connection with its nuclear-weapon-free

---

[1] Resolution 2625 (XXV), annex.
[2] A/67/517-S/2012/760, annex.
[3] A/67/393-S/2012/721, annex.
[4] See A/55/56-S/2000/160.

status[5] as a contribution to the implementation of resolution 53/77 D, as well as their commitment to Mongolia to cooperate in the implementation of the resolution, in accordance with the principles of the Charter,

Mindful of the support expressed for Mongolia's nuclear-weapon-free status by the Heads of State and Government of Non-Aligned Countries at the Thirteenth Summit Conference of Heads of State or Government of Non-Aligned Countries, held in Kuala Lumpur on 24 and 25 February 2003,[6] the Fourteenth Conference, held in Havana on 15 and 16 September 2006,[7] the Fifteenth Summit Conference, held in Sharm el Sheikh, Egypt, from 11 to 16 July 2009,[8] the Sixteenth Conference, held in Tehran from 26 to 31 August 2012,[9] and the Seventeenth Conference, held on Margarita Island, Bolivarian Republic of Venezuela, from 13 to 18 September 2016, and by Ministers at the Fifteenth Ministerial Conference of the Movement of Non-Aligned Countries, held in Tehran on 29 and 30 July 2008,[10] the Sixteenth Ministerial Conference and Commemorative Meeting, held in Nusa Dua, Bali, Indonesia, from 23 to 27 May 2011,[11] the Seventeenth Ministerial Conference, held in Algiers from 26 to 29 May 2014, and the Eighteenth Ministerial Conference, held in Baku from 5 to 6 April 2018,

Noting that the States parties and signatories to the treaties of Tlatelolco,[12] Rarotonga,[13] Bangkok[14] and Pelindaba[15] expressed their recognition and full support for Mongolia's international nuclear-weapon-free status at the first Conference of States Parties and Signatories to Treaties that Establish Nuclear-Weapon-Free Zones, held in Tlatelolco, Mexico, from 26 to 28 April 2005,[16]

Noting also that the States parties and signatories to the treaties of Tlatelolco, Rarotonga, Bangkok and Pelindaba and the Treaty on a Nuclear-Weapon-Free Zone in Central Asia expressed support for Mongolia's policy at the second Conference of States Parties and Signatories to Treaties that Establish Nuclear-Weapon-Free Zones and Mongolia, held in New York on 30 April 2010, and at the third Conference of States Parties and Signatories of Treaties that Establish Nuclear-Weapon-Free Zones and Mongolia, held in New York on 24 April 2015,

---

[5] A/55/530-S/2000/1052, annex.

[6] See A/57/759-S/2003/332, annex I.

[7] See A/61/472-S/2006/780, annex I.

[8] See A/63/965-S/2009/514, annex.

[9] See A/67/506-S/2012/752, annex I.

[10] See A/62/929, annex I.

[11] A/65/896-S/2011/407, annex V.

[12] United Nations, *Treaty Series*, vol. 634, No. 9068.

[13] *The United Nations Disarmament Yearbook*, vol. 10: 1985 (United Nations publication, Sales No. E.86.IX.7), appendix VII.

[14] United Nations, *Treaty Series*, vol. 1981, No. 33873.

[15] A/50/426, annex.

[16] See A/60/121, annex III.

Noting further other measures taken to implement resolution 71/43 at the national and international levels,

Welcoming Mongolia's active and positive role in developing peaceful, friendly and mutually beneficial relations with the States of the region and other States,

Having considered the report of the Secretary-General,[17]

1.   *Takes note* of the report of the Secretary-General;[17]

2.   *Expresses its appreciation* to the Secretary-General for the efforts to implement resolution 71/43;[18]

3.   *Welcomes* the declarations of 17 September 2012 by Mongolia[2] and the five nuclear-weapon States[3] on Mongolia's nuclear-weapon-free status as a concrete contribution to nuclear disarmament and the non-proliferation of nuclear weapons and the enhancement of confidence and predictability in the region;

4.   *Welcomes and supports* the measures taken by Mongolia to consolidate and strengthen this status;

5.   *Endorses and supports* Mongolia's good-neighbourly and balanced relationship with its neighbours as an important element of strengthening regional peace, security and stability;

6.   *Welcomes* the efforts made by Member States to cooperate with Mongolia in implementing resolution 71/43, as well as the progress made in consolidating Mongolia's international security;

7.   *Invites* Member States to continue to cooperate with Mongolia in taking the measures necessary to consolidate and strengthen Mongolia's independence, sovereignty and territorial integrity, the inviolability of its borders, its independent foreign policy, its economic security and its ecological balance, as well as its nuclear-weapon-free status;

8.   *Appeals* to the Member States of the Asia-Pacific region to support Mongolia's efforts to join the relevant regional security and economic arrangements;

9.   *Requests* the Secretary-General and relevant United Nations bodies to continue to provide assistance to Mongolia in taking the necessary measures mentioned in paragraph 7 above;

10.   *Requests* the Secretary-General to report to the General Assembly at its seventy-fifth session on the implementation of the present resolution;

11.   *Decides* to include in the provisional agenda of its seventy-fifth session, under the item entitled "General and complete disarmament", the

---

[17]   A/73/202.
[18]   Ibid., sect. IV.

sub-item entitled "Mongolia's international security and nuclear-weapon-free status".

Action by the General Assembly

Date: 5 December 2018   Meeting: 45th plenary meeting
Vote: Adopted without a vote   Report: A/73/510

Sponsors

Australia, Austria, China, France, Haiti, Ireland, Malta, **Mongolia**, United Kingdom, United States

Co-sponsors

Indonesia, Kazakhstan, Kyrgyzstan, Mexico, Morocco, Philippines, Uzbekistan, Viet Nam

Action by the First Committee

Date: 1 November 2018   Meeting: 26th meeting
Vote: Adopted without a vote   Draft resolution: A/C.1/73/L.19

Agenda item 101 (k)

73/45 Implementation of the Convention on the Prohibition of the Development, Production, Stockpiling and Use of Chemical Weapons and on Their Destruction

Text

The General Assembly,

Recalling its previous resolutions on the subject of chemical weapons, in particular resolution 72/43 of 4 December 2017,

Determined to achieve the effective prohibition of the development, production, acquisition, transfer, stockpiling and use of chemical weapons and their destruction,

Reaffirming its strong support for the Convention on the Prohibition of the Development, Production, Stockpiling and Use of Chemical Weapons and on Their Destruction[1] and for the Organisation for the Prohibition of Chemical Weapons and its deep appreciation of the Organisation, which was awarded the Nobel Peace Prize for 2013 for its extensive efforts to eliminate chemical weapons,

Re-emphasizing its unequivocal support for the decision of the Director General of the Organisation for the Prohibition of Chemical Weapons to continue the mission to establish the facts surrounding the allegations of the use of chemical weapons, including toxic chemicals, for hostile purposes in the Syrian Arab Republic, while stressing that the safety and security of mission personnel remains the top priority, and recalling the work, pursuant to Security Council resolutions 2235 (2015) of 7 August 2015 and 2319 (2016) of 17 November 2016, of the Joint Investigative Mechanism of the Organisation for the Prohibition of Chemical Weapons and the United Nations, which was established to identify to the greatest extent feasible individuals, entities, groups or Governments that were perpetrators, organizers, sponsors or otherwise involved in the use of chemicals as weapons, including chlorine or any other toxic chemical, in the Syrian Arab Republic, where the fact-finding mission of the Organisation for the Prohibition of Chemical Weapons determined that a specific incident in the Syrian Arab Republic involved or likely involved the use of chemicals as weapons,

Reaffirming the importance of the outcome of the Third Special Session of the Conference of the States Parties to Review the Operation of the Chemical Weapons Convention, held in The Hague from 8 to 19 April 2013 (the Third Review Conference), including its consensus final report, in which

---

[1] United Nations, *Treaty Series*, vol. 1974, No. 33757.

the Conference addressed all aspects of the Convention and made important recommendations on its continued implementation,

Emphasizing that the Third Review Conference welcomed the fact that the Convention is a unique multilateral agreement banning an entire category of weapons of mass destruction in a non-discriminatory and verifiable manner under strict and effective international control and noted with satisfaction that the Convention continues to be a remarkable success and an example of effective multilateralism,

Convinced that the Convention, 21 years after its entry into force, has reinforced its role as the international norm against chemical weapons, and that it constitutes a major contribution to:

(a)   International peace and security,

(b)   Eliminating chemical weapons and preventing their re-emergence,

(c)   The ultimate objective of general and complete disarmament under strict and effective international control,

(d)   Excluding completely, for the sake of all mankind, the possibility of the use of chemical weapons,

(e)   Promoting international cooperation and exchange in scientific and technical information in the field of chemical activities among States parties for peaceful purposes in order to enhance the economic and technological development of all States parties,

1.   *Reaffirms its condemnation in the strongest possible terms* of the use of chemical weapons by anyone under any circumstances, emphasizing that any use of chemical weapons anywhere, at any time, by anyone, under any circumstances is unacceptable and is and would be a violation of international law and expressing its strong conviction that those individuals responsible for the use of chemical weapons must and should be held accountable;

2.   *Condemns in the strongest possible terms* that chemical weapons have since 2012 been used in Iraq, Malaysia, the Syrian Arab Republic and the United Kingdom of Great Britain and Northern Ireland, including as reported by the Joint Investigative Mechanism of the Organisation for the Prohibition of Chemical Weapons and the United Nations in:

(a)   Its reports of 24 August 2016[2] and 21 October 2016,[3] which concluded that there was sufficient information to determine that the Syrian Arab Armed Forces were responsible for the attacks which released toxic substances in Talmenes, Syrian Arab Republic, on 21 April 2014, in Sarmin, Syrian Arab Republic, on 16 March 2015, and in Qmenas, Syrian Arab Republic, also on 16 March 2015, and that the so-called "Islamic State in

---

[2]   See S/2016/738/Rev.1.
[3]   See S/2016/888.

Iraq and the Levant" used sulfur mustard in Marea, Syrian Arab Republic, on 21 August 2015; and

(b)   Its report of 26 October 2017,[4] which concluded that there was sufficient information to be confident that Islamic State in Iraq and the Levant was responsible for the use of sulfur mustard at Umm Hawsh on 15 and 16 September 2016 and that the Syrian Arab Republic was responsible for the release of sarin at Khan Shaykhun on 4 April 2017;

and demands that the perpetrators immediately desist from any further use of chemical weapons;

3.   *Takes note with great concern in that regard* of the reports of the fact-finding mission of the Organisation for the Prohibition of Chemical Weapons regarding alleged incidents in Ltamenah, Syrian Arab Republic,[5] and regarding an alleged incident in Saraqib, Syrian Arab Republic,[6] as well as the interim report of the fact-finding mission of the Organisation regarding the incident of alleged use of toxic chemicals as a weapon in Douma, Syrian Arab Republic;[7]

4.   *Recalls* the adoption of decision C-SS-4/DEC.3 of the Fourth Special Session of the Conference of the States Parties, entitled "Addressing the threat from chemical weapons use", of 27 June 2018, and stresses the importance of its implementation, in accordance with the Convention on the Prohibition of the Development, Production, Stockpiling and Use of Chemical Weapons and on Their Destruction;[1]

5.   *Emphasizes* that the universality of the Convention is essential to achieving its object and purpose and to enhancing the security of States parties, as well as to international peace and security, underlines the fact that the objectives of the Convention will not be fully realized as long as there remains even a single State not party to the Convention that could possess or acquire such weapons, and calls upon all States that have not yet done so to become parties to the Convention without delay;

6.   *Underlines* the fact that the full, effective and non-discriminatory implementation of all articles of the Convention makes a major contribution to international peace and security through the elimination of existing stockpiles of chemical weapons and the prohibition of their acquisition and use, and provides for assistance and protection in the event of use or threat of use of chemical weapons and for international cooperation for peaceful purposes in the field of chemical activities;

---

[4] See S/2017/904.

[5] See S/2017/931, annex, and S/2018/620, annex.

[6] See S/2018/478, annex.

[7] See S/2018/732, annex.

7.   *Notes* the impact of scientific and technological progress on the effective implementation of the Convention and the importance for the Organisation for the Prohibition of Chemical Weapons and its policymaking organs of taking due account of such developments;

8.   *Reaffirms* that the obligation of the States parties to complete the destruction of chemical weapons stockpiles and the destruction or conversion of chemical weapons production facilities in accordance with the provisions of the Convention and the Annex on Implementation and Verification (Verification Annex) and under the verification of the Technical Secretariat of the Organisation for the Prohibition of Chemical Weapons is essential for the realization of the object and purpose of the Convention;

9.   *Stresses* the importance to the Convention that all possessors of chemical weapons, chemical weapons production facilities or chemical weapons development facilities, including previously declared possessor States, should be among the States parties to the Convention, and welcomes progress to that end;

10.   *Recalls* that the Third Special Session of the Conference of the States Parties to Review the Operation of the Chemical Weapons Convention expressed concern regarding the statement made by the Director General of the Organisation for the Prohibition of Chemical Weapons in his report to the Executive Council of the Organisation at its sixty-eighth session, provided in accordance with paragraph 2 of decision C-16/DEC.11 of 1 December 2011 adopted by the Conference of the States Parties at its sixteenth session, that three possessor States parties, namely, Libya, the Russian Federation and the United States of America, had been unable to fully meet the final extended deadline of 29 April 2012 for the destruction of their chemical weapons stockpiles, and also expressed determination that the destruction of all categories of chemical weapons should be completed in the shortest time possible in accordance with the provisions of the Convention and the Verification Annex, and with the full application of the relevant decisions that have been taken;

11.   *Welcomes* the confirmation by the Director General of the Organisation for the Prohibition of Chemical Weapons expressed in his report of 5 October 2017,[8] based upon information received from the Russian Federation and independent information received from the inspectors of the Organisation, regarding the completion of the full destruction of chemical weapons declared by the Russian Federation;

12.   *Also welcomes* the completed destruction of Libya's remaining category 2 chemical weapons, as reported by the Director General of the Organisation for the Prohibition of Chemical Weapons in his report of

---

[8] EC-86/DG.31.

22 December 2017,[9] as well as the completed destruction by Iraq of its entire declared stockpile of chemical weapons remnants, as reported by the Director General in his report of 28 February 2018;[10]

13. *Notes with concern* that, along with the threat of the possible production, acquisition and use of chemical weapons by States, the international community also faces the danger of the production, acquisition and use of chemical weapons by non-State actors, including terrorists, concerns which have highlighted the necessity of achieving universal adherence to the Convention, as well as the high level of readiness of the Organisation for the Prohibition of Chemical Weapons, and stresses that the full and effective implementation of all provisions of the Convention, including those on national implementation (article VII) and assistance and protection (article X), constitutes an important contribution to the efforts of the United Nations in the global fight against terrorism in all its forms and manifestations;

14. *Notes* that the effective application of the verification system builds confidence in compliance with the Convention by States parties;

15. *Stresses* the importance of the Organisation for the Prohibition of Chemical Weapons in verifying compliance with the provisions of the Convention as well as in promoting the timely and efficient accomplishment of all its objectives;

16. *Expresses grave concern* that, despite the verified destruction of all 27 chemical weapons production facilities declared by the Syrian Arab Republic, the Technical Secretariat, as reported by the Director General, cannot fully verify that the Syrian Arab Republic has submitted a declaration that can be considered accurate and complete in accordance with the Convention or Executive Council decision EC-M-33/DEC.1 as well as with the conclusion of decision C-SS-4/DEC.3, of the Fourth Special Session of the Conference of the States Parties that the Syrian Arab Republic failed to declare and destroy all of its chemical weapons and chemical weapons production facilities, and underscores the importance of such full verification;

17. *Urges* all States parties to the Convention to meet in full and on time their obligations under the Convention and to support the Organisation for the Prohibition of Chemical Weapons in its implementation activities;

18. *Welcomes* the progress made in the national implementation of article VII obligations, commends the States parties and the Technical Secretariat for assisting other States parties, on request, with the implementation of the follow-up to the plan of action regarding article VII

---

[9] EC-87/DG.6.
[10] EC-87/DG.18.

obligations, and urges States parties that have not fulfilled their obligations under article VII to do so without further delay, in accordance with their constitutional processes;

19. *Emphasizes* the continuing relevance and importance of the provisions of article X of the Convention, welcomes the activities of the Organisation for the Prohibition of Chemical Weapons in relation to assistance and protection against chemical weapons, supports further efforts by both States parties and the Technical Secretariat to promote a high level of readiness to respond to chemical weapons threats as articulated in article X, and welcomes the effectiveness and efficiency of the increased focus on making full use of regional and subregional capacities and expertise, including taking advantage of established training centres;

20. *Reaffirms* that the provisions of the Convention shall be implemented in a manner that avoids hampering the economic or technological development of States parties and international cooperation in the field of chemical activities for purposes not prohibited under the Convention, including the international exchange of scientific and technical information, and chemicals and equipment for the production, processing or use of chemicals for purposes not prohibited under the Convention;

21. *Emphasizes* the importance of the provisions of article XI of the Convention relating to the economic and technological development of States parties, recalls that the full, effective and non-discriminatory implementation of those provisions contributes to universality, and reaffirms the undertaking of the States parties to foster international cooperation for peaceful purposes in the field of chemical activities of the States parties and the importance of that cooperation and its contribution to the promotion of the Convention as a whole;

22. *Notes with appreciation* the ongoing work of the Organisation for the Prohibition of Chemical Weapons to achieve the object and purpose of the Convention, to ensure the full implementation of its provisions, including those for international verification of compliance with it, and to provide a forum for consultation and cooperation among States parties;

23. *Stresses* the importance of the continued work related to the Fourth Special Session of the Conference of the States Parties to Review the Operation of the Chemical Weapons Convention;

24. *Welcomes* the cooperation between the United Nations and the Organisation for the Prohibition of Chemical Weapons within the framework of the relationship agreement between the United Nations and the Organisation,[11] in accordance with the provisions of the Convention;

---

[11] United Nations, *Treaty Series*, vol. 2160, No. 1240.

25. *Decides* to include in the provisional agenda of its seventy-fourth session, under the item entitled "General and complete disarmament", the sub-item entitled "Implementation of the Convention on the Prohibition of the Development, Production, Stockpiling and Use of Chemical Weapons and on Their Destruction".

Action by the General Assembly

Date: 5 December 2018   Meeting: 45th plenary meeting
Vote: 152-7-22   Report: A/73/510
       134-7-25, p.p. 4
       122-13-26, o.p. 2
       122-13-30, o.p. 3
       112-18-35, o.p. 4
       110-15-38, o.p. 16

Sponsors

Poland

Recorded vote

As a whole

In favour:

Afghanistan, Albania, Andorra, Angola, Antigua and Barbuda, Argentina, Australia, Austria, Azerbaijan, Bahamas, Bahrain, Bangladesh, Barbados, Belgium, Belize, Benin, Bhutan, Bosnia and Herzegovina, Botswana, Brazil, Brunei Darussalam, Bulgaria, Burkina Faso, Cabo Verde, Cameroon, Canada, Central African Republic, Chile, Colombia, Congo, Costa Rica, Côte d'Ivoire, Croatia, Cyprus, Czechia, Denmark, Djibouti, Dominican Republic, Ecuador, El Salvador, Equatorial Guinea, Eritrea, Estonia, Eswatini, Ethiopia, Fiji, Finland, France, Gabon, Gambia, Georgia, Germany, Ghana, Greece, Grenada, Guatemala, Guinea, Guinea-Bissau, Guyana, Haiti, Honduras, Hungary, Iceland, India, Indonesia, Iraq, Ireland, Israel, Italy, Jamaica, Japan, Jordan, Kuwait, Lao People's Democratic Republic, Latvia, Lesotho, Liberia, Libya, Liechtenstein, Lithuania, Luxembourg, Malawi, Malaysia, Maldives, Malta, Marshall Islands, Mauritania, Mauritius, Mexico, Micronesia (Federated States of), Monaco, Mongolia, Montenegro, Morocco, Mozambique, Namibia, Nepal, Netherlands, New Zealand, Nigeria, Norway, Oman, Pakistan, Palau, Panama, Papua New Guinea, Paraguay, Peru, Philippines, Poland, Portugal, Qatar, Republic of Korea, Republic of Moldova, Romania, Saint Lucia, Saint Vincent and the Grenadines, Samoa, San Marino, Sao Tome and Principe, Saudi Arabia, Senegal, Seychelles, Sierra Leone, Singapore, Slovakia, Slovenia, Solomon Islands, South Africa, Spain, Sri Lanka, Sudan, Sweden,

Switzerland, Tajikistan, Thailand, the former Yugoslav Republic of Macedonia, Timor-Leste, Togo, Trinidad and Tobago, Tunisia, Turkey, Tuvalu, Ukraine, United Arab Emirates, United Kingdom, United States, Uruguay, Vanuatu, Viet Nam, Yemen, Zambia

Against:

Cambodia, China, Iran (Islamic Republic of), Nicaragua, Russian Federation, Syrian Arab Republic, Zimbabwe

Abstaining:

Algeria, Armenia, Belarus, Bolivia (Plurinational State of), Burundi, Comoros, Cuba, Egypt, Kazakhstan, Kenya, Kyrgyzstan, Lebanon, Madagascar, Mali, Myanmar, Niger, Rwanda, Suriname, Uganda, United Republic of Tanzania, Uzbekistan, Venezuela (Bolivarian Republic of)

*Fourth preambular paragraph**

In favour:

Albania, Andorra, Angola, Antigua and Barbuda, Argentina, Australia, Austria, Bahamas, Bahrain, Barbados, Belgium, Belize, Benin, Bhutan, Bosnia and Herzegovina, Botswana, Brazil, Brunei Darussalam, Bulgaria, Burundi, Cabo Verde, Canada, Chile, Colombia, Comoros, Costa Rica, Côte d'Ivoire, Croatia, Cyprus, Czechia, Denmark, Dominican Republic, El Salvador, Equatorial Guinea, Estonia, Eswatini, Ethiopia, Fiji, Finland, France, Georgia, Germany, Ghana, Greece, Guatemala, Guinea, Guinea-Bissau, Guyana, Haiti, Honduras, Hungary, Iceland, India, Indonesia, Ireland, Israel, Italy, Jamaica, Japan, Kuwait, Latvia, Lesotho, Liberia, Libya, Liechtenstein, Lithuania, Luxembourg, Madagascar, Malawi, Malaysia, Maldives, Malta, Marshall Islands, Mauritania, Mauritius, Mexico, Micronesia (Federated States of), Monaco, Mongolia, Montenegro, Morocco, Mozambique, Myanmar, Namibia, Nepal, Netherlands, New Zealand, Nicaragua, Niger, Nigeria, Norway, Pakistan, Panama, Papua New Guinea, Paraguay, Peru, Poland, Portugal, Qatar, Republic of Korea, Republic of Moldova, Romania, Saint Lucia, Saint Vincent and the Grenadines, Samoa, San Marino, Sao Tome and Principe, Saudi Arabia, Senegal, Sierra Leone, Singapore, Slovakia, Slovenia, South Africa, Spain, Sri Lanka, Sweden, Switzerland, Thailand, the former Yugoslav Republic of Macedonia, Timor-Leste, Togo, Trinidad and Tobago, Tunisia, Turkey, Ukraine, United Arab Emirates, United Kingdom, United States, Uruguay, Vanuatu, Viet Nam, Yemen, Zambia

---

* Subsequently, the delegation of the Bangladesh informed the Secretariat that it had intended to vote in favour, the delegation of Nicaragua had intended to vote against. The voting tally above does not reflect this information.

Against:

Belarus, Cambodia, Democratic People's Republic of Korea, Iran (Islamic Republic of), Russian Federation, Syrian Arab Republic, Zimbabwe

Abstaining:

Algeria, Armenia, Azerbaijan, Bolivia (Plurinational State of), China, Cuba, Egypt, Iraq, Jordan, Kazakhstan, Kenya, Kyrgyzstan, Lebanon, Mali, Oman, Philippines, Rwanda, Seychelles, Sudan, Suriname, Tajikistan, Uganda, United Republic of Tanzania, Uzbekistan, Venezuela (Bolivarian Republic of)

Operative paragraph 2**

In favour:

Albania, Andorra, Angola, Antigua and Barbuda, Argentina, Australia, Austria, Bahamas, Bahrain, Barbados, Belgium, Belize, Benin, Bhutan, Bosnia and Herzegovina, Botswana, Brazil, Brunei Darussalam, Bulgaria, Cabo Verde, Canada, Chile, Colombia, Costa Rica, Côte d'Ivoire, Croatia, Cyprus, Czechia, Denmark, Dominican Republic, El Salvador, Equatorial Guinea, Estonia, Eswatini, Finland, France, Georgia, Germany, Ghana, Greece, Guatemala, Guinea, Guinea-Bissau, Guyana, Haiti, Honduras, Hungary, Iceland, Indonesia, Iraq, Ireland, Israel, Italy, Jamaica, Japan, Kuwait, Latvia, Lesotho, Liberia, Libya, Liechtenstein, Lithuania, Luxembourg, Madagascar, Malawi, Malaysia, Maldives, Malta, Marshall Islands, Mauritania, Mexico, Micronesia (Federated States of), Monaco, Mongolia, Montenegro, Morocco, Mozambique, Myanmar, Namibia, Nepal, Netherlands, New Zealand, Norway, Panama, Papua New Guinea, Paraguay, Peru, Poland, Portugal, Qatar, Republic of Korea, Republic of Moldova, Romania, Saint Lucia, Saint Vincent and the Grenadines, Samoa, San Marino, Sao Tome and Principe, Saudi Arabia, Sierra Leone, Singapore, Slovakia, Slovenia, Spain, Sri Lanka, Sweden, Switzerland, Thailand, the former Yugoslav Republic of Macedonia, Timor-Leste, Togo, Trinidad and Tobago, Tunisia, Turkey, Ukraine, United Arab Emirates, United Kingdom, United States, Uruguay, Vanuatu, Yemen, Zambia

Against:

Belarus, Bolivia (Plurinational State of), Cambodia, China, Cuba, Democratic People's Republic of Korea, Iran (Islamic Republic of), Kyrgyzstan, Nicaragua, Russian Federation, Syrian Arab Republic, Venezuela (Bolivarian Republic of), Zimbabwe

---

** Subsequently, the delegations of the Bangladesh and Benin informed the Secretariat that they had intended to abstain. The voting tally above does not reflect this information.

Abstaining:

> Algeria, Armenia, Azerbaijan, Ecuador, Egypt, Ethiopia, Fiji, India, Jordan, Kazakhstan, Kenya, Lebanon, Mali, Niger, Nigeria, Oman, Pakistan, Philippines, South Africa, Sudan, Suriname, Tajikistan, Uganda, United Republic of Tanzania, Uzbekistan, Viet Nam

Operative paragraph 3***

In favour:

> Albania, Andorra, Angola, Antigua and Barbuda, Argentina, Australia, Austria, Bahamas, Bahrain, Barbados, Belgium, Belize, Benin, Bhutan, Bosnia and Herzegovina, Botswana, Brazil, Brunei Darussalam, Bulgaria, Cabo Verde, Canada, Chile, Colombia, Costa Rica, Côte d'Ivoire, Croatia, Cyprus, Czechia, Denmark, Dominican Republic, El Salvador, Equatorial Guinea, Estonia, Eswatini, Ethiopia, Fiji, Finland, France, Georgia, Germany, Ghana, Greece, Guatemala, Guinea, Guinea-Bissau, Guyana, Haiti, Honduras, Hungary, Iceland, Ireland, Israel, Italy, Jamaica, Japan, Kuwait, Latvia, Lesotho, Liberia, Libya, Liechtenstein, Lithuania, Luxembourg, Malawi, Malaysia, Maldives, Malta, Marshall Islands, Mauritania, Mauritius, Mexico, Micronesia (Federated States of), Monaco, Mongolia, Montenegro, Morocco, Mozambique, Myanmar, Namibia, Nepal, Netherlands, New Zealand, Norway, Panama, Papua New Guinea, Paraguay, Peru, Poland, Portugal, Qatar, Republic of Korea, Republic of Moldova, Romania, Saint Lucia, Saint Vincent and the Grenadines, Samoa, San Marino, Sao Tome and Principe, Saudi Arabia, Sierra Leone, Singapore, Slovakia, Slovenia, Spain, Sri Lanka, Sweden, Switzerland, Thailand, the former Yugoslav Republic of Macedonia, Timor-Leste, Togo, Trinidad and Tobago, Tunisia, Turkey, Ukraine, United Arab Emirates, United Kingdom, United States, Uruguay, Vanuatu, Yemen, Zambia

Against:

> Belarus, Bolivia (Plurinational State of), Cambodia, China, Cuba, Democratic People's Republic of Korea, Iran (Islamic Republic of), Nicaragua, Russian Federation, Sudan, Syrian Arab Republic, Venezuela (Bolivarian Republic of), Zimbabwe

Abstaining:

> Algeria, Armenia, Azerbaijan, Burundi, Comoros, Ecuador, Egypt, India, Indonesia, Iraq, Jordan, Kazakhstan, Kenya, Kyrgyzstan, Lebanon, Madagascar, Mali, Niger, Nigeria, Oman, Pakistan, Philippines, Rwanda, South Africa, Suriname, Tajikistan, Uganda, United Republic of Tanzania, Uzbekistan, Viet Nam

---

*** Subsequently, the delegation of Bangladesh informed the Secretariat that it had intended to vote in favour, the delegation of Benin had intended to abstain. The voting tally above does not reflect this information.

Operative paragraph 4****

In favour:

Albania, Andorra, Angola, Antigua and Barbuda, Argentina, Australia, Austria, Bahamas, Bahrain, Barbados, Belgium, Belize, Bhutan, Bosnia and Herzegovina, Botswana, Bulgaria, Cabo Verde, Canada, Chile, Colombia, Costa Rica, Côte d'Ivoire, Croatia, Cyprus, Czechia, Denmark, Djibouti, Dominican Republic, El Salvador, Equatorial Guinea, Estonia, Fiji, Finland, France, Georgia, Germany, Ghana, Greece, Guatemala, Guinea, Guinea-Bissau, Guyana, Haiti, Honduras, Hungary, Iceland, Ireland, Israel, Italy, Japan, Kuwait, Latvia, Liberia, Libya, Liechtenstein, Lithuania, Luxembourg, Malawi, Maldives, Malta, Marshall Islands, Mauritania, Mauritius, Mexico, Micronesia (Federated States of), Monaco, Montenegro, Morocco, Mozambique, Namibia, Nepal, Netherlands, New Zealand, Norway, Panama, Papua New Guinea, Paraguay, Peru, Poland, Portugal, Qatar, Republic of Korea, Republic of Moldova, Romania, Saint Lucia, Saint Vincent and the Grenadines, Samoa, San Marino, Sao Tome and Principe, Saudi Arabia, Sierra Leone, Singapore, Slovakia, Slovenia, Spain, Sri Lanka, Sweden, Switzerland, the former Yugoslav Republic of Macedonia, Timor-Leste, Togo, Trinidad and Tobago, Tunisia, Turkey, Ukraine, United Arab Emirates, United Kingdom, United States, Uruguay, Vanuatu, Yemen, Zambia

Against:

Belarus, Bolivia (Plurinational State of), Cambodia, China, Comoros, Cuba, Democratic People's Republic of Korea, India, Iran (Islamic Republic of), Kazakhstan, Kyrgyzstan, Lao People's Democratic Republic, Myanmar, Nicaragua, Russian Federation, Syrian Arab Republic, Venezuela (Bolivarian Republic of), Viet Nam

Abstaining:

Algeria, Azerbaijan, Benin, Brazil, Brunei Darussalam, Burundi, Ecuador, Egypt, Eswatini, Ethiopia, Indonesia, Iraq, Jamaica, Jordan, Kenya, Lebanon, Madagascar, Malaysia, Mali, Mongolia, Niger, Nigeria, Oman, Pakistan, Philippines, Rwanda, South Africa, Sudan, Suriname, Tajikistan, Thailand, Uganda, United Republic of Tanzania, Uzbekistan, Zimbabwe

Operative paragraph 16*****

In favour:

Albania, Andorra, Angola, Antigua and Barbuda, Argentina, Australia, Austria, Bahamas, Bahrain, Barbados, Belgium, Belize, Bhutan,

---

**** Subsequently, the delegation of Bangladesh informed the Secretariat that it had intended to abstain. The voting tally above does not reflect this information.

***** Subsequently, the delegation of Bangladesh informed the Secretariat that it had intended to abstain. The voting tally above does not reflect this information.

Bosnia and Herzegovina, Botswana, Bulgaria, Cabo Verde, Canada, Chile, Colombia, Costa Rica, Côte d'Ivoire, Croatia, Cyprus, Czechia, Denmark, Dominican Republic, El Salvador, Estonia, Ethiopia, Finland, France, Georgia, Germany, Greece, Guatemala, Guinea, Guinea-Bissau, Guyana, Haiti, Honduras, Hungary, Iceland, Ireland, Israel, Italy, Jamaica, Japan, Kuwait, Latvia, Lesotho, Liberia, Libya, Liechtenstein, Lithuania, Luxembourg, Malawi, Maldives, Malta, Marshall Islands, Mauritania, Mexico, Micronesia (Federated States of), Monaco, Montenegro, Morocco, Mozambique, Namibia, Nepal, Netherlands, New Zealand, Norway, Panama, Papua New Guinea, Paraguay, Peru, Poland, Portugal, Qatar, Republic of Korea, Republic of Moldova, Romania, Saint Lucia, Saint Vincent and the Grenadines, Samoa, San Marino, Sao Tome and Principe, Saudi Arabia, Sierra Leone, Singapore, Slovakia, Slovenia, Spain, Sri Lanka, Sweden, Switzerland, the former Yugoslav Republic of Macedonia, Timor-Leste, Togo, Trinidad and Tobago, Tunisia, Turkey, Ukraine, United Arab Emirates, United Kingdom, United States, Uruguay, Vanuatu, Yemen, Zambia

Against:

Belarus, Bolivia (Plurinational State of), Cambodia, China, Comoros, Cuba, Democratic People's Republic of Korea, Iran (Islamic Republic of), Myanmar, Nicaragua, Russian Federation, Sudan, Syrian Arab Republic, Venezuela (Bolivarian Republic of), Zimbabwe

Abstaining:

Algeria, Azerbaijan, Benin, Brazil, Brunei Darussalam, Burundi, Ecuador, Egypt, Equatorial Guinea, Eswatini, Fiji, Ghana, India, Indonesia, Iraq, Jordan, Kazakhstan, Kenya, Kyrgyzstan, Lao People's Democratic Republic, Lebanon, Madagascar, Malaysia, Mali, Mongolia, Niger, Nigeria, Oman, Pakistan, Philippines, South Africa, Suriname, Tajikistan, Thailand, Uganda, United Republic of Tanzania, Uzbekistan, Viet Nam

Action by the First Committee

Date:	5 November 2018	Meeting:	28th meeting
Vote:	148-7-23	Draft resolution:	A/C.1/73/L.20
	128-7-30, p.p. 4		
	120-14-32, o.p. 2		
	123-13-33, o.p. 3		
	113-19-34, o.p. 4		
	112-15-39, o.p. 16		

Agenda item 101 (gg)

73/46　Women, disarmament, non-proliferation and arms control

Text

The General Assembly,

Recalling that the Charter of the United Nations reaffirms the equal rights of women and men,

Recalling also its resolutions 65/69 of 8 December 2010, 67/48 of 3 December 2012, 68/33 of 5 December 2013, 69/61 of 2 December 2014 and 71/56 of 5 December 2016,

Recalling further General Assembly and Security Council resolutions on the issue of women and peace and security,

Recalling the 2015 review of the women and peace and security agenda,

Reaffirming the Sustainable Development Goals relevant to the promotion of women, disarmament, non-proliferation and arms control, and acknowledging that the success of efforts to achieve sustainable development and disarmament depends on the full and effective inclusion of women in all aspects of these efforts,

Welcoming the call for the full and meaningful participation of women in efforts to prevent, combat and eradicate the illicit transfer of small arms, pursuant to Security Council resolutions 2106 (2013) of 24 June 2013, 2117 (2013) of 26 September 2013, 2122 (2013) of 18 October 2013 and 2220 (2015) of 22 May 2015,

Reaffirming that the equal, full and effective participation of both women and men is one of the essential factors for the promotion and attainment of sustainable peace and security,

Recognizing the valuable contribution of women to practical disarmament measures carried out at the local, national, subregional and regional levels in the prevention and reduction of armed violence and armed conflict, and in promoting disarmament, non-proliferation and arms control,

Recognizing also that the role of women in disarmament, non-proliferation and arms control should be further developed and in particular the need to facilitate the participation and representation of women in policymaking, planning and implementation processes related to disarmament, non-proliferation and arms control,

Recalling the entry into force of the Arms Trade Treaty,[1] and therefore encouraging States parties to fully implement all the provisions of the Treaty,

---

[1] See resolution 67/234 B.

including the provisions on serious acts of gender-based violence and on violence against children,

Noting with appreciation the efforts of Member States to increase the participation of women in their national and regional coordination mechanisms on disarmament-related matters, including in efforts to prevent, combat and eradicate the illicit trade in small arms and light weapons in all its aspects,

Recognizing the important role played by civil society organizations in promoting the role of women in disarmament, non-proliferation and arms control,

1. *Urges* Member States, relevant subregional and regional organizations, the United Nations and the specialized agencies to promote equal opportunities for the representation of women in all decision-making processes with regard to matters related to disarmament, non-proliferation and arms control, in particular as it relates to the prevention and reduction of armed violence and armed conflict;

2. *Welcomes* the report of the Secretary-General on the measures taken by Member States to implement General Assembly resolution 71/56;[2]

3. *Also welcomes* the continuing efforts of the United Nations organs, agencies, funds and programmes to accord high priority to the issue of women and peace and security, and in this regard notes the role of the United Nations Entity for Gender Equality and the Empowerment of Women (UN-Women) in promoting the implementation of all resolutions related to women in the context of peace and security;

4. *Encourages* Member States to better understand the impact of armed violence, in particular the impact of the illicit trafficking in small arms and light weapons on women and girls, through, inter alia, the development of national action plans on women and peace and security and strengthening the collection of data disaggregated by sex and age;

5. *Urges* Member States to support and strengthen the effective participation of women in organizations in the field of disarmament at the local, national, subregional and regional levels;

6. *Calls upon* all States to empower women, including through capacity-building efforts, as appropriate, to participate in the design and implementation of disarmament, non-proliferation and arms control efforts;

7. *Encourages* States to seriously consider increasing funding for policies and programmes that take account of the differing impacts of illicit small arms and light weapons on women, men, girls and boys;

---

[2] A/73/115.

8.   *Calls upon* all States to develop appropriate and effective national risk assessment criteria to facilitate the prevention of the use of arms to commit violence against women and children;

9.   *Requests* the relevant United Nations organs, agencies, funds and programmes to assist States, upon request, in promoting the role of women in disarmament, non-proliferation and arms control, including in preventing, combating and eradicating the illicit trade in small arms and light weapons;

10.   *Requests* the Secretary-General to seek the views of Member States on ways and means of promoting the role of women in disarmament, non-proliferation and arms control and to report to the General Assembly at its seventy-fifth session on the implementation of the present resolution;

11.   *Decides* to include in the provisional agenda of its seventy-fifth session, under the item entitled "General and complete disarmament", the sub-item entitled "Women, disarmament, non-proliferation and arms control".

Action by the General Assembly

Date: 5 December 2018   Meeting: 45th plenary meeting
Vote: Adopted without a vote   Report: A/73/510
       149-0-23, p.p. 10

Sponsors

Albania, Antigua and Barbuda, Argentina, Australia, Austria, Bahamas, Belgium, Belize, Bosnia and Herzegovina, Bulgaria, Canada, Central African Republic, Chile, Costa Rica, Croatia, Cyprus, Czechia, Denmark, Dominican Republic, El Salvador, Estonia, Finland, France, Greece, Grenada, Guatemala, Guyana, Haiti, Hungary, Iceland, Ireland, Italy, Jamaica, Japan, Latvia, Liechtenstein, Lithuania, Luxembourg, Madagascar, Malawi, Malta, Mongolia, Montenegro, Namibia, Nepal, Netherlands, New Zealand, Nigeria, Norway, Panama, Peru, Philippines, Poland, Portugal, Republic of Moldova, Romania, Saint Lucia, Saint Vincent and the Grenadines, Samoa, San Marino, Senegal, Serbia, Slovakia, Slovenia, South Africa, Spain, Suriname, Sweden, Switzerland, Thailand, Togo, **Trinidad and Tobago**, United Kingdom, Uruguay

Co-sponsors

Andorra, Bangladesh, Brazil, Burkina Faso, Congo, Equatorial Guinea, Eritrea, Germany, Ghana, Guinea-Bissau, Honduras, Lebanon, Micronesia (Federated States of), Monaco, Papua New Guinea, Paraguay, Republic of Korea, Saint Kitts and Nevis, the former Yugoslav Republic of Macedonia, Tunisia, Tuvalu, Ukraine, Zambia

Recorded vote

Tenth preambular paragraph

In favour:

Afghanistan, Albania, Algeria, Andorra, Angola, Antigua and Barbuda, Argentina, Australia, Austria, Bahamas, Bahrain, Bangladesh, Barbados, Belgium, Belize, Benin, Bosnia and Herzegovina, Botswana, Brazil, Brunei Darussalam, Bulgaria, Burkina Faso, Burundi, Cabo Verde, Cambodia, Canada, Chile, China, Colombia, Comoros, Costa Rica, Côte d'Ivoire, Croatia, Cyprus, Czechia, Democratic Republic of the Congo, Denmark, Djibouti, Dominican Republic, El Salvador, Equatorial Guinea, Eritrea, Estonia, Eswatini, Ethiopia, Fiji, Finland, France, Gambia, Georgia, Germany, Ghana, Greece, Guatemala, Guinea, Guinea-Bissau, Guyana, Haiti, Honduras, Hungary, Iceland, Iraq, Ireland, Israel, Italy, Jamaica, Japan, Jordan, Kazakhstan, Kenya, Latvia, Lebanon, Lesotho, Liberia, Libya, Liechtenstein, Lithuania, Luxembourg, Madagascar, Malawi, Malaysia, Maldives, Mali, Malta, Marshall Islands, Mauritania, Mauritius, Mexico, Micronesia (Federated States of), Monaco, Mongolia, Montenegro, Morocco, Mozambique, Namibia, Nepal, Netherlands, New Zealand, Nigeria, Norway, Oman, Pakistan, Palau, Panama, Papua New Guinea, Paraguay, Peru, Philippines, Poland, Portugal, Republic of Korea, Republic of Moldova, Romania, Saint Lucia, Saint Vincent and the Grenadines, Samoa, San Marino, Sao Tome and Principe, Saudi Arabia, Senegal, Serbia, Seychelles, Sierra Leone, Singapore, Slovakia, Slovenia, South Africa, Spain, Sudan, Suriname, Sweden, Switzerland, Thailand, the former Yugoslav Republic of Macedonia, Timor-Leste, Togo, Trinidad and Tobago, Tunisia, Turkey, Tuvalu, Ukraine, United Arab Emirates, United Kingdom, United Republic of Tanzania, United States, Uruguay, Vanuatu, Yemen, Zambia

Against:

None

Abstaining:

Armenia, Azerbaijan, Belarus, Bhutan, Bolivia (Plurinational State of), Cuba, Democratic People's Republic of Korea, Ecuador, Egypt, India, Indonesia, Iran (Islamic Republic of), Kuwait, Lao People's Democratic Republic, Myanmar, Nicaragua, Qatar, Russian Federation, Sri Lanka, Syrian Arab Republic, Uganda, Venezuela (Bolivarian Republic of), Zimbabwe

Action by the First Committee

Date:	8 November 2018	Meeting:	30th meeting
Vote:	Adopted without a vote 149-0-23, p.p. 10	Draft resolution:	A/C.1/73/L.21

Agenda item 101 (jj)

73/47   Humanitarian consequences of nuclear weapons

Text

The General Assembly,

Recalling its resolutions 70/47 of 7 December 2015, 71/46 of 5 December 2016 and 72/30 of 4 December 2017,

Reiterating the deep concern about the catastrophic consequences of nuclear weapons,

Stressing that the immense and uncontrollable destructive capability and indiscriminate nature of nuclear weapons cause unacceptable humanitarian consequences, as has been demonstrated through their past use and testing,

Recalling that concern about the humanitarian consequences of nuclear weapons has been reflected in numerous United Nations resolutions, including the first resolution adopted by the General Assembly, on 24 January 1946,

Recalling also that at the first special session of the General Assembly devoted to disarmament, in 1978, the Assembly stressed that nuclear weapons posed the greatest danger to mankind and to the survival of civilization,[1]

Welcoming the renewed interest and resolve of the international community, together with the International Committee of the Red Cross and international humanitarian organizations, to address the catastrophic consequences of nuclear weapons,

Recalling that the 2010 Review Conference of the Parties to the Treaty on the Non-Proliferation of Nuclear Weapons expressed deep concern at the catastrophic humanitarian consequences of any use of nuclear weapons,[2]

Noting the resolution of 26 November 2011 of the Council of Delegates of the International Red Cross and Red Crescent Movement entitled "Working towards the elimination of nuclear weapons",

Recalling the joint statements on the humanitarian consequences of nuclear weapons delivered to the General Assembly and during the 2010–2015 cycle of the review of the Treaty on the Non-Proliferation of Nuclear Weapons,[3]

Welcoming the facts-based discussions on the effects of a nuclear weapon detonation that were held at the conferences on the humanitarian impact of

---

[1] See resolution S-10/2.

[2] See *2010 Review Conference of the Parties to the Treaty on the Non-Proliferation of Nuclear Weapons, Final Document*, vol. I (NPT/CONF.2010/50 (Vol. I)), part I, *Conclusions and recommendations for follow-on actions*.

[3] United Nations, *Treaty Series*, vol. 729, No. 10485.

nuclear weapons, convened by Norway, on 4 and 5 March 2013, Mexico, on 13 and 14 February 2014, and Austria, on 8 and 9 December 2014,

Cognizant that a key message from experts and international organizations at those conferences was that no State or international body could address the immediate humanitarian emergency caused by a nuclear weapon detonation or provide adequate assistance to victims,

Firmly believing that it is in the interest of all States to engage in discussions on the humanitarian consequences of nuclear weapons with the aim of further broadening and deepening the understanding of this matter, and welcoming civil society's ongoing engagement,

Reaffirming the role of civil society, in partnership with Governments, in raising awareness about the unacceptable humanitarian consequences of nuclear weapons,

Emphasizing that the catastrophic consequences of nuclear weapons affect not only Governments but each and every citizen of our interconnected world and have deep implications for human survival, for the environment, for socioeconomic development, for our economies and for the health of future generations,

1. *Stresses* that it is in the interest of the very survival of humanity that nuclear weapons never be used again, under any circumstances;

2. *Emphasizes* that the only way to guarantee that nuclear weapons will never be used again is their total elimination;

3. *Stresses* that the catastrophic effects of a nuclear weapon detonation, whether by accident, miscalculation or design, cannot be adequately addressed;

4. *Expresses its firm belief* that awareness of the catastrophic consequences of nuclear weapons must underpin all approaches and efforts towards nuclear disarmament;

5. *Calls upon* all States, in their shared responsibility, to prevent the use of nuclear weapons, to prevent their vertical and horizontal proliferation and to achieve nuclear disarmament;

6. *Urges* States to exert all efforts to totally eliminate the threat of these weapons of mass destruction;

7. *Decides* to include in the provisional agenda of its seventy-fourth session, under the item entitled "General and complete disarmament", the sub-item entitled "Humanitarian consequences of nuclear weapons".

Action by the General Assembly

Date: 5 December 2018   Meeting: 45th plenary meeting
Vote: 142-15-26   Report: A/73/510

Sponsors

Algeria, Angola, Antigua and Barbuda, **Austria**, Bahamas, Belize, Benin, Bolivia (Plurinational State of), Brazil, Cabo Verde, Central African Republic, Chile, Costa Rica, Democratic Republic of the Congo, Dominican Republic, Egypt, El Salvador, Eritrea, Eswatini, Ghana, Guatemala, Guyana, Honduras, Indonesia, Ireland, Jamaica, Kazakhstan, Libya, Liechtenstein, Madagascar, Malawi, Malaysia, Malta, Mexico, Mongolia, Myanmar, Namibia, Nepal, New Zealand, Nicaragua, Nigeria, Panama, Papua New Guinea, Paraguay, Peru, Philippines, Saint Vincent and the Grenadines, Samoa, San Marino, Sierra Leone, South Africa, Sudan, Suriname, Sweden, Switzerland, Thailand, Togo, Trinidad and Tobago, Uruguay, Viet Nam, Zimbabwe

Co-sponsors

Andorra, Bahrain, Bangladesh, Burkina Faso, Colombia, Côte d'Ivoire, Djibouti, Fiji, Iraq, Lebanon, Morocco, Mozambique, Oman, Palau, Republic of Moldova, Sao Tome and Principe, Saudi Arabia, Seychelles, Singapore, Tunisia, Tuvalu, United Arab Emirates, Venezuela (Bolivarian Republic of)

Recorded vote

In favour:

Afghanistan, Algeria, Andorra, Angola, Antigua and Barbuda, Argentina, Austria, Azerbaijan, Bahamas, Bahrain, Bangladesh, Barbados, Belarus, Belize, Benin, Bhutan, Bolivia (Plurinational State of), Botswana, Brazil, Brunei Darussalam, Burkina Faso, Burundi, Cabo Verde, Cambodia, Cameroon, Central African Republic, Chile, Colombia, Comoros, Congo, Costa Rica, Côte d'Ivoire, Cuba, Cyprus, Democratic Republic of the Congo, Djibouti, Dominica, Dominican Republic, Ecuador, Egypt, El Salvador, Equatorial Guinea, Eritrea, Eswatini, Ethiopia, Fiji, Finland, Gambia, Ghana, Greece, Grenada, Guatemala, Guinea, Guinea-Bissau, Guyana, Honduras, India, Indonesia, Iran (Islamic Republic of), Iraq, Ireland, Jamaica, Japan, Jordan, Kazakhstan, Kenya, Kuwait, Kyrgyzstan, Lao People's Democratic Republic, Lebanon, Lesotho, Liberia, Libya, Liechtenstein, Madagascar, Malawi, Malaysia, Maldives, Malta, Marshall Islands, Mauritania, Mauritius, Mexico, Mongolia, Morocco, Mozambique, Myanmar, Namibia, Nauru, Nepal, New Zealand, Nicaragua, Niger, Nigeria, Oman, Palau, Panama, Papua New Guinea, Paraguay, Peru, Philippines, Qatar, Republic of Moldova, Saint Lucia, Saint Vincent and the Grenadines, Samoa, San Marino, Sao Tome and Principe, Saudi Arabia, Senegal, Serbia, Seychelles, Sierra Leone, Singapore, Solomon Islands, South Africa, Sri Lanka, Sudan, Suriname, Sweden, Switzerland, Syrian Arab Republic, Tajikistan, Thailand, the former Yugoslav Republic of Macedonia, Timor-Leste, Togo, Tonga,

Trinidad and Tobago, Tunisia, Tuvalu, Uganda, United Arab Emirates, United Republic of Tanzania, Uruguay, Uzbekistan, Vanuatu, Venezuela (Bolivarian Republic of), Viet Nam, Yemen, Zambia, Zimbabwe

Against:

Czechia, Estonia, France, Hungary, Israel, Latvia, Lithuania, Monaco, Poland, Republic of Korea, Romania, Russian Federation, Turkey, United Kingdom, United States

Abstaining:

Albania, Armenia, Australia, Belgium, Bosnia and Herzegovina, Bulgaria, Canada, China, Croatia, Democratic People's Republic of Korea, Denmark, Georgia, Germany, Iceland, Italy, Luxembourg, Mali, Montenegro, Netherlands, Norway, Pakistan, Portugal, Slovakia, Slovenia, Spain, Ukraine

Action by the First Committee

Date: 1 November 2018	Meeting: 26th meeting
Vote: 143-15-26	Draft resolution: A/C.1/73/L.23

Agenda item 101 (oo)

73/48   Treaty on the Prohibition of Nuclear Weapons

Text

The General Assembly,

Recalling its resolution 72/31 of 4 December 2017,

1.   *Welcomes* the adoption of the Treaty on the Prohibition of Nuclear Weapons[1] on 7 July 2017;

2.   *Notes* that the Treaty has been open for signature at United Nations Headquarters in New York since 20 September 2017;

3.   *Welcomes* that already 69 States had signed the Treaty and 19 States had ratified or acceded to it as at 17 October 2018;

4.   *Calls upon* all States that have not yet done so to sign, ratify, accept, approve or accede to the Treaty at the earliest possible date;

5.   *Calls upon* those States in a position to do so to promote adherence to the Treaty through bilateral, subregional, regional and multilateral contacts, outreach and other means;

6.   *Requests* the Secretary-General, as depositary of the Treaty, to report to the General Assembly at its seventy-fourth session on the status of signature and ratification, acceptance, approval or accession of the Treaty;

7.   *Decides* to include in the provisional agenda of its seventy-fourth session, under the item entitled "General and complete disarmament", the sub-item entitled "Treaty on the Prohibition of Nuclear Weapons".

Action by the General Assembly

Date: 5 December 2018   Meeting: 45th plenary meeting
Vote: 126-41-16   Report: A/73/510

Sponsors

Algeria, Angola, Antigua and Barbuda, **Austria**, Benin, Bolivia (Plurinational State of), Brazil, Chile, Costa Rica, Cuba, Democratic Republic of the Congo, Dominican Republic, Ecuador, El Salvador, Eswatini, Ghana, Guatemala, Guyana, Honduras, Indonesia, Ireland, Jamaica, Kazakhstan, Liechtenstein, Madagascar, Malawi, Mexico, Namibia, Nepal, New Zealand, Nicaragua, Nigeria, Palau, Panama, Paraguay, Peru, Philippines, Saint Vincent and the Grenadines, Samoa, San Marino, Senegal, Seychelles, Sierra Leone, South Africa, Thailand,

---

[1]   A/CONF.229/2017/8.

Trinidad and Tobago, Uganda, Uruguay, Vanuatu, Venezuela (Bolivarian Republic of), Viet Nam, Zambia, Zimbabwe

Co-sponsors

Bangladesh, Belize, Cabo Verde, Central African Republic, Congo, Côte d'Ivoire, Gambia, Lao People's Democratic Republic, Libya, Malaysia, Mongolia, Papua New Guinea, Saint Lucia, Sao Tome and Principe, Togo, Turkmenistan

*Recorded vote**

In favour:

Algeria, Andorra, Angola, Antigua and Barbuda, Austria, Azerbaijan, Bahamas, Bahrain, Bangladesh, Barbados, Belize, Benin, Bhutan, Bolivia (Plurinational State of), Botswana, Brazil, Brunei Darussalam, Burkina Faso, Burundi, Cabo Verde, Cambodia, Cameroon, Central African Republic, Chile, Colombia, Comoros, Congo, Costa Rica, Côte d'Ivoire, Cuba, Cyprus, Democratic Republic of the Congo, Djibouti, Dominica, Dominican Republic, Ecuador, Egypt, El Salvador, Equatorial Guinea, Eritrea, Eswatini, Ethiopia, Fiji, Gabon, Gambia, Ghana, Grenada, Guatemala, Guinea, Guinea-Bissau, Guyana, Honduras, Indonesia, Iran (Islamic Republic of), Iraq, Ireland, Jamaica, Jordan, Kazakhstan, Kenya, Kuwait, Lao People's Democratic Republic, Lebanon, Lesotho, Liberia, Libya, Liechtenstein, Madagascar, Malawi, Malaysia, Maldives, Malta, Mauritania, Mauritius, Mexico, Mongolia, Morocco, Mozambique, Myanmar, Namibia, Nepal, New Zealand, Nicaragua, Niger, Nigeria, Oman, Palau, Panama, Papua New Guinea, Paraguay, Peru, Philippines, Qatar, Republic of Moldova, Rwanda, Saint Lucia, Saint Vincent and the Grenadines, Samoa, San Marino, Sao Tome and Principe, Saudi Arabia, Senegal, Seychelles, Sierra Leone, Solomon Islands, South Africa, Sri Lanka, Sudan, Suriname, Thailand, Timor-Leste, Togo, Trinidad and Tobago, Tunisia, Turkmenistan, Tuvalu, Uganda, United Arab Emirates, United Republic of Tanzania, Uruguay, Vanuatu, Venezuela (Bolivarian Republic of), Viet Nam, Yemen, Zambia, Zimbabwe

Against:

Albania, Australia, Belgium, Bosnia and Herzegovina, Bulgaria, Canada, China, Croatia, Czechia, Denmark, Estonia, France, Germany, Greece, Hungary, Iceland, India, Israel, Italy, Japan, Latvia, Lithuania, Luxembourg, Micronesia (Federated States of), Monaco, Montenegro, Netherlands, Norway, Pakistan, Poland, Portugal, Republic of Korea, Romania, Russian Federation, Slovakia, Slovenia, Spain, the former

---

* Subsequently, the delegation of Saint Kitts and Nevis informed the Secretariat that it had intended to vote in favour. The voting tally above does not reflect this information.

Yugoslav Republic of Macedonia, Turkey, United Kingdom, United States

Abstaining:

Argentina, Armenia, Belarus, Democratic People's Republic of Korea, Finland, Georgia, Kyrgyzstan, Mali, Marshall Islands, Serbia, Singapore, Sweden, Switzerland, Tajikistan, Ukraine, Uzbekistan

Action by the First Committee

Date: 1 November 2018   Meeting: 26th meeting
Vote: 122-41-16   Draft resolution: A/C.1/73/L.24

Agenda item 101 (y)

73/49 The Hague Code of Conduct against Ballistic Missile Proliferation

Text

The General Assembly,

Concerned about the increasing regional and global security challenges caused, inter alia, by the ongoing proliferation of ballistic missiles capable of delivering weapons of mass destruction,

Bearing in mind the purposes and principles of the United Nations and its role and responsibility in the field of international peace and security in accordance with the Charter of the United Nations,

Emphasizing the significance of regional and international efforts to prevent and curb comprehensively the proliferation of ballistic missile systems capable of delivering weapons of mass destruction, as a contribution to international peace and security,

Welcoming the adoption of the Hague Code of Conduct against Ballistic Missile Proliferation on 25 November 2002 at The Hague,[1] and convinced that the Code of Conduct will contribute to enhancing transparency and confidence among States,

Recalling its resolutions 59/91 of 3 December 2004, 60/62 of 8 December 2005, 63/64 of 2 December 2008, 65/73 of 8 December 2010, 67/42 of 3 December 2012, 69/44 of 2 December 2014 and 71/33 of 5 December 2016 entitled "The Hague Code of Conduct against Ballistic Missile Proliferation",

Recalling also that the proliferation of ballistic missiles capable of delivering weapons of mass destruction, as recognized by the Security Council in its resolution 1540 (2004) of 28 April 2004 and subsequent resolutions, constitutes a threat to international peace and security,

Confirming its commitment to the Declaration on International Cooperation in the Exploration and Use of Outer Space for the Benefit and in the Interest of All States, Taking into Particular Account the Needs of Developing Countries, as contained in the annex to its resolution 51/122 of 13 December 1996,

Recognizing that States should not be excluded from utilizing the benefits of space for peaceful purposes, but that in reaping such benefits and in conducting related cooperation they must not contribute to the proliferation of ballistic missiles capable of carrying weapons of mass destruction,

---

[1] A/57/724, enclosure.

Noting the efforts of subscribing States, undertaken in cooperation with the Office for Disarmament Affairs of the Secretariat, to raise awareness of the Code of Conduct through the preparation of educational material,

Mindful of the need to combat the proliferation of weapons of mass destruction and their means of delivery,

1.   *Welcomes* the fact that 139 States have so far subscribed to the Hague Code of Conduct against Ballistic Missile Proliferation[1] as a practical step against the proliferation of weapons of mass destruction and their means of delivery;

2.   *Also welcomes* the advancement of the universalization process of the Code of Conduct, and underscores the importance of further advancing, at both the regional and the international levels, the universalization of the Code;

3.   *Invites* all States that have not yet subscribed to the Code of Conduct, in particular those possessing space launch vehicle and ballistic missile capabilities and those developing corresponding national programmes, to do so, bearing in mind the right to use space for peaceful purposes;

4.   *Encourages* States that have already subscribed to the Code of Conduct to make efforts to increase participation in the Code and to further improve its implementation;

5.   *Notes* progress in the implementation of the Code of Conduct, which contributes to enhancing transparency and building confidence among States through the submission of pre-launch notifications and annual declarations on space launch vehicle and ballistic missile policies, and underlines the importance of further steps in this direction;

6.   *Encourages* the exploration of further ways and means to deal effectively with the problem of the proliferation of ballistic missiles capable of delivering weapons of mass destruction, to take the measures necessary to avoid contributing to such delivery systems, and to continue to deepen the relationship between the Code of Conduct and the United Nations;

7.   *Decides* to include in the provisional agenda of its seventy-fifth session, under the item entitled "General and complete disarmament", the sub-item entitled "The Hague Code of Conduct against Ballistic Missile Proliferation".

Action by the General Assembly

Date: 5 December 2018   Meeting: 45th plenary meeting
Vote: 171-1-12   Report: A/73/510

Sponsors

Albania, Argentina, Australia, Austria, Belgium, Bosnia and Herzegovina, Bulgaria, Canada, Chile, Costa Rica, Croatia, Cyprus,

Czechia, Denmark, Eritrea, Estonia, Finland, France, Georgia, Germany, Greece, Guatemala, Hungary, Iceland, Ireland, Italy, Japan, Kazakhstan, Latvia, Liechtenstein, Lithuania, Luxembourg, Malta, Mongolia, Montenegro, Netherlands, New Zealand, Norway, Peru, Philippines, Poland, Portugal, Romania, Samoa, San Marino, Serbia, Slovakia, Slovenia, Spain, **Sweden**, Switzerland

Co-sponsors

Andorra, Armenia, Burkina Faso, Ecuador, Guyana, India, Iraq, Micronesia (Federated States of), Monaco, Morocco, Paraguay, Republic of Korea, Republic of Moldova, Seychelles, Singapore, the former Yugoslav Republic of Macedonia, Turkey, United Kingdom, United States

Recorded vote

In favour:

Afghanistan, Albania, Andorra, Angola, Antigua and Barbuda, Argentina, Armenia, Australia, Austria, Azerbaijan, Bahamas, Bahrain, Bangladesh, Barbados, Belarus, Belgium, Belize, Benin, Bhutan, Bolivia (Plurinational State of), Bosnia and Herzegovina, Botswana, Brazil, Brunei Darussalam, Bulgaria, Burkina Faso, Burundi, Cabo Verde, Cambodia, Cameroon, Canada, Central African Republic, Chile, Colombia, Comoros, Congo, Costa Rica, Côte d'Ivoire, Croatia, Cyprus, Czechia, Democratic Republic of the Congo, Denmark, Dominica, Dominican Republic, Ecuador, El Salvador, Equatorial Guinea, Eritrea, Estonia, Eswatini, Fiji, Finland, France, Gabon, Gambia, Georgia, Germany, Ghana, Greece, Grenada, Guatemala, Guinea, Guinea-Bissau, Guyana, Haiti, Honduras, Hungary, Iceland, India, Iraq, Ireland, Israel, Italy, Jamaica, Japan, Jordan, Kazakhstan, Kenya, Kyrgyzstan, Lao People's Democratic Republic, Latvia, Lesotho, Liberia, Libya, Liechtenstein, Lithuania, Luxembourg, Madagascar, Malawi, Malaysia, Maldives, Mali, Malta, Marshall Islands, Mauritania, Mauritius, Mexico, Micronesia (Federated States of), Monaco, Mongolia, Montenegro, Morocco, Mozambique, Myanmar, Namibia, Nepal, Netherlands, New Zealand, Nicaragua, Niger, Nigeria, Norway, Palau, Panama, Papua New Guinea, Paraguay, Peru, Philippines, Poland, Portugal, Republic of Korea, Republic of Moldova, Romania, Russian Federation, Rwanda, Saint Lucia, Saint Vincent and the Grenadines, Samoa, San Marino, Sao Tome and Principe, Saudi Arabia, Senegal, Serbia, Seychelles, Sierra Leone, Singapore, Slovakia, Slovenia, Solomon Islands, South Africa, Spain, Sri Lanka, Sudan, Suriname, Sweden, Switzerland, Tajikistan, Thailand, the former Yugoslav Republic of Macedonia, Timor-Leste, Togo, Tonga, Trinidad and Tobago, Tunisia, Turkey, Turkmenistan, Tuvalu, Uganda, Ukraine, United Arab Emirates, United Kingdom,

United Republic of Tanzania, United States, Uruguay, Uzbekistan, Vanuatu, Venezuela (Bolivarian Republic of), Viet Nam, Zambia, Zimbabwe

Against:
Iran (Islamic Republic of)

Abstaining:
Algeria, China, Cuba, Egypt, Indonesia, Kuwait, Lebanon, Oman, Pakistan, Qatar, Syrian Arab Republic, Yemen

Action by the First Committee

Date:	1 November 2018	Meeting:	26th meeting
Vote:	171-1-12	Draft resolution:	A/C.1/73/L.25

Agenda item 101 (b)

73/50 Nuclear disarmament

Text

The General Assembly,

Recalling its resolution 49/75 E of 15 December 1994 on a step-by-step reduction of the nuclear threat, and its resolutions 50/70 P of 12 December 1995, 51/45 O of 10 December 1996, 52/38 L of 9 December 1997, 53/77 X of 4 December 1998, 54/54 P of 1 December 1999, 55/33 T of 20 November 2000, 56/24 R of 29 November 2001, 57/79 of 22 November 2002, 58/56 of 8 December 2003, 59/77 of 3 December 2004, 60/70 of 8 December 2005, 61/78 of 6 December 2006, 62/42 of 5 December 2007, 63/46 of 2 December 2008, 64/53 of 2 December 2009, 65/56 of 8 December 2010, 66/51 of 2 December 2011, 67/60 of 3 December 2012, 68/47 of 5 December 2013, 69/48 of 2 December 2014, 70/52 of 7 December 2015, 71/63 of 5 December 2016 and 72/38 of 4 December 2017 on nuclear disarmament,

Reaffirming the commitment of the international community to the goal of the total elimination of nuclear weapons and the establishment of a nuclear-weapon-free world,

Bearing in mind that the Convention on the Prohibition of the Development, Production and Stockpiling of Bacteriological (Biological) and Toxin Weapons and on Their Destruction of 1972[1] and the Convention on the Prohibition of the Development, Production, Stockpiling and Use of Chemical Weapons and on Their Destruction of 1993[2] have already established legal regimes on the complete prohibition of biological and chemical weapons, respectively, and determined to achieve a comprehensive nuclear weapons convention on the prohibition of the development, testing, production, stockpiling, loan, transfer, use and threat of use of nuclear weapons and on their destruction, and to conclude such an international convention at an early date,

Recognizing the urgent need to take concrete practical steps towards achieving the establishment of a world free of nuclear weapons,

Bearing in mind paragraph 50 of the Final Document of the Tenth Special Session of the General Assembly, the first special session devoted to disarmament,[3] calling for the urgent negotiation of agreements for the cessation of the qualitative improvement and development of nuclear-weapon systems and for a comprehensive and phased programme with agreed time frames, wherever feasible, for the progressive and balanced reduction of

---

[1] United Nations, *Treaty Series*, vol. 1015, No. 14860.

[2] Ibid., vol. 1974, No. 33757.

[3] Resolution S-10/2.

nuclear weapons and their means of delivery, leading to their ultimate and complete elimination at the earliest possible time,

Reaffirming the conviction of the States parties to the Treaty on the Non-Proliferation of Nuclear Weapons[4] that the Treaty is a cornerstone of nuclear non-proliferation and nuclear disarmament, and the importance of the decision on strengthening the review process for the Treaty, the decision on principles and objectives for nuclear non-proliferation and disarmament, the decision on the extension of the Treaty and the resolution on the Middle East, adopted by the 1995 Review and Extension Conference of the Parties to the Treaty on the Non-Proliferation of Nuclear Weapons,[5]

Stressing the importance of the 13 steps for the systematic and progressive efforts to achieve the objective of nuclear disarmament leading to the total elimination of nuclear weapons, as agreed to by the States parties in the Final Document of the 2000 Review Conference of the Parties to the Treaty on the Non-Proliferation of Nuclear Weapons,[6]

Recognizing the important work done at the 2010 Review Conference of the Parties to the Treaty on the Non-Proliferation of Nuclear Weapons,[7] and affirming its 22-point action plan on nuclear disarmament as an impetus to intensify work aimed at beginning negotiations for a nuclear weapons convention,

Expressing deep concern that the 2015 Review Conference of the Parties to the Treaty on the Non-Proliferation of Nuclear Weapons, held from 27 April to 22 May 2015, did not reach agreement on a substantive final document,

Reaffirming the continued validity of agreements reached at the 1995 Review and Extension Conference and the 2000 and 2010 Review Conferences until all their objectives are achieved, and calling for their full and immediate fulfilment, including the action plan on nuclear disarmament adopted at the 2010 Review Conference,

Reiterating the highest priority accorded to nuclear disarmament in the Final Document of the Tenth Special Session of the General Assembly and by the international community,

---

[4] United Nations, *Treaty Series*, vol. 729, No. 10485.

[5] See *1995 Review and Extension Conference of the Parties to the Treaty on the Non-Proliferation of Nuclear Weapons, Final Document, Part I* (NPT/CONF.1995/32 (Part I) and NPT/CONF.1995/32 (Part I)/Corr.2), annex.

[6] *2000 Review Conference of the Parties to the Treaty on the Non-Proliferation of Nuclear Weapons, Final Document*, vol. I (NPT/CONF.2000/28 (Parts I and II)), part I, section entitled "Article VI and eighth to twelfth preambular paragraphs", para. 15.

[7] *2010 Review Conference of the Parties to the Treaty on the Non-Proliferation of Nuclear Weapons, Final Document*, vols. I–III (NPT/CONF.2010/50 (Vol. I), NPT/CONF.2010/50 (Vol. II) and NPT/CONF.2010/50 (Vol. III)).

Reiterating its call for an early entry into force of the Comprehensive Nuclear-Test-Ban Treaty,[8]

Noting the new strategic arms reduction treaty between the Russian Federation and the United States of America, in order to achieve further cuts in their deployed and non-deployed strategic nuclear weapons, and stressing that such cuts should be irreversible, verifiable and transparent,

Noting also the statements by nuclear-weapon States of their intention to pursue actions in achieving a world free of nuclear weapons, as well as the steps taken to reduce the role and number of nuclear weapons, and urging nuclear-weapon States to take further measures for progress on nuclear disarmament within a specified framework of time,

Recognizing the complementarity of bilateral, plurilateral and multilateral negotiations on nuclear disarmament, and that bilateral negotiations can never replace multilateral negotiations in this respect,

Noting the support expressed in the Conference on Disarmament and in the General Assembly for the elaboration of an international convention to assure non-nuclear-weapon States, without exception or discrimination, against the use or threat of use of nuclear weapons under any circumstances, and the multilateral efforts in the Conference to reach agreement on such an international convention at an early date,

Recalling the advisory opinion of the International Court of Justice on the legality of the threat or use of nuclear weapons, issued on 8 July 1996,[9] and welcoming the unanimous reaffirmation by all judges of the Court that there exists an obligation for all States to pursue in good faith and bring to a conclusion negotiations leading to nuclear disarmament in all its aspects under strict and effective international control,

Recalling also paragraph 176 of the Final Document of the Seventeenth Conference of Heads of State or Government of Non-Aligned Countries, held on Margarita Island, Bolivarian Republic of Venezuela, from 13 to 18 September 2016, in which the Conference on Disarmament was called upon to agree on a balanced and comprehensive programme of work by, inter alia, establishing an ad hoc committee on nuclear disarmament as soon as possible and as the highest priority, while the necessity was emphasized of starting negotiations in the Conference on Disarmament, without further delay, on a comprehensive nuclear weapons convention that sets, inter alia, a phased programme for the complete elimination of nuclear weapons within a specified framework of time,

---

[8] See resolution 50/245 and A/50/1027.

[9] A/51/218, annex.

Noting the adoption of the programme of work for the 2009 session by the Conference on Disarmament on 29 May 2009,[10] after years of stalemate, and regretting that the Conference did not succeed in reaching consensus on a programme of work for its 2018 session,

Welcoming the proposals submitted by the States members of the Conference on Disarmament that are members of the Group of 21 on the follow-up to the 2013 high-level meeting of the General Assembly on nuclear disarmament, pursuant to Assembly resolution 68/32 of 5 December 2013, as contained in documents of the Conference,[11]

Reaffirming the importance and validity of the Conference on Disarmament as the sole multilateral disarmament negotiating forum, and expressing the need to adopt and implement a balanced and comprehensive programme of work on the basis of its agenda and dealing with, inter alia, four core issues, in accordance with the rules of procedure,[12] and by taking into consideration the security concerns of all States,

Reaffirming also the specific mandate conferred upon the Disarmament Commission by the General Assembly, in its decision 52/492 of 8 September 1998, to discuss the subject of nuclear disarmament as one of its main substantive agenda items,

Recalling the United Nations Millennium Declaration,[13] in which Heads of State and Government resolved to strive for the elimination of weapons of mass destruction, in particular nuclear weapons, and to keep all options open for achieving that aim, including the possibility of convening an international conference to identify ways of eliminating nuclear dangers,

Underlining the importance of convening, as a priority, a United Nations high-level international conference on nuclear disarmament to review the progress made in this regard,

Recalling the high-level meeting of the General Assembly on nuclear disarmament held on 26 September 2013, and the strong support for nuclear disarmament expressed therein,

Welcoming the commemoration of 26 September as the International Day for the Total Elimination of Nuclear Weapons, devoted to furthering this objective, as declared by the General Assembly in its resolution 68/32 and subsequently welcomed in its resolutions 69/58 of 2 December 2014, 70/34 of 7 December 2015, 71/71 of 5 December 2016 and 72/251 of 24 December 2017,

---

[10] See *Official Records of the General Assembly, Sixty-fourth Session, Supplement No. 27* (A/64/27), para. 18.

[11] See CD/1999 and CD/2067.

[12] CD/8/Rev.9.

[13] Resolution 55/2.

Taking note of the declaration of the States members of the Agency for the Prohibition of Nuclear Weapons in Latin America and the Caribbean on the International Day for the Total Elimination of Nuclear Weapons, in Mexico City on 26 September 2018,[14]

Expressing deep concern about the catastrophic humanitarian consequences of any use of nuclear weapons,

Noting the successful convening of the first, second and third Conferences on the Humanitarian Impact of Nuclear Weapons, in Oslo on 4 and 5 March 2013, in Nayarit, Mexico, on 13 and 14 February 2014, and in Vienna on 8 and 9 December 2014, and noting also that 127 nations have formally endorsed the Humanitarian Pledge issued following the third Conference,[15]

Welcoming the signing by the nuclear-weapon States, namely, China, France, the Russian Federation, the United Kingdom of Great Britain and Northern Ireland and the United States of America, of the Protocol to the Treaty on a Nuclear-Weapon-Free Zone in Central Asia, in New York on 6 May 2014,

Welcoming also the proclamation of Latin America and the Caribbean as a Zone of Peace on 29 January 2014 during the Second Summit of the Community of Latin American and Caribbean States, held in Havana on 28 and 29 January 2014,

Welcoming further the successful adoption of the Treaty on the Prohibition of Nuclear Weapons[16] on 7 July 2017,

Reaffirming that, in accordance with the Charter of the United Nations, States should refrain from the use or threat of use of nuclear weapons in settling their disputes in international relations,

Seized of the danger of the use of weapons of mass destruction, particularly nuclear weapons, in terrorist acts and the urgent need for concerted international efforts to control and overcome it,

1. *Urges* all nuclear-weapon States to take effective disarmament measures to achieve the total elimination of all nuclear weapons at the earliest possible time;

2. *Reaffirms* that nuclear disarmament and nuclear non-proliferation are substantively interrelated and mutually reinforcing, that the two processes must go hand in hand and that there is a genuine need for a systematic and progressive process of nuclear disarmament;

---

[14] A/73/403, annex.
[15] See CD/2039.
[16] A/CONF.229/2017/8.

3. *Welcomes and encourages* the efforts to establish new nuclear-weapon-free zones in different parts of the world, including the establishment of a Middle East zone free of nuclear weapons, on the basis of agreements or arrangements freely arrived at among the States of the regions concerned, which is an effective measure for limiting the further spread of nuclear weapons geographically and contributes to the cause of nuclear disarmament;

4. *Encourages* States parties to the Treaty on the South-East Asia Nuclear-Weapon-Free Zone[17] and the nuclear-weapon States to intensify ongoing efforts to resolve all outstanding issues, in accordance with the objectives and principles of the Treaty;

5. *Recognizes* that there is a genuine need to diminish the role of nuclear weapons in strategic doctrines and security policies to minimize the risk that these weapons will ever be used and to facilitate the process of their total elimination;

6. *Urges* the nuclear-weapon States to stop immediately the qualitative improvement, development, production and stockpiling of nuclear warheads and their delivery systems;

7. *Also urges* the nuclear-weapon States, as an interim measure, to de-alert and deactivate immediately their nuclear weapons and to take other concrete measures to reduce further the operational status of their nuclear-weapon systems, while stressing that reductions in deployments and in operational status cannot substitute for irreversible cuts in and the total elimination of nuclear weapons;

8. *Reiterates its call upon* the nuclear-weapon States to carry out effective nuclear disarmament measures with a view to achieving the total elimination of nuclear weapons within a specified framework of time;

9. *Calls upon* the nuclear-weapon States, pending the achievement of the total elimination of nuclear weapons, to agree on an internationally and legally binding instrument on a joint undertaking not to be the first to use nuclear weapons;

10. *Urges* the nuclear-weapon States to commence plurilateral negotiations among themselves at an appropriate stage on further deep reductions of their nuclear weapons, in an irreversible, verifiable and transparent manner, as an effective measure of nuclear disarmament;

11. *Underlines* the importance of applying the principles of transparency, irreversibility and verifiability to the process of nuclear disarmament;

12. *Also underlines* the importance of the unequivocal undertaking by the nuclear-weapon States, in the Final Document of the 2000 Review

---

[17] United Nations, *Treaty Series*, vol. 1981, No. 33873.

Conference of the Parties to the Treaty on the Non-Proliferation of Nuclear Weapons, to accomplish the total elimination of their nuclear arsenals leading to nuclear disarmament, to which all States parties are committed under article VI of the Treaty,[6] and the reaffirmation by the States parties that the total elimination of nuclear weapons is the only absolute guarantee against the use or threat of use of nuclear weapons;[18]

13.   *Calls for* the full and effective implementation of the 13 practical steps for nuclear disarmament contained in the Final Document of the 2000 Review Conference;[6]

14.   *Also calls for* the full implementation of the action plan as set out in the conclusions and recommendations for follow-on actions of the Final Document of the 2010 Review Conference of the Parties to the Treaty on the Non-Proliferation of Nuclear Weapons, particularly the 22-point action plan on nuclear disarmament;[7]

15.   *Urges* the nuclear-weapon States to carry out further reductions of non-strategic nuclear weapons, including on unilateral initiatives and as an integral part of the nuclear arms reduction and disarmament process;

16.   *Calls for* the immediate commencement of negotiations in the Conference on Disarmament, in the context of an agreed, comprehensive and balanced programme of work, on a non-discriminatory, multilateral and internationally and effectively verifiable treaty banning the production of fissile material for nuclear weapons or other nuclear explosive devices on the basis of the report of the Special Coordinator[19] and the mandate contained therein;

17.   *Urges* the Conference on Disarmament to commence as early as possible its substantive work during its 2019 session, on the basis of a comprehensive and balanced programme of work that takes into consideration all the real and existing priorities in the field of disarmament and arms control, including the immediate commencement of negotiations on a comprehensive nuclear weapons convention;

18.   *Calls for* the conclusion of an international legal instrument on unconditional security assurances to non-nuclear-weapon States against the threat or use of nuclear weapons under any circumstances;

19.   *Also calls for* the early entry into force, universalization and strict observance of the Comprehensive Nuclear-Test-Ban Treaty[8] as a contribution to nuclear disarmament, while welcoming the latest signatory to the Treaty, Tuvalu, and its latest ratification, by Thailand, on 25 September 2018;

---

[18] *2000 Review Conference of the Parties to the Treaty on the Non-Proliferation of Nuclear Weapons, Final Document*, vol. I (NPT/CONF.2000/28 (Parts I and II)), part I, section entitled "Article VII and the security of non-nuclear-weapon States", para. 2.
[19] CD/1299.

20. *Reiterates its call upon* the Conference on Disarmament to establish, as soon as possible and as the highest priority, an ad hoc committee on nuclear disarmament in 2019 and to commence negotiations on a phased programme of nuclear disarmament leading to the total elimination of nuclear weapons within a specified framework of time;

21. *Calls for* the convening, as soon as possible, of a United Nations high-level international conference on nuclear disarmament to review the progress made in this regard;

22. *Requests* the Secretary-General to submit to the General Assembly at its seventy-fourth session a report on the implementation of the present resolution;

23. *Decides* to include in the provisional agenda of its seventy-fourth session, under the item entitled "General and complete disarmament", the sub-item entitled "Nuclear disarmament".

Action by the General Assembly

Date: 5 December 2018   Meeting: 45th plenary meeting
Vote: 125-40-18   Report: A/73/510
      116-38-15, p.p. 32
      167-2-6, o.p. 16

Sponsors

Belize, Bolivia (Plurinational State of), Brazil, Cuba, Ecuador, El Salvador, Eritrea, Eswatini, Honduras, Indonesia, Lao People's Democratic Republic, Malawi, Mongolia, **Myanmar**, Namibia, Nepal, Nicaragua, Philippines, Samoa, Singapore, Thailand, Venezuela (Bolivarian Republic of), Viet Nam, Zambia, Zimbabwe

Co-sponsors

Bhutan, Brunei Darussalam, Burkina Faso, Cambodia, Central African Republic, Fiji, Ghana, Kazakhstan, Mozambique, Nigeria, Seychelles, Sri Lanka, Timor-Leste

Recorded vote

As a whole

In favour:

Afghanistan, Algeria, Angola, Antigua and Barbuda, Argentina, Azerbaijan, Bahamas, Bahrain, Bangladesh, Barbados, Belize, Benin, Bhutan, Bolivia (Plurinational State of), Botswana, Brazil, Brunei Darussalam, Burkina Faso, Burundi, Cabo Verde, Cambodia, Cameroon, Central African Republic, China, Colombia, Comoros, Congo, Costa Rica, Côte d'Ivoire, Cuba, Democratic People's Republic of Korea,

Democratic Republic of the Congo, Djibouti, Dominica, Dominican Republic, Ecuador, Egypt, El Salvador, Equatorial Guinea, Eritrea, Eswatini, Ethiopia, Fiji, Gabon, Ghana, Grenada, Guatemala, Guinea, Guinea-Bissau, Guyana, Honduras, Indonesia, Iran (Islamic Republic of), Iraq, Jamaica, Jordan, Kazakhstan, Kenya, Kuwait, Kyrgyzstan, Lao People's Democratic Republic, Lebanon, Lesotho, Liberia, Libya, Madagascar, Malawi, Malaysia, Maldives, Mali, Mauritania, Mauritius, Mexico, Mongolia, Morocco, Mozambique, Myanmar, Namibia, Nepal, Nicaragua, Niger, Nigeria, Oman, Palau, Panama, Papua New Guinea, Paraguay, Peru, Philippines, Qatar, Rwanda, Saint Lucia, Saint Vincent and the Grenadines, Samoa, Sao Tome and Principe, Saudi Arabia, Senegal, Seychelles, Sierra Leone, Singapore, Solomon Islands, Sri Lanka, Sudan, Suriname, Switzerland, Syrian Arab Republic, Tajikistan, Thailand, Timor-Leste, Togo, Tonga, Trinidad and Tobago, Tunisia, Tuvalu, Uganda, United Arab Emirates, United Republic of Tanzania, Uruguay, Uzbekistan, Vanuatu, Venezuela (Bolivarian Republic of), Viet Nam, Yemen, Zambia, Zimbabwe

Against:

Albania, Australia, Belgium, Bosnia and Herzegovina, Bulgaria, Canada, Croatia, Czechia, Denmark, Estonia, Finland, France, Georgia, Germany, Greece, Hungary, Iceland, Israel, Italy, Latvia, Lithuania, Luxembourg, Micronesia (Federated States of), Monaco, Montenegro, Netherlands, Norway, Poland, Portugal, Republic of Korea, Romania, Russian Federation, Slovakia, Slovenia, Spain, the former Yugoslav Republic of Macedonia, Turkey, Ukraine, United Kingdom, United States

Abstaining:

Andorra, Armenia, Austria, Belarus, Cyprus, India, Ireland, Japan, Liechtenstein, Malta, Marshall Islands, New Zealand, Pakistan, Republic of Moldova, San Marino, Serbia, South Africa, Sweden

Thirty-second preambular paragraph

In favour:

Algeria, Angola, Antigua and Barbuda, Argentina, Austria, Azerbaijan, Bahamas, Bahrain, Bangladesh, Barbados, Belize, Benin, Bhutan, Bolivia (Plurinational State of), Botswana, Brazil, Brunei Darussalam, Burkina Faso, Burundi, Cabo Verde, Cambodia, Chile, Colombia, Comoros, Costa Rica, Côte d'Ivoire, Cuba, Cyprus, Democratic Republic of the Congo, Djibouti, Dominican Republic, Ecuador, Egypt, El Salvador, Equatorial Guinea, Eritrea, Eswatini, Ethiopia, Fiji, Gambia, Ghana, Guatemala, Guinea, Guinea-Bissau, Guyana, Honduras, Indonesia, Iran (Islamic Republic of), Iraq, Ireland, Jamaica, Jordan, Kazakhstan, Kenya, Kuwait, Lao People's Democratic Republic, Lebanon, Lesotho, Libya, Liechtenstein, Madagascar, Malawi, Malaysia, Maldives,

Mali, Malta, Mauritania, Mexico, Mongolia, Morocco, Mozambique, Myanmar, Namibia, Nepal, New Zealand, Nicaragua, Niger, Nigeria, Oman, Panama, Papua New Guinea, Paraguay, Peru, Philippines, Qatar, Republic of Moldova, Rwanda, Saint Lucia, Saint Vincent and the Grenadines, Samoa, San Marino, Sao Tome and Principe, Saudi Arabia, Senegal, Singapore, Solomon Islands, South Africa, Sri Lanka, Sudan, Suriname, Thailand, Timor-Leste, Togo, Trinidad and Tobago, Tunisia, Tuvalu, Uganda, United Arab Emirates, United Republic of Tanzania, Uruguay, Vanuatu, Venezuela (Bolivarian Republic of), Viet Nam, Yemen, Zambia, Zimbabwe

Against:

Albania, Australia, Belgium, Bosnia and Herzegovina, Bulgaria, Canada, China, Croatia, Czechia, Denmark, Estonia, France, Georgia, Germany, Greece, Hungary, Iceland, Israel, Italy, Latvia, Lithuania, Luxembourg, Monaco, Montenegro, Netherlands, Norway, Poland, Portugal, Republic of Korea, Romania, Russian Federation, Slovakia, Slovenia, Spain, Turkey, Ukraine, United Kingdom, United States

Abstaining:

Andorra, Armenia, Belarus, Democratic People's Republic of Korea, Finland, India, Japan, Kyrgyzstan, Liberia, Pakistan, Serbia, Sierra Leone, Sweden, Switzerland, the former Yugoslav Republic of Macedonia

Operative paragraph 16

In favour:

Albania, Algeria, Andorra, Angola, Antigua and Barbuda, Argentina, Armenia, Australia, Austria, Azerbaijan, Bahamas, Bahrain, Bangladesh, Barbados, Belarus, Belgium, Belize, Benin, Bhutan, Bolivia (Plurinational State of), Bosnia and Herzegovina, Botswana, Brazil, Brunei Darussalam, Bulgaria, Burkina Faso, Burundi, Cabo Verde, Cambodia, Canada, Chile, China, Colombia, Comoros, Costa Rica, Côte d'Ivoire, Croatia, Cuba, Cyprus, Czechia, Democratic Republic of the Congo, Denmark, Djibouti, Dominican Republic, Ecuador, Egypt, El Salvador, Equatorial Guinea, Eritrea, Estonia, Eswatini, Ethiopia, Fiji, Finland, Gambia, Germany, Ghana, Greece, Guatemala, Guinea, Guinea-Bissau, Guyana, Honduras, Hungary, Iceland, India, Indonesia, Iran (Islamic Republic of), Iraq, Ireland, Italy, Jamaica, Japan, Jordan, Kazakhstan, Kenya, Kuwait, Kyrgyzstan, Lao People's Democratic Republic, Latvia, Lebanon, Lesotho, Liberia, Libya, Liechtenstein, Lithuania, Luxembourg, Madagascar, Malawi, Malaysia, Maldives, Mali, Malta, Mauritania, Mauritius, Mexico, Micronesia (Federated States of), Monaco, Mongolia, Montenegro, Morocco, Mozambique, Myanmar, Namibia, Nepal, Netherlands, New Zealand, Nicaragua,

Niger, Nigeria, Norway, Oman, Panama, Papua New Guinea, Paraguay, Peru, Philippines, Poland, Portugal, Qatar, Republic of Korea, Republic of Moldova, Romania, Rwanda, Saint Lucia, Saint Vincent and the Grenadines, Samoa, San Marino, Sao Tome and Principe, Saudi Arabia, Senegal, Serbia, Seychelles, Sierra Leone, Singapore, Slovakia, Slovenia, Solomon Islands, South Africa, Spain, Sri Lanka, Sudan, Suriname, Sweden, Switzerland, Syrian Arab Republic, Tajikistan, Thailand, the former Yugoslav Republic of Macedonia, Timor-Leste, Togo, Trinidad and Tobago, Tunisia, Turkey, Tuvalu, Uganda, Ukraine, United Arab Emirates, United Republic of Tanzania, Uruguay, Uzbekistan, Vanuatu, Venezuela (Bolivarian Republic of), Viet Nam, Yemen, Zambia, Zimbabwe

Against:

Pakistan, Russian Federation

Abstaining:

Democratic People's Republic of Korea, France, Israel, Marshall Islands, United Kingdom, United States

Action by the First Committee

Date:	1 November 2018	Meeting:	26th meeting
Vote:	120-41-21	Draft resolution:	A/C.1/73/L.28
	117-37-19, p.p. 32		
	168-2-8, o.p. 16		

Agenda item 101 (z)

73/51 Information on confidence-building measures in the field of conventional arms

Text

The General Assembly,

Guided by the purposes and principles enshrined in the Charter of the United Nations,

Bearing in mind the contribution of confidence-building measures in the field of conventional arms, adopted on the initiative and with the agreement of the States concerned, to the improvement of the overall international peace and security situation,

Convinced that the relationship between the development of confidence-building measures in the field of conventional arms and the international security environment can also be mutually reinforcing,

Considering the important role that confidence-building measures in the field of conventional arms can also play in creating favourable conditions for progress in the field of disarmament,

Recognizing that the exchange of information on confidence-building measures in the field of conventional arms contributes to mutual understanding and confidence among Member States,

Underlining that confidence-building measures in the field of conventional arms are key tools in strengthening conflict prevention and reducing armed violence, thereby contributing to the achievement of Sustainable Development Goal 16 of the 2030 Agenda for Sustainable Development,[1]

Recalling its resolutions 59/92 of 3 December 2004, 60/82 of 8 December 2005, 61/79 of 6 December 2006, 63/57 of 2 December 2008, 65/63 of 8 December 2010, 67/49 of 3 December 2012, 69/64 of 2 December 2014 and 71/35 of 5 December 2016,

1. *Welcomes* all confidence-building measures in the field of conventional arms already undertaken by Member States;

2. *Encourages* Member States to continue to adopt and apply confidence-building measures in the field of conventional arms;

3. *Invites* Member States to submit to the Secretariat, on a voluntary basis, information on confidence-building measures in the field of conventional arms;

---

[1] Resolution 70/1.

4.	*Encourages* Member States to establish or continue dialogues on confidence-building measures in the field of conventional arms;

5.	*Appreciates* the continuing operation of the Secretariat database containing information provided by Member States,[2] and requests the Secretary-General to keep the database updated and to assist Member States, at their request, in confidence-building activities and in the organization of seminars, courses and workshops aimed at enhancing the knowledge of new developments in this field;

6.	*Welcomes* the adoption by the Disarmament Commission in April 2017 of recommendations on practical confidence-building measures in the field of conventional weapons;[3]

7.	*Notes* that, in those recommendations, Member States are encouraged, as appropriate, and on a voluntary basis, to exchange information on confidence-building measures in the field of conventional weapons at the bilateral, subregional, regional and international levels and to draw lessons learned from other mechanisms;

8.	*Decides* to include in the provisional agenda of its seventy-fifth session, under the item entitled "General and complete disarmament", the sub-item entitled "Information on confidence-building measures in the field of conventional arms".

Action by the General Assembly

Date: 5 December 2018   Meeting: 45th plenary meeting
Vote: Adopted without a vote   Report: A/73/510

Sponsors

Albania, **Argentina**, Australia, Austria, Bulgaria, Canada, Chile, Costa Rica, Croatia, Cyprus, Czechia, Denmark, El Salvador, Estonia, Finland, France, Georgia, Ghana, Greece, Guatemala, Honduras, Ireland, Italy, Jamaica, Japan, Latvia, Luxembourg, Malta, Montenegro, Netherlands, Norway, Peru, Philippines, Poland, Portugal, Romania, San Marino, Serbia, Slovakia, Spain, Suriname, Sweden, Switzerland, Thailand, Uruguay

Co-sponsors

Andorra, Armenia, Belarus, Belgium, Belize, Benin, Bosnia and Herzegovina, Brazil, Burkina Faso, Chad, Colombia, Dominican Republic, Ecuador, Equatorial Guinea, Germany, Guinea-Bissau, Guyana, Haiti, Hungary, Iceland, Indonesia, Kazakhstan, Lithuania,

---

[2]	See www.un.org/disarmament/cbms.
[3]	*Official Records of the General Assembly, Seventy-second Session, Supplement No. 42* (A/72/42), annex.

Malaysia, Mexico, Monaco, Panama, Paraguay, Republic of Korea, Republic of Moldova, Russian Federation, Slovenia, the former Yugoslav Republic of Macedonia, Turkey, Ukraine, United Kingdom

Action by the First Committee

Date: 6 November 2018   Meeting: 29th meeting
Vote: Adopted without a vote   Draft resolution: A/C.1/73/L.29

Agenda item 101 (n)

73/52 Assistance to States for curbing the illicit traffic in small arms and light weapons and collecting them

Text

The General Assembly,

Recalling its resolution 72/40 of 4 December 2017,

Deeply concerned by the magnitude of human casualty and suffering, especially among children, caused by the illicit proliferation and use of small arms and light weapons,

Concerned by the negative impact that the illicit proliferation and use of those weapons continue to have on the efforts of States in the Sahelo-Saharan subregion in the areas of poverty eradication, sustainable development and the maintenance of peace, security and stability,

Bearing in mind the Bamako Declaration on an African Common Position on the Illicit Proliferation, Circulation and Trafficking of Small Arms and Light Weapons, adopted in Bamako on 1 December 2000,[1]

Recalling the report of the Secretary-General entitled "In larger freedom: towards development, security and human rights for all",[2] in which he emphasized that States must strive just as hard to eliminate the threat of small arms and light weapons as they do to eliminate the threat of weapons of mass destruction,

Recalling also the International Instrument to Enable States to Identify and Trace, in a Timely and Reliable Manner, Illicit Small Arms and Light Weapons, adopted on 8 December 2005,[3]

Recalling further the expression of support in the 2005 World Summit Outcome for the implementation of the Programme of Action to Prevent, Combat and Eradicate the Illicit Trade in Small Arms and Light Weapons in All Its Aspects,[4]

Recalling the adoption, on 14 June 2006 in Abuja at the thirtieth ordinary summit of the Economic Community of West African States, of the Convention on Small Arms and Light Weapons, Their Ammunition and Other Related Materials, in replacement of the moratorium on the importation, exportation and manufacture of small arms and light weapons in West Africa,

Recalling also the entry into force of the Convention on 29 September 2009,

---

[1] A/CONF.192/PC/23, annex.
[2] A/59/2005.
[3] See decision 60/519 and A/60/88 and A/60/88/Corr.2, annex.
[4] Resolution 60/1, para. 94.

Recalling further the decision taken by the Economic Community to establish the Small Arms Unit, responsible for advocating appropriate policies and developing and implementing programmes, as well as the establishment of the Economic Community's Small Arms Control Programme, launched on 6 June 2006 in Bamako, in replacement of the Programme for Coordination and Assistance for Security and Development,

Taking note of the latest report of the Secretary-General on the illicit trade in small arms and light weapons in all its aspects and assistance to States for curbing the illicit traffic in small arms and light weapons and collecting them,[5]

Recalling, in that regard, the decision of the European Union to significantly support the Economic Community in its efforts to combat the illicit proliferation of small arms and light weapons,

Recognizing the important role that civil society organizations play, by raising public awareness, in efforts to curb the illicit traffic in small arms and light weapons,

Recalling the report of the sixth Biennial Meeting of States to Consider the Implementation of the Programme of Action to Prevent, Combat and Eradicate the Illicit Trade in Small Arms and Light Weapons in All Its Aspects, held in New York from 6 to 10 June 2016,[6]

Recalling also the report of the third United Nations Conference to Review Progress Made in the Implementation of the Programme of Action to Prevent, Combat and Eradicate the Illicit Trade in Small Arms and Light Weapons in All Its Aspects, held in New York from 18 to 29 June 2018,[7]

Welcoming the inclusion of small arms and light weapons in the scope of the Arms Trade Treaty,[8] as well as the inclusion of international assistance in its provisions,

1. *Commends* the United Nations and international, regional and other organizations for their assistance to States for curbing the illicit traffic in small arms and light weapons and collecting them;

2. *Encourages* the Secretary-General to pursue his efforts in the context of the implementation of General Assembly resolution 49/75 G of 15 December 1994 and the recommendations of the United Nations advisory missions aimed at curbing the illicit circulation of small arms and light weapons and collecting them in the affected States that so request, with the support of the United Nations Regional Centre for Peace and Disarmament in Africa and in close cooperation with the African Union;

---

[5] A/73/168.

[6] A/CONF.192/BMS/2016/2.

[7] A/CONF.192/2018/RC/3.

[8] See resolution 67/234 B.

3. *Encourages* the international community to support the implementation of the Economic Community of West African States Convention on Small Arms and Light Weapons, Their Ammunition and Other Related Materials;

4. *Encourages* the countries of the Sahelo-Saharan subregion to facilitate the effective functioning of national commissions to combat the illicit proliferation of small arms and light weapons, and in that regard invites the international community to lend its support wherever possible;

5. *Encourages* the collaboration of civil society organizations and associations in the efforts of the national commissions to combat the illicit traffic in small arms and light weapons and in the implementation of the Programme of Action to Prevent, Combat and Eradicate the Illicit Trade in Small Arms and Light Weapons in All Its Aspects;[9]

6. *Encourages* cooperation among State organs, international organizations and civil society in support of programmes and projects aimed at combating the illicit traffic in small arms and light weapons and collecting them;

7. *Calls upon* the international community to provide technical and financial support to strengthen the capacity of civil society organizations to take action to help to combat the illicit trade in small arms and light weapons;

8. *Invites* the Secretary-General and those States and organizations that are in a position to do so to continue to provide assistance to States for curbing the illicit traffic in small arms and light weapons and collecting them;

9. *Requests* the Secretary-General to continue to consider the matter and to report to the General Assembly at its seventy-fourth session on the implementation of the present resolution;

10. *Decides* to include in the provisional agenda of its seventy-fourth session, under the item entitled "General and complete disarmament", the sub-item entitled "Assistance to States for curbing the illicit traffic in small arms and light weapons and collecting them".

Action by the General Assembly

Date: 5 December 2018   Meeting: 45th plenary meeting
Vote: Adopted without a vote   Report: A/73/510

Sponsors

Albania, Australia, Austria, Belgium, Bulgaria, Canada, Croatia, Cyprus, Czechia, Democratic Republic of the Congo, Denmark, Djibouti, Eritrea,

---

[9] *Report of the United Nations Conference on the Illicit Trade in Small Arms and Light Weapons in All Its Aspects, New York, 9–20 July 2001* (A/CONF.192/15), chap. IV, para. 24.

Estonia, Finland, France, Georgia, Greece, Guatemala, Haiti, Honduras, Ireland, Italy, Latvia, Lithuania, Luxembourg, **Mali** (on behalf of the States Members of the United Nations that are members of the Economic Community of West African States), Mauritania, Montenegro, Namibia, Netherlands, New Zealand, Norway, Poland, Portugal, Romania, San Marino, Serbia, Slovakia, Spain, Sweden, Thailand, Uganda

Co-sponsors

Andorra, Bosnia and Herzegovina, Central African Republic, Chad, Colombia, Comoros, Equatorial Guinea, Guyana, Hungary, Iceland, Madagascar, Maldives, Malta, Monaco, Panama, Republic of Moldova, Slovenia, the former Yugoslav Republic of Macedonia, Tunisia, Turkey, United Kingdom, Uruguay, Zambia, Zimbabwe

Action by the First Committee

Date: 6 November 2018   Meeting: 29th meeting
Vote: Adopted without a vote   Draft resolution: A/C.1/73/L.32

Agenda item 101 (j)

73/53   Consolidation of peace through practical disarmament measures

Text

The General Assembly,

Recalling its resolutions 51/45 N of 10 December 1996, 52/38 G of 9 December 1997, 53/77 M of 4 December 1998, 54/54 H of 1 December 1999, 55/33 G of 20 November 2000, 56/24 P of 29 November 2001 and 57/81 of 22 November 2002, its decision 58/519 of 8 December 2003, as well as its resolutions 59/82 of 3 December 2004, 61/76 of 6 December 2006, 63/62 of 2 December 2008, 65/67 of 8 December 2010, 67/50 of 3 December 2012, 69/60 of 2 December 2014 and 71/64 of 5 December 2016, entitled "Consolidation of peace through practical disarmament measures",

Convinced that a comprehensive and integrated approach towards certain practical disarmament measures often is a prerequisite to maintaining and consolidating peace and security and thus provides a basis for effective post-conflict peacebuilding; such measures include collection and responsible disposal, preferably through destruction, of weapons obtained through illicit trafficking or illicit manufacture as well as of stockpiled weapons and ammunition declared by competent national authorities to be surplus to requirements, particularly with regard to small arms and light weapons, unless another form of disposition or use has been officially authorized and provided that such weapons have been duly marked and registered; confidence-building measures; disarmament, demobilization and reintegration of former combatants; demining; and conversion,

Noting with satisfaction that the international community is more than ever applying such practical disarmament measures, especially with regard to the growing problems arising from the excessive accumulation and uncontrolled spread of small arms and light weapons, including their ammunition, which pose a threat to peace and security and reduce the prospects for economic and social development in many regions, particularly in post-conflict situations,

Welcoming the evolution of the "second generation" concept for disarmament, demobilization and reintegration, which takes into account increasingly complex peacekeeping environments characterized by, inter alia, political instability and a prevalence of weapons and ammunition, and which integrates innovative approaches, such as fostering community violence reduction programmes, to better address needs on the ground,

Recalling Security Council resolution 2171 (2014) of 21 August 2014, in which the Council affirmed that a comprehensive conflict prevention strategy should include practical disarmament and other measures to contribute to combating the proliferation of and illicit trade in arms,

Recalling also its resolution 71/56 of 5 December 2016 on women, disarmament, non-proliferation and arms control, in which it recognized the valuable contribution of women to practical disarmament measures carried out at the local, national, subregional and regional levels in the prevention and reduction of armed violence and armed conflict, and in promoting disarmament, non-proliferation and arms control,

Emphasizing that the meaningful participation of women must be ensured in disarmament, including mine action and the control of small arms and light weapons,

Welcoming the work of the United Nations Coordinating Action on Small Arms mechanism, which was established by the Secretary-General to bring about a holistic and multidisciplinary approach to the complex and multifaceted global problems related to small arms,

Welcoming also the report of the third United Nations Conference to Review Progress Made in the Implementation of the Programme of Action to Prevent, Combat and Eradicate the Illicit Trade in Small Arms and Light Weapons in All Its Aspects,[1] in which the Review Conference, inter alia, underlined the importance of the full and effective implementation of the Programme of Action[2] and the International Instrument to Enable States to Identify and Trace, in a Timely and Reliable Manner, Illicit Small Arms and Light Weapons (the International Tracing Instrument)[3] for attaining Goal 16 and target 16.4 of the 2030 Agenda for Sustainable Development,[4] and called for the further strengthening of international cooperation and assistance for the implementation of the Programme of Action and the International Tracing Instrument,

Reaffirming the importance of the early designation of the President of the Review Conference and the Chair of future meetings on the Programme of Action and the International Tracing Instrument, and encouraging the relevant regional group to make such a nomination, if possible, at least one year in advance of the meeting,

Welcoming the practice of the Office for Disarmament Affairs of the Secretariat in regularly providing information in presentations, in hard copy and online, regarding requests for assistance from States as presented in their

---

[1] A/CONF.192/2018/RC/3.

[2] *Report of the United Nations Conference on the Illicit Trade in Small Arms and Light Weapons in All Its Aspects, New York, 9–20 July 2001* (A/CONF.192/15), chap. IV, para. 24.

[3] See decision 60/519 and A/60/88 and A/60/88/Corr.2, annex.

[4] Resolution 70/1.

national reports under the Programme of Action,[5] with a view to facilitating the matching of assistance needs with available resources,

Welcoming also the sustainable operation of the flexible, voluntary United Nations Trust Facility Supporting Cooperation on Arms Regulation, pursuant to the Programme of Action and the outcome of the second United Nations Conference to Review Progress Made in the Implementation of the Programme of Action,[6]

1.   *Takes note* of the report of the Secretary-General submitted pursuant to resolution 71/64;[7]

2.   *Welcomes* the ongoing efforts of United Nations-mandated peacekeeping missions, as appropriate and with the consent of the host State, to include practical disarmament measures aimed at addressing the illicit trafficking in small arms and light weapons, including through weapons collection, disarmament, demobilization, and reintegration programmes and enhancing physical security and stockpile management practices, as well as relevant training programmes, with a view to promoting and implementing an integrated comprehensive and effective weapons management strategy that would contribute to a sustainable peacebuilding process, and, in so doing, strive to achieve the goals set out in Security Council resolution 1325 (2000) of 31 October 2000 on women and peace and security;

3.   *Also welcomes* the expert discussions organized within the Group of Interested States for Practical Disarmament Measures in 2017 and 2018;

4.   *Encourages* Member States in a position to do so to financially contribute to the United Nations Trust Facility Supporting Cooperation on Arms Regulation;

5.   *Encourages* States parties to the Arms Trade Treaty[8] in a position to do so to financially contribute to the Treaty voluntary trust fund;

6.   *Welcomes* the synergies within the multi-stakeholder process, including Governments, the United Nations system, regional and subregional organizations and institutions, as well as non-governmental organizations, in support of practical disarmament measures and the Programme of Action to Prevent, Combat and Eradicate the Illicit Trade in Small Arms and Light Weapons in All Its Aspects;[2]

7.   *Decides* to remain attentive to the matter.

---

[5]   Available at https://smallarms.un-arm.org/international-assistance.

[6]   A/CONF.192/2012/RC/4, annexes I and II.

[7]   A/73/168.

[8]   See resolution 67/234 B.

Action by the General Assembly

Date: 5 December 2018   Meeting: 45th plenary meeting
Vote: Adopted without a vote   Report: A/73/510
168-2-7, p.p. 9

Sponsors

Albania, Argentina, Australia, Austria, Belgium, Bosnia and Herzegovina, Bulgaria, Costa Rica, Croatia, Cyprus, Czechia, Denmark, Estonia, Finland, France, **Germany**, Greece, Haiti, Hungary, Iceland, Ireland, Italy, Japan, Latvia, Liechtenstein, Lithuania, Luxembourg, Malta, Mongolia, Montenegro, Netherlands, Norway, Portugal, Republic of Moldova, Romania, San Marino, Serbia, Slovakia, Slovenia, Spain, Sweden, Switzerland, United Kingdom

Co-sponsors

Andorra, Canada, Guatemala, Micronesia (Federated States of), Monaco, Poland, Republic of Korea, Turkey, Ukraine

Recorded vote

Ninth preambular paragraph*

In favour:

Afghanistan, Albania, Algeria, Andorra, Angola, Antigua and Barbuda, Argentina, Armenia, Australia, Austria, Azerbaijan, Bahamas, Bahrain, Bangladesh, Barbados, Belarus, Belgium, Belize, Benin, Bhutan, Bosnia and Herzegovina, Botswana, Brazil, Brunei Darussalam, Bulgaria, Burkina Faso, Burundi, Cabo Verde, Cambodia, Canada, Chile, China, Colombia, Comoros, Costa Rica, Côte d'Ivoire, Croatia, Cyprus, Czechia, Democratic Republic of the Congo, Denmark, Djibouti, Dominican Republic, Ecuador, Egypt, El Salvador, Equatorial Guinea, Eritrea, Estonia, Eswatini, Ethiopia, Fiji, Finland, France, Gambia, Georgia, Germany, Ghana, Greece, Guatemala, Guinea, Guinea-Bissau, Guyana, Haiti, Honduras, Hungary, Iceland, India, Indonesia, Iraq, Ireland, Italy, Jamaica, Japan, Jordan, Kazakhstan, Kenya, Kuwait, Kyrgyzstan, Lao People's Democratic Republic, Latvia, Lebanon, Lesotho, Liberia, Libya, Liechtenstein, Lithuania, Luxembourg, Madagascar, Malawi, Malaysia, Maldives, Mali, Malta, Marshall Islands, Mauritania, Mauritius, Mexico, Micronesia (Federated States of), Monaco, Mongolia, Montenegro, Morocco, Mozambique, Myanmar, Namibia, Nepal, Netherlands, New Zealand, Niger, Nigeria, Norway, Oman, Pakistan, Palau, Panama, Papua New Guinea, Peru, Philippines,

---

* Subsequently, the delegation of Egypt informed the Secretariat that it had intended to abstain. The voting tally above does not reflect this information.

Poland, Portugal, Qatar, Republic of Korea, Republic of Moldova, Romania, Russian Federation, Rwanda, Saint Lucia, Saint Vincent and the Grenadines, Samoa, San Marino, Sao Tome and Principe, Saudi Arabia, Senegal, Serbia, Seychelles, Sierra Leone, Singapore, Slovakia, Slovenia, Solomon Islands, South Africa, Spain, Sri Lanka, Sudan, Suriname, Sweden, Switzerland, Thailand, the former Yugoslav Republic of Macedonia, Timor-Leste, Togo, Trinidad and Tobago, Tunisia, Turkey, Tuvalu, Uganda, Ukraine, United Arab Emirates, United Kingdom, United Republic of Tanzania, Uruguay, Uzbekistan, Vanuatu, Viet Nam, Yemen, Zambia, Zimbabwe

Against:

Israel, United States

Abstaining:

Bolivia (Plurinational State of), Cuba, Democratic People's Republic of Korea, Iran (Islamic Republic of), Nicaragua, Syrian Arab Republic, Venezuela (Bolivarian Republic of)

Action by the First Committee

Date: 8 November 2018   Meeting: 30th meeting
Vote: Adopted without a vote   Draft resolution: A/C.1/73/L.35
       162-2-8, p.p. 9

Agenda item 101 (II)

73/54   Implementation of the Convention on Cluster Munitions

Text

The General Assembly,

Recalling its resolutions 63/71 of 2 December 2008 on the Convention on Cluster Munitions and 70/54 of 7 December 2015, 71/45 of 5 December 2016 and 72/54 of 4 December 2017 on the implementation of the Convention,

Reaffirming its determination to put an end for all time to the suffering and casualties caused by cluster munitions at the time of their use, when they fail to function as intended or when they are abandoned,

Deploring the recent cases of cluster munitions use and related civilian casualties, and calling upon those who continue to use cluster munitions to cease any such activity immediately,

Conscious that cluster munition remnants kill or maim civilians, including women and children, obstruct economic and social development, including through the loss of livelihood, impede post-conflict rehabilitation and reconstruction, delay or prevent the return of refugees and internally displaced persons, can have a negative impact on national and international peacebuilding and humanitarian assistance efforts, and have other severe consequences for many years after use,

Concerned about the dangers presented by the large national stockpiles of cluster munitions retained for operational use, and determined to ensure their rapid destruction,

Recognizing the impact of cluster munitions on women, men, girls and boys and the importance of relevant States providing adequate, gender- and age-sensitive assistance to victims of cluster munitions,

Believing it necessary to contribute effectively in an efficient, coordinated manner to resolving the challenge of removing cluster munition remnants located throughout the world, and to ensure their destruction,

Mindful of the need to coordinate adequately efforts undertaken in various forums, including through the Convention on the Rights of Persons with Disabilities,[1] to address the rights and needs of victims of various types of weapons, and resolved to avoid discrimination among victims of various types of weapons,

Reaffirming that in cases not covered by the Convention on Cluster Munitions[2] or by other international agreements, civilians and combatants

---

[1] United Nations, *Treaty Series*, vol. 2515, No. 44910.

[2] Ibid., vol. 2688, No. 47713.

remain under the protection and authority of the principles of international law, derived from established custom, from the principles of humanity and from the dictates of public conscience,

Welcoming the steps taken nationally, regionally and globally in recent years aimed at prohibiting, restricting or suspending the use, stockpiling, production and transfer of cluster munitions, and welcoming in this regard that, since 2014, all Central American States have joined the Convention, thus fulfilling their aspiration to become the first cluster munitions-free region in the world,

Stressing the role of public conscience in furthering the principles of humanity, as evidenced by the global call for an end to civilian suffering caused by cluster munitions, and recognizing the efforts to that end undertaken by the United Nations, the International Committee of the Red Cross, the Cluster Munition Coalition and numerous other non-governmental organizations around the world,

Noting that a total of 120 States have joined the Convention, 104 as States parties and 16 as signatories,

Recalling that 2018 marks the tenth anniversary of the Convention, and emphasizing the need to make further efforts in accelerating the universalization process,

Taking note of the initiative of the Secretary-General, *Securing Our Common Future: An Agenda for Disarmament*, in particular part III entitled "Disarmament that saves lives",

Taking note also of the 2015 Dubrovnik Declaration[3] and the Dubrovnik Action Plan[4] adopted at the first Review Conference of States Parties to the Convention on Cluster Munitions, held in Dubrovnik, Croatia, from 7 to 11 September 2015,

Taking note further of the political declaration establishing 2030 as a target date to implement all individual and collective outstanding obligations under the Convention as adopted by consensus under the presidency of the Netherlands at the sixth Meeting of States Parties to the Convention on Cluster Munitions, held in Geneva from 5 to 7 September 2016,

Welcoming the dialogue undertaken by the German presidency of the seventh Meeting of States Parties with States not parties to the Convention, including the military-to-military dialogue, in support of universal adherence to the Convention, and recognizing the assistance that the country coalition concept can provide to affected countries in the implementation of their obligations under the Convention,

---

[3] CCM/CONF/2015/7 and CCM/CONF/2015/7/Corr.1, annex I.
[4] Ibid., annex III.

Recognizing the importance of full involvement and equal opportunities for the meaningful participation of women and men in disarmament processes, policy and programming decisions related to the Convention,

1.   *Urges* all States outside the Convention on Cluster Munitions[2] to join as soon as possible, whether by ratifying or acceding to it, and all States parties that are in a position to do so to promote adherence to the Convention through bilateral, subregional and multilateral contacts, outreach and other means;

2.   *Stresses* the importance of the full and effective implementation of and compliance with the Convention, including through the implementation of the Dubrovnik Action Plan;[4]

3.   *Expresses strong concern* regarding the number of allegations, reports or documented evidence of the use of cluster munitions in different parts of the world, related civilian casualties and other consequences that impede the achievement of sustainable development;

4.   *Urges* all States parties to provide the Secretary-General with complete and timely information as required under article 7 of the Convention in order to promote transparency and compliance with the Convention;

5.   *Invites* all States that have not ratified the Convention or acceded to it to provide, on a voluntary basis, information that could make the clearance and destruction of cluster munition remnants and related activities more effective;

6.   *Reiterates* the invitation to States not parties to participate in a continued dialogue on issues relevant to the Convention in order to enhance its humanitarian impact and to promote its universalization, as well as to engage in a military-to-military dialogue in order to address specific security issues related to cluster munitions;

7.   *Reiterates its invitation and encouragement* to all States parties, interested States, the United Nations, other relevant international organizations or institutions, regional organizations, the International Committee of the Red Cross, the Cluster Munition Coalition and other relevant non-governmental organizations to participate in the future meetings of States parties to the Convention;

8.   *Calls upon* States parties and participating States to address issues arising from outstanding dues, including options to ensure sustainable financing for the meetings and prompt payment of respective shares of the estimated costs;

9.   *Decides* to include in the provisional agenda of its seventy-fourth session, under the item entitled "General and complete disarmament", the sub-item entitled "Implementation of the Convention on Cluster Munitions".

Action by the General Assembly

Date: 5 December 2018   Meeting: 45th plenary meeting
Vote: 144-1-38   Report: A/73/510
      153-0-18, p.p. 14

Sponsors

Australia, Austria, Belgium, Bosnia and Herzegovina, Bulgaria, Chile, Costa Rica, Croatia, Czechia, Denmark, France, Germany, Iceland, Ireland, Italy, Lao People's Democratic Republic, Lebanon, Liechtenstein, Luxembourg, Malta, Montenegro, Namibia, Netherlands, New Zealand, Nicaragua, Norway, Portugal, San Marino, Slovakia, Slovenia, Spain, **Sri Lanka**, Sweden, Switzerland

Co-sponsors

Andorra, Ecuador, Equatorial Guinea, Guyana, Hungary, Monaco, Philippines, Republic of Moldova, the former Yugoslav Republic of Macedonia, United Kingdom

Recorded vote

As a whole

In favour:

Afghanistan, Albania, Algeria, Andorra, Angola, Antigua and Barbuda, Australia, Austria, Azerbaijan, Bahamas, Bangladesh, Barbados, Belgium, Belize, Benin, Bhutan, Bolivia (Plurinational State of), Bosnia and Herzegovina, Botswana, Brunei Darussalam, Bulgaria, Burkina Faso, Burundi, Cabo Verde, Cameroon, Canada, Central African Republic, Chile, Colombia, Comoros, Congo, Costa Rica, Côte d'Ivoire, Croatia, Cuba, Czechia, Democratic Republic of the Congo, Denmark, Djibouti, Dominica, Dominican Republic, Ecuador, El Salvador, Equatorial Guinea, Eritrea, Eswatini, Ethiopia, Fiji, France, Gabon, Gambia, Germany, Ghana, Grenada, Guatemala, Guinea, Guinea-Bissau, Guyana, Haiti, Honduras, Hungary, Iceland, Indonesia, Iraq, Ireland, Italy, Jamaica, Japan, Jordan, Kazakhstan, Kenya, Kyrgyzstan, Lao People's Democratic Republic, Lebanon, Lesotho, Liberia, Libya, Liechtenstein, Lithuania, Luxembourg, Madagascar, Malawi, Malaysia, Maldives, Mali, Malta, Marshall Islands, Mauritania, Mauritius, Mexico, Micronesia (Federated States of), Monaco, Mongolia, Montenegro, Mozambique, Namibia, Netherlands, New Zealand, Nicaragua, Niger, Nigeria, Norway, Palau, Panama, Papua New Guinea, Paraguay, Peru, Philippines, Portugal, Republic of Moldova, Rwanda, Saint Lucia, Saint Vincent and the Grenadines, Samoa, San Marino, Sao Tome and Principe, Senegal, Seychelles, Sierra Leone, Singapore, Slovakia, Slovenia, Solomon Islands, South Africa, Spain, Sri Lanka, Sudan,

Suriname, Sweden, Switzerland, Thailand, the former Yugoslav Republic of Macedonia, Timor-Leste, Togo, Trinidad and Tobago, Tunisia, Tuvalu, United Kingdom, United Republic of Tanzania, Uruguay, Vanuatu, Venezuela (Bolivarian Republic of), Yemen, Zambia

Against:

Zimbabwe

Abstaining:

Argentina, Armenia, Bahrain, Belarus, Brazil, China, Cyprus, Egypt, Estonia, Finland, Georgia, Greece, India, Iran (Islamic Republic of), Israel, Kuwait, Latvia, Morocco, Myanmar, Nepal, Oman, Pakistan, Poland, Qatar, Republic of Korea, Romania, Russian Federation, Saudi Arabia, Serbia, Syrian Arab Republic, Tajikistan, Turkey, Uganda, Ukraine, United Arab Emirates, United States, Uzbekistan, Viet Nam

Fourteenth preambular paragraph*

In favour:

Albania, Algeria, Andorra, Angola, Antigua and Barbuda, Argentina, Australia, Austria, Bahamas, Bangladesh, Barbados, Belarus, Belgium, Belize, Benin, Bhutan, Bolivia (Plurinational State of), Bosnia and Herzegovina, Botswana, Brazil, Brunei Darussalam, Bulgaria, Burkina Faso, Burundi, Cabo Verde, Canada, Chile, China, Colombia, Comoros, Costa Rica, Côte d'Ivoire, Croatia, Cuba, Cyprus, Czechia, Democratic People's Republic of Korea, Democratic Republic of the Congo, Denmark, Djibouti, Dominica, Dominican Republic, Ecuador, Egypt, El Salvador, Equatorial Guinea, Eritrea, Estonia, Eswatini, Ethiopia, Fiji, Finland, France, Gambia, Germany, Ghana, Grenada, Guatemala, Guinea, Guinea-Bissau, Guyana, Haiti, Honduras, Hungary, Iceland, India, Indonesia, Iraq, Ireland, Italy, Jamaica, Japan, Jordan, Kazakhstan, Kenya, Lao People's Democratic Republic, Lebanon, Lesotho, Liberia, Libya, Liechtenstein, Lithuania, Luxembourg, Madagascar, Malawi, Malaysia, Maldives, Mali, Malta, Mauritania, Mauritius, Mexico, Monaco, Mongolia, Montenegro, Morocco, Mozambique, Myanmar, Namibia, Netherlands, New Zealand, Nicaragua, Niger, Nigeria, Norway, Pakistan, Panama, Papua New Guinea, Paraguay, Peru, Philippines, Poland, Portugal, Republic of Korea, Republic of Moldova, Romania, Rwanda, Saint Lucia, Saint Vincent and the Grenadines, Samoa, San Marino, Sao Tome and Principe, Senegal, Serbia, Seychelles, Sierra Leone, Singapore, Slovakia, Slovenia, South Africa, Spain, Sri Lanka, Sudan, Suriname, Sweden, Switzerland, Thailand, the former Yugoslav Republic of Macedonia, Timor-Leste, Togo, Trinidad and Tobago, Tunisia, Turkey, Tuvalu, Uganda, United Kingdom, United Republic

---

* Subsequently, the delegation of Greece informed the Secretariat that it had intended to vote in favour. The voting tally above does not reflect this information.

of Tanzania, Uruguay, Vanuatu, Venezuela (Bolivarian Republic of), Yemen, Zambia, Zimbabwe

Against:
None

Abstaining:
Armenia, Azerbaijan, Bahrain, Georgia, Greece, Israel, Kuwait, Latvia, Nepal, Oman, Qatar, Russian Federation, Saudi Arabia, Syrian Arab Republic, Ukraine, United Arab Emirates, United States, Viet Nam

Action by the First Committee

Date:	6 November 2018	Meeting:	29th meeting
Vote:	139-1-39	Draft resolution:	A/C.1/72/L.39
	152-0-17, p.p. 14		

Agenda item 101 (w)

73/55   Measures to prevent terrorists from acquiring weapons of mass destruction

Text

The General Assembly,

Recalling its resolution 72/42 of 4 December 2017,

Recognizing the determination of the international community to combat terrorism, as evidenced in relevant General Assembly and Security Council resolutions,

Deeply concerned by the growing risk of linkages between terrorism and weapons of mass destruction, and in particular by the fact that terrorists may seek to acquire weapons of mass destruction,

Cognizant of the steps taken by States to implement Security Council resolution 1540 (2004) of 28 April 2004 on the non-proliferation of weapons of mass destruction,

Taking note of Security Council resolution 2325 (2016) of 15 December 2016 on the non-proliferation of weapons of mass destruction,

Welcoming the entry into force on 7 July 2007 of the International Convention for the Suppression of Acts of Nuclear Terrorism,[1]

Welcoming also the adoption, by consensus, of amendments to strengthen the Convention on the Physical Protection of Nuclear Material[2] by the International Atomic Energy Agency on 8 July 2005, and their entry into force on 8 May 2016,

Noting the support expressed in the Final Document of the Seventeenth Conference of Heads of State or Government of Non-Aligned Countries, held on Margarita Island, Bolivarian Republic of Venezuela, from 13 to 18 September 2016, for measures to prevent terrorists from acquiring weapons of mass destruction,

Noting also that the Group of Eight, the European Union, the Regional Forum of the Association of Southeast Asian Nations and others have taken into account in their deliberations the dangers posed by the likely acquisition by terrorists of weapons of mass destruction and the need for international cooperation in combating it, and that the Global Initiative to Combat Nuclear Terrorism has been launched jointly by the Russian Federation and the United States of America,

---

[1] United Nations, *Treaty Series*, vol. 2445, No. 44004.
[2] Ibid., vol. 1456, No. 24631.

Noting further the holding of the Nuclear Security Summit on 12 and 13 April 2010 in Washington, D.C., on 26 and 27 March 2012 in Seoul, on 24 and 25 March 2014 in The Hague and on 31 March and 1 April 2016 in Washington, D.C.,

Noting the holding of the high-level meeting on countering nuclear terrorism, with a focus on strengthening the legal framework, in New York on 28 September 2012,

Acknowledging the consideration of issues relating to terrorism and weapons of mass destruction by the Advisory Board on Disarmament Matters,[3]

Taking note of the holding by the International Atomic Energy Agency of the International Conference on Nuclear Security: Commitments and Actions, in Vienna in December 2016, and the first International Conference on Nuclear Security: Enhancing Global Efforts, in Vienna in July 2013, and the relevant resolutions adopted by the General Conference of the Agency at its sixty-second regular session,

Taking note also of the Code of Conduct on the Safety and Security of Radioactive Sources, approved by the Board of Governors of the International Atomic Energy Agency on 8 September 2003, and the supplementary Guidance on the Management of Disused Radioactive Sources, approved by the Board of Governors of the Agency on 11 September 2017,

Taking note further of the 2005 World Summit Outcome adopted at the high-level plenary meeting of the General Assembly on 16 September 2005[4] and the adoption of the United Nations Global Counter-Terrorism Strategy on 8 September 2006,[5]

Taking note of the report of the Secretary-General submitted pursuant to paragraph 5 of resolution 72/42,[6]

Mindful of the urgent need for addressing, within the United Nations framework and through international cooperation, this threat to humanity,

Emphasizing that progress is urgently needed in the area of disarmament and non-proliferation in order to maintain international peace and security and to contribute to global efforts against terrorism,

1. *Calls upon* all Member States to support international efforts to prevent terrorists from acquiring weapons of mass destruction and their means of delivery;

2. *Appeals* to all Member States to consider early accession to and ratification of the International Convention for the Suppression of Acts of

---

[3] See A/59/361.
[4] Resolution 60/1.
[5] Resolution 60/288.
[6] A/73/112.

Nuclear Terrorism,[1] and encourages States parties to the Convention to review its implementation;

3.   *Urges* all Member States to take and strengthen national measures, as appropriate, to prevent terrorists from acquiring weapons of mass destruction, their means of delivery and materials and technologies related to their manufacture;

4.   *Encourages* cooperation among and between Member States and relevant regional and international organizations for strengthening national capacities in this regard;

5.   *Requests* the Secretary-General to compile a report on measures already taken by international organizations on issues relating to the linkage between the fight against terrorism and the proliferation of weapons of mass destruction and to seek the views of Member States on additional relevant measures, including national measures, for tackling the global threat posed by the acquisition by terrorists of weapons of mass destruction and to report to the General Assembly at its seventy-fourth session;

6.   *Decides* to include in the provisional agenda of its seventy-fourth session, under the item entitled "General and complete disarmament", the sub-item entitled "Measures to prevent terrorists from acquiring weapons of mass destruction".

Action by the General Assembly

Date: 5 December 2018   Meeting: 45th plenary meeting
Vote: Adopted without a vote   Report: A/73/510

Sponsors

Albania, Angola, Argentina, Australia, Austria, Azerbaijan, Bhutan, Bulgaria, Canada, Costa Rica, Croatia, Cyprus, Czechia, Denmark, Estonia, Finland, Georgia, Germany, Ghana, Greece, Guatemala, Honduras, Hungary, **India**, Ireland, Italy, Jamaica, Latvia, Lithuania, Luxembourg, Madagascar, Malawi, Mongolia, Myanmar, Nepal, Netherlands, New Zealand, Norway, Paraguay, Philippines, Poland, Portugal, Romania, Samoa, San Marino, Serbia, Sierra Leone, Slovakia, Spain, Sweden, the former Yugoslav Republic of Macedonia, Thailand, United Kingdom, United States

Co-sponsors

Armenia, Bangladesh, Belgium, Benin, Bosnia and Herzegovina, Central African Republic, Chile, Democratic Republic of the Congo, Equatorial Guinea, Eritrea, France, Guyana, Haiti, Iceland, Iraq, Kazakhstan, Kyrgyzstan, Liechtenstein, Maldives, Malta, Mauritius, Monaco, Montenegro, Namibia, Nigeria, Republic of Korea, Republic of Moldova, Senegal, Seychelles, Singapore, Slovenia, Sri Lanka, Togo, Tunisia, Turkey, Ukraine

Action by the First Committee

Date:	5 November 2018	Meeting:	28th meeting
Vote:	Adopted without a vote	Draft resolution:	A/C.1/73/L.42

Agenda item 101 (p)

73/56   Reducing nuclear danger

Text

The General Assembly,

Bearing in mind that the use of nuclear weapons poses the most serious threat to humankind and to the survival of civilization,

Reaffirming that any use or threat of use of nuclear weapons would constitute a violation of the Charter of the United Nations,

Convinced that the proliferation of nuclear weapons in all its aspects would seriously enhance the danger of nuclear war,

Convinced also that nuclear disarmament and the complete elimination of nuclear weapons are essential to remove the danger of nuclear war,

Considering that, until nuclear weapons cease to exist, it is imperative on the part of the nuclear-weapon States to adopt measures that assure non-nuclear-weapon States against the use or threat of use of nuclear weapons,

Considering also that the hair-trigger alert of nuclear weapons carries unacceptable risks of unintentional or accidental use of nuclear weapons, which would have catastrophic consequences for all humankind,

Emphasizing the need to adopt measures to avoid accidental, unauthorized or unexplained incidents arising from computer anomalies or other technical malfunctions,

Conscious that limited steps relating to de-alerting and de-targeting have been taken by the nuclear-weapon States and that further practical, realistic and mutually reinforcing steps are necessary to contribute to the improvement in the international climate for negotiations leading to the elimination of nuclear weapons,

Mindful that a diminishing role for nuclear weapons in the security policies of nuclear-weapon States would have a positive impact on international peace and security and improve the conditions for the further reduction and the elimination of nuclear weapons,

Reiterating the highest priority accorded to nuclear disarmament in the Final Document of the Tenth Special Session of the General Assembly[1] and by the international community,

Recalling the advisory opinion of the International Court of Justice on the legality of the threat or use of nuclear weapons[2] that there exists an obligation for all States to pursue in good faith and bring to a conclusion

---

[1]   Resolution S-10/2.
[2]   A/51/218, annex.

negotiations leading to nuclear disarmament in all its aspects under strict and effective international control,

Recalling also the call, in the United Nations Millennium Declaration,[3] to seek to eliminate the dangers posed by weapons of mass destruction and the resolve to strive for the elimination of weapons of mass destruction, particularly nuclear weapons, including the possibility of convening an international conference to identify ways of eliminating nuclear dangers,

1.   *Calls for* a review of nuclear doctrines and, in this context, immediate and urgent steps to reduce the risks of unintentional and accidental use of nuclear weapons, including through de-alerting and de-targeting nuclear weapons;

2.   *Requests* the five nuclear-weapon States to take measures towards the implementation of paragraph 1 above;

3.   *Calls upon* Member States to take the measures necessary to prevent the proliferation of nuclear weapons in all its aspects and to promote nuclear disarmament, with the objective of eliminating nuclear weapons;

4.   *Takes note* of the report of the Secretary-General submitted pursuant to paragraph 5 of its resolution 72/41 of 4 December 2017;[4]

5.   *Requests* the Secretary-General to intensify efforts and support initiatives that would contribute to the full implementation of the seven recommendations identified in the report of the Advisory Board on Disarmament Matters that would significantly reduce the risk of nuclear war,[5] and also to continue to encourage Member States to consider the convening of an international conference, as proposed in the United Nations Millennium Declaration,[3] to identify ways of eliminating nuclear dangers, and to report thereon to the General Assembly at its seventy-fourth session;

6.   *Decides* to include in the provisional agenda of its seventy-fourth session, under the item entitled "General and complete disarmament", the sub-item entitled "Reducing nuclear danger".

Action by the General Assembly

Date: 5 December 2018   Meeting: 45th plenary meeting
Vote: 126-49-11   Report: A/73/510

Sponsors

Angola, Bhutan, Cuba, Ecuador, **India**, Malawi, Myanmar, Namibia, Nepal, Nicaragua, Samoa, Viet Nam

Co-sponsors

Bangladesh, Bolivia (Plurinational State of), Central African Republic, Indonesia, Malaysia, Maldives, Mauritius, Seychelles, Sri Lanka

---

[3] Resolution 55/2.
[4] A/73/116.
[5] A/56/400, para. 3.

Recorded vote

In favour:

Afghanistan, Algeria, Angola, Antigua and Barbuda, Azerbaijan, Bahamas, Bahrain, Bangladesh, Barbados, Belize, Benin, Bhutan, Bolivia (Plurinational State of), Botswana, Brazil, Brunei Darussalam, Burkina Faso, Burundi, Cabo Verde, Cambodia, Cameroon, Central African Republic, Chile, Colombia, Comoros, Costa Rica, Côte d'Ivoire, Cuba, Democratic People's Republic of Korea, Democratic Republic of the Congo, Djibouti, Dominica, Dominican Republic, Ecuador, Egypt, El Salvador, Equatorial Guinea, Eritrea, Eswatini, Ethiopia, Fiji, Gabon, Gambia, Ghana, Grenada, Guatemala, Guinea, Guinea-Bissau, Guyana, Honduras, India, Indonesia, Iran (Islamic Republic of), Iraq, Jamaica, Jordan, Kazakhstan, Kenya, Kuwait, Kyrgyzstan, Lao People's Democratic Republic, Lebanon, Lesotho, Liberia, Libya, Madagascar, Malawi, Malaysia, Maldives, Mauritania, Mauritius, Mexico, Mongolia, Morocco, Mozambique, Myanmar, Namibia, Nauru, Nepal, Nicaragua, Niger, Nigeria, Oman, Pakistan, Palau, Panama, Papua New Guinea, Paraguay, Peru, Philippines, Qatar, Rwanda, Saint Lucia, Saint Vincent and the Grenadines, Samoa, Sao Tome and Principe, Saudi Arabia, Senegal, Seychelles, Sierra Leone, Singapore, Solomon Islands, South Africa, Sri Lanka, Sudan, Suriname, Syrian Arab Republic, Tajikistan, Thailand, Timor-Leste, Togo, Tonga, Trinidad and Tobago, Tunisia, Turkmenistan, Tuvalu, Uganda, United Arab Emirates, United Republic of Tanzania, Uruguay, Vanuatu, Venezuela (Bolivarian Republic of), Viet Nam, Yemen, Zambia, Zimbabwe

Against:

Albania, Andorra, Australia, Austria, Belgium, Bosnia and Herzegovina, Bulgaria, Canada, Croatia, Cyprus, Czechia, Denmark, Estonia, Finland, France, Germany, Greece, Hungary, Iceland, Ireland, Israel, Italy, Latvia, Liechtenstein, Lithuania, Luxembourg, Malta, Micronesia (Federated States of), Monaco, Montenegro, Netherlands, New Zealand, Norway, Poland, Portugal, Republic of Korea, Republic of Moldova, Romania, San Marino, Slovakia, Slovenia, Spain, Sweden, Switzerland, the former Yugoslav Republic of Macedonia, Turkey, Ukraine, United Kingdom, United States

Abstaining:

Argentina, Armenia, Belarus, China, Georgia, Japan, Mali, Marshall Islands, Russian Federation, Serbia, Uzbekistan

Action by the First Committee

Date: 1 November 2018   Meeting: 26th meeting
Vote: 127-49-10   Draft resolution: A/C.1/73/L.43

Agenda item 101 (mm)

73/57   Universal Declaration on the Achievement of a Nuclear-Weapon-Free-World

Text

The General Assembly,

Recalling its longstanding support for the total elimination of all nuclear weapons and its resolution 70/57 of 7 December 2015, by which it adopted the Universal Declaration on the Achievement of a Nuclear-Weapon-Free World,

Recognizing the need to achieve a world without nuclear weapons,

Emphasizing, in this regard, the fundamental role of the agreement on the Final Document of the Tenth Special Session of the General Assembly of 30 June 1978,[1] in which it is stated, inter alia, that "effective measures of nuclear disarmament and the prevention of nuclear war have the highest priority",

Emphasizing also the crucial role of the Treaty on the Non-Proliferation of Nuclear Weapons[2] in achieving nuclear disarmament and nuclear non-proliferation, and recalling in particular the unequivocal undertaking by the nuclear-weapon States to accomplish the total elimination of their nuclear arsenals, leading to nuclear disarmament, in accordance with commitments made under article VI of the Treaty, agreed to at the 2000 Review Conference of the Parties to the Treaty on the Non-Proliferation of Nuclear Weapons and reaffirmed by the 2010 Review Conference,

Bearing in mind the advisory opinion of the International Court of Justice on the legality of the threat or use of nuclear weapons, issued on 8 July 1996,[3] in which the Court concluded unanimously that there exists an obligation to pursue in good faith and bring to a conclusion negotiations leading to nuclear disarmament in all its aspects under strict and effective international control,

Acknowledging the significant contribution made towards realizing the objectives of nuclear disarmament and non-proliferation, pending the total elimination of nuclear weapons, through the establishment of nuclear-weapon-free zones, although they are not an end in themselves, and reaffirming the political decision of 115 States parties to the treaties that establish nuclear-weapon-free zones and Mongolia to reject nuclear weapons,

Noting the adoption, with a vote, of the Treaty on the Prohibition of Nuclear Weapons, on 7 July 2017 at the United Nations conference to

---

[1] Resolution S-10/2.

[2] United Nations, *Treaty Series*, vol. 729, No. 10485.

[3] A/51/218, annex.

negotiate a legally binding instrument to prohibit nuclear weapons, leading towards their total elimination,[4]

Recalling the relevant principles and agreements of international humanitarian law and the laws of war, and noting the expression of deep concern by the 2010 Review Conference at the catastrophic humanitarian consequences of any use of nuclear weapons,[5]

Taking into account, in this context, the Secretary-General's disarmament agenda, *Securing Our Common Future: An Agenda for Disarmament*, announced in May 2018,

1. *Recalls* the adoption of the Universal Declaration on the Achievement of a Nuclear-Weapon-Free World, annexed to resolution 70/57;

2. *Invites* States, agencies and organizations of the United Nations system and intergovernmental and non-governmental organizations to disseminate the Declaration and to promote its implementation;

3. *Requests* the Secretary-General to seek the views of Member States on the efforts they have made and measures they have taken with respect to the implementation of the Declaration, and also requests the Secretary-General to submit to the General Assembly at its seventy-sixth session a report on the implementation of the Declaration;

4. *Decides* to include in the provisional agenda of its seventy-sixth session, under the item entitled "General and complete disarmament", the sub-item entitled "Universal Declaration on the Achievement of a Nuclear-Weapon-Free World".

Action by the General Assembly

Date: 5 December 2018	Meeting: 45th plenary meeting
Vote: 138-21-26	Report: A/73/510
128-20-25, p.p. 7	
136-3-35, p.p. 9	

Sponsors

Afghanistan, Algeria, Azerbaijan, Belarus, Bolivia (Plurinational State of), Eritrea, Guatemala, **Kazakhstan**, Malawi, Nicaragua, Palau, Sierra Leone, Tuvalu, Uganda, Venezuela (Bolivarian Republic of)

Co-sponsors

Angola, Bangladesh, Central African Republic, Comoros, Democratic Republic of the Congo, Djibouti, Dominican Republic, Egypt, Guinea,

---

[4] A/CONF.229/2017/8.

[5] See *2010 Review Conference of the Parties to the Treaty on the Non-Proliferation of Nuclear Weapons, Final Document*, vol. I (NPT/CONF.2010/50 (Vol. I)), part I, *Conclusions and recommendations for follow-on actions*.

Indonesia, Iran (Islamic Republic of), Kuwait, Kyrgyzstan, Morocco, Myanmar, Namibia, Paraguay, Qatar, Saudi Arabia, Seychelles, Tajikistan, Timor-Leste, Turkmenistan, Uruguay, Uzbekistan, Zambia

Recorded vote

As a whole

In favour:

Afghanistan, Algeria, Angola, Antigua and Barbuda, Argentina, Austria, Azerbaijan, Bahamas, Bahrain, Bangladesh, Barbados, Belarus, Belize, Benin, Bhutan, Bolivia (Plurinational State of), Botswana, Brazil, Brunei Darussalam, Burkina Faso, Burundi, Cabo Verde, Cambodia, Cameroon, Central African Republic, Chile, Colombia, Comoros, Congo, Costa Rica, Côte d'Ivoire, Cuba, Cyprus, Democratic People's Republic of Korea, Democratic Republic of the Congo, Djibouti, Dominica, Dominican Republic, Ecuador, Egypt, El Salvador, Equatorial Guinea, Eritrea, Eswatini, Ethiopia, Fiji, Gabon, Gambia, Ghana, Grenada, Guatemala, Guinea, Guinea-Bissau, Guyana, Honduras, India, Indonesia, Iran (Islamic Republic of), Iraq, Ireland, Jamaica, Jordan, Kazakhstan, Kenya, Kuwait, Kyrgyzstan, Lao People's Democratic Republic, Lebanon, Lesotho, Liberia, Libya, Liechtenstein, Madagascar, Malawi, Malaysia, Maldives, Mali, Malta, Marshall Islands, Mauritania, Mauritius, Mexico, Mongolia, Morocco, Mozambique, Myanmar, Namibia, Nepal, Nicaragua, Niger, Nigeria, Oman, Palau, Panama, Papua New Guinea, Paraguay, Peru, Philippines, Qatar, Republic of Moldova, Rwanda, Saint Lucia, Saint Vincent and the Grenadines, Samoa, San Marino, Sao Tome and Principe, Saudi Arabia, Senegal, Serbia, Seychelles, Sierra Leone, Singapore, Solomon Islands, South Africa, Sri Lanka, Sudan, Suriname, Syrian Arab Republic, Tajikistan, Thailand, Timor-Leste, Togo, Tonga, Trinidad and Tobago, Tunisia, Turkmenistan, Tuvalu, Uganda, United Arab Emirates, United Republic of Tanzania, Uruguay, Uzbekistan, Vanuatu, Venezuela (Bolivarian Republic of), Viet Nam, Yemen, Zambia, Zimbabwe

Against:

Albania, Belgium, Czechia, Denmark, Estonia, France, Germany, Hungary, Israel, Italy, Latvia, Lithuania, Luxembourg, Monaco, Netherlands, Poland, Republic of Korea, Slovakia, Slovenia, United Kingdom, United States

Abstaining:

Andorra, Armenia, Australia, Bosnia and Herzegovina, Bulgaria, Canada, China, Croatia, Finland, Georgia, Greece, Iceland, Japan, Montenegro, New Zealand, Norway, Pakistan, Portugal, Romania, Russian Federation, Spain, Sweden, Switzerland, the former Yugoslav Republic of Macedonia, Turkey, Ukraine

Seventh preambular paragraph

In favour:

Afghanistan, Algeria, Angola, Antigua and Barbuda, Argentina, Austria, Azerbaijan, Bahamas, Bahrain, Bangladesh, Barbados, Belarus, Belize, Benin, Bhutan, Bolivia (Plurinational State of), Botswana, Brazil, Brunei Darussalam, Burkina Faso, Burundi, Cabo Verde, Cambodia, Chile, Colombia, Comoros, Costa Rica, Côte d'Ivoire, Cuba, Cyprus, Democratic Republic of the Congo, Djibouti, Dominican Republic, Ecuador, Egypt, El Salvador, Equatorial Guinea, Eritrea, Eswatini, Ethiopia, Fiji, Gambia, Ghana, Guatemala, Guinea, Guinea-Bissau, Guyana, Honduras, Indonesia, Iran (Islamic Republic of), Iraq, Ireland, Jamaica, Jordan, Kazakhstan, Kenya, Kuwait, Lao People's Democratic Republic, Lebanon, Lesotho, Liberia, Libya, Liechtenstein, Madagascar, Malawi, Malaysia, Maldives, Mali, Malta, Mauritania, Mauritius, Mexico, Mongolia, Morocco, Mozambique, Myanmar, Namibia, Nepal, Netherlands, New Zealand, Nicaragua, Niger, Nigeria, Oman, Panama, Papua New Guinea, Paraguay, Peru, Philippines, Qatar, Republic of Moldova, Rwanda, Saint Lucia, Saint Vincent and the Grenadines, Samoa, San Marino, Sao Tome and Principe, Saudi Arabia, Senegal, Seychelles, Sierra Leone, Singapore, Solomon Islands, South Africa, Sri Lanka, Sudan, Suriname, Sweden, Switzerland, Tajikistan, Thailand, Timor-Leste, Togo, Trinidad and Tobago, Tunisia, Turkmenistan, Tuvalu, Uganda, United Arab Emirates, United Republic of Tanzania, Uruguay, Uzbekistan, Vanuatu, Venezuela (Bolivarian Republic of), Viet Nam, Yemen, Zambia, Zimbabwe

Against:

Albania, China, Croatia, Czechia, Denmark, Estonia, France, Hungary, Israel, Latvia, Lithuania, Luxembourg, Monaco, Poland, Romania, Russian Federation, Slovakia, Slovenia, United Kingdom, United States

Abstaining:

Andorra, Armenia, Australia, Belgium, Bosnia and Herzegovina, Bulgaria, Canada, Democratic People's Republic of Korea, Finland, Georgia, Germany, Greece, Iceland, India, Italy, Japan, Montenegro, Norway, Pakistan, Portugal, Serbia, Spain, the former Yugoslav Republic of Macedonia, Turkey, Ukraine

Ninth preambular paragraph*

In favour:

Algeria, Angola, Antigua and Barbuda, Argentina, Australia, Austria, Azerbaijan, Bahamas, Bahrain, Bangladesh, Barbados, Belarus, Belize,

---

* Subsequently, the delegations of Norway and Sweden of informed the Secretariat that they had intended to vote in favour. The voting tally above does not reflect this information.

Benin, Bhutan, Bolivia (Plurinational State of), Botswana, Brazil, Brunei Darussalam, Burkina Faso, Burundi, Cabo Verde, Cambodia, Canada, Chile, China, Colombia, Comoros, Costa Rica, Côte d'Ivoire, Cuba, Cyprus, Democratic People's Republic of Korea, Democratic Republic of the Congo, Djibouti, Dominican Republic, Ecuador, Egypt, El Salvador, Equatorial Guinea, Eritrea, Eswatini, Ethiopia, Fiji, Finland, Gambia, Ghana, Guatemala, Guinea, Guinea-Bissau, Guyana, Honduras, India, Indonesia, Iraq, Ireland, Jamaica, Japan, Jordan, Kazakhstan, Kenya, Kuwait, Kyrgyzstan, Lao People's Democratic Republic, Lebanon, Lesotho, Liberia, Libya, Liechtenstein, Madagascar, Malawi, Malaysia, Maldives, Mali, Malta, Mauritania, Mauritius, Mexico, Mongolia, Morocco, Mozambique, Myanmar, Namibia, Nepal, Netherlands, New Zealand, Nicaragua, Niger, Nigeria, Oman, Pakistan, Panama, Papua New Guinea, Paraguay, Peru, Philippines, Qatar, Republic of Korea, Republic of Moldova, Rwanda, Saint Lucia, Saint Vincent and the Grenadines, Samoa, San Marino, Sao Tome and Principe, Saudi Arabia, Senegal, Serbia, Seychelles, Sierra Leone, Singapore, Solomon Islands, South Africa, Sri Lanka, Sudan, Suriname, Switzerland, Tajikistan, Thailand, Timor-Leste, Togo, Trinidad and Tobago, Tunisia, Turkmenistan, Tuvalu, Uganda, United Arab Emirates, United Republic of Tanzania, Uruguay, Uzbekistan, Vanuatu, Venezuela (Bolivarian Republic of), Viet Nam, Yemen, Zambia, Zimbabwe

Against:

France, United Kingdom, United States

Abstaining:

Albania, Andorra, Armenia, Belgium, Bosnia and Herzegovina, Bulgaria, Croatia, Czechia, Denmark, Estonia, Georgia, Germany, Greece, Hungary, Iceland, Israel, Italy, Latvia, Lithuania, Luxembourg, Monaco, Montenegro, Norway, Poland, Portugal, Romania, Russian Federation, Slovakia, Slovenia, Spain, Sweden, Syrian Arab Republic, the former Yugoslav Republic of Macedonia, Turkey, Ukraine

Action by the First Committee

Date: 1 November 2018   Meeting: 26th meeting
Vote: 135-21-27   Draft resolution: A/C.1/73/L.46
     126-21-26, p.p. 7
     137-3-36, p.p. 9

Agenda item 101 (o)

73/58 Treaty on a Nuclear-Weapon-Free Zone in Central Asia

Text

The General Assembly,

Recalling its resolutions 65/49 of 8 December 2010, 67/31 of 3 December 2012, 69/36 of 2 December 2014 and 71/65 of 5 December 2016,

Convinced that the establishment of nuclear-weapon-free zones contributes to the achievement of general and complete disarmament, and emphasizing the importance of internationally recognized treaties on the establishment of such zones in different regions of the world in the strengthening of the non-proliferation regime,

Considering that the Treaty on a Nuclear-Weapon-Free Zone in Central Asia, on the basis of arrangements freely arrived at among the States of the region,[1] constitutes an important step towards strengthening the nuclear non-proliferation regime and ensuring regional and international peace and security,

Considering also that the Treaty is an effective contribution to combating international terrorism and preventing nuclear materials and technologies from falling into the hands of non-State actors, primarily terrorists,

Reaffirming the universally recognized role of the United Nations in the establishment of nuclear-weapon-free zones,

Emphasizing the role of the Treaty in promoting cooperation in the peaceful uses of nuclear energy and in the environmental rehabilitation of territories affected by radioactive contamination, and the importance of stepping up efforts to ensure the safe and reliable storage of radioactive waste in the Central Asian States,

Recognizing the importance of the Treaty, and emphasizing its significance in the attainment of peace and security,

1.　*Welcomes* the entry into force on 21 March 2009 of the Treaty on a Nuclear-Weapon-Free Zone in Central Asia;

2.　*Also welcomes* the signing of the Protocol to the Treaty on a Nuclear-Weapon-Free Zone in Central Asia on 6 May 2014 by nuclear-weapon States and the ratification of this instrument by four of them, and calls for early completion of the ratification process;

3.　*Further welcomes* the submission at the 2015 Review Conference of the Parties to the Treaty on the Non-Proliferation of Nuclear Weapons of

---

[1] Kazakhstan, Kyrgyzstan, Tajikistan, Turkmenistan and Uzbekistan.

two working papers, on the Treaty and on the environmental consequences of uranium mining;

4. *Welcomes* the convening of consultative meetings of States parties to the Treaty, on 15 October 2009 in Ashgabat, 15 March 2011 in Tashkent, 12 June 2012 in Astana, 27 June 2013 in Astana, 25 July 2014 in Almaty, Kazakhstan, and 27 February 2015 in Bishkek, which identified joint activities by the Central Asian States to ensure the fulfilment of the obligations set out in the Treaty and to develop cooperation on disarmament issues with international bodies, as well as the adoption of an action plan of the States parties to the Treaty to strengthen nuclear security, prevent the proliferation of nuclear materials and counter nuclear terrorism in Central Asia;

5. *Decides* to include in the provisional agenda of its seventy-fifth session, under the item entitled "General and complete disarmament", the sub-item entitled "Treaty on a Nuclear-Weapon-Free Zone in Central Asia".

Action by the General Assembly

Date: 5 December 2018   Meeting: 45th plenary meeting
Vote: Adopted without a vote   Report: A/73/510

Sponsors

Angola, Australia, Austria, Belgium, Croatia, Cyprus, Czechia, Denmark, Egypt, Estonia, Finland, France, Germany, Greece, Ireland, Kazakhstan, Kyrgyzstan, Latvia, Lithuania, Luxembourg, Mongolia, Netherlands, Poland, Portugal, Romania, Slovakia, Spain, Sweden, Tajikistan, Turkmenistan, United Kingdom, **Uzbekistan**

Co-sponsors

Albania, Belarus, Bulgaria, Canada, China, Congo, Hungary, Indonesia, Italy, Japan, Mexico, Republic of Korea, Republic of Moldova, Russian Federation, Slovenia, Turkey, Ukraine

Action by the First Committee

Date: 1 November 2018   Meeting: 26th meeting
Vote: Adopted without a vote   Draft resolution: A/C.1/73/L.48

Agenda item 101 (u)

73/59   Disarmament and non-proliferation education

Text

The General Assembly,

Recalling its resolutions 55/33 E of 20 November 2000, 57/60 of 22 November 2002, 59/93 of 3 December 2004, 61/73 of 6 December 2006, 63/70 of 2 December 2008, 65/77 of 8 December 2010, 67/47 of 3 December 2012, 69/65 of 2 December 2014 and 71/57 of 5 December 2016,

Welcoming the report of the Secretary-General on disarmament and non-proliferation education,[1] in which the Secretary-General reported on the implementation of the recommendations contained in the United Nations study on disarmament and non-proliferation education,[2] and recalling that 2018 marks the sixteenth anniversary of that report,

Recognizing the usefulness of the disarmament and non-proliferation education website "Disarmament education: resources for learning", which is updated on a regular basis by the Office for Disarmament Affairs of the Secretariat, including to provide information in all its sections, such as presentations, interviews in the *Disarmament Today* series of podcasts, which include the experiences of the hibakusha, the atomic bomb survivors, films and publications on disarmament issues, and encouraging the use of new communications technologies and social media for the promotion of disarmament and non-proliferation education,

Emphasizing that the Secretary-General concludes in his report that efforts need to be continued to implement the recommendations of the study and follow the good examples of how they are being implemented to stimulate even further long-term results,

Desirous of stressing the urgency of promoting concerted international efforts at disarmament and non-proliferation, in particular in the field of nuclear disarmament and non-proliferation, with a view to strengthening international security and enhancing sustainable development,

Conscious of the need to combat the negative effects of cultures of violence and complacency in the face of current dangers in this field through long-term programmes of education and training,

Remaining convinced that the need for disarmament and non-proliferation education, particularly among youth, has never been greater, not only on the subject of weapons of mass destruction but also in the field of small arms and light weapons, terrorism and other challenges to international security and

---

[1] A/73/119.
[2] A/57/124.

the process of disarmament, as well as on the relevance of implementing the recommendations contained in the United Nations study,

Recognizing the importance of the participation of civil society, including academic and non-governmental organizations, which plays an active role in the promotion of disarmament and non-proliferation education,

1. *Expresses its appreciation* to the Member States, the United Nations and other international and regional organizations, civil society and academic and non-governmental organizations, which, within their purview, implemented the recommendations made in the United Nations study,[2] as discussed in the report of the Secretary-General reviewing the implementation of the recommendations,[1] and encourages them once again to continue to apply those recommendations and report to the Secretary-General on steps taken to implement them;

2. *Requests* the Secretary-General to prepare a report reviewing the results of the implementation of the recommendations and possible new opportunities for promoting disarmament and non-proliferation education, and to submit it to the General Assembly at its seventy-fifth session;

3. *Expresses its appreciation* to the Secretary-General for his disarmament agenda, *Securing Our Common Future: An Agenda for Disarmament*, and notes the proposed actions therein to further advance disarmament and non-proliferation education;

4. *Reiterates* the request to the Secretary-General to utilize electronic means to the fullest extent possible in the dissemination, in as many official languages as feasible, of information related to his report and any other information that the Office for Disarmament Affairs gathers on an ongoing basis with regard to the implementation of the recommendations of the United Nations study;

5. *Requests* the Secretary-General to maintain and update the website "Disarmament education: resources for learning", including the *Disarmament Today* series of podcasts, as an efficient and effective tool to promote disarmament and non-proliferation education;

6. *Decides* to include in the provisional agenda of its seventy-fifth session, under the item entitled "General and complete disarmament", the sub-item entitled "Disarmament and non-proliferation education".

Action by the General Assembly

Date:	5 December 2018	Meeting:	45th plenary meeting
Vote:	Adopted without a vote 171-0-3, o.p. 3	Report:	A/73/510

Sponsors

Argentina, Australia, Austria, Belgium, Bulgaria, Canada, Chile, Costa Rica, Croatia, Czechia, Denmark, Ecuador, El Salvador, Germany, Greece, Guatemala, Haiti, Honduras, Ireland, Italy, Japan, Latvia, Luxembourg, Malta, **Mexico**, Mongolia, Netherlands, Norway, Peru, Poland, Portugal, Romania, Spain, Sweden, Thailand, United Kingdom, United States, Uruguay

Co-sponsors

Bangladesh, Equatorial Guinea, Estonia, Hungary, Iceland, Indonesia, Iran (Islamic Republic of), Lebanon, Malaysia, Montenegro, Paraguay, Philippines, Republic of Moldova, Slovenia, Turkey, Ukraine

Recorded vote

Operative paragraph 3

In favour:

Afghanistan, Albania, Algeria, Andorra, Angola, Antigua and Barbuda, Argentina, Australia, Austria, Bahamas, Bahrain, Bangladesh, Barbados, Belarus, Belgium, Belize, Benin, Bhutan, Bolivia (Plurinational State of), Bosnia and Herzegovina, Botswana, Brazil, Brunei Darussalam, Bulgaria, Burkina Faso, Burundi, Cabo Verde, Cambodia, Canada, Chile, China, Colombia, Comoros, Costa Rica, Côte d'Ivoire, Croatia, Cuba, Cyprus, Czechia, Democratic People's Republic of Korea, Democratic Republic of the Congo, Denmark, Djibouti, Dominican Republic, Ecuador, Egypt, El Salvador, Equatorial Guinea, Eritrea, Estonia, Eswatini, Ethiopia, Fiji, Finland, France, Gambia, Georgia, Germany, Ghana, Greece, Guatemala, Guinea, Guinea-Bissau, Guyana, Haiti, Honduras, Hungary, Iceland, India, Indonesia, Iraq, Ireland, Italy, Jamaica, Japan, Jordan, Kazakhstan, Kenya, Kuwait, Lao People's Democratic Republic, Latvia, Lebanon, Lesotho, Liberia, Libya, Liechtenstein, Lithuania, Luxembourg, Madagascar, Malawi, Malaysia, Maldives, Mali, Malta, Marshall Islands, Mauritania, Mauritius, Mexico, Micronesia (Federated States of), Monaco, Mongolia, Montenegro, Morocco, Mozambique, Myanmar, Namibia, Nepal, Netherlands, New Zealand, Nicaragua, Niger, Nigeria, Norway, Oman, Pakistan, Panama, Papua New Guinea, Paraguay, Peru, Philippines, Poland, Portugal, Qatar, Republic of Korea, Republic of Moldova, Romania, Rwanda, Saint Lucia, Saint Vincent and the Grenadines, Samoa, San Marino, Sao Tome and Principe, Saudi Arabia, Senegal, Serbia, Seychelles, Sierra Leone, Singapore, Slovakia, Slovenia, Solomon Islands, South Africa, Spain, Sri Lanka, Sudan, Suriname, Sweden, Switzerland, Tajikistan, Thailand, the former Yugoslav Republic of Macedonia, Timor-Leste, Togo, Trinidad and Tobago, Tunisia, Turkey, Tuvalu, Uganda, Ukraine, United Arab

Emirates, United Kingdom, United Republic of Tanzania, United States, Uruguay, Uzbekistan, Vanuatu, Venezuela (Bolivarian Republic of), Viet Nam, Yemen, Zambia, Zimbabwe

Against:
None

Abstaining:
Israel, Russian Federation, Syrian Arab Republic

Action by the First Committee

Date: 8 November 2018   Meeting: 30th meeting
Vote: Adopted without a vote   Draft resolution: A/C.1/73/L.49
166-0-4, o.p. 3

Agenda item 101

73/60   Decreasing the operational readiness of nuclear weapons systems

Text

The General Assembly,

Recalling its resolutions 62/36 of 5 December 2007, 63/41 of 2 December 2008, 65/71 of 8 December 2010, 67/46 of 3 December 2012, 69/42 of 2 December 2014 and 71/53 of 5 December 2016,

Recalling also that the maintenance of nuclear weapons on high alert was a feature of cold war nuclear postures, and welcoming the increased confidence and transparency since the cessation of the cold war, while noting with concern the recent deterioration in the international security climate,

Concerned that several thousand nuclear weapons remain on high alert, ready to be launched within minutes,

Noting the continuing engagement in multilateral disarmament forums in support of further reductions to the operational status of nuclear weapons systems,

Recognizing that the maintenance of nuclear weapons systems at a high level of readiness increases the risk of the unintentional or accidental use of such weapons, which would have catastrophic humanitarian consequences,

Recognizing also that reductions in deployments and the lowering of operational status contribute to the maintenance of international peace and security, as well as to the process of nuclear disarmament, through the enhancement of confidence-building and transparency measures and a diminishing role for nuclear weapons in security policies,

Welcoming the steps taken by some States in support of nuclear disarmament, including de-targeting initiatives, increasing the amount of preparation time required for deployment and other measures to diminish further the possibility of nuclear launches resulting from accidents, unauthorized actions or misperceptions,

Recalling the adoption by consensus of the conclusions and recommendations for follow-on actions by the 2010 Review Conference of the Parties to the Treaty on the Non-Proliferation of Nuclear Weapons,[1] including the commitments of the nuclear-weapon States to promptly engage with a view to, inter alia, considering the legitimate interest of non-nuclear-weapon States in further reducing the operational status of nuclear weapons systems in ways that promote international stability and security,

---

[1] See *2010 Review Conference of the Parties to the Treaty on the Non-Proliferation of Nuclear Weapons, Final Document*, vol. I (NPT/CONF.2010/50 (Vol. I)), part I.

Encouraging, in this regard, continued dialogue among the nuclear-weapon States to advance their nuclear non-proliferation and disarmament commitments under the action plan of the 2010 Review Conference,[1] and acknowledging the potential of this process for leading to deeper engagement on nuclear disarmament and greater mutual confidence,

Taking note of the references to operational readiness in reports of the nuclear-weapon States during the last review cycle of the Treaty on the Non-Proliferation of Nuclear Weapons,

Welcoming all opportunities to address the further reduction of the operational status of nuclear weapons systems as a step leading to nuclear disarmament,

1.　*Calls for* practical and concrete steps to be taken, unilaterally, bilaterally or multilaterally, to decrease the operational readiness of nuclear weapons systems, with a view to ensuring that all nuclear weapons are removed from high alert status;

2.　*Looks forward* to the issue of the lowering of the operational readiness of nuclear weapons systems being addressed further during the current review cycle of the Treaty on the Non-Proliferation of Nuclear Weapons;

3.　*Urges* States to update the General Assembly on progress made in the implementation of the present resolution;

4.　*Decides* to remain seized of the matter.

Action by the General Assembly

Date: 5 December 2018　　　Meeting: 45th plenary meeting
Vote: 175-5-5　　　　　　　Report:　 A/73/510
　　　 164-2-7, p.p. 8

Sponsors

Austria, Belgium, Chile, Eswatini, Finland, Ghana, Ireland, Luxembourg, Malaysia, Malta, **New Zealand**, Nigeria, Samoa, San Marino, Sweden, Switzerland, Zambia

Co-sponsors

Australia, Bangladesh, Burkina Faso, Canada, Ecuador, Germany, Iceland, Liechtenstein, Mexico, Netherlands, Norway, Paraguay, Republic of Moldova, Spain, Thailand

Recorded vote

As a whole

In favour:
> Afghanistan, Albania, Algeria, Andorra, Angola, Antigua and Barbuda, Argentina, Armenia, Australia, Austria, Azerbaijan, Bahamas, Bahrain, Bangladesh, Barbados, Belarus, Belgium, Belize, Benin, Bhutan, Bolivia (Plurinational State of), Bosnia and Herzegovina, Botswana, Brazil, Brunei Darussalam, Bulgaria, Burkina Faso, Burundi, Cabo Verde, Cambodia, Cameroon, Canada, Central African Republic, Chile, China, Colombia, Congo, Costa Rica, Côte d'Ivoire, Croatia, Cuba, Cyprus, Czechia, Democratic Republic of the Congo, Denmark, Djibouti, Dominica, Dominican Republic, Ecuador, Egypt, El Salvador, Equatorial Guinea, Eritrea, Estonia, Eswatini, Ethiopia, Fiji, Finland, Gabon, Gambia, Georgia, Germany, Ghana, Greece, Grenada, Guatemala, Guinea, Guinea-Bissau, Guyana, Honduras, Hungary, Iceland, India, Indonesia, Iran (Islamic Republic of), Iraq, Ireland, Italy, Jamaica, Japan, Jordan, Kazakhstan, Kenya, Kuwait, Kyrgyzstan, Lao People's Democratic Republic, Latvia, Lebanon, Lesotho, Liberia, Libya, Liechtenstein, Luxembourg, Madagascar, Malawi, Malaysia, Maldives, Mali, Malta, Marshall Islands, Mauritania, Mauritius, Mexico, Mongolia, Montenegro, Morocco, Mozambique, Myanmar, Namibia, Nepal, Netherlands, New Zealand, Nicaragua, Niger, Nigeria, Norway, Oman, Pakistan, Palau, Panama, Papua New Guinea, Paraguay, Peru, Philippines, Poland, Portugal, Qatar, Republic of Moldova, Romania, Rwanda, Saint Lucia, Saint Vincent and the Grenadines, Samoa, San Marino, Sao Tome and Principe, Saudi Arabia, Senegal, Serbia, Seychelles, Sierra Leone, Singapore, Slovakia, Slovenia, Solomon Islands, South Africa, Spain, Sri Lanka, Sudan, Suriname, Sweden, Switzerland, Syrian Arab Republic, Tajikistan, Thailand, the former Yugoslav Republic of Macedonia, Timor-Leste, Togo, Tonga, Trinidad and Tobago, Tunisia, Turkey, Turkmenistan, Tuvalu, Uganda, Ukraine, United Arab Emirates, United Republic of Tanzania, Uruguay, Uzbekistan, Vanuatu, Venezuela (Bolivarian Republic of), Viet Nam, Yemen, Zambia, Zimbabwe

Against:
> Comoros, France, Russian Federation, United Kingdom, United States

Abstaining:
> Democratic People's Republic of Korea, Israel, Lithuania, Micronesia (Federated States of), Republic of Korea

Eighth preambular paragraph

In favour:

Afghanistan, Albania, Algeria, Andorra, Angola, Antigua and Barbuda, Argentina, Armenia, Australia, Austria, Azerbaijan, Bahamas, Bahrain, Bangladesh, Barbados, Belarus, Belgium, Belize, Benin, Bhutan, Bolivia (Plurinational State of), Bosnia and Herzegovina, Botswana, Brazil, Brunei Darussalam, Bulgaria, Burkina Faso, Burundi, Cabo Verde, Cambodia, Canada, Chile, China, Colombia, Comoros, Costa Rica, Côte d'Ivoire, Croatia, Cuba, Cyprus, Czechia, Democratic Republic of the Congo, Denmark, Djibouti, Dominican Republic, Ecuador, Egypt, El Salvador, Equatorial Guinea, Eritrea, Estonia, Eswatini, Ethiopia, Fiji, Finland, Gambia, Georgia, Germany, Ghana, Greece, Guatemala, Guinea, Guinea-Bissau, Guyana, Honduras, Hungary, Iceland, Indonesia, Iran (Islamic Republic of), Iraq, Ireland, Italy, Jamaica, Japan, Jordan, Kazakhstan, Kenya, Kuwait, Kyrgyzstan, Lao People's Democratic Republic, Latvia, Lebanon, Lesotho, Liberia, Libya, Liechtenstein, Luxembourg, Madagascar, Malawi, Malaysia, Maldives, Mali, Malta, Mauritania, Mauritius, Mexico, Mongolia, Montenegro, Morocco, Mozambique, Myanmar, Namibia, Nepal, Netherlands, New Zealand, Nicaragua, Niger, Nigeria, Norway, Oman, Panama, Papua New Guinea, Paraguay, Peru, Philippines, Poland, Portugal, Qatar, Republic of Moldova, Romania, Rwanda, Saint Lucia, Saint Vincent and the Grenadines, Samoa, San Marino, Sao Tome and Principe, Saudi Arabia, Senegal, Serbia, Seychelles, Sierra Leone, Singapore, Slovakia, Slovenia, Solomon Islands, South Africa, Spain, Sri Lanka, Sudan, Suriname, Sweden, Switzerland, Syrian Arab Republic, Tajikistan, Thailand, the former Yugoslav Republic of Macedonia, Togo, Trinidad and Tobago, Tunisia, Turkey, Turkmenistan, Tuvalu, Uganda, Ukraine, United Arab Emirates, United Republic of Tanzania, Uruguay, Uzbekistan, Vanuatu, Venezuela (Bolivarian Republic of), Viet Nam, Yemen, Zambia, Zimbabwe

Against:

Russian Federation, United States

Abstaining:

France, India, Israel, Lithuania, Pakistan, Republic of Korea, United Kingdom

Action by the First Committee

Date:	1 November 2018	Meeting:	26th meeting
Vote:	173-4-7	Draft resolution:	A/C.1/73/L.52
	166-2-10, p.p. 8		

Agenda item 101 (m)

73/61 Implementation of the Convention on the Prohibition of the Use, Stockpiling, Production and Transfer of Anti-personnel Mines and on Their Destruction

Text

The General Assembly,

Recalling its resolutions 54/54 B of 1 December 1999, 55/33 V of 20 November 2000, 56/24 M of 29 November 2001, 57/74 of 22 November 2002, 58/53 of 8 December 2003, 59/84 of 3 December 2004, 60/80 of 8 December 2005, 61/84 of 6 December 2006, 62/41 of 5 December 2007, 63/42 of 2 December 2008, 64/56 of 2 December 2009, 65/48 of 8 December 2010, 66/29 of 2 December 2011, 67/32 of 3 December 2012, 68/30 of 5 December 2013, 69/34 of 2 December 2014, 70/55 of 7 December 2015, 71/34 of 5 December 2016 and 72/53 of 4 December 2017,

Reaffirming its determination to put an end to the suffering and casualties caused by anti-personnel mines, which kill or injure thousands of people – women, girls, boys and men – every year, and which place people living in affected areas at risk and hinder the development of their communities,

Believing it necessary to do the utmost to contribute in an efficient and coordinated manner to facing the challenge of removing anti-personnel mines placed throughout the world and to assure their destruction,

Wishing to do the utmost to ensure assistance for the care and rehabilitation, including the social and economic reintegration, of mine victims,

Noting with satisfaction the work undertaken to implement the Convention on the Prohibition of the Use, Stockpiling, Production and Transfer of Anti-Personnel Mines and on Their Destruction[1] and the substantial progress made towards addressing the global anti-personnel landmine problem,

Recalling the first to sixteenth meetings of the States parties to the Convention, held in Maputo (1999), Geneva (2000), Managua (2001), Geneva (2002), Bangkok (2003), Zagreb (2005), Geneva (2006), the Dead Sea (2007), Geneva (2008 and 2010), Phnom Penh (2011), Geneva (2012, 2013 and 2015), Santiago (2016) and Vienna (2017), and the First, Second and Third Review Conferences of the States Parties to the Convention, held in Nairobi (2004), Cartagena, Colombia (2009), and Maputo (2014),

---

[1] United Nations, *Treaty Series*, vol. 2056, No. 35597.

Recalling also that, at the Third Review Conference of the States Parties to the Convention, the international community reviewed the implementation of the Convention and the States parties adopted a declaration and an action plan for the period 2014–2019 to support enhanced implementation and promotion of the Convention,

Underlining the importance of cooperation and assistance in the implementation of the Convention, including through the so-called individualized approach, which offers mine-affected countries a platform for presenting their challenges,

Stressing the need to take into account gender aspects in mine action,

Noting with satisfaction that 164 States have ratified or acceded to the Convention and have formally accepted the obligations of the Convention,

Emphasizing the desirability of attracting the adherence of all States to the Convention, and determined to work strenuously towards the promotion of its universalization and norms,

Noting with regret that anti-personnel mines continue to be used in some conflicts around the world, causing human suffering and impeding post-conflict development,

1.   *Invites* all States that have not signed the Convention on the Prohibition of the Use, Stockpiling, Production and Transfer of Anti-Personnel Mines and on Their Destruction[1] to accede to it without delay;

2.   *Urges* the one remaining State that has signed but has not ratified the Convention to ratify it without delay;

3.   *Stresses* the importance of the full and effective implementation of and compliance with the Convention, including through the continued implementation of the action plan for the period 2014–2019;

4.   *Expresses strong concern* regarding the use of anti-personnel mines in various parts of the world, including use highlighted in recent allegations, reports and documented evidence;

5.   *Urges* all States parties to provide the Secretary-General with complete and timely information as required under article 7 of the Convention in order to promote transparency and compliance with the Convention;

6.   *Invites* all States that have not ratified the Convention or acceded to it to provide, on a voluntary basis, information to make global mine action efforts more effective;

7.   *Renews its call upon* all States and other relevant parties to work together to promote, support and advance the care, rehabilitation and social and economic reintegration of mine victims, mine risk education programmes and the removal and destruction of anti-personnel mines placed or stockpiled throughout the world;

8. *Urges* all States to remain seized of the issue at the highest political level and, where in a position to do so, to promote adherence to the Convention through bilateral, subregional, regional and multilateral contacts, outreach, seminars and other means;

9. *Invites and encourages* all interested States, the United Nations, other relevant international organizations or institutions, regional organizations, the International Committee of the Red Cross and relevant non-governmental organizations to attend the Seventeenth Meeting of the States Parties to the Convention, to be held in Geneva from 26 to 30 November 2018, and to participate in the future programme of meetings of the States parties to the Convention;

10. *Requests* the Secretary-General, in accordance with article 12, paragraph 1, of the Convention, to undertake the preparations necessary to convene the Fourth Review Conference of the States Parties to the Convention and, on behalf of the States parties and in accordance with article 12, paragraph 3, of the Convention, to invite States not parties to the Convention, as well as the United Nations, other relevant international organizations or institutions, regional organizations, the International Committee of the Red Cross and relevant non-governmental organizations, to attend the Fourth Review Conference as observers;

11. *Calls upon* States parties and participating States to address issues arising from outstanding dues and from recently implemented United Nations financial and accounting practices, and to proceed promptly with the payment of their share of the estimated costs;

12. *Decides* to include in the provisional agenda of its seventy-fourth session, under the item entitled "General and complete disarmament", the sub-item entitled "Implementation of the Convention on the Prohibition of the Use, Stockpiling, Production and Transfer of Anti-Personnel Mines and on Their Destruction".

Action by the General Assembly

Date: 5 December 2018   Meeting: 45th plenary meeting
Vote: 169-0-16   Report: A/73/510

Sponsors

Afghanistan, Austria, Norway

Recorded vote

In favour:

Afghanistan, Albania, Algeria, Andorra, Angola, Antigua and Barbuda, Argentina, Armenia, Australia, Austria, Azerbaijan, Bahamas, Bahrain, Bangladesh, Barbados, Belarus, Belgium, Belize, Benin, Bhutan, Bolivia (Plurinational State of), Bosnia and Herzegovina, Botswana,

Brazil, Brunei Darussalam, Bulgaria, Burkina Faso, Burundi, Cabo Verde, Cambodia, Cameroon, Canada, Central African Republic, Chile, China, Colombia, Comoros, Congo, Costa Rica, Côte d'Ivoire, Croatia, Cyprus, Czechia, Democratic Republic of the Congo, Denmark, Djibouti, Dominica, Dominican Republic, Ecuador, El Salvador, Equatorial Guinea, Eritrea, Estonia, Eswatini, Ethiopia, Fiji, Finland, France, Gabon, Gambia, Georgia, Germany, Ghana, Greece, Grenada, Guatemala, Guinea, Guinea-Bissau, Guyana, Haiti, Honduras, Hungary, Iceland, Indonesia, Iraq, Ireland, Italy, Jamaica, Japan, Jordan, Kazakhstan, Kenya, Kuwait, Kyrgyzstan, Lao People's Democratic Republic, Latvia, Lesotho, Liberia, Libya, Liechtenstein, Lithuania, Luxembourg, Madagascar, Malawi, Malaysia, Maldives, Mali, Malta, Marshall Islands, Mauritania, Mauritius, Mexico, Micronesia (Federated States of), Monaco, Mongolia, Montenegro, Morocco, Mozambique, Namibia, Netherlands, New Zealand, Nicaragua, Niger, Nigeria, Norway, Oman, Panama, Papua New Guinea, Paraguay, Peru, Philippines, Poland, Portugal, Qatar, Republic of Moldova, Romania, Rwanda, Saint Lucia, Saint Vincent and the Grenadines, Samoa, San Marino, Sao Tome and Principe, Senegal, Serbia, Seychelles, Sierra Leone, Singapore, Slovakia, Slovenia, Solomon Islands, South Africa, Spain, Sri Lanka, Sudan, Suriname, Sweden, Switzerland, Tajikistan, Thailand, the former Yugoslav Republic of Macedonia, Timor-Leste, Togo, Tonga, Trinidad and Tobago, Tunisia, Turkey, Turkmenistan, Tuvalu, Uganda, Ukraine, United Arab Emirates, United Kingdom, United Republic of Tanzania, Uruguay, Vanuatu, Venezuela (Bolivarian Republic of), Yemen, Zambia, Zimbabwe

Against:
None

Abstaining:
Cuba, Democratic People's Republic of Korea, Egypt, India, Iran (Islamic Republic of), Israel, Myanmar, Nepal, Pakistan, Palau, Republic of Korea, Russian Federation, Saudi Arabia, Syrian Arab Republic, United States, Viet Nam

Action by the First Committee

Date: 8 November 2018   Meeting: 31st meeting
Vote: 154-0-17   Draft resolution: A/C.1/73/L.53/Rev.1

Agenda item 101 (ee)

73/62   United action with renewed determination towards the total elimination of nuclear weapons

Text

The General Assembly,

Reaffirming its commitment towards a peaceful and secure world free of nuclear weapons,

Recalling its resolution 72/50 of 4 December 2017,

Reaffirming the crucial importance of the Treaty on the Non-Proliferation of Nuclear Weapons[1] as the cornerstone of the international nuclear non-proliferation regime and an essential foundation for the pursuit of nuclear disarmament, nuclear non-proliferation and the peaceful uses of nuclear energy,

Reaffirming also its determination to further strengthen the universality of the regime of the Treaty on the Non-Proliferation of Nuclear Weapons, and recalling that nuclear disarmament, non-proliferation and peaceful uses of nuclear energy are mutually reinforcing and are essential for strengthening the Treaty regime,

Stressing the essential role of the Treaty on the Non-Proliferation of Nuclear Weapons, 2018 being the fiftieth anniversary of its opening for signature, in the maintenance of international peace, security and stability, as well as its centrality to the rules-based international order, and recalling the achievements and the significance of the Treaty as the cornerstone of the international nuclear disarmament and non-proliferation regime, which has contributed to the achievement of major reductions in the nuclear arsenals of nuclear-weapon States,

Stressing also the importance of the Review Conference of the Parties to the Treaty on the Non-Proliferation of Nuclear Weapons to be held in 2020, on the occasion of the fiftieth anniversary of the entry into force of the Treaty, and of its review cycle towards the 2020 Review Conference,

Reaffirming that the enhancement of international peace and security and the promotion of nuclear disarmament are mutually reinforcing and that it is in the common interest of all States to improve the international security environment and pursue a world free of nuclear weapons in line with article VI of the Treaty on the Non-Proliferation of Nuclear Weapons,

Emphasizing the crucial importance of rebuilding trust and enhancing cooperation among all States in order to make substantive progress in

---

[1] United Nations, *Treaty Series*, vol. 729, No. 10485.

nuclear disarmament and non-proliferation, bearing in mind there are various approaches towards the realization of a world free of nuclear weapons,

Mindful, in this regard, that civility in discourse and respect for divergent views contribute to facilitating a meaningful and realistic dialogue, which enables the international community to reduce nuclear dangers and move forward towards a world free of nuclear weapons,

Recognizing the importance of ensuring the equitable representation and participation of both women and men in disarmament discussions to enable a truly comprehensive approach to nuclear non-proliferation and disarmament,

Expressing grave concern over the recent developments in regional security situations and the growing dangers posed by the proliferation of weapons of mass destruction, including nuclear weapons, and by related proliferation networks,

Noting that the ultimate objective of the efforts of States in the disarmament process is general and complete disarmament under strict and effective international control,

Reaffirming the commitment to achieving the complete, verifiable and irreversible denuclearization of the Democratic People's Republic of Korea, including the dismantlement of its nuclear weapons, ballistic missiles and related nuclear and ballistic missile programmes, and the cessation of all related activities, in accordance with Security Council resolutions,

Welcoming the inter-Korean summits held on 27 April, 26 May and 18 to 20 September 2018 and the meeting between the President of the United States of America and the Chairman of the Workers' Party of the Democratic People's Republic of Korea of 12 June 2018 as a positive step toward the final, fully verified denuclearization of the Democratic People's Republic of Korea,

Recalling, in this context, that the repeated unlawful nuclear tests and frequent missile launches using United Nations-proscribed ballistic missile technology by the Democratic People's Republic of Korea pose unprecedented, grave and imminent threats to the peace and security of the region and the world, present grave challenges to the regime centred on the Treaty on the Non-Proliferation of Nuclear Weapons, and constitute clear and repeated violations of the relevant Security Council resolutions, and reiterating the resolute opposition of the international community to the possession of nuclear weapons by the Democratic People's Republic of Korea,

Recognizing that the relevant Security Council resolutions, including resolution 2397 (2017) of 22 December 2017, express the Council's firm opposition to the unlawful nuclear and missile programmes of the Democratic People's Republic of Korea in violation of the relevant Council resolutions and the Council's determination to take further significant measures in the event of a further nuclear test or ballistic missile launch by the Democratic People's Republic of Korea,

Reaffirming that further consolidation of the international regime for nuclear non-proliferation, is, inter alia, essential to international peace and security,

Stressing the importance of the decisions and the resolution on the Middle East of the 1995 Review and Extension Conference of the Parties to the Treaty on the Non-Proliferation of Nuclear Weapons[2] and the Final Documents of the 2000[3] and 2010[4] Review Conferences of the Parties to the Treaty on the Non-Proliferation of Nuclear Weapons, and reaffirming its support for the establishment of a Middle East zone free of nuclear weapons and all other weapons of mass destruction and their delivery systems, on the basis of arrangements freely arrived at by the States of the region and in accordance with the 1995 resolution on the Middle East, and for the resumption of dialogue towards this end involving the States concerned,

Expressing deep concern at the catastrophic humanitarian consequences of nuclear weapons use, and reaffirming the need for all States to comply at all times with applicable international law, including international humanitarian law, while convinced that every effort should be made to avoid the use of nuclear weapons,

Recognizing that the catastrophic humanitarian consequences that would result from the use of nuclear weapons should be fully understood by all, and noting in this regard that efforts should be made to increase such understanding,

Welcoming the visits of political leaders to Hiroshima and Nagasaki, in particular the recent visit to Nagasaki by the Secretary-General of the United Nations,

Recalling that nuclear and radiological terrorism remains a pressing and evolving challenge to the international community, and reaffirming the central role of the International Atomic Energy Agency in nuclear security,

1.   *Renews* the determination of all States to take united action towards the total elimination of nuclear weapons through the easing of international tension and the strengthening of trust between States as envisioned in

---

[2] *1995 Review and Extension Conference of the Parties to the Treaty on the Non-Proliferation of Nuclear Weapons, Final Document, Part I* (NPT/CONF.1995/32 (Part I) and NPT/CONF.1995/32 (Part I)/Corr.2), annex.

[3] *2000 Review Conference of the Parties to the Treaty on the Non-Proliferation of Nuclear Weapons, Final Document*, vols. I–III (NPT/CONF.2000/28 (Parts I and II), NPT/CONF.2000/28 (Part III) and NPT/CONF.2000/28 (Part IV)).

[4] *2010 Review Conference of the Parties to the Treaty on the Non-Proliferation of Nuclear Weapons, Final Document*, vols. I–III (NPT/CONF.2010/50 (Vol. I), NPT/CONF.2010/50 (Vol. II) and NPT/CONF.2010/50 (Vol. III)).

the preamble to the Treaty on the Non-Proliferation of Nuclear Weapons[1] in order to facilitate disarmament and through strengthening the nuclear non-proliferation regime;

2.   *Reaffirms*, in this regard, the unequivocal undertaking of the nuclear-weapon States to fully implement the Treaty on the Non-Proliferation of Nuclear Weapons in all its aspects, including article VI, towards the goal of the total elimination of nuclear weapons, recalling the Final Document of the 2000 Review Conference of the Parties to the Treaty on the Non-Proliferation of Nuclear Weapons;[3]

3.   *Calls upon* all States parties to the Treaty on the Non-Proliferation of Nuclear Weapons to comply with their obligations under all the articles of the Treaty and to implement, with due consideration to developments in global security, steps agreed to in the Final Documents of the 1995 Review and Extension Conference of the Parties to the Treaty on the Non-Proliferation of Nuclear Weapons[2] and the 2000 and 2010[4] Review Conferences;

4.   *Encourages* all States to exert their utmost efforts towards the success of the 2020 Review Conference of the Parties to the Treaty on the Non-Proliferation of Nuclear Weapons, welcoming the successful convening of the first and second sessions of the Preparatory Committee for the Review Conference, which were held, respectively, in Vienna in May 2017 and in Geneva in April and May 2018;

5.   *Calls upon* all States not parties to the Treaty on the Non-Proliferation of Nuclear Weapons to accede as non-nuclear-weapon States to the Treaty promptly and without any conditions to achieve its universality and, pending their accession to the Treaty, to adhere to its terms and to take practical steps in support of the Treaty;

6.   *Encourages* all States to further engage in meaningful dialogue that facilitates practical, concrete and effective measures on nuclear disarmament and non-proliferation, and calls for efforts to foster a dialogue through interactive discussion to improve understanding and develop measures that enable States to address the security environment and improve confidence and trust among all States;

7.   *Emphasizes* that deep concerns about the humanitarian consequences of the use of nuclear weapons continue to be a key factor that underpins efforts by all States towards a world free of nuclear weapons;

8.   *Calls upon* all States to apply the principles of irreversibility, verifiability and transparency in the process of nuclear disarmament and non-proliferation;

9.   *Also calls upon* all States to take further practical steps and effective measures towards the total elimination of nuclear weapons, based on the principle of undiminished and increased security for all;

10. *Stresses* that increased transparency will build confidence and trust at the regional and international levels and contribute to establishing a common ground for dialogue and negotiation, which could allow further reductions in nuclear weapons towards their total elimination;

11. *Encourages* the nuclear-weapon States to build upon and expand their efforts to enhance transparency and to increase mutual confidence, including, inter alia, by providing more frequent and further detailed reporting on nuclear weapons and delivery systems dismantled and reduced as part of nuclear disarmament efforts throughout the review process of the Treaty on the Non-Proliferation of Nuclear Weapons towards the 2020 Review Conference of the Parties to the Treaty;

12. *Calls upon* all States to make utmost efforts to ease international tension, strengthen trust between States and improve the international security environment with a view to facilitating further nuclear reductions, placing special emphasis, among others, on the following actions:

(a) Continued implementation of the Treaty on Measures for the Further Reduction and Limitation of Strategic Offensive Arms (New START Treaty), welcoming the fact that 5 February 2018 marked the date on which the central limits on strategic nuclear arsenals under the Treaty took effect, and further welcoming the respective announcements of the Russian Federation and the United States of America that each had by that date met those central limits;

(b) Continuing dialogues between the Russian Federation and the United States of America that could enable the commencement of negotiations to achieve greater reductions in their stockpiles of nuclear weapons;

(c) Efforts by all States possessing nuclear weapons to reduce and ultimately eliminate all types of nuclear weapons, deployed and non-deployed, including through unilateral, bilateral, regional and multilateral measures;

(d) Regular discussions among the nuclear-weapon States and other States, through which the international security environment could be improved with a view to facilitating further nuclear disarmament measures;

(e) Continuous review by the States concerned of their military and security concepts, doctrines and policies with a view to reducing further the role and significance of nuclear weapons therein, taking into account the security environment;

13. *Urges* all States possessing nuclear weapons to continue to undertake all efforts necessary to comprehensively address the risks of unintended nuclear detonations;

14. *Recognizes* the legitimate interest of non-nuclear-weapon States that are party to the Treaty on the Non-Proliferation of Nuclear Weapons and in compliance with their nuclear non-proliferation obligations in receiving

unequivocal and legally binding security assurances from nuclear-weapon States which could strengthen the nuclear non-proliferation regime;

15. *Recalls* Security Council resolution 984 (1995) of 11 April 1995, noting the unilateral statements by each of the nuclear-weapon States, and calls upon all nuclear-weapon States to fully respect their commitments with regard to security assurances;

16. *Encourages* the establishment of further nuclear-weapon-free zones, where appropriate, on the basis of arrangements freely arrived at by the States of the region concerned and in accordance with the 1999 guidelines of the Disarmament Commission,[5] and recognizes that, by signing and ratifying relevant protocols that contain negative security assurances, nuclear-weapon States would undertake individual legally binding commitments with respect to the status of such zones and not to use or threaten to use nuclear weapons against States that are party to such treaties;

17. *Also encourages* further efforts towards the establishment of a Middle East zone free of nuclear weapons and all other weapons of mass destruction and their delivery systems, on the basis of arrangements freely arrived at by the States of the region and in accordance with the 1995 resolution on the Middle East,[2] and the resumption of dialogue towards that end involving the States concerned;

18. *Acknowledges* the widespread call for the early entry into force of the Comprehensive Nuclear-Test-Ban Treaty,[6] while recalling that all States, in particular the eight remaining States in annex 2 thereof, have been urged to take individual initiatives to sign and ratify that Treaty without waiting for any other States to do so, and urges all States to maintain all existing moratoria on nuclear-weapon test explosions or any other nuclear explosions and declare their political will to do so, so long as the Treaty has not entered into force;

19. *Commends* the accomplishments of and continued support by States for the Preparatory Commission for the Comprehensive Nuclear-Test-Ban Treaty Organization since the opening for signature of the Treaty, in particular the significant progress made in the establishment of the International Monitoring System and the International Data Centre;

20. *Urges* all States concerned to immediately commence negotiations on a treaty banning the production of fissile material for nuclear weapons or other nuclear explosive devices and its early conclusion on the basis of document CD/1299 of 24 March 1995 and the mandate contained therein, taking into consideration the report of the Group of Government Experts requested in paragraph 3 of resolution 67/53 of 3 December 2012,[7] the report

---

[5] See *Official Records of the General Assembly, Fifty-fourth Session, Supplement No. 42* (A/54/42).

[6] See resolution 50/245 and A/50/1027.

[7] A/70/81.

of the high-level fissile material cut-off treaty expert preparatory group requested in paragraph 2 of resolution 71/259 of 23 December 2016,[8] as well as the report of subsidiary body 2 of the Conference on Disarmament, adopted on 5 September 2018;[9]

21. *Urges* all States concerned to declare and maintain a moratorium on the production of fissile material for use in nuclear weapons or other nuclear explosive devices, pending the entry into force of the treaty;

22. *Welcomes* the efforts undertaken towards the development of nuclear disarmament verification capabilities that can contribute to the pursuit of a world free of nuclear weapons, including the Group of Governmental Experts mandated pursuant to resolution 71/67 of 14 December 2016 and the International Partnership for Nuclear Disarmament Verification, and stresses in this regard the importance of cooperation between nuclear-weapon States and non-nuclear-weapon States;

23. *While noting with appreciation* the decision of the Conference on Disarmament at its 2018 session on the establishment of the subsidiary bodies, calls upon the Conference on Disarmament to further intensify consultations and to explore possibilities for overcoming its ongoing deadlock of two decades by adopting and implementing a programme of work at the earliest possible date during its 2019 session;

24. *Encourages* all States to implement the recommendations contained in the report of the Secretary-General on the United Nations study on disarmament and non-proliferation education,[10] in support of achieving a world free of nuclear weapons;

25. *Encourages* every effort to raise awareness of the realities of the use of nuclear weapons, including through, among others, visits by leaders, youth and others to and interactions with communities and people, including the hibakusha (those who have suffered the use of nuclear weapons) that pass on their experiences to the future generations;

26. *Reaffirms* the responsibility of all States for the full implementation of all relevant Security Council resolutions and the obligations of the Democratic People's Republic of Korea to achieve complete, verifiable and irreversible denuclearization in accordance with relevant Security Council resolutions;

27. *Urges* the Democratic People's Republic of Korea to fulfil its commitment made at the inter-Korean summits held on 27 April, 26 May and 18 to 20 September 2018 and the meeting of 12 June 2018 between the President of the United States of America and the Chairman of the Workers'

---

[8] A/73/159.
[9] CD/2139.
[10] A/57/124.

Party of the Democratic People's Republic of Korea for the final, fully verified denuclearization of the Democratic People's Republic of Korea;

28. *Condemns in the strongest terms* all nuclear tests and launches using ballistic missile technology and other activities in furtherance of the development of nuclear and ballistic missile technology by the Democratic People's Republic of Korea, which cannot have the status of a nuclear-weapon State in accordance with the Treaty on the Non-Proliferation of Nuclear Weapons, and strongly urges the Democratic People's Republic of Korea to refrain from conducting any further nuclear tests as a step toward complete, verifiable and irreversible denuclearization, to sign and ratify the Comprehensive Nuclear-Test-Ban Treaty without further delay and without waiting for any other States to do so and to abandon all ongoing nuclear activities immediately in a complete, verifiable and irreversible manner, and calls upon the Democratic People's Republic of Korea to fully comply with all relevant Security Council resolutions, to implement the joint statement of the Six-Party Talks of 19 September 2005 and to return at an early date to full compliance with the Treaty, including that of the International Atomic Energy Agency safeguards;

29. *Calls upon* all States to redouble their efforts to prevent and curb the proliferation of nuclear weapons and their means of delivery and to fully respect and comply with any obligations undertaken to forswear nuclear weapons;

30. *Also calls upon* all States to establish and enforce effective domestic controls to prevent proliferation of nuclear weapons, and encourages cooperation among States and technical assistance to enhance international partnership and capacity-building in non-proliferation efforts;

31. *Stresses* the fundamental role of the International Atomic Energy Agency safeguards and the importance of the universalization of the comprehensive safeguards agreements, and, while noting that it is the sovereign decision of any State to conclude an additional protocol, strongly encourages all States that have not done so to conclude and bring into force as soon as possible an additional protocol based on the Model Additional Protocol to the Agreement(s) between States and the International Atomic Energy Agency for the Application of Safeguards, approved by the Board of Governors of the Agency on 15 May 1997;

32. *Calls upon* all States to fully implement relevant Security Council resolutions, including Council resolutions 1540 (2004) of 28 April 2004 and 2325 (2016) of 15 December 2016, based on the outcome of the comprehensive review of the status of implementation of Council resolution 1540 (2004);

33. *Encourages* all States to attach more importance to, and enhance the security of, nuclear and other radiological materials, and to further strengthen the global nuclear security architecture;

34. *Decides* to include in the provisional agenda of its seventy-fourth session, under the item entitled "General and complete disarmament", the sub-item entitled "United action with renewed determination towards the total elimination of nuclear weapons".

Action by the General Assembly

Date:	5 December 2018	Meeting:	45th plenary meeting
Vote:	162-4-23	Report:	A/73/510
	167-3-10, p.p. 19		
	168-2-6, p.p. 20		
	150-5-21, o.p. 2		
	147-8-22, o.p. 3		
	175-3-2, o.p. 5		
	162-3-10, o.p. 7		
	152-1-26, o.p. 10		
	148-2-27, o.p. 12		
	170-3-4, o.p. 13		
	159-2-20, o.p. 18		
	174-1-5, o.p. 20		
	173-2-4, o.p. 21		
	172-0-8, o.p. 31		

Sponsors

Australia, Bulgaria, Croatia, Czechia, Dominican Republic, Estonia, Finland, Georgia, Germany, Greece, Haiti, Honduras, Hungary, Italy, **Japan**, Latvia, Luxembourg, Montenegro, Nepal, Nicaragua, Palau, Panama, Paraguay, Poland, Portugal, Romania, Senegal, Seychelles, Slovakia, Slovenia, Spain, the former Yugoslav Republic of Macedonia, Vanuatu, Zambia

Co-sponsors

Afghanistan, Albania, Andorra, Antigua and Barbuda, Belgium, Belize, Benin, Canada, Colombia, Comoros, Cyprus, Denmark, Fiji, Guinea, Iceland, Lithuania, Madagascar, Malawi, Marshall Islands, Mauritania, Micronesia (Federated States of), Netherlands, Norway, Republic of Moldova, Sao Tome and Principe, Singapore, Solomon Islands, Togo, Turkey, Tuvalu, Uganda, United Arab Emirates, United Kingdom, Uruguay, Uzbekistan

Recorded vote

As a whole

In favour:

Afghanistan, Albania, Andorra, Angola, Antigua and Barbuda, Argentina, Armenia, Australia, Azerbaijan, Bahamas, Bahrain, Bangladesh, Barbados, Belarus, Belgium, Belize, Benin, Bhutan, Bolivia (Plurinational State of), Bosnia and Herzegovina, Botswana, Brunei Darussalam, Bulgaria, Burkina Faso, Burundi, Cabo Verde, Cambodia, Cameroon, Canada, Central African Republic, Chile, Colombia, Comoros, Congo, Côte d'Ivoire, Croatia, Cyprus, Czechia, Democratic Republic of the Congo, Denmark, Djibouti, Dominica, Dominican Republic, El Salvador, Equatorial Guinea, Eritrea, Estonia, Eswatini, Ethiopia, Fiji, Finland, Gabon, Gambia, Georgia, Germany, Ghana, Greece, Grenada, Guatemala, Guinea, Guinea-Bissau, Guyana, Haiti, Honduras, Hungary, Iceland, Indonesia, Iraq, Italy, Jamaica, Japan, Jordan, Kazakhstan, Kenya, Kuwait, Kyrgyzstan, Lao People's Democratic Republic, Latvia, Lebanon, Lesotho, Liberia, Libya, Lithuania, Luxembourg, Madagascar, Malawi, Malaysia, Maldives, Mali, Malta, Marshall Islands, Mauritania, Mauritius, Micronesia (Federated States of), Monaco, Mongolia, Montenegro, Morocco, Mozambique, Namibia, Nauru, Nepal, Netherlands, Nicaragua, Niger, Norway, Oman, Palau, Panama, Papua New Guinea, Paraguay, Peru, Philippines, Poland, Portugal, Qatar, Republic of Moldova, Romania, Rwanda, Saint Kitts and Nevis, Saint Lucia, Saint Vincent and the Grenadines, Samoa, San Marino, Sao Tome and Principe, Saudi Arabia, Senegal, Serbia, Seychelles, Sierra Leone, Singapore, Slovakia, Slovenia, Solomon Islands, South Sudan, Spain, Sri Lanka, Sudan, Suriname, Sweden, Switzerland, Tajikistan, Thailand, the former Yugoslav Republic of Macedonia, Timor-Leste, Togo, Tonga, Trinidad and Tobago, Tunisia, Turkey, Turkmenistan, Tuvalu, Uganda, Ukraine, United Arab Emirates, United Kingdom, United Republic of Tanzania, Uruguay, Vanuatu, Viet Nam, Yemen, Zambia

Against:

China, Democratic People's Republic of Korea, Russian Federation, Syrian Arab Republic

Abstaining:

Algeria, Austria, Brazil, Costa Rica, Cuba, Ecuador, Egypt, France, India, Iran (Islamic Republic of), Ireland, Israel, Liechtenstein, Mexico, Myanmar, New Zealand, Nigeria, Pakistan, Republic of Korea, South Africa, United States, Venezuela (Bolivarian Republic of), Zimbabwe

Nineteenth preambular paragraph

In favour:

Afghanistan, Albania, Algeria, Andorra, Angola, Antigua and Barbuda, Argentina, Armenia, Australia, Austria, Azerbaijan, Bahamas, Bahrain, Bangladesh, Barbados, Belarus, Belgium, Belize, Benin, Bhutan, Bolivia (Plurinational State of), Bosnia and Herzegovina, Botswana, Brazil, Brunei Darussalam, Bulgaria, Burkina Faso, Burundi, Cabo Verde, Cambodia, Cameroon, Canada, Chile, Colombia, Comoros, Costa Rica, Côte d'Ivoire, Croatia, Cuba, Cyprus, Czechia, Democratic Republic of the Congo, Denmark, Djibouti, Dominica, Dominican Republic, Ecuador, Egypt, El Salvador, Equatorial Guinea, Eritrea, Estonia, Eswatini, Ethiopia, Fiji, Finland, Gabon, Gambia, Georgia, Germany, Ghana, Greece, Guatemala, Guinea, Guinea-Bissau, Guyana, Haiti, Honduras, Hungary, Iceland, India, Indonesia, Iran (Islamic Republic of), Iraq, Italy, Jamaica, Japan, Jordan, Kazakhstan, Kenya, Kuwait, Kyrgyzstan, Lao People's Democratic Republic, Latvia, Lebanon, Lesotho, Liberia, Libya, Lithuania, Luxembourg, Madagascar, Malawi, Malaysia, Maldives, Mali, Malta, Marshall Islands, Mauritania, Mauritius, Mexico, Micronesia (Federated States of), Mongolia, Montenegro, Morocco, Mozambique, Myanmar, Namibia, Nepal, Netherlands, Nicaragua, Niger, Nigeria, Norway, Oman, Panama, Papua New Guinea, Paraguay, Peru, Philippines, Poland, Portugal, Qatar, Republic of Moldova, Romania, Rwanda, Saint Lucia, Saint Vincent and the Grenadines, Samoa, San Marino, Sao Tome and Principe, Saudi Arabia, Senegal, Serbia, Seychelles, Sierra Leone, Singapore, Slovakia, Slovenia, Solomon Islands, South Sudan, Spain, Sri Lanka, Sudan, Suriname, Sweden, Tajikistan, Thailand, the former Yugoslav Republic of Macedonia, Timor-Leste, Togo, Trinidad and Tobago, Tunisia, Turkey, Turkmenistan, Tuvalu, Uganda, Ukraine, United Arab Emirates, United Kingdom, United Republic of Tanzania, Uruguay, Uzbekistan, Vanuatu, Venezuela (Bolivarian Republic of), Viet Nam, Yemen, Zambia

Against:

France, Russian Federation, South Africa

Abstaining:

China, Ireland, Israel, Liechtenstein, Monaco, New Zealand, Pakistan, Switzerland, United States, Zimbabwe

Twentieth preambular paragraph

In favour:

Afghanistan, Albania, Algeria, Andorra, Angola, Antigua and Barbuda, Argentina, Armenia, Australia, Austria, Azerbaijan, Bahamas, Bahrain, Bangladesh, Barbados, Belarus, Belgium, Belize, Benin, Bhutan, Bolivia (Plurinational State of), Bosnia and Herzegovina, Botswana,

Brazil, Brunei Darussalam, Bulgaria, Burkina Faso, Burundi, Cabo Verde, Cambodia, Canada, Chile, Colombia, Comoros, Costa Rica, Côte d'Ivoire, Croatia, Cuba, Cyprus, Czechia, Democratic Republic of the Congo, Denmark, Djibouti, Dominica, Dominican Republic, Ecuador, Egypt, El Salvador, Equatorial Guinea, Eritrea, Estonia, Eswatini, Ethiopia, Fiji, Finland, Gabon, Gambia, Georgia, Germany, Ghana, Greece, Guatemala, Guinea, Guinea-Bissau, Guyana, Haiti, Honduras, Hungary, Iceland, India, Indonesia, Iran (Islamic Republic of), Iraq, Ireland, Italy, Jamaica, Japan, Jordan, Kazakhstan, Kenya, Kuwait, Kyrgyzstan, Lao People's Democratic Republic, Latvia, Lebanon, Lesotho, Liberia, Libya, Liechtenstein, Lithuania, Luxembourg, Madagascar, Malaysia, Maldives, Malta, Marshall Islands, Mauritania, Mauritius, Mexico, Micronesia (Federated States of), Mongolia, Montenegro, Morocco, Mozambique, Myanmar, Namibia, Nepal, Netherlands, New Zealand, Nicaragua, Niger, Nigeria, Norway, Oman, Panama, Papua New Guinea, Paraguay, Peru, Poland, Portugal, Qatar, Republic of Moldova, Romania, Saint Lucia, Saint Vincent and the Grenadines, Samoa, San Marino, Sao Tome and Principe, Saudi Arabia, Senegal, Serbia, Seychelles, Sierra Leone, Singapore, Slovakia, Slovenia, Solomon Islands, South Africa, South Sudan, Spain, Sri Lanka, Sudan, Suriname, Sweden, Switzerland, Tajikistan, Thailand, the former Yugoslav Republic of Macedonia, Timor-Leste, Togo, Trinidad and Tobago, Tunisia, Turkey, Turkmenistan, Tuvalu, Uganda, Ukraine, United Arab Emirates, United Kingdom, United Republic of Tanzania, Uruguay, Uzbekistan, Vanuatu, Venezuela (Bolivarian Republic of), Viet Nam, Yemen, Zambia, Zimbabwe

Against:
France, Russian Federation

Abstaining:
China, Israel, Mali, Pakistan, Philippines, United States

Operative paragraph 2

In favour:
Afghanistan, Albania, Andorra, Angola, Antigua and Barbuda, Argentina, Armenia, Australia, Azerbaijan, Bahamas, Bahrain, Bangladesh, Barbados, Belarus, Belgium, Belize, Benin, Bhutan, Bolivia (Plurinational State of), Bosnia and Herzegovina, Botswana, Brunei Darussalam, Bulgaria, Burundi, Cambodia, Canada, China, Colombia, Comoros, Côte d'Ivoire, Croatia, Cyprus, Czechia, Democratic Republic of the Congo, Denmark, Djibouti, Dominica, Dominican Republic, Ecuador, El Salvador, Equatorial Guinea, Eritrea, Estonia, Eswatini, Ethiopia, Fiji, Finland, Gabon, Georgia, Germany, Greece, Guatemala, Guinea, Guinea-Bissau, Guyana, Haiti, Honduras, Hungary, Iceland,

Indonesia, Iraq, Italy, Jamaica, Japan, Jordan, Kazakhstan, Kenya, Kuwait, Kyrgyzstan, Lao People's Democratic Republic, Latvia, Lebanon, Lesotho, Liberia, Libya, Lithuania, Luxembourg, Madagascar, Malawi, Maldives, Mali, Malta, Marshall Islands, Mauritania, Mauritius, Micronesia (Federated States of), Monaco, Mongolia, Montenegro, Morocco, Mozambique, Myanmar, Namibia, Nepal, Netherlands, Nicaragua, Niger, Norway, Oman, Panama, Papua New Guinea, Paraguay, Peru, Philippines, Poland, Portugal, Qatar, Republic of Korea, Republic of Moldova, Romania, Rwanda, Saint Lucia, Saint Vincent and the Grenadines, Samoa, San Marino, Sao Tome and Principe, Saudi Arabia, Senegal, Serbia, Seychelles, Sierra Leone, Singapore, Slovakia, Slovenia, Solomon Islands, South Sudan, Spain, Sri Lanka, Sudan, Tajikistan, the former Yugoslav Republic of Macedonia, Timor-Leste, Togo, Trinidad and Tobago, Tunisia, Turkey, Turkmenistan, Tuvalu, Uganda, Ukraine, United Arab Emirates, United Kingdom, United Republic of Tanzania, Uruguay, Uzbekistan, Vanuatu, Viet Nam, Yemen, Zambia, Zimbabwe

Against:

Austria, Liechtenstein, New Zealand, South Africa, United States

Abstaining:

Algeria, Brazil, Chile, Costa Rica, Cuba, Egypt, France, Ghana, India, Iran (Islamic Republic of), Ireland, Israel, Malaysia, Mexico, Nigeria, Pakistan, Russian Federation, Sweden, Switzerland, Thailand, Venezuela (Bolivarian Republic of)

Operative paragraph 3

In favour:

Afghanistan, Albania, Andorra, Angola, Antigua and Barbuda, Argentina, Armenia, Australia, Azerbaijan, Bahamas, Bahrain, Bangladesh, Barbados, Belarus, Belgium, Belize, Benin, Bhutan, Bosnia and Herzegovina, Botswana, Brunei Darussalam, Bulgaria, Burundi, Cambodia, Canada, Chile, China, Colombia, Comoros, Côte d'Ivoire, Croatia, Cyprus, Czechia, Democratic Republic of the Congo, Denmark, Dominica, Dominican Republic, Equatorial Guinea, Eritrea, Estonia, Eswatini, Ethiopia, Fiji, Finland, Gabon, Georgia, Germany, Greece, Guatemala, Guinea, Guinea-Bissau, Guyana, Haiti, Honduras, Hungary, Iceland, Indonesia, Iraq, Italy, Jamaica, Japan, Jordan, Kazakhstan, Kenya, Kuwait, Kyrgyzstan, Lao People's Democratic Republic, Latvia, Lebanon, Lesotho, Liberia, Libya, Lithuania, Luxembourg, Madagascar, Malawi, Maldives, Mali, Malta, Marshall Islands, Mauritania, Mauritius, Micronesia (Federated States of), Monaco, Mongolia, Montenegro, Morocco, Mozambique, Myanmar, Namibia, Nepal, Netherlands, Nicaragua, Niger, Norway, Oman, Panama, Papua New Guinea,

Paraguay, Peru, Poland, Portugal, Qatar, Republic of Korea, Republic of Moldova, Romania, Russian Federation, Rwanda, Saint Lucia, Saint Vincent and the Grenadines, Samoa, Sao Tome and Principe, Saudi Arabia, Senegal, Serbia, Seychelles, Sierra Leone, Singapore, Slovakia, Slovenia, Solomon Islands, South Sudan, Spain, Sri Lanka, Sudan, Suriname, Tajikistan, the former Yugoslav Republic of Macedonia, Timor-Leste, Togo, Trinidad and Tobago, Tunisia, Turkey, Turkmenistan, Tuvalu, Uganda, Ukraine, United Arab Emirates, United Kingdom, United Republic of Tanzania, Uruguay, Uzbekistan, Vanuatu, Viet Nam, Yemen, Zambia, Zimbabwe

Against:

Austria, Ireland, Liechtenstein, New Zealand, South Africa, Sweden, Switzerland, United States

Abstaining:

Algeria, Bolivia (Plurinational State of), Brazil, Costa Rica, Cuba, Djibouti, Ecuador, Egypt, El Salvador, France, Ghana, India, Iran (Islamic Republic of), Israel, Malaysia, Mexico, Nigeria, Pakistan, Philippines, San Marino, Thailand, Venezuela (Bolivarian Republic of)

Operative paragraph 5

In favour:

Afghanistan, Albania, Algeria, Andorra, Angola, Antigua and Barbuda, Argentina, Armenia, Australia, Austria, Azerbaijan, Bahamas, Bahrain, Bangladesh, Barbados, Belarus, Belgium, Belize, Benin, Bolivia (Plurinational State of), Bosnia and Herzegovina, Botswana, Brazil, Brunei Darussalam, Bulgaria, Burkina Faso, Burundi, Cabo Verde, Cambodia, Canada, Chile, China, Colombia, Comoros, Congo, Costa Rica, Côte d'Ivoire, Croatia, Cuba, Cyprus, Czechia, Democratic Republic of the Congo, Denmark, Djibouti, Dominica, Dominican Republic, Ecuador, Egypt, El Salvador, Equatorial Guinea, Eritrea, Estonia, Eswatini, Ethiopia, Finland, France, Gabon, Gambia, Georgia, Germany, Ghana, Greece, Guatemala, Guinea, Guinea-Bissau, Guyana, Haiti, Honduras, Hungary, Iceland, Indonesia, Iran (Islamic Republic of), Iraq, Ireland, Italy, Jamaica, Japan, Jordan, Kazakhstan, Kenya, Kuwait, Kyrgyzstan, Lao People's Democratic Republic, Latvia, Lebanon, Lesotho, Liberia, Libya, Liechtenstein, Lithuania, Luxembourg, Madagascar, Malawi, Malaysia, Maldives, Mali, Malta, Marshall Islands, Mauritania, Mauritius, Mexico, Micronesia (Federated States of), Monaco, Mongolia, Montenegro, Morocco, Mozambique, Myanmar, Namibia, Nepal, Netherlands, New Zealand, Nicaragua, Niger, Nigeria, Norway, Oman, Panama, Papua New Guinea, Paraguay, Peru, Philippines, Poland, Portugal, Qatar, Republic of Korea, Republic of Moldova, Romania, Russian Federation, Rwanda, Saint Lucia, Saint

Vincent and the Grenadines, Samoa, San Marino, Sao Tome and Principe, Saudi Arabia, Senegal, Serbia, Seychelles, Sierra Leone, Singapore, Slovakia, Slovenia, Solomon Islands, South Africa, South Sudan, Spain, Sri Lanka, Sudan, Suriname, Sweden, Switzerland, Tajikistan, Thailand, the former Yugoslav Republic of Macedonia, Timor-Leste, Togo, Trinidad and Tobago, Tunisia, Turkey, Turkmenistan, Tuvalu, Uganda, Ukraine, United Arab Emirates, United Kingdom, United Republic of Tanzania, Uruguay, Uzbekistan, Vanuatu, Venezuela (Bolivarian Republic of), Viet Nam, Yemen, Zambia, Zimbabwe

Against:
India, Israel, Pakistan

Abstaining:
Bhutan, United States

Operative paragraph 7

In favour:
Afghanistan, Albania, Algeria, Andorra, Angola, Antigua and Barbuda, Argentina, Armenia, Australia, Austria, Azerbaijan, Bahamas, Bahrain, Bangladesh, Barbados, Belarus, Belgium, Belize, Benin, Bhutan, Bolivia (Plurinational State of), Bosnia and Herzegovina, Botswana, Brazil, Brunei Darussalam, Bulgaria, Burkina Faso, Burundi, Cabo Verde, Cambodia, Canada, Chile, Colombia, Comoros, Costa Rica, Côte d'Ivoire, Croatia, Cuba, Cyprus, Czechia, Democratic Republic of the Congo, Denmark, Djibouti, Dominica, Dominican Republic, Ecuador, Egypt, El Salvador, Equatorial Guinea, Eritrea, Estonia, Eswatini, Ethiopia, Fiji, Finland, Gabon, Gambia, Georgia, Germany, Ghana, Greece, Guatemala, Guinea, Guinea-Bissau, Guyana, Haiti, Honduras, Hungary, Iceland, India, Indonesia, Iran (Islamic Republic of), Iraq, Italy, Jamaica, Japan, Jordan, Kenya, Kuwait, Kyrgyzstan, Lao People's Democratic Republic, Latvia, Lebanon, Lesotho, Liberia, Libya, Liechtenstein, Lithuania, Luxembourg, Madagascar, Malawi, Maldives, Malta, Marshall Islands, Mauritania, Mauritius, Mexico, Micronesia (Federated States of), Mongolia, Montenegro, Morocco, Mozambique, Myanmar, Namibia, Nepal, Netherlands, Nicaragua, Niger, Nigeria, Norway, Oman, Panama, Papua New Guinea, Paraguay, Peru, Poland, Portugal, Qatar, Republic of Moldova, Romania, Saint Lucia, Saint Vincent and the Grenadines, Samoa, San Marino, Sao Tome and Principe, Saudi Arabia, Senegal, Serbia, Seychelles, Sierra Leone, Singapore, Slovakia, Slovenia, Solomon Islands, South Sudan, Spain, Sri Lanka, Sudan, Suriname, Sweden, Tajikistan, Thailand, the former Yugoslav Republic of Macedonia, Timor-Leste, Togo, Trinidad and Tobago, Tunisia, Turkey, Turkmenistan, Tuvalu, Uganda, Ukraine, United Arab Emirates, United Kingdom, United Republic of Tanzania,

Uruguay, Vanuatu, Venezuela (Bolivarian Republic of), Viet Nam, Yemen, Zambia, Zimbabwe

Against:

France, Russian Federation, South Africa

Abstaining:

China, Ireland, Israel, Malaysia, Mali, New Zealand, Pakistan, Philippines, Switzerland, United States

Operative paragraph 10

In favour:

Afghanistan, Albania, Andorra, Antigua and Barbuda, Argentina, Armenia, Australia, Azerbaijan, Bahamas, Bahrain, Bangladesh, Barbados, Belarus, Belgium, Belize, Benin, Bhutan, Bosnia and Herzegovina, Botswana, Brunei Darussalam, Bulgaria, Burundi, Cabo Verde, Cambodia, Canada, Chile, Colombia, Comoros, Côte d'Ivoire, Croatia, Cyprus, Czechia, Democratic Republic of the Congo, Denmark, Djibouti, Dominica, Dominican Republic, Eritrea, Estonia, Eswatini, Ethiopia, Fiji, Finland, Gabon, Gambia, Georgia, Germany, Greece, Guatemala, Guinea, Guinea-Bissau, Guyana, Haiti, Honduras, Hungary, Iceland, Indonesia, Iraq, Italy, Jamaica, Japan, Jordan, Kazakhstan, Kenya, Kuwait, Kyrgyzstan, Lao People's Democratic Republic, Latvia, Lebanon, Lesotho, Liberia, Libya, Lithuania, Luxembourg, Madagascar, Malawi, Malaysia, Maldives, Mali, Malta, Marshall Islands, Mauritania, Mauritius, Micronesia (Federated States of), Monaco, Mongolia, Montenegro, Morocco, Mozambique, Myanmar, Namibia, Nepal, Netherlands, Nicaragua, Niger, Norway, Oman, Pakistan, Panama, Papua New Guinea, Paraguay, Peru, Philippines, Poland, Portugal, Qatar, Republic of Korea, Republic of Moldova, Romania, Russian Federation, Saint Kitts and Nevis, Saint Lucia, Saint Vincent and the Grenadines, Samoa, San Marino, Saudi Arabia, Senegal, Serbia, Seychelles, Sierra Leone, Singapore, Slovakia, Slovenia, Solomon Islands, South Sudan, Spain, Sri Lanka, Sudan, Suriname, Tajikistan, Thailand, the former Yugoslav Republic of Macedonia, Timor-Leste, Togo, Trinidad and Tobago, Tunisia, Turkey, Turkmenistan, Tuvalu, Uganda, Ukraine, United Arab Emirates, United Kingdom, United Republic of Tanzania, United States, Uruguay, Uzbekistan, Vanuatu, Viet Nam, Yemen, Zambia, Zimbabwe

Against:

France

Abstaining:

Algeria, Angola, Austria, Bolivia (Plurinational State of), Brazil, China, Costa Rica, Cuba, Ecuador, Egypt, El Salvador, Equatorial Guinea, Ghana, India, Iran (Islamic Republic of), Ireland, Israel, Liechtenstein,

Mexico, New Zealand, Nigeria, Sao Tome and Principe, South Africa, Sweden, Switzerland, Venezuela (Bolivarian Republic of)

Operative paragraph 12*

In favour:

Afghanistan, Albania, Andorra, Antigua and Barbuda, Argentina, Armenia, Australia, Azerbaijan, Bahamas, Bahrain, Bangladesh, Barbados, Belarus, Belgium, Belize, Benin, Bhutan, Bosnia and Herzegovina, Botswana, Brunei Darussalam, Bulgaria, Burundi, Cabo Verde, Cambodia, Canada, China, Colombia, Comoros, Côte d'Ivoire, Croatia, Cyprus, Czechia, Democratic Republic of the Congo, Denmark, Djibouti, Dominica, Dominican Republic, Equatorial Guinea, Estonia, Eswatini, Ethiopia, Fiji, Finland, Gabon, Georgia, Germany, Ghana, Greece, Guatemala, Guinea, Guinea-Bissau, Guyana, Haiti, Honduras, Hungary, Iceland, Indonesia, Iraq, Italy, Jamaica, Japan, Jordan, Kazakhstan, Kenya, Kuwait, Kyrgyzstan, Lao People's Democratic Republic, Latvia, Lebanon, Lesotho, Liberia, Libya, Lithuania, Luxembourg, Madagascar, Malawi, Malaysia, Maldives, Mali, Malta, Marshall Islands, Mauritania, Mauritius, Micronesia (Federated States of), Monaco, Mongolia, Montenegro, Morocco, Mozambique, Myanmar, Namibia, Nepal, Netherlands, Nicaragua, Niger, Norway, Oman, Pakistan, Panama, Papua New Guinea, Paraguay, Peru, Poland, Portugal, Qatar, Republic of Korea, Republic of Moldova, Romania, Saint Kitts and Nevis, Saint Lucia, Saint Vincent and the Grenadines, Samoa, Saudi Arabia, Senegal, Serbia, Seychelles, Sierra Leone, Singapore, Slovakia, Slovenia, Solomon Islands, South Sudan, Spain, Sri Lanka, Sudan, Suriname, Sweden, Tajikistan, the former Yugoslav Republic of Macedonia, Timor-Leste, Togo, Trinidad and Tobago, Tunisia, Turkey, Turkmenistan, Tuvalu, Uganda, Ukraine, United Arab Emirates, United Kingdom, United Republic of Tanzania, United States, Uruguay, Uzbekistan, Vanuatu, Viet Nam, Yemen, Zambia

Against:

France, South Africa

Abstaining:

Algeria, Angola, Austria, Bolivia (Plurinational State of), Brazil, Chile, Costa Rica, Cuba, Ecuador, Egypt, El Salvador, India, Iran (Islamic Republic of), Ireland, Israel, Liechtenstein, Mexico, New Zealand, Nigeria, Philippines, Russian Federation, San Marino, Sao Tome and Principe, Switzerland, Thailand, Venezuela (Bolivarian Republic of), Zimbabwe

---

* Subsequently, the delegation of Sweden informed the Secretariat that it had intended to abstain. The voting tally above does not reflect this information.

Operative paragraph 13

In favour:

> Afghanistan, Albania, Algeria, Andorra, Angola, Antigua and Barbuda, Argentina, Armenia, Australia, Austria, Azerbaijan, Bahamas, Bahrain, Bangladesh, Barbados, Belarus, Belgium, Belize, Benin, Bhutan, Bolivia (Plurinational State of), Bosnia and Herzegovina, Botswana, Brazil, Brunei Darussalam, Bulgaria, Burkina Faso, Burundi, Cabo Verde, Cambodia, Canada, Chile, Colombia, Comoros, Costa Rica, Côte d'Ivoire, Croatia, Cuba, Cyprus, Czechia, Democratic Republic of the Congo, Denmark, Djibouti, Dominica, Dominican Republic, Ecuador, Egypt, El Salvador, Equatorial Guinea, Eritrea, Estonia, Eswatini, Ethiopia, Fiji, Finland, Gambia, Georgia, Germany, Ghana, Greece, Guatemala, Guinea-Bissau, Guyana, Haiti, Honduras, Hungary, Iceland, India, Indonesia, Iraq, Ireland, Israel, Italy, Jamaica, Japan, Jordan, Kazakhstan, Kenya, Kuwait, Kyrgyzstan, Lao People's Democratic Republic, Latvia, Lebanon, Lesotho, Liberia, Libya, Liechtenstein, Lithuania, Luxembourg, Madagascar, Malawi, Malaysia, Maldives, Malta, Marshall Islands, Mauritania, Mauritius, Mexico, Micronesia (Federated States of), Mongolia, Montenegro, Morocco, Mozambique, Myanmar, Namibia, Nepal, Netherlands, New Zealand, Nicaragua, Niger, Nigeria, Norway, Oman, Panama, Papua New Guinea, Paraguay, Peru, Philippines, Poland, Portugal, Qatar, Republic of Moldova, Romania, Saint Kitts and Nevis, Saint Lucia, Saint Vincent and the Grenadines, Samoa, San Marino, Sao Tome and Principe, Saudi Arabia, Senegal, Serbia, Seychelles, Sierra Leone, Singapore, Slovakia, Slovenia, Solomon Islands, South Africa, South Sudan, Spain, Sri Lanka, Sudan, Suriname, Sweden, Switzerland, Tajikistan, Thailand, the former Yugoslav Republic of Macedonia, Timor-Leste, Togo, Trinidad and Tobago, Tunisia, Turkey, Turkmenistan, Tuvalu, Uganda, Ukraine, United Arab Emirates, United Kingdom, United Republic of Tanzania, United States, Uruguay, Uzbekistan, Vanuatu, Venezuela (Bolivarian Republic of), Viet Nam, Yemen, Zambia, Zimbabwe

Against:

> China, France, Russian Federation

Abstaining:

> Iran (Islamic Republic of), Mali, Pakistan, Republic of Korea

Operative paragraph 18

In favour:

> Afghanistan, Albania, Andorra, Antigua and Barbuda, Argentina, Armenia, Australia, Azerbaijan, Bahamas, Bahrain, Bangladesh, Barbados, Belarus, Belgium, Belize, Benin, Bhutan, Bolivia (Plurinational State of), Bosnia and Herzegovina, Botswana, Brunei

Darussalam, Bulgaria, Burkina Faso, Burundi, Cabo Verde, Cambodia, Canada, Chile, China, Colombia, Comoros, Côte d'Ivoire, Croatia, Cyprus, Czechia, Democratic Republic of the Congo, Denmark, Djibouti, Dominica, Dominican Republic, Ecuador, Equatorial Guinea, Eritrea, Estonia, Eswatini, Ethiopia, Fiji, Finland, France, Gabon, Gambia, Georgia, Germany, Ghana, Greece, Guatemala, Guinea, Guinea-Bissau, Guyana, Haiti, Honduras, Hungary, Iceland, Indonesia, Iraq, Italy, Jamaica, Japan, Jordan, Kazakhstan, Kenya, Kuwait, Kyrgyzstan, Lao People's Democratic Republic, Latvia, Lebanon, Lesotho, Liberia, Libya, Lithuania, Luxembourg, Madagascar, Malawi, Maldives, Mali, Malta, Marshall Islands, Mauritania, Mexico, Micronesia (Federated States of), Monaco, Mongolia, Montenegro, Morocco, Mozambique, Myanmar, Namibia, Nepal, Netherlands, New Zealand, Nicaragua, Niger, Norway, Oman, Pakistan, Panama, Papua New Guinea, Paraguay, Peru, Poland, Portugal, Qatar, Republic of Korea, Republic of Moldova, Romania, Russian Federation, Rwanda, Saint Kitts and Nevis, Saint Lucia, Saint Vincent and the Grenadines, Samoa, San Marino, Sao Tome and Principe, Saudi Arabia, Senegal, Serbia, Seychelles, Sierra Leone, Singapore, Slovakia, Slovenia, Solomon Islands, South Sudan, Spain, Sri Lanka, Sudan, Suriname, Tajikistan, the former Yugoslav Republic of Macedonia, Timor-Leste, Togo, Trinidad and Tobago, Tunisia, Turkey, Turkmenistan, Tuvalu, Uganda, Ukraine, United Arab Emirates, United Kingdom, United Republic of Tanzania, Uruguay, Uzbekistan, Vanuatu, Venezuela (Bolivarian Republic of), Viet Nam, Yemen, Zambia, Zimbabwe

Against:
South Africa, United States

Abstaining:
Algeria, Angola, Austria, Brazil, Costa Rica, Cuba, Egypt, El Salvador, India, Iran (Islamic Republic of), Ireland, Israel, Liechtenstein, Malaysia, Mauritius, Nigeria, Philippines, Sweden, Switzerland, Thailand

Operative paragraph 20

In favour:
Afghanistan, Albania, Algeria, Andorra, Angola, Antigua and Barbuda, Argentina, Armenia, Australia, Austria, Azerbaijan, Bahamas, Bahrain, Bangladesh, Barbados, Belarus, Belgium, Belize, Benin, Bhutan, Bolivia (Plurinational State of), Bosnia and Herzegovina, Botswana, Brazil, Brunei Darussalam, Bulgaria, Burkina Faso, Burundi, Cabo Verde, Cambodia, Canada, Chile, China, Colombia, Comoros, Costa Rica, Côte d'Ivoire, Croatia, Cuba, Cyprus, Czechia, Democratic Republic of the Congo, Denmark, Djibouti, Dominica, Dominican Republic, Ecuador, El Salvador, Equatorial Guinea, Eritrea, Estonia, Eswatini, Ethiopia, Fiji,

Finland, France, Gabon, Gambia, Germany, Ghana, Greece, Guatemala, Guinea, Guinea-Bissau, Guyana, Haiti, Honduras, Hungary, Iceland, India, Indonesia, Iraq, Ireland, Italy, Jamaica, Japan, Jordan, Kazakhstan, Kenya, Kuwait, Kyrgyzstan, Lao People's Democratic Republic, Latvia, Lebanon, Lesotho, Liberia, Libya, Liechtenstein, Lithuania, Luxembourg, Madagascar, Malawi, Malaysia, Maldives, Mali, Malta, Marshall Islands, Mauritania, Mauritius, Mexico, Micronesia (Federated States of), Monaco, Mongolia, Montenegro, Morocco, Mozambique, Myanmar, Namibia, Nepal, Netherlands, New Zealand, Nicaragua, Niger, Nigeria, Norway, Oman, Panama, Papua New Guinea, Paraguay, Peru, Philippines, Poland, Portugal, Qatar, Republic of Korea, Republic of Moldova, Romania, Russian Federation, Rwanda, Saint Kitts and Nevis, Saint Lucia, Saint Vincent and the Grenadines, Samoa, San Marino, Sao Tome and Principe, Saudi Arabia, Senegal, Serbia, Seychelles, Sierra Leone, Singapore, Slovakia, Slovenia, Solomon Islands, South Africa, South Sudan, Spain, Sri Lanka, Sudan, Suriname, Sweden, Switzerland, Tajikistan, the former Yugoslav Republic of Macedonia, Timor-Leste, Togo, Trinidad and Tobago, Tunisia, Turkey, Turkmenistan, Tuvalu, Uganda, Ukraine, United Arab Emirates, United Kingdom, United Republic of Tanzania, United States, Uruguay, Uzbekistan, Vanuatu, Venezuela (Bolivarian Republic of), Viet Nam, Yemen, Zambia

Against:

Pakistan

Abstaining:

Egypt, Iran (Islamic Republic of), Israel, Thailand, Zimbabwe

Operative paragraph 21

In favour:

Afghanistan, Albania, Algeria, Andorra, Angola, Antigua and Barbuda, Argentina, Armenia, Australia, Austria, Azerbaijan, Bahamas, Bahrain, Bangladesh, Barbados, Belarus, Belgium, Belize, Benin, Bhutan, Bolivia (Plurinational State of), Bosnia and Herzegovina, Botswana, Brazil, Brunei Darussalam, Bulgaria, Burkina Faso, Burundi, Cabo Verde, Cambodia, Canada, Chile, Colombia, Comoros, Costa Rica, Côte d'Ivoire, Croatia, Cuba, Cyprus, Czechia, Democratic Republic of the Congo, Denmark, Djibouti, Dominica, Dominican Republic, Ecuador, Egypt, El Salvador, Equatorial Guinea, Eritrea, Estonia, Eswatini, Ethiopia, Fiji, Finland, France, Gabon, Gambia, Georgia, Germany, Ghana, Greece, Guatemala, Guinea, Guinea-Bissau, Guyana, Haiti, Honduras, Hungary, Iceland, Indonesia, Iran (Islamic Republic of), Iraq, Ireland, Italy, Jamaica, Japan, Jordan, Kazakhstan, Kenya, Kuwait, Kyrgyzstan, Lao People's Democratic Republic, Latvia, Lebanon, Lesotho, Liberia, Libya, Liechtenstein, Lithuania, Luxembourg,

Madagascar, Malawi, Malaysia, Maldives, Mali, Malta, Marshall Islands, Mauritania, Mauritius, Mexico, Micronesia (Federated States of), Monaco, Mongolia, Montenegro, Morocco, Mozambique, Namibia, Nepal, Netherlands, New Zealand, Nicaragua, Niger, Nigeria, Norway, Oman, Panama, Papua New Guinea, Paraguay, Peru, Philippines, Poland, Portugal, Qatar, Republic of Korea, Republic of Moldova, Romania, Russian Federation, Rwanda, Saint Kitts and Nevis, Saint Lucia, Saint Vincent and the Grenadines, Samoa, San Marino, Sao Tome and Principe, Saudi Arabia, Senegal, Serbia, Seychelles, Sierra Leone, Singapore, Slovakia, Slovenia, South Africa, South Sudan, Spain, Sri Lanka, Sudan, Suriname, Sweden, Switzerland, Tajikistan, the former Yugoslav Republic of Macedonia, Timor-Leste, Togo, Trinidad and Tobago, Tunisia, Turkey, Turkmenistan, Tuvalu, Uganda, Ukraine, United Arab Emirates, United Kingdom, United Republic of Tanzania, United States, Uruguay, Vanuatu, Venezuela (Bolivarian Republic of), Viet Nam, Yemen, Zambia, Zimbabwe

Against:
China, Pakistan

Abstaining:
India, Israel, Myanmar, Thailand

Operative paragraph 31

In favour:
Afghanistan, Albania, Algeria, Andorra, Angola, Antigua and Barbuda, Argentina, Armenia, Australia, Austria, Azerbaijan, Bahamas, Bahrain, Bangladesh, Barbados, Belarus, Belgium, Belize, Benin, Bhutan, Bolivia (Plurinational State of), Bosnia and Herzegovina, Botswana, Brunei Darussalam, Bulgaria, Burkina Faso, Burundi, Cabo Verde, Cambodia, Canada, Chile, China, Colombia, Comoros, Costa Rica, Côte d'Ivoire, Croatia, Cuba, Cyprus, Czechia, Democratic Republic of the Congo, Denmark, Djibouti, Dominica, Dominican Republic, Ecuador, El Salvador, Equatorial Guinea, Eritrea, Estonia, Eswatini, Ethiopia, Fiji, Finland, France, Gabon, Gambia, Georgia, Germany, Ghana, Greece, Guatemala, Guinea, Guinea-Bissau, Guyana, Haiti, Honduras, Hungary, Iceland, Indonesia, Iraq, Ireland, Italy, Jamaica, Japan, Jordan, Kazakhstan, Kenya, Kuwait, Kyrgyzstan, Lao People's Democratic Republic, Latvia, Lebanon, Lesotho, Liberia, Libya, Liechtenstein, Lithuania, Luxembourg, Madagascar, Malawi, Malaysia, Maldives, Mali, Malta, Marshall Islands, Mauritania, Mauritius, Mexico, Micronesia (Federated States of), Monaco, Mongolia, Montenegro, Morocco, Mozambique, Namibia, Nepal, Netherlands, New Zealand, Nicaragua, Niger, Nigeria, Norway, Oman, Panama, Papua New Guinea, Paraguay, Peru, Philippines, Poland, Portugal, Qatar, Republic of Korea,

Republic of Moldova, Romania, Russian Federation, Rwanda, Saint Kitts and Nevis, Saint Lucia, Saint Vincent and the Grenadines, Samoa, San Marino, Sao Tome and Principe, Saudi Arabia, Senegal, Serbia, Seychelles, Sierra Leone, Singapore, Slovakia, Slovenia, Solomon Islands, South Africa, South Sudan, Spain, Sri Lanka, Sudan, Sweden, Switzerland, Tajikistan, Thailand, the former Yugoslav Republic of Macedonia, Timor-Leste, Togo, Trinidad and Tobago, Tunisia, Turkey, Turkmenistan, Tuvalu, Uganda, Ukraine, United Arab Emirates, United Kingdom, United Republic of Tanzania, United States, Uruguay, Uzbekistan, Vanuatu, Viet Nam, Yemen, Zambia, Zimbabwe

Against:

None

Abstaining:

Brazil, Egypt, India, Iran (Islamic Republic of), Israel, Myanmar, Pakistan, Venezuela (Bolivarian Republic of)

Action by the First Committee

Date: 1 November 2018 Meeting: 26th meeting
Vote: 160-4-24   Draft resolution: A/C.1/73/L.54
   164-3-12, p.p. 19
   170-2-7, p.p. 20
   145-5-23, o.p. 2
   139-8-29, o.p. 3
   173-3-5, o.p. 5
   165-4-11, o.p. 7
   152-1-23, o.p. 10
   147-2-26, o.p. 12
   170-3-6, o.p. 13
   158-2-19, o.p. 18
   172-2-5, o.p. 20
   172-2-5, o.p. 21
   170-0-9, o.p. 31

Agenda item 101 (ff)

73/63 Preventing and combating illicit brokering activities

Text

The General Assembly,

Recalling its resolutions 69/62 of 2 December 2014 and 71/36 of 5 December 2016,

Noting the threat to international peace and security posed by illicit brokering activities circumventing the international arms control and non-proliferation framework,

Concerned that, if proper measures are not taken, the illicit brokering of arms in all its aspects will adversely affect the maintenance of international peace and security, and prolong conflicts, and could be an obstacle to sustainable economic and social development and result in illicit transfers of conventional arms and the acquisition of weapons of mass destruction by non-State actors,

Recognizing the need for Member States to prevent and combat illicit brokering activities, which covers not only conventional arms but also materials, equipment and technology that could contribute to the proliferation of weapons of mass destruction and their means of delivery,

Reaffirming that efforts to prevent and combat illicit brokering activities should not hamper the legitimate arms trade and international cooperation with respect to materials, equipment and technology for peaceful purposes,

Recalling Security Council resolution 1540 (2004) of 28 April 2004, in particular paragraph 3, in which the Council determined that all States shall develop and maintain appropriate effective border controls and law enforcement efforts to detect, deter, prevent and combat, including through international cooperation when necessary, illicit trafficking in and brokering of materials related to nuclear, chemical or biological weapons and their means of delivery, in accordance with their national legal authorities and legislation and consistent with international law, and taking note of the comprehensive review of the status of implementation of resolution 1540 (2004) conducted in 2016,

Noting international efforts to prevent and combat illicit arms brokering, in particular in small arms and light weapons, as demonstrated by the adoption in 2001 of the Programme of Action to Prevent, Combat and Eradicate the Illicit Trade in Small Arms and Light Weapons in All Its Aspects,[1] and the entry into force in 2005 of the Protocol against the Illicit Manufacturing of

---

[1] *Report of the United Nations Conference on the Illicit Trade in Small Arms and Light Weapons in All Its Aspects, New York, 9–20 July 2001* (A/CONF.192/15), chap. IV, para. 24.

and Trafficking in Firearms, Their Parts and Components and Ammunition, supplementing the United Nations Convention against Transnational Organized Crime,[2]

Welcoming efforts to implement the Programme of Action and the International Instrument to Enable States to Identify and Trace, in a Timely and Reliable Manner, Illicit Small Arms and Light Weapons,[3] including the holding of mandated meetings to review their implementation and the submission by Member States of national reports,

Recognizing the importance of States parties to the Arms Trade Treaty[4] taking measures, pursuant to their national laws, to regulate brokering taking place under their jurisdiction, in accordance with article 10 of the Treaty,

Taking note of Security Council resolutions 2117 (2013) of 26 September 2013 and 2220 (2015) of 22 May 2015 on small arms and light weapons, in which the Council encouraged cooperation and information-sharing on suspect brokering activities to address the illicit transfer, destabilizing accumulation and misuse of small arms and light weapons,

Taking note also of the report issued on 30 August 2007 by the Group of Governmental Experts established pursuant to General Assembly resolution 60/81 of 8 December 2005 to consider further steps to enhance international cooperation in preventing, combating and eradicating illicit brokering in small arms and light weapons[5] as an international initiative within the framework of the United Nations,

Underlining the inherent right of Member States to determine the specific scope and content of domestic regulations in accordance with their legislative frameworks and export control systems, consistent with international law,

Welcoming the efforts made by Member States to implement laws and/or administrative measures to regulate arms brokering within their legal systems,

Encouraging cooperation among Member States to prevent and combat illicit trafficking in nuclear materials, and recognizing in this regard existing efforts at all levels, consistent with international law,

Welcoming the technical guidance and capacity-building assistance provided by the International Atomic Energy Agency to enhance nuclear security globally,

Encouraging Member States in a position to do so to share their experience and practices in relation to the control of illicit brokering and to further enhance international cooperation to this end,

---

[2] United Nations, *Treaty Series*, vol. 2326, No. 39574.
[3] See decision 60/519 and A/60/88 and A/60/88/Corr.2, annex.
[4] See resolution 67/234 B.
[5] A/62/163 and A/62/163/Corr.1.

Noting with satisfaction the awareness-raising activities of the United Nations Institute for Disarmament Research, which contribute to efforts aimed at preventing and combating illicit brokering activities,

Acknowledging the constructive role that civil society can play in raising awareness and providing practical expertise on the prevention of illicit brokering activities,

1. *Underlines* the commitment of Member States to address the threat posed by illicit brokering activities;

2. *Encourages* Member States to fully implement relevant international treaties, instruments and resolutions to prevent and combat illicit brokering activities, and implement, where appropriate, the recommendations contained in the report of the Group of Governmental Experts;[5]

3. *Calls upon* Member States to establish appropriate national laws and/or measures to prevent and combat the illicit brokering of conventional arms and materials, equipment and technology that could contribute to the proliferation of weapons of mass destruction and their means of delivery, in a manner consistent with international law;

4. *Acknowledges* that national efforts to prevent and combat illicit brokering activities can be reinforced by such efforts at the regional and subregional levels;

5. *Emphasizes* the importance of international cooperation and assistance, capacity-building and information-sharing in preventing and combating illicit brokering activities, and encourages Member States to take such measures as appropriate and in a manner consistent with international law;

6. *Encourages* Member States to draw, where appropriate, on the relevant expertise of civil society in developing effective measures to prevent and combat illicit brokering activities.

Action by the General Assembly

Date:	5 December 2018	Meeting:	45th plenary meeting
Vote:	185-1-2	Report:	A/73/510
	157-0-19, p.p. 9		

Sponsors

Albania, Argentina, **Australia**, Austria, Belgium, Bulgaria, Canada, Croatia, Cyprus, Czechia, Denmark, Estonia, Finland, France, Germany, Greece, Haiti, Hungary, Ireland, Italy, Jamaica, Japan, Latvia, Lithuania, Luxembourg, Malta, Montenegro, Netherlands, Poland, Portugal, **Republic of Korea**, Romania, San Marino, Serbia, Slovakia, Spain, Sweden

Co-sponsors

Bosnia and Herzegovina, Central African Republic, Chile, Iceland, Malawi, Monaco, Norway, Republic of Moldova, Slovenia, the former Yugoslav Republic of Macedonia, Ukraine, United Kingdom, United States

Recorded vote

As a whole

In favour:

Afghanistan, Albania, Algeria, Andorra, Angola, Antigua and Barbuda, Argentina, Armenia, Australia, Austria, Azerbaijan, Bahamas, Bahrain, Bangladesh, Barbados, Belarus, Belgium, Belize, Benin, Bhutan, Bolivia (Plurinational State of), Bosnia and Herzegovina, Botswana, Brazil, Brunei Darussalam, Bulgaria, Burkina Faso, Burundi, Cabo Verde, Cambodia, Cameroon, Canada, Central African Republic, Chile, China, Colombia, Comoros, Congo, Costa Rica, Côte d'Ivoire, Croatia, Cuba, Cyprus, Czechia, Democratic Republic of the Congo, Denmark, Djibouti, Dominica, Dominican Republic, Ecuador, El Salvador, Equatorial Guinea, Eritrea, Estonia, Eswatini, Ethiopia, Fiji, Finland, France, Gabon, Gambia, Georgia, Germany, Ghana, Greece, Grenada, Guatemala, Guinea, Guinea-Bissau, Guyana, Haiti, Honduras, Hungary, Iceland, India, Indonesia, Iraq, Ireland, Israel, Italy, Jamaica, Japan, Jordan, Kazakhstan, Kenya, Kuwait, Kyrgyzstan, Lao People's Democratic Republic, Latvia, Lebanon, Lesotho, Liberia, Libya, Liechtenstein, Lithuania, Luxembourg, Madagascar, Malawi, Malaysia, Maldives, Mali, Malta, Marshall Islands, Mauritania, Mauritius, Mexico, Micronesia (Federated States of), Monaco, Mongolia, Montenegro, Morocco, Mozambique, Myanmar, Namibia, Nepal, Netherlands, New Zealand, Nicaragua, Niger, Nigeria, Norway, Oman, Pakistan, Palau, Panama, Papua New Guinea, Paraguay, Peru, Philippines, Poland, Portugal, Qatar, Republic of Korea, Republic of Moldova, Romania, Russian Federation, Rwanda, Saint Kitts and Nevis, Saint Lucia, Saint Vincent and the Grenadines, Samoa, San Marino, Sao Tome and Principe, Saudi Arabia, Senegal, Serbia, Seychelles, Sierra Leone, Singapore, Slovakia, Slovenia, Solomon Islands, South Africa, Spain, Sri Lanka, Sudan, Suriname, Sweden, Switzerland, Syrian Arab Republic, Tajikistan, Thailand, the former Yugoslav Republic of Macedonia, Timor-Leste, Togo, Tonga, Trinidad and Tobago, Tunisia, Turkey, Turkmenistan, Tuvalu, Uganda, Ukraine, United Arab Emirates, United Kingdom, United Republic of Tanzania, United States, Uruguay, Uzbekistan, Vanuatu, Venezuela (Bolivarian Republic of), Viet Nam, Yemen, Zambia, Zimbabwe

Against:
Democratic People's Republic of Korea

Abstaining:
Egypt, Iran (Islamic Republic of)

Ninth preambular paragraph

In favour:
> Afghanistan, Albania, Algeria, Andorra, Angola, Antigua and Barbuda, Argentina, Australia, Austria, Bahamas, Bahrain, Bangladesh, Barbados, Belgium, Belize, Benin, Bhutan, Bosnia and Herzegovina, Botswana, Brazil, Brunei Darussalam, Bulgaria, Burkina Faso, Burundi, Cabo Verde, Cambodia, Canada, Chile, China, Colombia, Comoros, Costa Rica, Côte d'Ivoire, Croatia, Cyprus, Czechia, Denmark, Djibouti, Dominican Republic, El Salvador, Equatorial Guinea, Eritrea, Estonia, Eswatini, Ethiopia, Fiji, Finland, France, Gabon, Gambia, Georgia, Germany, Ghana, Greece, Guatemala, Guinea, Guinea-Bissau, Guyana, Haiti, Honduras, Hungary, Iceland, Ireland, Israel, Italy, Jamaica, Japan, Jordan, Kazakhstan, Kenya, Kuwait, Latvia, Lebanon, Lesotho, Liberia, Libya, Liechtenstein, Lithuania, Luxembourg, Madagascar, Malawi, Malaysia, Maldives, Mali, Malta, Marshall Islands, Mauritania, Mauritius, Mexico, Micronesia (Federated States of), Monaco, Mongolia, Montenegro, Morocco, Mozambique, Myanmar, Namibia, Nepal, Netherlands, New Zealand, Niger, Nigeria, Norway, Oman, Pakistan, Palau, Panama, Papua New Guinea, Paraguay, Peru, Philippines, Poland, Portugal, Qatar, Republic of Korea, Republic of Moldova, Romania, Rwanda, Saint Kitts and Nevis, Saint Lucia, Saint Vincent and the Grenadines, Samoa, San Marino, Sao Tome and Principe, Saudi Arabia, Senegal, Serbia, Seychelles, Sierra Leone, Singapore, Slovakia, Slovenia, Solomon Islands, South Africa, Spain, Sudan, Suriname, Sweden, Switzerland, Thailand, the former Yugoslav Republic of Macedonia, Timor-Leste, Togo, Trinidad and Tobago, Tunisia, Turkey, Turkmenistan, Tuvalu, Ukraine, United Arab Emirates, United Kingdom, United Republic of Tanzania, United States, Uruguay, Vanuatu, Yemen, Zambia

Against:
> None

Abstaining:
> Azerbaijan, Belarus, Bolivia (Plurinational State of), Cuba, Democratic People's Republic of Korea, Ecuador, Egypt, India, Indonesia, Iran (Islamic Republic of), Iraq, Nicaragua, Russian Federation, Sri Lanka, Syrian Arab Republic, Tajikistan, Uganda, Venezuela (Bolivarian Republic of), Zimbabwe

Action by the First Committee

Date:	6 November 2018	Meeting:	29th meeting
Vote:	177-1-2	Draft resolution:	A/C.1/73/L.55
	149-0-20, p.p. 9		

Agenda item 101 (i)

73/64   Follow-up to the advisory opinion of the International Court of Justice on the legality of the threat or use of nuclear weapons

Text

The General Assembly,

Recalling its resolutions 49/75 K of 15 December 1994, 51/45 M of 10 December 1996, 52/38 O of 9 December 1997, 53/77 W of 4 December 1998, 54/54 Q of 1 December 1999, 55/33 X of 20 November 2000, 56/24 S of 29 November 2001, 57/85 of 22 November 2002, 58/46 of 8 December 2003, 59/83 of 3 December 2004, 60/76 of 8 December 2005, 61/83 of 6 December 2006, 62/39 of 5 December 2007, 63/49 of 2 December 2008, 64/55 of 2 December 2009, 65/76 of 8 December 2010, 66/46 of 2 December 2011, 67/33 of 3 December 2012, 68/42 of 5 December 2013, 69/43 of 2 December 2014, 70/56 of 7 December 2015, 71/58 of 5 December 2016 and 72/58 of 4 December 2017,

Convinced that the continuing existence of nuclear weapons poses a threat to humanity and all life on Earth, and recognizing that the only defence against a nuclear catastrophe is the total elimination of nuclear weapons and the certainty that they will never be produced again,

Reaffirming the commitment of the international community to the realization of the goal of a nuclear-weapon-free world through the total elimination of nuclear weapons,

Mindful of the solemn obligations of States parties, in particular the obligations undertaken in article VI of the Treaty on the Non-Proliferation of Nuclear Weapons,[1] to pursue negotiations in good faith on effective measures relating to cessation of the nuclear arms race at an early date and to nuclear disarmament,

Recalling the principles and objectives for nuclear non-proliferation and disarmament adopted at the 1995 Review and Extension Conference of the Parties to the Treaty on the Non-Proliferation of Nuclear Weapons,[2] the unequivocal commitment of nuclear-weapon States to accomplish the total elimination of their nuclear arsenals leading to nuclear disarmament, agreed at the 2000 Review Conference of the Parties to the Treaty on the

---

[1]   United Nations, *Treaty Series*, vol. 729, No. 10485.

[2]   *1995 Review and Extension Conference of the Parties to the Treaty on the Non-Proliferation of Nuclear Weapons, Final Document, Part I* (NPT/CONF.1995/32 (Part I) and NPT/CONF.1995/32 (Part I)/Corr.2), annex, decision 2.

Non-Proliferation of Nuclear Weapons,[3] and the action points agreed at the 2010 Review Conference of the Parties to the Treaty on the Non-Proliferation of Nuclear Weapons as part of the conclusions and recommendations for follow-on actions on nuclear disarmament,[4]

Sharing the deep concern at the catastrophic humanitarian consequences of any use of nuclear weapons, and in this context reaffirming the need for all States at all times to comply with applicable international law, including international humanitarian law,

Calling upon all nuclear-weapon States to undertake concrete disarmament efforts, and stressing that all States need to make special efforts to achieve and maintain a world without nuclear weapons,

Recalling the five-point proposal for nuclear disarmament of the Secretary-General, in which he proposes, inter alia, the consideration of negotiations on a nuclear weapons convention or agreement on a framework of separate mutually reinforcing instruments, backed by a strong system of verification,

Noting continued efforts towards realizing nuclear disarmament, including through the Secretary-General's disarmament agenda, *Securing Our Common Future: An Agenda for Disarmament,*

Recalling the adoption of the Comprehensive Nuclear-Test-Ban Treaty in its resolution 50/245 of 10 September 1996, and expressing its satisfaction at the increasing number of States that have signed and ratified the Treaty,

Recognizing with satisfaction that the Antarctic Treaty,[5] the treaties of Tlatelolco,[6] Rarotonga,[7] Bangkok[8] and Pelindaba[9] and the Treaty on a Nuclear-Weapon-Free Zone in Central Asia, as well as Mongolia's nuclear-weapon-free status, are gradually freeing the entire southern hemisphere and adjacent areas covered by those treaties from nuclear weapons,

Recognizing the need for a multilaterally negotiated and legally binding instrument to assure non-nuclear-weapon States against the threat or use of nuclear weapons pending the total elimination of nuclear weapons,

Reaffirming the central role of the Conference on Disarmament as the sole multilateral disarmament negotiating forum,

---

[3] See *2000 Review Conference of the Parties to the Treaty on the Non-Proliferation of Nuclear Weapons, Final Document*, vol. I (NPT/CONF.2000/28 (Parts I and II)), part I, section entitled "Article VI and eighth to twelfth preambular paragraphs", para. 15.

[4] See *2010 Review Conference of the Parties to the Treaty on the Non-Proliferation of Nuclear Weapons, Final Document*, vol. I (NPT/CONF.2010/50 (Vol. I)), part I.

[5] United Nations, *Treaty Series*, vol. 402, No. 5778.

[6] Ibid., vol. 634, No. 9068.

[7] *The United Nations Disarmament Yearbook*, vol. 10: 1985 (United Nations publication, Sales No. E.86.IX.7), appendix VII.

[8] United Nations, *Treaty Series*, vol. 1981, No. 33873.

[9] A/50/426, annex.

Emphasizing the need for the Conference on Disarmament to commence negotiations on a phased programme for the complete elimination of nuclear weapons with a specified framework of time,

Stressing the urgent need for the nuclear-weapon States to accelerate concrete progress on the 13 practical steps to implement article VI of the Treaty on the Non-Proliferation of Nuclear Weapons leading to nuclear disarmament, contained in the Final Document of the 2000 Review Conference,

Recalling the Model Nuclear Weapons Convention submitted to the Secretary-General by Costa Rica and Malaysia in 2007 and circulated by the Secretary-General,[10]

Welcoming the adoption on 7 July 2017 of the Treaty on the Prohibition of Nuclear Weapons,[11] which has contributed to achieving the objective of a legally binding prohibition of the development, production, testing, deployment, stockpiling, threat or use of nuclear weapons and their destruction under effective international control,

Recalling the advisory opinion of the International Court of Justice on the legality of the threat or use of nuclear weapons, issued on 8 July 1996,[12]

1. *Underlines* once again the unanimous conclusion of the International Court of Justice that there exists an obligation to pursue in good faith and bring to a conclusion negotiations leading to nuclear disarmament in all its aspects under strict and effective international control;

2. *Calls once again upon* all States to immediately engage in multilateral negotiations leading to nuclear disarmament in all its aspects under strict and effective international control, including under the Treaty on the Prohibition of Nuclear Weapons;[11]

3. *Requests* all States to inform the Secretary-General of the efforts and measures which they have taken with respect to the implementation of the present resolution and nuclear disarmament, and requests the Secretary-General to apprise the General Assembly of that information at its seventy-fourth session;

4. *Decides* to include in the provisional agenda of its seventy-fourth session, under the item entitled "General and complete disarmament", the sub-item entitled "Follow-up to the advisory opinion of the International Court of Justice on the legality of the threat or use of nuclear weapons".

---

[10] A/62/650, annex.
[11] A/CONF.229/2017/8.
[12] A/51/218, annex.

Action by the General Assembly

Date: 5 December 2018   Meeting: 45th plenary meeting
Vote: 138-32-17   Report: A/73/510
      138-2-31, p.p. 9
      118-35-20, p.p. 17
      121-35-18, o.p. 2

Sponsors

Algeria, Belize, Bolivia (Plurinational State of), Brunei Darussalam, Costa Rica, Cuba, Egypt, Guatemala, Honduras, Iran (Islamic Republic of), Iraq, Lao People's Democratic Republic, Malawi, **Malaysia**, Myanmar, Nepal, Nicaragua, Peru, Philippines, Samoa, Singapore, Thailand, Uruguay, Viet Nam, Zimbabwe

Co-sponsors

Bahamas, Bangladesh, Burkina Faso, Cambodia, Chile, Côte d'Ivoire, Ecuador, El Salvador, Indonesia, Jamaica, Kazakhstan, Lebanon, Madagascar, Maldives, Mexico, Morocco, Palau, Sri Lanka, Timor-Leste, Tunisia, Venezuela (Bolivarian Republic of)

Recorded vote

As a whole

In favour:

Afghanistan, Algeria, Andorra, Angola, Antigua and Barbuda, Argentina, Austria, Azerbaijan, Bahamas, Bahrain, Bangladesh, Barbados, Belize, Benin, Bhutan, Bolivia (Plurinational State of), Botswana, Brazil, Brunei Darussalam, Burkina Faso, Burundi, Cabo Verde, Cambodia, Cameroon, Central African Republic, Chile, China, Colombia, Comoros, Congo, Costa Rica, Côte d'Ivoire, Cuba, Cyprus, Democratic Republic of the Congo, Djibouti, Dominica, Dominican Republic, Ecuador, Egypt, El Salvador, Equatorial Guinea, Eritrea, Ethiopia, Fiji, Gabon, Gambia, Ghana, Grenada, Guatemala, Guinea, Guinea-Bissau, Guyana, Honduras, Indonesia, Iran (Islamic Republic of), Iraq, Ireland, Jamaica, Jordan, Kazakhstan, Kenya, Kuwait, Kyrgyzstan, Lao People's Democratic Republic, Lebanon, Lesotho, Liberia, Libya, Liechtenstein, Madagascar, Malawi, Malaysia, Maldives, Mali, Malta, Mauritania, Mauritius, Mexico, Mongolia, Morocco, Mozambique, Myanmar, Namibia, Nepal, New Zealand, Nicaragua, Niger, Nigeria, Oman, Pakistan, Palau, Panama, Papua New Guinea, Paraguay, Peru, Philippines, Qatar, Republic of Moldova, Rwanda, Saint Kitts and Nevis, Saint Lucia, Saint Vincent and the Grenadines, Samoa, San Marino, Sao Tome and Principe, Saudi Arabia, Senegal, Seychelles, Sierra Leone, Singapore, Solomon Islands, South Africa, Sri Lanka, Sudan, Suriname, Sweden, Switzerland, Syrian

Arab Republic, Tajikistan, Thailand, Timor-Leste, Togo, Tonga, Trinidad and Tobago, Tunisia, Turkmenistan, Tuvalu, Uganda, United Arab Emirates, United Republic of Tanzania, Uruguay, Vanuatu, Venezuela (Bolivarian Republic of), Viet Nam, Yemen, Zambia, Zimbabwe

Against:

Albania, Australia, Belgium, Bulgaria, Croatia, Czechia, Denmark, Estonia, France, Germany, Greece, Hungary, Israel, Italy, Latvia, Lithuania, Luxembourg, Monaco, Montenegro, Netherlands, Norway, Poland, Portugal, Republic of Korea, Romania, Russian Federation, Slovakia, Slovenia, Spain, Turkey, United Kingdom, United States

Abstaining:

Armenia, Belarus, Bosnia and Herzegovina, Canada, Democratic People's Republic of Korea, Eswatini, Finland, Georgia, Iceland, India, Japan, Marshall Islands, Micronesia (Federated States of), Serbia, the former Yugoslav Republic of Macedonia, Ukraine, Uzbekistan

Ninth preambular paragraph

In favour:

Algeria, Andorra, Angola, Antigua and Barbuda, Argentina, Australia, Austria, Azerbaijan, Bahamas, Bahrain, Bangladesh, Barbados, Belarus, Belize, Benin, Bhutan, Bolivia (Plurinational State of), Botswana, Brazil, Brunei Darussalam, Burkina Faso, Burundi, Cabo Verde, Cambodia, Canada, Chile, China, Colombia, Comoros, Costa Rica, Côte d'Ivoire, Cuba, Cyprus, Democratic People's Republic of Korea, Democratic Republic of the Congo, Djibouti, Dominican Republic, Ecuador, Egypt, El Salvador, Equatorial Guinea, Eritrea, Eswatini, Ethiopia, Fiji, Finland, Gambia, Ghana, Guatemala, Guinea, Guinea-Bissau, Guyana, Honduras, India, Indonesia, Iraq, Ireland, Jamaica, Japan, Jordan, Kazakhstan, Kenya, Kuwait, Kyrgyzstan, Lao People's Democratic Republic, Lebanon, Lesotho, Liberia, Libya, Liechtenstein, Madagascar, Malawi, Malaysia, Maldives, Mali, Malta, Mauritania, Mauritius, Mexico, Mongolia, Morocco, Mozambique, Myanmar, Namibia, Nepal, Netherlands, New Zealand, Nicaragua, Niger, Nigeria, Oman, Pakistan, Panama, Papua New Guinea, Paraguay, Peru, Philippines, Qatar, Republic of Korea, Republic of Moldova, Saint Kitts and Nevis, Saint Lucia, Saint Vincent and the Grenadines, Samoa, San Marino, Sao Tome and Principe, Saudi Arabia, Senegal, Serbia, Seychelles, Sierra Leone, Singapore, Solomon Islands, South Africa, Sri Lanka, Sudan, Suriname, Sweden, Switzerland, Tajikistan, Thailand, Timor-Leste, Togo, Trinidad and Tobago, Tunisia, Turkmenistan, Tuvalu, Uganda, United Arab Emirates, United Republic of Tanzania, Uruguay, Uzbekistan, Vanuatu, Venezuela (Bolivarian Republic of), Viet Nam, Yemen, Zambia, Zimbabwe

Against:

France, United States

Abstaining:

> Albania, Armenia, Belgium, Bosnia and Herzegovina, Bulgaria, Croatia, Czechia, Denmark, Estonia, Georgia, Germany, Greece, Hungary, Israel, Italy, Latvia, Lithuania, Luxembourg, Montenegro, Poland, Portugal, Romania, Russian Federation, Slovakia, Slovenia, Spain, Syrian Arab Republic, the former Yugoslav Republic of Macedonia, Turkey, Ukraine, United Kingdom

Seventeenth preambular paragraph

In favour:

> Afghanistan, Algeria, Andorra, Angola, Antigua and Barbuda, Argentina, Austria, Azerbaijan, Bahamas, Bahrain, Bangladesh, Barbados, Belize, Benin, Bhutan, Bolivia (Plurinational State of), Botswana, Brazil, Brunei Darussalam, Burkina Faso, Burundi, Cabo Verde, Cambodia, Chile, Colombia, Comoros, Costa Rica, Côte d'Ivoire, Cuba, Cyprus, Democratic Republic of the Congo, Djibouti, Dominican Republic, Ecuador, Egypt, El Salvador, Eritrea, Ethiopia, Fiji, Gambia, Ghana, Guatemala, Guinea, Guinea-Bissau, Guyana, Honduras, Indonesia, Iran (Islamic Republic of), Iraq, Ireland, Jamaica, Jordan, Kazakhstan, Kenya, Kuwait, Lao People's Democratic Republic, Lebanon, Lesotho, Libya, Liechtenstein, Madagascar, Malawi, Malaysia, Maldives, Mali, Malta, Mauritania, Mauritius, Mexico, Mongolia, Morocco, Mozambique, Myanmar, Namibia, Nepal, New Zealand, Nicaragua, Niger, Nigeria, Oman, Panama, Papua New Guinea, Paraguay, Peru, Philippines, Qatar, Republic of Moldova, Saint Kitts and Nevis, Saint Lucia, Saint Vincent and the Grenadines, Samoa, San Marino, Sao Tome and Principe, Saudi Arabia, Senegal, Singapore, Solomon Islands, South Africa, Sri Lanka, Sudan, Suriname, Thailand, Timor-Leste, Togo, Trinidad and Tobago, Tunisia, Turkmenistan, Tuvalu, Uganda, United Arab Emirates, United Republic of Tanzania, Uruguay, Vanuatu, Venezuela (Bolivarian Republic of), Viet Nam, Yemen, Zambia, Zimbabwe

Against:

> Albania, Australia, Belgium, Bulgaria, Canada, China, Croatia, Czechia, Denmark, Estonia, France, Germany, Greece, Hungary, Iceland, Israel, Italy, Latvia, Lithuania, Luxembourg, Monaco, Montenegro, Netherlands, Norway, Poland, Portugal, Republic of Korea, Romania, Russian Federation, Slovakia, Slovenia, Spain, Turkey, United Kingdom, United States

Abstaining:

> Armenia, Belarus, Bosnia and Herzegovina, Democratic People's Republic of Korea, Equatorial Guinea, Eswatini, Finland, Georgia, India, Japan, Kyrgyzstan, Liberia, Pakistan, Serbia, Sweden, Switzerland, Tajikistan, the former Yugoslav Republic of Macedonia, Ukraine, Uzbekistan

Operative paragraph 2

In favour:

Afghanistan, Algeria, Andorra, Angola, Antigua and Barbuda, Argentina, Austria, Azerbaijan, Bahamas, Bahrain, Bangladesh, Barbados, Belize, Benin, Bhutan, Bolivia (Plurinational State of), Botswana, Brazil, Brunei Darussalam, Burkina Faso, Burundi, Cabo Verde, Cambodia, Chile, Colombia, Comoros, Costa Rica, Côte d'Ivoire, Cuba, Cyprus, Democratic Republic of the Congo, Djibouti, Dominican Republic, Ecuador, Egypt, El Salvador, Eritrea, Ethiopia, Fiji, Gambia, Ghana, Guatemala, Guinea, Guinea-Bissau, Guyana, Honduras, Indonesia, Iran (Islamic Republic of), Iraq, Ireland, Jamaica, Jordan, Kazakhstan, Kenya, Kuwait, Lao People's Democratic Republic, Lebanon, Lesotho, Liberia, Libya, Liechtenstein, Madagascar, Malawi, Malaysia, Maldives, Mali, Malta, Mauritania, Mauritius, Mexico, Mongolia, Morocco, Mozambique, Myanmar, Namibia, Nepal, New Zealand, Nicaragua, Niger, Nigeria, Oman, Panama, Papua New Guinea, Paraguay, Peru, Philippines, Qatar, Republic of Moldova, Saint Kitts and Nevis, Saint Lucia, Saint Vincent and the Grenadines, Samoa, San Marino, Sao Tome and Principe, Saudi Arabia, Senegal, Sierra Leone, Singapore, Solomon Islands, South Africa, Sri Lanka, Sudan, Suriname, Syrian Arab Republic, Thailand, Timor-Leste, Togo, Trinidad and Tobago, Tunisia, Turkmenistan, Tuvalu, Uganda, United Arab Emirates, United Republic of Tanzania, Uruguay, Vanuatu, Venezuela (Bolivarian Republic of), Viet Nam, Yemen, Zambia, Zimbabwe

Against:

Albania, Australia, Belgium, Bulgaria, Canada, China, Croatia, Czechia, Denmark, Estonia, France, Germany, Greece, Hungary, Iceland, Israel, Italy, Latvia, Lithuania, Luxembourg, Monaco, Montenegro, Netherlands, Norway, Poland, Portugal, Republic of Korea, Romania, Russian Federation, Slovakia, Slovenia, Spain, Turkey, United Kingdom, United States

Abstaining:

Armenia, Belarus, Bosnia and Herzegovina, Democratic People's Republic of Korea, Equatorial Guinea, Eswatini, Finland, Georgia, India, Japan, Kyrgyzstan, Pakistan, Serbia, Sweden, Switzerland, Tajikistan, the former Yugoslav Republic of Macedonia, Ukraine

Action by the First Committee

Date: 1 November 2018 Meeting: 26th meeting
Vote: 131-31-19 Draft resolution: A/C.1/73/L.57/Rev.1
   137-1-35, p.p. 9
   118-34-23, p.p. 17
   120-34-22, o.p. 2

Agenda item 101 (a)

73/65   Treaty banning the production of fissile material for nuclear weapons or other nuclear explosive devices

Text

The General Assembly,

Recalling its resolutions 48/75 L of 16 December 1993, 53/77 I of 4 December 1998, 55/33 Y of 20 November 2000, 56/24 J of 29 November 2001, 57/80 of 22 November 2002, 58/57 of 8 December 2003, 59/81 of 3 December 2004, 64/29 of 2 December 2009, 65/65 of 8 December 2010, 66/44 of 2 December 2011 and 67/53 of 3 December 2012, its decisions 68/518 of 5 December 2013 and 69/516 of 2 December 2014, its resolutions 70/39 of 7 December 2015 and 71/259 of 23 December 2016, as well as its decision 72/513 of 4 December 2017, on the subject of a treaty banning the production of fissile material for nuclear weapons or other nuclear explosive devices,

Recalling also document CD/1299 of 24 March 1995, which indicated that all members of the Conference on Disarmament had agreed that the mandate to negotiate a treaty banning the production of fissile material for nuclear weapons or other nuclear explosive devices would not preclude any delegation from raising for consideration, in negotiations, any issue noted therein,

Reaffirming the importance of ensuring continued international commitment and high-level attention to making practical progress on achieving a world without nuclear weapons and on non-proliferation in all its aspects,

Mindful of the continuing importance and relevance of the Conference on Disarmament, and recalling the past achievements of that body in successfully negotiating non-proliferation and disarmament agreements,

Taking into account the adoption by consensus of the report of subsidiary body 2 of the Conference on Disarmament on prevention of nuclear war, including all related matters, with a general focus on a ban of the production of fissile materials for nuclear weapons and other explosive devices,[1]

Looking forward to the Conference again fulfilling its mandate as the world's single multilateral disarmament negotiating forum,

Convinced that a non-discriminatory, multilateral and effectively verifiable treaty banning the production of fissile material for nuclear weapons

---

[1] CD/2139.

or other nuclear explosive devices would represent a significant practical contribution to nuclear disarmament and non-proliferation efforts,

Recognizing the essential role of fissile material in the manufacture of nuclear weapons or other nuclear explosive devices and the long-standing efforts of the international community to negotiate a treaty that would ban its production for such purposes,

Recognizing also that a future treaty should not prohibit the production of fissile material for non-proscribed military purposes or civilian use, consistent with the obligations of States parties, or interfere in any other way with a State's right to peaceful uses of nuclear energy,

Recalling action 15 of the conclusions and recommendations for follow-on actions agreed by consensus at the 2010 Review Conference of the Parties to the Treaty on the Non-Proliferation of Nuclear Weapons[2] that, inter alia, the Conference on Disarmament should, within the context of an agreed, comprehensive and balanced programme of work, immediately begin negotiation of a treaty banning the production of fissile material for use in nuclear weapons or other nuclear explosive devices in accordance with the report of the Special Coordinator of 1995 (CD/1299) and the mandate contained therein,

Underlining that the consensus report of the Group of Governmental Experts, mandated in resolution 67/53, as contained in document A/70/81, and the deliberations which underpin it, serve as a valuable reference for States and should be a useful resource for negotiators of a treaty banning the production of fissile material for nuclear weapons or other nuclear explosive devices,

Noting with appreciation the work accomplished in 2017 and 2018 by the high-level fissile material cut-off treaty expert preparatory group convened by the Secretary General following resolution 71/259, on the basis of equitable geographic distribution, to consider and make recommendations on substantial elements of a future non-discriminatory, multilateral and effectively verifiable treaty banning the production of fissile material for nuclear weapons or other nuclear explosive devices, on the basis of document CD/1299 and the mandate contained therein,

Welcoming the participation of Member States in informal consultative meetings, organized by the Chair of the high-level fissile material cut-off treaty expert preparatory group, which were open-ended so that all Member States could engage in interactive discussions and share their views on a treaty banning the production of fissile material for nuclear weapons or other nuclear explosive devices,

---

[2] See *2010 Review Conference of the Parties to the Treaty on the Non-Proliferation of Nuclear Weapons, Final Document*, vol. I (NPT/CONF.2010/50 (Vol. I)), part I, *Conclusions and recommendations for follow-on actions.*

Convinced that the report of the high-level fissile material cut-off treaty expert preparatory group, mandated in resolution 71/259, as contained in document A/73/159, read in conjunction with document A/70/81, should be taken into account by future negotiators in their deliberations,

Recognizing the importance of concerted efforts to ensure that both women and men can participate equally, fully and effectively in the negotiation process of a future treaty,

1.   *Urges* the Conference on Disarmament to agree on and implement at its earliest opportunity a programme of work that includes the immediate commencement of negotiations on a treaty banning the production of fissile material for nuclear weapons or other nuclear explosive devices on the basis of document CD/1299 and the mandate contained therein;

2.   *Welcomes* the adoption by consensus of the report of the high-level fissile material cut-off treaty expert preparatory group, mandated in resolution 71/259, as contained in document A/73/159;

3.   *Calls upon* the Secretary-General to transmit the report of the high-level fissile material cut-off treaty expert preparatory group to the Conference on Disarmament prior to its 2019 session;

4.   *Urges* Member States to give due consideration to the report of the high-level fissile material cut-off treaty expert preparatory group, in conjunction with document A/70/81, including its call that further consideration be given to measures that might facilitate the commencement of treaty negotiations and enhance confidence, and calls upon the Conference on Disarmament to fully examine the report and consider further action as appropriate;

5.   *Urges* the Conference on Disarmament to carry out further expert work to elaborate on all relevant aspects of a treaty banning the production of fissile material for nuclear weapons or other nuclear explosive devices, including how the various approaches to verification of a treaty would work in practice, and to assess the resource implications associated with the use in a treaty of the various potential elements;

6.   *Calls upon* future negotiators of a treaty to take into account the work of the high-level fissile material cut-off treaty expert preparatory group, in conjunction with the work of the Group of Governmental Experts, as appropriate in their deliberations;

7.   *Decides* to include in the provisional agenda of its seventy-fourth session, under the item entitled "General and complete disarmament", the sub-item entitled "Treaty banning the production of fissile material for nuclear weapons or other nuclear explosive devices".

Action by the General Assembly

Date: 5 December 2018   Meeting: 45th plenary meeting
Vote: 182-1-5   Report: A/73/510

Sponsors

Canada, Germany, Netherlands

Recorded vote

In favour:

Afghanistan, Albania, Algeria, Andorra, Angola, Argentina, Armenia, Australia, Austria, Azerbaijan, Bahamas, Bahrain, Bangladesh, Barbados, Belarus, Belgium, Belize, Benin, Bhutan, Bolivia (Plurinational State of), Bosnia and Herzegovina, Botswana, Brazil, Brunei Darussalam, Bulgaria, Burkina Faso, Burundi, Cabo Verde, Cambodia, Cameroon, Canada, Central African Republic, Chile, China, Colombia, Comoros, Congo, Costa Rica, Côte d'Ivoire, Croatia, Cuba, Cyprus, Czechia, Democratic Republic of the Congo, Denmark, Djibouti, Dominica, Dominican Republic, Ecuador, El Salvador, Equatorial Guinea, Eritrea, Estonia, Eswatini, Ethiopia, Fiji, Finland, France, Gabon, Gambia, Georgia, Germany, Ghana, Greece, Grenada, Guatemala, Guinea, Guinea-Bissau, Guyana, Haiti, Honduras, Hungary, Iceland, India, Indonesia, Iraq, Ireland, Italy, Jamaica, Japan, Jordan, Kazakhstan, Kenya, Kuwait, Kyrgyzstan, Lao People's Democratic Republic, Latvia, Lebanon, Lesotho, Liberia, Libya, Liechtenstein, Lithuania, Luxembourg, Madagascar, Malawi, Malaysia, Maldives, Mali, Malta, Marshall Islands, Mauritania, Mauritius, Mexico, Micronesia (Federated States of), Monaco, Mongolia, Montenegro, Morocco, Mozambique, Myanmar, Namibia, Nauru, Nepal, Netherlands, New Zealand, Nicaragua, Niger, Nigeria, Norway, Oman, Palau, Panama, Papua New Guinea, Paraguay, Peru, Philippines, Poland, Portugal, Qatar, Republic of Korea, Republic of Moldova, Romania, Russian Federation, Rwanda, Saint Kitts and Nevis, Saint Lucia, Saint Vincent and the Grenadines, Samoa, San Marino, Sao Tome and Principe, Saudi Arabia, Senegal, Serbia, Seychelles, Sierra Leone, Singapore, Slovakia, Slovenia, Solomon Islands, South Africa, Spain, Sri Lanka, Sudan, Suriname, Sweden, Switzerland, Tajikistan, Thailand, the former Yugoslav Republic of Macedonia, Timor-Leste, Togo, Tonga, Trinidad and Tobago, Tunisia, Turkey, Turkmenistan, Tuvalu, Uganda, Ukraine, United Arab Emirates, United Kingdom, United Republic of Tanzania, United States, Uruguay, Uzbekistan, Vanuatu, Venezuela (Bolivarian Republic of), Viet Nam, Yemen, Zambia, Zimbabwe

Against:

Pakistan

Abstaining:
> Democratic People's Republic of Korea, Egypt, Iran (Islamic Republic of), Israel, Syrian Arab Republic

Action by the First Committee

Date: 1 November 2018	Meeting:	26th meeting
Vote: 180-1-5	Draft resolution:	A/C.1/73/L.58

Agenda item 101 (dd)

73/66   Preventing the acquisition by terrorists of radioactive sources

Text

The General Assembly,

Recalling its resolutions 62/46 of 5 December 2007, 65/74 of 8 December 2010, 67/51 of 3 December 2012, 69/50 of 2 December 2014 and 71/66 of 5 December 2016,

Recognizing the essential contribution of radioactive sources to social and economic development, and the benefits drawn from their use for all States,

Recognizing also the determination of the international community to combat terrorism, as evident in relevant General Assembly and Security Council resolutions,

Noting with satisfaction the continued international efforts to strengthen further the security of radioactive sources worldwide,

Mindful of the responsibilities of every Member State, in accordance with their national legal frameworks and international obligations, to maintain effective nuclear safety and security, asserting that responsibility for nuclear security within a State rests entirely with that State, and noting the important contribution of international cooperation in supporting the efforts of States to fulfil their responsibilities,

Deeply concerned by the threat of terrorism and the risk that terrorists may acquire, traffic in or use radioactive sources in radiological dispersion devices,

Deeply concerned also by the potential threat to human health and the environment that would result from the use of such devices by terrorists,

Noting with concern the occurrence of nuclear and radioactive materials that are outside of regulatory control or being trafficked,

Recalling the importance of international conventions aimed at preventing and suppressing such a risk, in particular the International Convention for the Suppression of Acts of Nuclear Terrorism, adopted on 13 April 2005,[1] and the Convention on the Physical Protection of Nuclear Material, adopted on 26 October 1979,[2] as well as its Amendment, adopted on 8 July 2005,[3] which entered into force on 8 May 2016,

---

[1] United Nations, *Treaty Series*, vol. 2445, No. 44004.
[2] Ibid., vol. 1456, No. 24631.
[3] See International Atomic Energy Agency, document GOV/INF/2005/10-GC(49)/INF/6, attachment.

Noting that actions of the international community to combat the proliferation of weapons of mass destruction and prevent access by non-State actors to weapons of mass destruction and related material, notably Security Council resolutions 1540 (2004) of 28 April 2004, 1977 (2011) of 20 April 2011 and 2325 (2016) of 15 December 2016, constitute contributions to the prevention of acts of terrorism using such materials,

Taking note of resolutions GC(62)/RES/6 and GC(62)/RES/7, adopted on 20 September 2018 by the General Conference of the International Atomic Energy Agency at its sixty-second regular session, which address measures to strengthen international cooperation in nuclear, radiation, transport and waste safety and measures to enhance nuclear security,

Stressing the importance of the role of the International Atomic Energy Agency in promoting and reinforcing the safety and security of radioactive sources, in particular by establishing technical guidance and supporting States in the improvement of national legal and regulatory infrastructure, and in strengthening coordination and complementarities among various nuclear or radiological security activities,

Noting the organization by the International Atomic Energy Agency of the International Conference on Nuclear Security: Enhancing Global Efforts, held in Vienna from 1 to 5 July 2013, the International Conference on the Safety and Security of Radioactive Sources: Maintaining the Continuous Global Control of Sources throughout their Life Cycle, held in Abu Dhabi from 27 to 31 October 2013, and the International Conference on Nuclear Security: Commitments and Actions, held in Vienna from 5 to 9 December 2016, as well as the upcoming International Conference on the Security of Radioactive Material: The Way Forward for Prevention and Detection, to be held in Vienna from 3 to 7 December 2018,

Noting also the utility of the Incident and Trafficking Database as a voluntary mechanism for the international exchange of information on incidents and illicit trafficking of nuclear and other radioactive material, encouraging the International Atomic Energy Agency to further facilitate, including through designated points of contact, the timely exchange of information, including through secured electronic access to information contained in the Database, and encouraging also all States to join and participate actively in the Database programme in support of their national efforts to prevent, detect and respond to radioactive and nuclear materials that may have fallen out of regulatory control,

Noting further the importance of the Joint Convention on the Safety of Spent Fuel Management and on the Safety of Radioactive Waste Management[4] with respect to its provisions on the safety of disused sealed sources,

---

[4] United Nations, *Treaty Series*, vol. 2153, No. 37605.

Highlighting the importance of the Code of Conduct on the Safety and Security of Radioactive Sources, of its supplementary Guidance on the Import and Export of Radioactive Sources and of its supplementary Guidance on the Management of Disused Radioactive Sources as valuable instruments for enhancing the safety and security of radioactive sources, noting that 137 States members of the International Atomic Energy Agency have made a political commitment to implement the provisions of the Code and 114 States have made a similar commitment to the supplementary Guidance on the Import and Export of Radioactive Sources, while recognizing that they are not legally binding,

Noting that a number of States have not yet become parties to the pertinent international instruments,

Taking note of the Nuclear Security Plan for 2018–2021 of the International Atomic Energy Agency, and encouraging Member States to make voluntary contributions to the International Atomic Energy Agency Nuclear Security Fund,

Welcoming the fact that Member States have taken multilateral actions to address the security of radioactive sources, as reflected in General Assembly resolution 72/5 of 10 November 2017,

Noting the various international efforts and partnerships to enhance nuclear and radiological security, encouraging further efforts to secure radioactive sources, and noting also in this respect guidance and recommendations of the International Atomic Energy Agency with regard to safe and secure management of radioactive sources,

Taking note of the findings of the International Conference on the Safety and Security of Radioactive Sources of 2013, which, inter alia, call for further assessment of the merits of developing an international convention on the safety and security of radioactive sources so that Member States can make the best-informed decisions on the matter,

Noting that the Radiological and Nuclear Terrorism Prevention Unit of the International Criminal Police Organization (INTERPOL) works with nations to strengthen capabilities to counter radioactive source smuggling and prevent terrorists from acquiring such materials, and that INTERPOL Operation Fail Safe promotes the sharing of sensitive law-enforcement information on known nuclear smugglers,

Welcoming the ongoing individual and collective efforts of Member States to take into account in their deliberations the dangers posed by the lack or insufficiency of control over radioactive sources, and recognizing the need for States to take more effective measures to strengthen those controls in accordance with their national legal authorities and legislation and consistent with international law,

Mindful of the urgent need to address, within the United Nations framework and through international cooperation, this rising concern for international security,

1.   *Calls upon* Member States to support international efforts to prevent the acquisition and use by terrorists of radioactive sources and, if necessary, suppress such acts, in accordance with their national legal authorities and legislation and consistent with international law;

2.   *Encourages* all Member States that have not yet done so to become party to the International Convention for the Suppression of Acts of Nuclear Terrorism[1] as soon as possible, in accordance with their legal and constitutional processes;

3.   *Invites* Member States, in coordination with the International Atomic Energy Agency and in accordance with its statute, to consider the merits of conducting an evaluation of the existing international framework applicable to the security of radioactive sources and, if necessary, to explore possible options for its potential strengthening;

4.   *Urges* Member States to take and strengthen national measures and capabilities, as appropriate, to prevent the acquisition and use by terrorists of radioactive sources as well as terrorist attacks on nuclear plants and facilities which would result in radioactive releases, and, if necessary, to suppress such acts, in particular by taking effective measures to account for, control, secure and physically protect such facilities, materials and sources in accordance with their national legal authorities and legislation and consistent with their international obligations;

5.   *Encourages* Member States to enhance their national capacities with appropriate means of detection and related architecture or systems, including through international cooperation and assistance in conformity with international law and regulations, with a view to preventing, detecting and responding to illicit trafficking in radioactive sources;

6.   *Invites* Member States, in particular those producing and distributing radioactive sources, to support and endorse the efforts of the International Atomic Energy Agency to enhance the safety and security of radioactive sources, as described in General Conference resolutions GC(62)/RES/6 and GC(62)/RES/7, and to enhance the security of radioactive sources, as described in the Nuclear Security Plan for 2018–2021;

7.   *Urges* all States to work towards following the guidance contained in the non-legally binding International Atomic Energy Agency Code of Conduct on the Safety and Security of Radioactive Sources, including, as appropriate, the supplementary Guidance on the Import and Export of Radioactive Sources and the supplementary Guidance on the Management of Disused Radioactive Sources, and encourages Member States to notify the

Director General of the Agency of their intention to do so pursuant to General Conference resolutions GC(62)/RES/6 and GC(62)/RES/7;

8.   *Encourages* Member States to work with the International Atomic Energy Agency to enhance the non-legally binding international framework for the security of radioactive sources, especially on the safe and secure management of disused radioactive sources, in accordance with relevant resolutions of the Agency, in particular resolutions GC(62)/RES/6 and GC(62)/RES/7;

9.   *Recognizes* the value of information exchange on national approaches to controlling radioactive sources, and takes note of the endorsement by the Board of Governors of the International Atomic Energy Agency of a proposal for a formalized process for a voluntary periodic exchange on information and lessons learned and for the evaluation of progress made by States towards implementing the provisions of the Code of Conduct on the Safety and Security of Radioactive Sources;

10.   *Welcomes* the endorsement of the Guidance on the Management of Disused Radioactive Sources by the General Conference of the International Atomic Energy Agency in its resolution GC(61)/RES/8 adopted on 21 September 2017 at its sixty-first session;

11.   *Encourages* Member States to participate, on a voluntary basis, in the Incident and Trafficking Database programme of the International Atomic Energy Agency;

12.   *Welcomes* the efforts undertaken by Member States, including through international cooperation under the auspices of the International Atomic Energy Agency, to search for, locate, recover and secure lost or orphaned radioactive sources within their State jurisdiction or territory, encourages continued efforts in this way, and also encourages cooperation among and between Member States and through relevant international and, where appropriate, regional organizations aimed at strengthening national capacities in this regard;

13.   *Encourages* Member States, in accordance with their national laws, policies and priorities, to provide support for scientific research to develop technically and economically appropriate technologies with the capability to further improve the security of radioactive sources or reduce the risk of acquisition by terrorists and of malicious use of radioactive sources, including by, on a voluntary basis and when technically feasible and economically realistic, developing technologies that do not rely on high-activity radioactive sources and developing exchanges on alternative technologies, without unduly hindering the beneficial uses of radioactive sources;

14.   *Invites* all Member States to participate, on a voluntary basis, in the annual meeting of the ad hoc working group of stakeholder States involved with alternative technologies to high-activity radioactive sources;

15.   *Decides* to include in the provisional agenda of its seventy-fifth session, under the item entitled "General and complete disarmament", the sub-item entitled "Preventing the acquisition by terrorists of radioactive sources".

Action by the General Assembly

Date: 5 December 2018   Meeting: 45th plenary meeting
Vote: Adopted without a vote   Report: A/73/510

Sponsors

Australia, Bulgaria, Croatia, Cyprus, Czechia, Denmark, Estonia, Finland, **France**, **Germany**, Ghana, Greece, Haiti, Hungary, Iceland, Japan, Lithuania, Luxembourg, Montenegro, Namibia, Netherlands, Poland, Portugal, Romania, Slovakia, Spain, Sweden, United Kingdom

Co-sponsors

Albania, Andorra, Argentina, Belgium, Bosnia and Herzegovina, Canada, Equatorial Guinea, Guinea, Honduras, Ireland, Italy, Latvia, Malta, Monaco, Morocco, Norway, Paraguay, Republic of Korea, Republic of Moldova, San Marino, Slovenia, Switzerland, the former Yugoslav Republic of Macedonia, United States, Uruguay

Action by the First Committee

Date: 5 November 2018   Meeting: 28th meeting
Vote: Adopted without a vote   Draft resolution: A/C.1/73/L.59

Agenda item 101 (ii)

73/67 Countering the threat posed by improvised explosive devices

Text

The General Assembly,

Recalling its resolutions 70/46 of 7 December 2015, 71/72 of 5 December 2016 and 72/36 of 4 December 2017,

Expressing grave concern over the devastation caused by the increasing use of improvised explosive devices by illegal armed groups, terrorists and other unauthorized recipients,[1] which has affected a large number of countries and has resulted in thousands of casualties, both civilian and military, and, in this regard, stressing the need for all actors to comply with applicable international law at all times,

Expressing concern over the increased use of and sophistication of the design and means of detonation of improvised explosive devices,

Expressing profound concern at the indiscriminate use and effects of improvised explosive devices and at the increasing humanitarian impact of such attacks on civilian populations worldwide, in particular through the perpetration of terrorist acts, and noting the need for a comprehensive approach in addressing this concern,

Expressing concern at the serious harm that such improvised explosive device attacks have caused to United Nations staff and peacekeepers, and to humanitarian workers, by threatening their lives, increasing the cost of their activities, limiting their freedom of movement and affecting their ability to effectively deliver on their mandates,

Expressing concern also about the negative impact of these attacks on socioeconomic development, infrastructure and freedom of movement, and on the security and stability of States, and thus underlining the need to address this issue in order to achieve relevant goals and targets under the 2030 Agenda for Sustainable Development,[2] in particular target 16.1 on significantly reducing all forms of violence and related death rates everywhere,

Urging Member States to ensure that any measures taken or means employed to implement the present resolution comply with international law, in particular the Charter of the United Nations, applicable international humanitarian law and human rights law,

---

[1] See resolution 69/51, A/CONF.192/BMS/2014/2, A/71/187 and Security Council resolution 2370 (2017).

[2] Resolution 70/1.

Recognizing the importance of full involvement and equal opportunities for participation for both women and men in countering the threat posed by improvised explosive devices,

Underlining the importance of addressing the threat of improvised explosive devices and their differential impacts on women, girls, boys and men,

Recognizing that the wide spectrum of materials that can be used for the manufacture of improvised explosive devices, including those sourced from the military and civilian industry, contributes to their diverse nature and their deployment methods, which thus requires an appropriate approach to the formulation of measures to counter them,

Noting that the impact of improvised explosive devices spans a wide array of policy areas and that, owing to the extent of the cross-cutting nature of the issue, a whole-of-government approach focusing on the capacity of Governments to effectively bring together several policy strands for comprehensive action is essential,

Underlining the important role that States can play in raising awareness among private sector and other entities about the possible theft, diversion and misuse of their products to make improvised explosive devices, with a view to enabling those entities to develop effective strategies to counter the threat of improvised explosive devices,[3] including to prevent the adverse impact of the diversion of materials and the potential loss of revenue and risk to reputation, either in a partnership with governmental authorities, or through business-to-business processes or activities,

Noting existing industry-led initiatives that seek to increase industry oversight and accountability along the supply chain for precursor components, and encouraging States to engage, as appropriate, with private sector industry actors in supporting such initiatives,

Noting also the contribution of good governance, the promotion of human rights, the rule of law, adherence to the principles of the Charter and sustained and inclusive socioeconomic growth, including through effective measures and mechanisms for persons belonging to vulnerable groups, as important elements in comprehensively addressing the issue of improvised explosive devices, in particular in post-conflict situations,

Stressing the paramount need to prevent illegal armed groups, terrorists and other unauthorized recipients from, and identify the networks that support them in, obtaining, handling, financing, storing, using or seeking access to all types of explosives, whether military or civilian, as well as other military or civilian materials and components that can be used to manufacture improvised explosive devices, including detonators, detonating cords and chemical

---

[3] See the Guiding Principles on Business and Human Rights: Implementing the United Nations "Protect, Respect and Remedy" Framework (A/HRC/17/31, annex).

components, while at the same time avoiding any undue restrictions on the legitimate use of those materials,

Recalling, in this context, relevant resolutions on the prevention of the acquisition of weapons by terrorists, including improvised explosive device components, and their transfer to and between terrorists, associated groups and other illegal armed groups and criminals,[4]

Recalling also relevant resolutions on improvised explosive device threat mitigation, including those addressing the indiscriminate use of improvised explosive devices and the impact on peacekeeping operations, special political missions and humanitarian responses,[5]

Stressing the importance of effectively securing conventional ammunition stockpiles in order to mitigate the risk of their diversion to illicit use as materials for improvised explosive devices, and noting the voluntary, practical International Ammunition Technical Guidelines in this regard,

Stressing also the importance of engagement by all Member States in a comprehensive and coordinated community of action to counter the global threat posed by improvised explosive devices in the hands of illegal armed groups, terrorists and other unauthorized recipients, taking into account national capacities,

Noting that, at the global level, organizations across many sectors have expertise that can contribute to a useful set of measures for the mitigation of improvised explosive devices, and noting also the value of considered and coordinated efforts by various stakeholders, including intergovernmental and regional organizations and industry associations, with a view to investing effectively in coordination and information exchange,

Noting also the discussions on the issue of improvised explosive devices by the informal group of experts under the Protocol on Prohibitions or Restrictions on the Use of Mines, Booby Traps and Other Devices as amended on 3 May 1996 (Amended Protocol II)[6] and on the technical annex to the Protocol on Explosive Remnants of War (Protocol V)[7] to the Convention on Prohibitions or Restrictions on the Use of Certain Conventional Weapons Which May Be Deemed to Be Excessively Injurious or to Have Indiscriminate Effects,[8] and further noting that, for States parties thereto, anti-personnel mines of an improvised nature also fall within the scope of the Convention on the Prohibition of the Use, Stockpiling, Production and Transfer of Anti-Personnel Mines and on Their Destruction,[9]

---

[4] See Security Council resolution 2370 (2017).
[5] See Security Council resolution 2365 (2017).
[6] United Nations, *Treaty Series*, vol. 2048, No. 22495.
[7] Ibid., vol. 2399, No. 22495.
[8] Ibid., vol. 1342, No. 22495.
[9] Ibid., vol. 2056, No. 35597.

Noting further the multilateral efforts to counter improvised explosive devices of the Programme Global Shield, led by the World Customs Organization and assisted by the International Criminal Police Organization (INTERPOL) and the United Nations Office on Drugs and Crime, to prevent the smuggling and illicit diversion of precursor chemicals that could be used to build improvised explosive devices, the network of regional and multilateral communities of action established by States to counter improvised explosive devices, the research on those devices undertaken by the United Nations Institute for Disarmament Research and the work undertaken by the Mine Action Service of the United Nations to mitigate the threat posed by those devices to civilians, United Nations staff, peacekeepers and humanitarian personnel, in particular in the field,

Taking note of the International Convention for the Suppression of Terrorist Bombings[10] and the United Nations Global Counter-Terrorism Strategy[11] and the efforts undertaken to strengthen the capability of the United Nations system to assist Member States in implementing the Strategy, including through the establishment of the Office of Counter-Terrorism,[12]

Reaffirming the inherent right of Member States to individual or collective self-defence in accordance with Article 51 of the Charter,

1.   *Takes note* of the report of the Secretary-General submitted pursuant to resolution 72/36,[13] including the recommendations contained therein;

2.   *Recognizes* that existing approaches in multilateral arms regulation, while valuable, do not fully address the use of improvised explosive devices in conflict and immediate post-conflict environments, and therefore strongly urges States to develop and implement, where appropriate, all national measures, including outreach and partnerships with relevant actors, including the private sector, necessary to promote awareness, vigilance and good practices among their nationals, persons subject to their jurisdiction and firms incorporated in their territory or subject to their jurisdiction that are involved in the production, sale, supply, purchase, transfer and/or storage of precursor components and materials that could be used to make improvised explosive devices;

3.   *Strongly encourages* States, where appropriate, to develop and adopt their own national policy to counter improvised explosive devices that includes civilian-military cooperation, to strengthen their countermeasure capability, to prevent their territory from being used for terrorist purposes and to combat illegal armed groups, terrorists and other unauthorized

---

[10]   Ibid., vol. 2149, No. 37517.
[11]   Resolution 60/288.
[12]   See resolution 71/291.
[13]   A/73/156.

recipients in their use of improvised explosive devices, while bearing in mind their obligations under applicable international law, and notes that the policy could include measures to support international and regional efforts to prevent, protect against, respond to, recover from and mitigate attacks using improvised explosive devices and their widespread consequences;

4.   *Urges* all States, in particular those that have the capacity to do so, as well as the United Nations system and other relevant organizations and institutions supporting affected States, to increase attention to prevention and to provide support to reduce the risks posed by improvised explosive devices in a manner which takes into consideration the different needs of women, girls, boys and men;

5.   *Stresses* the need for States to take appropriate measures to strengthen the management of their national ammunition stockpiles to prevent the diversion of materials for making improvised explosive devices to illicit markets, illegal armed groups, terrorists and other unauthorized recipients, and encourages the application of the International Ammunition Technical Guidelines for the safer and more secure management of ammunition stockpiles, while also recognizing the importance of capacity-building, through both technical and financial assistance, in this regard, as well as the contributions made by various United Nations entities to that end;[14]

6.   *Underlines* that, for the issue of improvised explosive devices to be effectively addressed, it is essential to comprehend the importance of action needed at the local and community levels, engaging with community leaders and relevant civil society organizations through activities ranging from awareness-raising of the threat posed by such devices and of possible threat mitigation measures, in conjunction with distributors and local retailers, and intelligence-gathering, to establishing deradicalization programmes, and the need for Governments to engage continuously with local authorities and groups, and encourages States in a position to do so to support initiatives and efforts to that end;

7.   *Encourages* States to enhance, as appropriate, international and regional cooperation, including the sharing of information on good practices as appropriate and where relevant, in cooperation with the private sector, the International Criminal Police Organization (INTERPOL), the United Nations Office on Drugs and Crime and the World Customs Organization, in order to address the theft, diversion, loss and illicit use of materials for making improvised explosive devices, while ensuring the security of sensitive information that is shared;

---

[14] The General Assembly, in its resolution 66/42, welcomed the completion of the International Ammunition Technical Guidelines and the establishment of the "Safer Guard" knowledge resource management programme for the stockpile management of conventional ammunition.

8. *Encourages* States and the private sector to increase prevention efforts by taking measures to stem the transfer of knowledge of improvised explosive devices and their construction and use by illegal armed groups, terrorists and other unauthorized recipients, as well as measures to stem the illicit acquisition of components over the Internet;

9. *Encourages* States to increase prevention efforts by taking measures, including awareness-raising, support for research and data collection, to combat illicit procurement of components, explosives and materials for the construction of improvised explosive devices, including through the use of the "dark web";[15]

10. *Also encourages* States to participate, in accordance with their obligations and commitments, in the ongoing work on improvised explosive devices by the informal group of experts under the Protocol on Prohibitions or Restrictions on the Use of Mines, Booby Traps and Other Devices as amended on 3 May 1996 (Amended Protocol II)[6] to the Convention on Prohibitions or Restrictions on the Use of Certain Conventional Weapons Which May Be Deemed to Be Excessively Injurious or to Have Indiscriminate Effects,[8] while recognizing the role of the United Nations and other international organizations in providing technical support and insight for these discussions;

11. *Further encourages* States to participate, as appropriate, in a comprehensive and coordinated community of action to counter improvised explosive devices in accordance with their respective international obligations and commitments, and to consider supporting the Programme Global Shield of the World Customs Organization and other multilateral and regional efforts;

12. *Encourages* States, the United Nations and international, regional and other organizations with relevant expertise that are in a position to do so to render to interested States, upon their request, technical, financial and material assistance aimed at strengthening the capacity of such States to counter the threat of improvised explosive devices, including through assistance for the development of good practices for the protection of civilians from attacks using such devices and for the development of standards to ensure the safety of personnel involved in the disposal of improvised explosive devices, and to provide appropriate assistance to the victims of such attacks;

13. *Encourages* States to respond to the needs of today's peacekeepers to operate in new threat environments involving improvised explosive devices, including by providing, in consultation and cooperation with the Department of Peacekeeping Operations of the Secretariat, the appropriate training, capabilities, information and knowledge management and technology required to counter improvised explosive devices, and to ensure that adequate financial resources are allocated to meet such needs, takes note of the Guidelines on

---

[15] Content of the dark web exists on overlay networks which use the Internet but require specific software, configurations or authorizations that are not indexed by search engines.

Improvised Explosive Device Threat Mitigation in Mission Settings developed by the Department of Peacekeeping Operations and the Department of Field Support of the Secretariat,[16] and encourages the full implementation of the Guidelines in all peacekeeping operations;

14.   *Recognizes* that improvised explosive devices are being increasingly used in terrorist activities, takes note of the work of the Counter-Terrorism Committee Executive Directorate and the Office of Counter-Terrorism related to the prevention of the acquisition of weapons by terrorists, and encourages all relevant entities of the United Nations system to continue to address the issue of improvised explosive devices, as appropriate and in line with their respective mandates, and to coordinate their activities to that end;

15.   *Urges* Member States to comply fully with all relevant United Nations resolutions, including those related to preventing terrorist groups from using and accessing materials that can be used in the making of improvised explosive devices;[17]

16.   *Encourages* States and relevant international and regional organizations and non-governmental organizations, including international industry associations, to continue to build upon existing awareness, prevention and risk education campaigns regarding the urgent threat of improvised explosive devices and to disseminate threat mitigation measures;

17.   *Encourages* States and relevant international and regional organizations to engage, as appropriate, with private sector entities in discussions and initiatives on countering improvised explosive devices, including on issues such as accountability throughout the supply chain for dual-use components, traceability procedures, improving the regulation of explosive precursors, where possible and as appropriate, strengthening security for the transport and storage of explosives and of precursors, as well as enhancing the vetting procedures for personnel with access to explosives or to precursors useful to the manufacture of explosives, while avoiding undue restrictions on the legitimate use of and access to such materials;

18.   *Notes* the relevant research undertaken by the United Nations Institute for Disarmament Research, encourages it to continue research in the area of prevention strategies, and encourages States in a position to do so to continue to support its work in this area;

19.   *Strongly encourages* States to share information, on a voluntary basis, on the diversion of commercial-grade explosives and commercially available detonators to the illicit trade and transfers to illegal armed groups, terrorists and other unauthorized recipients, through relevant channels, including the INTERPOL Project Watchmaker, Chemical Anti-Smuggling

---

[16] Available at www.un.org/disarmament/convarms/ieds.

[17] Including Security Council resolutions 1373 (2001), 2160 (2014), 2161 (2014), 2199 (2015), 2253 (2015), 2255 (2015) and 2370 (2017).

Enforcement and Chemical Risk Identification and Mitigation programmes and the Programme Global Shield of the World Customs Organization;

20. *Encourages* States to share information related to countering the threat posed by improvised explosive devices;

21. *Takes into account* the existing initiatives at the international, regional and national levels to counter improvised explosive devices, and encourages the engagement by States in an open and inclusive dialogue on steps forward to harmonize diverse ongoing efforts, including those on raising awareness and preventive strategies;

22. *Urges* States in a position to do so to contribute funding to the diverse areas of work needed to effectively address the issue of improvised explosive devices, including research, clearance, ammunition stockpile management, preventing violent extremism as and when conducive to terrorism, awareness-raising, capacity-building, information management and victim assistance, through existing trust funds and arrangements, including those of the Office of Counter-Terrorism, the United Nations Institute for Disarmament Research and the Office for Disarmament Affairs and the United Nations voluntary trust fund for assistance in mine action, efforts undertaken under relevant conventions[18] or through regional or national programmes;

23. *Welcomes* the establishment by the Office for Disarmament Affairs, in coordination with other relevant entities, of an online information hub that provides impartial, authoritative information relevant to addressing the issue of improvised explosive devices in a comprehensive manner, and encourages States to utilize the hub to access existing initiatives, policies, documents and tools relevant to countering the threat posed by improvised explosive devices;

24. *Takes note* of the completion of the United Nations Improvised Explosive Device Disposal Standards, coordinated by the Mine Action Service of the United Nations in cooperation with national technical experts, applicable where the context or mandate is not humanitarian;

25. *Also takes note* of the ongoing update of the International Mine Action Standards with regard to improvised explosive devices, which serve as the guiding framework for humanitarian mine action operations, and urges the International Mine Action Standards Review Board to rapidly finalize the update;

26. *Notes* that the United Nations Policy on Survivor Assistance in Mine Action highlights the significance of integrating survivor assistance efforts into broader international and national frameworks, as well as the

---

[18] Convention on Prohibitions or Restrictions on the Use of Certain Conventional Weapons Which May Be Deemed to Be Excessively Injurious or to Have Indiscriminate Effects and Convention on the Prohibition of the Use, Stockpiling, Production and Transfer of Anti-Personnel Mines and on Their Destruction.

importance of sustained services and support to survivors, including the survivors of attacks involving improvised explosive devices;

27. *Also notes* the completion of the United Nations Peacekeeping Missions Military Explosive Ordnance Disposal Unit Manual and the Improvised Explosive Device Threat Mitigation Military and Police Handbook by the Office of Military Affairs of the Department of Peacekeeping Operations and the Mine Action Service, respectively, to support the capacity of United Nations peacekeepers to effectively address the risks posed by such devices;

28. *Encourages* States in a position to do so to support the United Nations Institute for Disarmament Research, in consultation with relevant bodies of the United Nations system, in developing a voluntary self-assessment tool to assist States in identifying gaps and challenges in their national regulation and preparedness regarding improvised explosive devices;

29. *Recognizes* the important contribution of civil society to addressing the issue of improvised explosive devices, including in clearance, awareness-raising, risk education, victim assistance and preventing violent extremism as and when conducive to terrorism, in particular at the local and community levels;

30. *Requests* the Secretary-General to report to the General Assembly at its seventy-fifth session on the implementation of the present resolution, focusing on awareness and prevention strategies, acknowledging and taking into account existing efforts, both inside and outside the United Nations, and seeking the views of Member States;

31. *Encourages* States to continue to hold open, informal consultations, where appropriate, focusing on raising awareness, prevention and coordination within the United Nations system and beyond, with information provided by States, international and regional organizations as well as experts from non-governmental organizations, including relevant private sector stakeholders, on efforts to prevent, counter and mitigate the threat posed by improvised explosive devices, which could assist the General Assembly in maintaining a comprehensive overview of relevant global activities;

32. *Decides* to include in the provisional agenda of its seventy-fifth session, under the item entitled "General and complete disarmament", the sub-item entitled "Countering the threat posed by improvised explosive devices".

Action by the General Assembly

    Date: 5 December 2018   Meeting: 45th plenary meeting
    Vote: Adopted without a vote   Report: A/73/510

Sponsors

Afghanistan, Australia, Bulgaria, Croatia, Czechia, Denmark, Estonia, Finland, France, Georgia, Germany, Greece, Latvia, Lithuania, Luxembourg, Montenegro, Netherlands, Poland, Portugal, Romania, Slovakia, Spain, Sweden

Co-sponsors

Armenia, Bangladesh, Belgium, Canada, Chad, Democratic Republic of the Congo, Hungary, Iceland, India, Iraq, Ireland, Italy, Kazakhstan, Norway, Republic of Moldova, Slovenia, Turkey, Turkmenistan, Ukraine, United States, Yemen

Action by the First Committee

Date: 6 November 2018   Meeting: 29th meeting
Vote: Adopted without a vote   Draft resolution: A/C.1/73/L.60

Agenda item 101 (kk)

73/68 Ethical imperatives for a nuclear-weapon-free world

Text

The General Assembly,

Recalling its resolution 70/50 of 7 December 2015, adopted on the occasion of the seventieth anniversary of the United Nations, which was established to save succeeding generations from the untold suffering of the scourge of war, and its resolution 72/37 of 4 December 2017,

Recalling also that the United Nations emerged at the time of the immense trail of death and destruction resulting from the Second World War, 73 years ago,

Recalling further the noble principles of the Charter of the United Nations, which enjoin the international community, individually and collectively, to spare no effort in promoting the ethical imperative of "in larger freedom", so that all peoples may enjoy freedom from want, freedom from fear and the freedom to live in dignity,

Convinced that, given the catastrophic humanitarian consequences and risks associated with a nuclear weapon detonation, Member States have long envisaged nuclear disarmament and nuclear non-proliferation as urgent and interlinked ethical imperatives in achieving the objectives of the Charter, which is reflected in the first resolution, resolution 1 (I), adopted by the General Assembly on 24 January 1946, aimed at the elimination from national armaments of atomic weapons and of all other major weapons adaptable to mass destruction,

Acknowledging, in this connection, the ethical imperatives outlined in the provisions of its resolutions and reports and those of other related international initiatives on the catastrophic humanitarian consequences and risks posed by a nuclear weapon detonation, including the declaration that the use of nuclear weapons would cause indiscriminate suffering and as such is a violation of the Charter and the laws of humanity and international law,[1] the condemnation of nuclear war as contrary to human conscience and a violation of the fundamental right to life,[2] the threat to the very survival of humankind posed by the existence of nuclear weapons,[3] the detrimental environmental effects of the use of nuclear weapons,[4] and the disquiet that was expressed

---

[1] See resolution 1653 (XVI).
[2] See resolution 38/75.
[3] See resolution S-10/2.
[4] See resolution 50/70 M.

at the continued spending on the development and maintenance of nuclear arsenals,[5]

Acknowledging also the preamble to and article VI of the Treaty on the Non-Proliferation of Nuclear Weapons[6] and the advisory opinion of the International Court of Justice on the legality of the threat or use of nuclear weapons,[7] in which the Court unanimously concluded that there exists an obligation to pursue in good faith and bring to a conclusion negotiations leading to nuclear disarmament in all its aspects under strict and effective international control,

Acknowledging further the United Nations Millennium Declaration,[8] in which Heads of State and Government resolved to strive for the elimination of weapons of mass destruction, particularly nuclear weapons, and to keep all options open for achieving that aim, including the possibility of convening an international conference to identify ways of eliminating nuclear dangers,

Concerned that, despite the long-standing recognition that it has accorded to these ethical imperatives and while much effort has been directed to addressing nuclear non-proliferation, limited progress has been made in meeting the nuclear disarmament obligations required to achieve and maintain the nuclear-weapon-free world that the international community demands,

Disappointed at the continued absence of progress towards multilateral negotiations on nuclear disarmament in the Conference on Disarmament, despite unrelenting efforts of Member States towards this end,

Noting with satisfaction the increasing awareness, renewed attention and growing momentum that has been generated by Member States and the international community since 2010 regarding the catastrophic humanitarian consequences and risks associated with nuclear weapons, which underpin the ethical imperatives for nuclear disarmament and the urgency of achieving and maintaining a nuclear-weapon-free world, together with all related international initiatives,

Recalling the adoption on 7 July 2017 of the Treaty on the Prohibition of Nuclear Weapons,[9] in which the ethical imperatives for nuclear disarmament are acknowledged,

Conscious of the absolute validity of multilateral diplomacy in relation to nuclear disarmament, and determined to promote multilateralism as essential to nuclear disarmament negotiations,

---

[5] See A/59/119.
[6] United Nations, *Treaty Series*, vol. 729, No. 10485.
[7] A/51/218, annex.
[8] Resolution 55/2.
[9] A/CONF.229/2017/8.

1. *Calls upon* all States to acknowledge the catastrophic humanitarian consequences and risks posed by a nuclear weapon detonation, whether by accident, miscalculation or design;

2. *Acknowledges* the ethical imperatives for nuclear disarmament and the urgency of achieving and maintaining a nuclear-weapon-free world, which is a "global public good of the highest order", serving both national and collective security interests;

3. *Declares* that:

(a) The global threat posed by nuclear weapons must urgently be eliminated;

(b) Discussions, decisions and actions on nuclear weapons must focus on the effects of these weapons on human beings and the environment and must be guided by the unspeakable suffering and unacceptable harm that they cause;

(c) Greater attention must be given to the impact of a nuclear weapon detonation on women and the importance of their participation in discussions, decisions and actions on nuclear weapons;

(d) Nuclear weapons serve to undermine collective security, heighten the risk of nuclear catastrophe, aggravate international tension and make conflict more dangerous;

(e) Arguments in favour of the retention of nuclear weapons have a negative impact on the credibility of the nuclear disarmament and non-proliferation regime;

(f) The long-term plans for the modernization of nuclear weapons arsenals run contrary to commitments and obligations to nuclear disarmament and engender perceptions of the indefinite possession of these weapons;

(g) In a world where basic human needs have not yet been met, the vast resources allocated to the modernization of nuclear weapons arsenals could instead be redirected to meeting the Sustainable Development Goals;[10]

(h) Given the humanitarian impact of nuclear weapons, it is inconceivable that any use of nuclear weapons, irrespective of the cause, would be compatible with the requirements of international humanitarian law or international law, or the laws of morality, or the dictates of public conscience;

(i) Given their indiscriminate nature and potential to annihilate humanity, nuclear weapons are inherently immoral;

4. *Notes* that all responsible States have a solemn duty to take decisions that serve to protect their people and each other from the ravages

---

[10] See resolution 70/1.

of a nuclear weapon detonation, and that the only way for States to do so is through the total elimination of nuclear weapons;

5. *Stresses* that all States share an ethical responsibility to act with urgency and determination, with the support of all relevant stakeholders, to take the effective measures, including legally binding measures, necessary to eliminate and prohibit all nuclear weapons, given their catastrophic humanitarian consequences and associated risks;

6. *Decides* to include in the provisional agenda of its seventy-fourth session, under the item entitled "General and complete disarmament", the sub-item entitled "Ethical imperatives for a nuclear-weapon-free world".

Action by the General Assembly

Date: 5 December 2018
Vote: 136-36-14
        122-29-18, p.p. 11

Meeting: 45th plenary meeting
Report: A/73/510

Sponsors

Algeria, Austria, Brazil, Costa Rica, Ecuador, Egypt, Ghana, Guatemala, Ireland, Lesotho, Mexico, Namibia, Nigeria, Panama, Peru, Samoa, **South Africa**, Thailand, Uganda, Uruguay, Viet Nam

Co-sponsors

Benin, El Salvador, Eswatini, Philippines, Seychelles, Togo

Recorded vote

As a whole

In favour:

Afghanistan, Algeria, Angola, Antigua and Barbuda, Argentina, Austria, Azerbaijan, Bahamas, Bahrain, Bangladesh, Barbados, Belarus, Belize, Benin, Bhutan, Bolivia (Plurinational State of), Botswana, Brazil, Brunei Darussalam, Burkina Faso, Burundi, Cabo Verde, Cambodia, Cameroon, Central African Republic, Chile, Colombia, Comoros, Congo, Costa Rica, Côte d'Ivoire, Cuba, Democratic Republic of the Congo, Djibouti, Dominica, Dominican Republic, Ecuador, Egypt, El Salvador, Equatorial Guinea, Eritrea, Eswatini, Ethiopia, Fiji, Gabon, Gambia, Ghana, Grenada, Guatemala, Guinea, Guinea-Bissau, Guyana, Honduras, Indonesia, Iran (Islamic Republic of), Iraq, Ireland, Jamaica, Jordan, Kazakhstan, Kenya, Kuwait, Kyrgyzstan, Lao People's Democratic Republic, Lebanon, Lesotho, Liberia, Libya, Liechtenstein, Madagascar, Malawi, Malaysia, Maldives, Mali, Malta, Marshall Islands, Mauritania, Mauritius, Mexico, Mongolia, Morocco, Mozambique, Myanmar, Namibia, Nauru, Nepal, New Zealand, Nicaragua, Niger, Nigeria,

Oman, Palau, Panama, Papua New Guinea, Paraguay, Peru, Philippines, Qatar, Republic of Moldova, Rwanda, Saint Kitts and Nevis, Saint Lucia, Saint Vincent and the Grenadines, Samoa, San Marino, Sao Tome and Principe, Saudi Arabia, Senegal, Seychelles, Sierra Leone, Singapore, Solomon Islands, South Africa, Sri Lanka, Sudan, Suriname, Syrian Arab Republic, Tajikistan, Thailand, Timor-Leste, Togo, Tonga, Trinidad and Tobago, Tunisia, Tuvalu, Uganda, United Arab Emirates, United Republic of Tanzania, Uruguay, Uzbekistan, Vanuatu, Venezuela (Bolivarian Republic of), Viet Nam, Yemen, Zambia, Zimbabwe

Against:

Albania, Australia, Belgium, Bulgaria, Canada, Croatia, Czechia, Denmark, Estonia, Finland, France, Germany, Greece, Hungary, Iceland, Israel, Italy, Latvia, Lithuania, Luxembourg, Monaco, Montenegro, Netherlands, Norway, Poland, Portugal, Republic of Korea, Romania, Russian Federation, Slovakia, Slovenia, Spain, Turkey, Ukraine, United Kingdom, United States

Abstaining:

Andorra, Armenia, Bosnia and Herzegovina, China, Cyprus, Democratic People's Republic of Korea, Georgia, India, Japan, Pakistan, Serbia, Sweden, Switzerland, the former Yugoslav Republic of Macedonia

Eleventh preambular paragraph

In favour:

Algeria, Angola, Argentina, Austria, Azerbaijan, Bahamas, Bahrain, Bangladesh, Barbados, Belize, Benin, Bhutan, Bolivia (Plurinational State of), Botswana, Brazil, Brunei Darussalam, Burkina Faso, Burundi, Cabo Verde, Cambodia, Chile, Colombia, Comoros, Costa Rica, Côte d'Ivoire, Cuba, Cyprus, Democratic Republic of the Congo, Djibouti, Dominican Republic, Ecuador, Egypt, El Salvador, Equatorial Guinea, Eritrea, Eswatini, Ethiopia, Fiji, Gambia, Ghana, Guatemala, Guinea, Guinea-Bissau, Guyana, Honduras, Indonesia, Iran (Islamic Republic of), Iraq, Ireland, Jamaica, Jordan, Kazakhstan, Kenya, Kuwait, Lao People's Democratic Republic, Lebanon, Lesotho, Liberia, Libya, Liechtenstein, Madagascar, Malawi, Malaysia, Maldives, Mali, Malta, Mauritania, Mauritius, Mexico, Mongolia, Morocco, Mozambique, Myanmar, Namibia, Nepal, New Zealand, Nicaragua, Niger, Nigeria, Oman, Palau, Panama, Papua New Guinea, Paraguay, Peru, Philippines, Qatar, Republic of Moldova, Rwanda, Saint Kitts and Nevis, Saint Lucia, Saint Vincent and the Grenadines, Samoa, San Marino, Sao Tome and Principe, Saudi Arabia, Senegal, Seychelles, Sierra Leone, Singapore, Solomon Islands, South Africa, Sri Lanka, Sudan, Suriname, Sweden, Switzerland, Thailand, Togo, Trinidad and Tobago, Tunisia, Tuvalu, Uganda, United Arab Emirates, United Republic of Tanzania, Uruguay,

Vanuatu, Venezuela (Bolivarian Republic of), Viet Nam, Yemen, Zambia, Zimbabwe

Against:

Albania, Australia, Belgium, Bulgaria, China, Croatia, Czechia, Denmark, Estonia, France, Germany, Greece, Hungary, Israel, Italy, Latvia, Lithuania, Luxembourg, Monaco, Montenegro, Poland, Portugal, Romania, Russian Federation, Slovakia, Slovenia, Ukraine, United Kingdom, United States

Abstaining:

Andorra, Armenia, Belarus, Bosnia and Herzegovina, Canada, Democratic People's Republic of Korea, Finland, Georgia, Iceland, India, Japan, Netherlands, Norway, Pakistan, Serbia, Spain, the former Yugoslav Republic of Macedonia, Turkey

Action by the First Committee

Date: 1 November 2018	Meeting: 26th meeting
Vote: 130-34-18	Draft resolution: A/C.1/73/L.62
121-29-22, p.p. 11	

Agenda item 101 (q)

73/69   The illicit trade in small arms and light weapons in all its aspects

Text

The General Assembly,

Recalling its resolution 72/57 of 4 December 2017, as well as all previous resolutions on the illicit trade in small arms and light weapons in all its aspects, including resolution 56/24 V of 24 December 2001,

Emphasizing the importance of the continued and full implementation of the Programme of Action to Prevent, Combat and Eradicate the Illicit Trade in Small Arms and Light Weapons in All Its Aspects, adopted by the United Nations Conference on the Illicit Trade in Small Arms and Light Weapons in All Its Aspects,[1] and recognizing its important contribution to international efforts on this matter,

Emphasizing also the importance of the continued and full implementation of the International Instrument to Enable States to Identify and Trace, in a Timely and Reliable Manner, Illicit Small Arms and Light Weapons (the International Tracing Instrument),[2]

Recalling the commitment of States to the Programme of Action as the main framework for measures within the activities of the international community to prevent, combat and eradicate the illicit trade in small arms and light weapons in all its aspects,

Underlining the need for States to enhance their efforts to build national capacity for the effective implementation of the Programme of Action and the International Tracing Instrument,

Mindful of the implementation of the outcomes adopted by the follow-up meetings on the Programme of Action,

Welcoming the successful conclusion of the third United Nations Conference to Review Progress Made in the Implementation of the Programme of Action to Prevent, Combat and Eradicate the Illicit Trade in Small Arms and Light Weapons in All Its Aspects (the third Review Conference), held in New York from 18 to 29 June 2018,

Recognizing the need for strengthened participation of women in decision-making and implementation processes relating to the Programme of Action and the International Tracing Instrument, and reaffirming the need for States to mainstream gender dimensions in their implementation efforts,

---

[1] *Report of the United Nations Conference on the Illicit Trade in Small Arms and Light Weapons in All Its Aspects, New York, 9–20 July 2001* (A/CONF.192/15), chap. IV, para. 24.

[2] See decision 60/519 and A/60/88 and A/60/88/Corr.2, annex.

Noting that web-based tools developed by the Secretariat, including its searchable database and the Modular Small-arms-control Implementation Compendium, and the tools developed by Member States could be used to assess progress made in the implementation of the Programme of Action,

Reaffirming the acknowledgement, by the third Review Conference in its outcome document,[3] of the proposal on the establishment of a dedicated fellowship training programme on small arms and light weapons in order to strengthen technical knowledge and expertise in areas relating to the implementation of the Programme of Action and the International Tracing Instrument, in particular in developing countries,

Reaffirming also the importance of the early designation of the Presidents of future review conferences and the Chairs of future biennial meetings of States,

Noting that voluntary national reports on the implementation of the Programme of Action can serve, inter alia, to provide a baseline for measuring progress in its implementation, build confidence and promote transparency, provide a basis for information exchange and action and serve to identify needs and opportunities for international assistance and cooperation, including the matching of needs with available resources and expertise,

Noting with satisfaction regional and subregional efforts being undertaken in support of the implementation of the Programme of Action, and commending the progress that has already been made in this regard, including the tackling of both supply and demand factors that are relevant to addressing the illicit trade in small arms and light weapons,

Reaffirming that international cooperation and assistance are an essential aspect of the full and effective implementation of the Programme of Action and the International Tracing Instrument,

Recognizing the efforts undertaken by non-governmental organizations in the provision of assistance to States for the implementation of the Programme of Action,

Recalling that Governments bear the primary responsibility for preventing, combating and eradicating the illicit trade in small arms and light weapons in all its aspects, in accordance with the sovereignty of States and their relevant international obligations,

Reiterating that illicit brokering in small arms and light weapons is a serious problem that the international community should address urgently,

Highlighting new challenges and potential opportunities with regard to effective marking, record-keeping and tracing resulting from developments in the manufacturing, technology and design of small arms and light weapons,

---

[3] A/CONF.192/2018/RC/3, annex.

and bearing in mind the different situations, capacities and priorities of States and regions,

Taking note of the report of the Secretary-General,[4] which includes an overview of the implementation of resolution 72/57,

Welcoming the inclusion of small arms and light weapons in the scope of the Arms Trade Treaty,[5]

Acknowledging efforts related to the transfer of conventional arms that may also contribute to the prevention and eradication of the illicit trade in small arms and light weapons,

1.   *Underlines* the fact that the issue of the illicit trade in small arms and light weapons in all its aspects requires concerted efforts at the national, regional and international levels to prevent, combat and eradicate the illicit manufacture, transfer and circulation of small arms and light weapons, and that their uncontrolled spread in many regions of the world has a wide range of humanitarian and socioeconomic consequences and poses a serious threat to peace, reconciliation, safety, security, stability and sustainable development at the individual, local, national, regional and international levels;

2.   *Recognizes* the urgent need to maintain and enhance national controls, in accordance with the Programme of Action to Prevent, Combat and Eradicate the Illicit Trade in Small Arms and Light Weapons in All Its Aspects,[1] to prevent, combat and eradicate the illicit trade in small arms and light weapons, including their diversion to illicit trade, illegal armed groups, terrorists and other unauthorized recipients, taking into account, inter alia, their adverse humanitarian and socioeconomic consequences for the affected States;

3.   *Calls upon* all States to implement the International Instrument to Enable States to Identify and Trace, in a Timely and Reliable Manner, Illicit Small Arms and Light Weapons (the International Tracing Instrument)[2] by, inter alia, including in their national reports the name and contact information of the national points of contact and information on national marking practices used to indicate country of manufacture and/or country of import, as applicable;

4.   *Encourages* all relevant initiatives, including those of the United Nations, other international organizations, regional and subregional organizations, non-governmental organizations and civil society, for the successful implementation of the Programme of Action, and calls upon all Member States to contribute towards the continued implementation of the Programme of Action at the national, regional and global levels;

5.   *Encourages* States to implement the recommendations contained in the report of the Group of Governmental Experts established pursuant to resolution 60/81 to consider further steps to enhance international cooperation

---

[4] A/73/168.

[5] See resolution 67/234 B.

in preventing, combating and eradicating illicit brokering in small arms and light weapons;[6]

6. *Endorses* the outcome of the third United Nations Conference to Review Progress Made in the Implementation of the Programme of Action to Prevent, Combat and Eradicate the Illicit Trade in Small Arms and Light Weapons in All Its Aspects, held in New York from 18 to 29 June 2018 (the third Review Conference);[3]

7. *Decides*, pursuant to the schedule of meetings for the period from 2018 to 2024 agreed upon at the third Review Conference, to convene a one-week biennial meeting of States in 2020 to consider key challenges and opportunities relating to the implementation of the Programme of Action and the International Tracing Instrument at the national, regional and global levels for the purposes of preventing and combating the diversion and the illicit international transfer of small arms and light weapons to unauthorized recipients, as well as a one-week biennial meeting of States in 2022;

8. *Also decides* to convene the fourth United Nations Conference to Review Progress Made in the Implementation of the Programme of Action to Prevent, Combat and Eradicate the Illicit Trade in Small Arms and Light Weapons in All Its Aspects in 2024, to be preceded by a preparatory committee meeting in early 2024 of not more than five days;

9. *Underlines* the importance of the full and effective implementation of the Programme of Action and the International Tracing Instrument for attaining Goal 16 and target 16.4 of the Sustainable Development Goals;[7]

10. *Emphasizes* that international cooperation and assistance remain essential to the full and effective implementation of the Programme of Action and the International Tracing Instrument, while being mindful of the need to ensure the adequacy, effectiveness and sustainability of international cooperation and assistance;

11. *Also emphasizes* the fact that initiatives by the international community with respect to international cooperation and assistance remain essential and complementary to national implementation efforts, as well as to those at the regional and global levels;

12. *Recognizes* the necessity for interested States to develop effective coordination mechanisms, where they do not exist, in order to match the needs of States with existing resources to enhance the implementation of the Programme of Action and to make international cooperation and assistance more effective, and in this regard encourages States to make use, as appropriate, of the Programme of Action Implementation Support System;

---

[6] See A/62/163 and A/62/163/Corr.1.

[7] See resolution 70/1.

13. *Encourages* States to consider, among other mechanisms, the coherent identification of needs, priorities, national plans and programmes that may require international cooperation and assistance from States and regional and international organizations in a position to do so;

14. *Also encourages* States, on a voluntary basis, to make increasing use of their national reports as another tool for communicating assistance needs and information on the resources and mechanisms available to address such needs, and encourages States in a position to render such assistance to make use of those national reports;

15. *Encourages* States, relevant international and regional organizations and civil society with the capacity to do so to cooperate with and provide assistance to other States, upon request, in the preparation of comprehensive reports on their implementation of the Programme of Action;

16. *Encourages* States to reinforce, as necessary, cross-border cooperation at the national, subregional and regional levels in addressing the common problem of the illicit trade in small arms and light weapons in all its aspects, with full respect for each State's sovereignty over its own borders;

17. *Also encourages* States to take full advantage of the benefits of cooperation with the United Nations regional centres for peace and disarmament, the World Customs Organization, the International Criminal Police Organization (INTERPOL) and the United Nations Office on Drugs and Crime, in accordance with their mandates and consistent with national priorities;

18. *Encourages* all efforts to build national capacity for the effective implementation of the Programme of Action, including those highlighted in the outcome document of the third Review Conference;

19. *Encourages* States to submit, on a voluntary basis, national reports on their implementation of the Programme of Action, notes that States will submit national reports on their implementation of the International Tracing Instrument, encourages those States in a position to do so to use the reporting template made available by the Office for Disarmament Affairs of the Secretariat, and reaffirms the utility of synchronizing such reports with biennial meetings of States and review conferences as a means of increasing the submission rate and improving the utility of reports, as well as contributing substantively to meeting discussions;

20. *Encourages* States in a position to do so to provide financial assistance, through a voluntary sponsorship fund, that could be distributed, upon request, to States otherwise unable to participate in meetings on the Programme of Action;

21. *Welcomes* the initiative of the Secretary-General to establish a multi-partner trust facility within the Peacebuilding Fund, dedicated to providing sustainable, cross-sectional, multi-year programming focused on

eradicating the illicit trade in small arms and light weapons in settings of conflict and pervasive crime, and encourages States in a position to do so to make voluntary contributions to the facility;

22. *Encourages* interested States and relevant international and regional organizations in a position to do so to convene regional meetings to consider and advance the implementation of the Programme of Action, as well as the International Tracing Instrument, including in preparation for the meetings on the Programme of Action;

23. *Encourages* civil society and relevant organizations to strengthen their cooperation and work with States at the respective national and regional levels to achieve the implementation of the Programme of Action;

24. *Requests* the Secretary-General to report to the General Assembly at its seventy-fourth session on the implementation of the present resolution and to take into account in that report, among other issues, the views of Member States with regard to the recent developments in small arms and light weapons manufacturing, technology and design, in particular polymer and modular weapons, including on their associated opportunities and challenges, as well as their impact on the effective implementation of the International Tracing Instrument, and to make recommendations on ways of addressing them;

25. *Decides* to include in the provisional agenda of its seventy-fourth session, under the item entitled "General and complete disarmament", the sub-item entitled "The illicit trade in small arms and light weapons in all its aspects".

Action by the General Assembly

Date:	5 December 2018	Meeting:	45th plenary meeting
Vote:	Adopted without a vote	Report:	A/73/510
	176-2-1, p.p. 7		
	176-2-0, o.p. 6		

Sponsors

Afghanistan, Angola, Argentina, Australia, Austria, Bahamas, Belgium, Bulgaria, Chile, Colombia, Costa Rica, Croatia, Cyprus, Czechia, Denmark, Dominican Republic, El Salvador, Estonia, France, Germany, Ghana, Greece, Guatemala, Haiti, Honduras, Italy, Jamaica, Japan, Latvia, Lithuania, Luxembourg, Namibia, Paraguay, Peru, Poland, Portugal, Romania, Samoa, San Marino, Slovakia, **South Africa**, Spain, Sweden, Switzerland, Trinidad and Tobago, Uganda, United Kingdom, Uruguay

Co-sponsors

Albania, Andorra, Bosnia and Herzegovina, Brazil, Burkina Faso, Congo, Democratic Republic of the Congo, Equatorial Guinea, Eritrea, Finland, Georgia, Guinea-Bissau, Guyana, Hungary, Iceland, Ireland, Liechtenstein,

Malta, Monaco, Montenegro, Netherlands, Nigeria, Norway, Panama, Papua New Guinea, Philippines, Republic of Korea, Republic of Moldova, Sao Tome and Principe, Serbia, Seychelles, Slovenia, Thailand, the former Yugoslav Republic of Macedonia, Togo, Tunisia, Turkey, Ukraine

Recorded vote

Seventh preambular paragraph

In favour:

Afghanistan, Albania, Algeria, Andorra, Angola, Antigua and Barbuda, Argentina, Armenia, Australia, Austria, Azerbaijan, Bahamas, Bahrain, Bangladesh, Barbados, Belarus, Belgium, Belize, Benin, Bhutan, Bolivia (Plurinational State of), Bosnia and Herzegovina, Botswana, Brazil, Brunei Darussalam, Bulgaria, Burkina Faso, Burundi, Cabo Verde, Cambodia, Canada, Central African Republic, Chile, China, Colombia, Comoros, Costa Rica, Côte d'Ivoire, Croatia, Cuba, Cyprus, Czechia, Democratic Republic of the Congo, Denmark, Djibouti, Dominican Republic, Ecuador, Egypt, El Salvador, Equatorial Guinea, Eritrea, Estonia, Eswatini, Ethiopia, Fiji, Finland, France, Gambia, Georgia, Germany, Ghana, Greece, Guatemala, Guinea, Guinea-Bissau, Guyana, Haiti, Honduras, Hungary, Iceland, India, Indonesia, Iran (Islamic Republic of), Iraq, Ireland, Italy, Jamaica, Japan, Jordan, Kazakhstan, Kenya, Kuwait, Kyrgyzstan, Lao People's Democratic Republic, Latvia, Lebanon, Lesotho, Liberia, Libya, Liechtenstein, Lithuania, Luxembourg, Madagascar, Malawi, Malaysia, Maldives, Mali, Malta, Marshall Islands, Mauritania, Mauritius, Mexico, Micronesia (Federated States of), Monaco, Mongolia, Montenegro, Morocco, Mozambique, Myanmar, Namibia, Nepal, Netherlands, New Zealand, Nicaragua, Niger, Nigeria, Norway, Oman, Pakistan, Palau, Panama, Papua New Guinea, Paraguay, Peru, Philippines, Poland, Portugal, Qatar, Republic of Korea, Republic of Moldova, Romania, Russian Federation, Rwanda, Saint Kitts and Nevis, Saint Lucia, Saint Vincent and the Grenadines, Samoa, San Marino, Sao Tome and Principe, Saudi Arabia, Senegal, Serbia, Seychelles, Sierra Leone, Singapore, Slovakia, Slovenia, Solomon Islands, South Africa, Spain, Sri Lanka, Sudan, Suriname, Sweden, Switzerland, Syrian Arab Republic, Tajikistan, Thailand, the former Yugoslav Republic of Macedonia, Timor-Leste, Togo, Trinidad and Tobago, Tunisia, Turkey, Uganda, United Arab Emirates, United Kingdom, United Republic of Tanzania, Uruguay, Uzbekistan, Vanuatu, Venezuela (Bolivarian Republic of), Viet Nam, Yemen, Zambia, Zimbabwe

Against:

Israel, United States

Abstaining:

Ukraine

Operative paragraph 6

In favour:

Afghanistan, Albania, Algeria, Andorra, Angola, Antigua and Barbuda, Argentina, Armenia, Australia, Austria, Azerbaijan, Bahamas, Bahrain, Bangladesh, Barbados, Belarus, Belgium, Belize, Benin, Bhutan, Bolivia (Plurinational State of), Bosnia and Herzegovina, Botswana, Brazil, Brunei Darussalam, Bulgaria, Burkina Faso, Burundi, Cabo Verde, Cambodia, Canada, Central African Republic, Chile, China, Colombia, Comoros, Costa Rica, Côte d'Ivoire, Croatia, Cuba, Cyprus, Czechia, Democratic Republic of the Congo, Denmark, Djibouti, Dominican Republic, Ecuador, Egypt, El Salvador, Equatorial Guinea, Eritrea, Estonia, Eswatini, Ethiopia, Fiji, Finland, France, Gambia, Georgia, Germany, Ghana, Greece, Guatemala, Guinea, Guinea-Bissau, Guyana, Haiti, Honduras, Hungary, Iceland, India, Indonesia, Iran (Islamic Republic of), Iraq, Ireland, Italy, Jamaica, Japan, Jordan, Kazakhstan, Kenya, Kuwait, Kyrgyzstan, Lao People's Democratic Republic, Latvia, Lebanon, Lesotho, Liberia, Libya, Liechtenstein, Lithuania, Luxembourg, Madagascar, Malawi, Malaysia, Maldives, Mali, Malta, Marshall Islands, Mauritania, Mauritius, Mexico, Micronesia (Federated States of), Monaco, Mongolia, Montenegro, Morocco, Mozambique, Myanmar, Namibia, Nepal, Netherlands, New Zealand, Nicaragua, Niger, Nigeria, Norway, Oman, Pakistan, Palau, Panama, Papua New Guinea, Paraguay, Peru, Philippines, Poland, Portugal, Qatar, Republic of Korea, Republic of Moldova, Romania, Russian Federation, Rwanda, Saint Kitts and Nevis, Saint Lucia, Saint Vincent and the Grenadines, Samoa, San Marino, Sao Tome and Principe, Saudi Arabia, Senegal, Serbia, Seychelles, Sierra Leone, Singapore, Slovakia, Slovenia, Solomon Islands, South Africa, Spain, Sri Lanka, Sudan, Suriname, Sweden, Switzerland, Syrian Arab Republic, Tajikistan, Thailand, the former Yugoslav Republic of Macedonia, Timor-Leste, Togo, Trinidad and Tobago, Tunisia, Turkey, Uganda, Ukraine, United Arab Emirates, United Kingdom, United Republic of Tanzania, Uruguay, Vanuatu, Venezuela (Bolivarian Republic of), Viet Nam, Yemen, Zambia, Zimbabwe

Against:

Israel, United States

Abstaining:

None

Action by the First Committee

Date: 6 November 2018　　　Meeting:　　　29th meeting

Vote: Adopted without a vote　Draft resolution:　A/C.1/73/L.63

173-2-1, p.p. 7

174-2-1, o.p. 6

Agenda item 101 (r)

73/70   Towards a nuclear-weapon-free world: accelerating the implementation of nuclear disarmament commitments

Text

The General Assembly,

Recalling its resolutions 1 (I) of 24 January 1946, 71/54 of 5 December 2016 and 72/39 of 4 December 2017,

Noting the twentieth anniversary of the launch of the New Agenda Coalition and the joint declaration outlining a new agenda for disarmament, adopted in Dublin on 9 June 1998,[1]

Recalling its resolution 72/243 of 22 December 2017, in which it decided to hold a high-level plenary meeting in 2018, the Nelson Mandela Peace Summit, in honour of the centenary of the birth of Nelson Mandela, welcoming the political declaration adopted by the Summit on 24 September 2018,[2] in which it recalled the firm plea made by Nelson Mandela in favour of the total elimination of nuclear weapons, and underscoring commitments towards that goal,

Welcoming the launch of the Secretary-General's disarmament agenda, *Securing Our Common Future: An Agenda for Disarmament*, in Geneva on 24 May 2018,

Reiterating its grave concern at the danger to humanity posed by nuclear weapons, which should inform all deliberations, decisions and actions relating to nuclear disarmament and nuclear non-proliferation,

Recalling the expression of deep concern by the 2010 Review Conference of the Parties to the Treaty on the Non-Proliferation of Nuclear Weapons at the catastrophic humanitarian consequences of any use of nuclear weapons, and its resolve to seek a safer world for all and to achieve the peace and security of a world without nuclear weapons,[3]

Noting with satisfaction the renewed attention to the catastrophic humanitarian consequences and risks associated with nuclear weapons that has been generated by the international community since 2010 and the growing awareness that these concerns should underpin the need for nuclear disarmament and the urgency of achieving and maintaining a nuclear-

---

[1] A/53/138, annex.

[2] Resolution 73/1.

[3] See *2010 Review Conference of the Parties to the Treaty on the Non-Proliferation of Nuclear Weapons, Final Document*, vol. I (NPT/CONF.2010/50 (Vol. I)), part I, *Conclusions and recommendations for follow-on actions.*

weapon-free world, and noting with satisfaction also the prominence accorded to the humanitarian impact of nuclear weapons in multilateral disarmament forums,

Recalling the discussions held at the Conferences on the Humanitarian Impact of Nuclear Weapons, hosted by Norway, on 4 and 5 March 2013, Mexico, on 13 and 14 February 2014, and Austria, on 8 and 9 December 2014, aimed at understanding and developing a greater awareness of the catastrophic consequences of nuclear weapon detonations which further reinforce the urgency of nuclear disarmament,

Emphasizing the compelling evidence, including that presented at the Conferences on the Humanitarian Impact of Nuclear Weapons, that has detailed the catastrophic consequences that would result from a nuclear weapon detonation, reaching well beyond national borders and also imperilling the achievement of the Sustainable Development Goals,[4] the lack of capacity of States and international organizations to deal with the aftermath and the risk of an occurrence, due to an accident, systems failure or human error,

Noting the strongly disproportionate and gendered impact of exposure to ionizing radiation for women and girls,

Welcoming the commemoration and promotion of 26 September as the International Day for the Total Elimination of Nuclear Weapons,

Welcoming also the adoption on 7 July 2017 of the Treaty on the Prohibition of Nuclear Weapons, negotiated by the United Nations conference to negotiate a legally binding instrument to prohibit nuclear weapons, leading towards their total elimination, pursuant to resolution 71/258 of 23 December 2016,[5]

Underlining the importance of nuclear disarmament and non-proliferation education,

Reaffirming that transparency, verifiability and irreversibility are cardinal principles applying to nuclear disarmament and nuclear non-proliferation, which are mutually reinforcing processes,

Recalling the decisions and the resolution adopted at the 1995 Review and Extension Conference of the Parties to the Treaty on the Non-Proliferation of Nuclear Weapons,[6] the basis upon which the Treaty was indefinitely

---

[4] See resolution 70/1.

[5] A/CONF.229/2017/8.

[6] See *1995 Review and Extension Conference of the Parties to the Treaty on the Non-Proliferation of Nuclear Weapons, Final Document, Part I* (NPT/CONF.1995/32 (Part I) and NPT/CONF.1995/32 (Part I)/Corr.2), annex.

extended, and the Final Documents of the 2000[7] and the 2010[8] Review Conferences of the Parties to the Treaty on the Non-Proliferation of Nuclear Weapons, and in particular the unequivocal undertaking by the nuclear-weapon States to accomplish the total elimination of their nuclear arsenals, leading to nuclear disarmament, in accordance with commitments made under article VI of the Treaty on the Non-Proliferation of Nuclear Weapons,[9]

Reaffirming the commitment of all States parties to the Treaty on the Non-Proliferation of Nuclear Weapons to applying the principles of irreversibility, verifiability and transparency in relation to the implementation of their treaty obligations,

Recognizing the continued vital importance of the entry into force of the Comprehensive Nuclear-Test-Ban Treaty[10] to the advancement of nuclear disarmament and nuclear non-proliferation objectives,

Recalling that the total elimination of nuclear weapons is the only absolute guarantee against the use or threat of use of nuclear weapons and the legitimate interest of non-nuclear-weapon States in receiving unequivocal and legally binding negative security assurances from nuclear-weapon States pending the total elimination of nuclear weapons,

Reaffirming the conviction that, pending the total elimination of nuclear weapons, the establishment and maintenance of nuclear-weapon-free zones enhances global and regional peace and security, strengthens the nuclear non-proliferation regime and contributes towards realizing the objectives of nuclear disarmament, and welcoming the Conferences of States Parties and Signatories to Treaties that Establish Nuclear-Weapon-Free Zones and Mongolia,

Urging States to continue to make real progress towards strengthening all existing nuclear-weapon-free zones, inter alia, through the ratification of existing treaties and relevant protocols and the withdrawal or revision of any reservations or interpretative declarations contrary to the object and purpose of the treaties establishing such zones,

Recalling the encouragement expressed at the 2010 Review Conference for the establishment of further nuclear-weapon-free zones, on the basis of arrangements freely arrived at among the States of the region concerned, reaffirming the expectation that this will be followed by concerted international efforts to create such zones in areas where they do not

---

[7] *2000 Review Conference of the Parties to the Treaty on the Non-Proliferation of Nuclear Weapons, Final Document*, vols. I–III (NPT/CONF.2000/28 (Parts I and II), NPT/CONF.2000/28 (Part III) and NPT/CONF.2000/28 (Part IV)).

[8] *2010 Review Conference of the Parties to the Treaty on the Non-Proliferation of Nuclear Weapons, Final Document*, vols. I–III (NPT/CONF.2010/50 (Vol. I), NPT/CONF.2010/50 (Vol. II), and NPT/CONF.2010/50 (Vol. III)).

[9] United Nations, *Treaty Series*, vol. 729, No. 10485.

[10] See resolution 50/245 and A/50/1027.

currently exist, especially in the Middle East, in this context noting with deep disappointment the non-fulfilment of the agreement at the 2010 Review Conference on practical steps to fully implement the 1995 resolution on the Middle East,[6] and disappointed that no agreement could be reached at the 2015 Review Conference of the Parties to the Treaty on the Non-Proliferation of Nuclear Weapons on this issue,

Deeply disappointed at the continued absence of progress towards multilateral nuclear disarmament at the Conference on Disarmament, which has been unable for the past 22 years to agree upon and implement a programme of work, and disappointed that the Disarmament Commission has not produced a substantive outcome on nuclear disarmament since 1999,

Deeply regretting the lack of any substantive outcome of the 2015 Review Conference,

Disappointed that the 2015 Review Conference missed an opportunity to strengthen the Treaty on the Non-Proliferation of Nuclear Weapons, enhance progress towards its full implementation and universality and monitor the implementation of commitments made and actions agreed upon at the 1995, 2000 and 2010 Review Conferences, and deeply concerned about the impact of this failure on the Treaty and the balance between its three pillars,

Noting with concern the rising tensions in international relations and the increased prominence being given by some States to nuclear weapons in their security doctrines, including through modernization programmes,

Noting the second session of the Preparatory Committee for the 2020 Review Conference of the Parties to the Treaty on the Non-Proliferation of Nuclear Weapons, held in Geneva from 23 April to 4 May 2018,

Emphasizing the importance of a constructive and successful preparatory process leading to the 2020 Review Conference, and urging all Member States to step up their efforts in this regard, and emphasizing also that it should contribute to strengthening the Treaty and making progress towards achieving its full implementation and universality, and monitor the implementation of commitments made and actions agreed upon at the 1995, 2000 and 2010 Review Conferences,

Welcoming that the Russian Federation and the United States of America have completed the nuclear weapon reductions agreed under the new strategic arms reduction treaty, while re-emphasizing the encouragement of the 2010 Review Conference to both States to continue discussions on follow-on measures in order to achieve deeper reductions in their nuclear arsenals,

Underlining the importance of multilateralism in relation to nuclear disarmament, while recognizing the value of unilateral, bilateral and regional initiatives and the importance of compliance with the terms of these initiatives,

1.   *Reiterates* that each article of the Treaty on the Non-Proliferation of Nuclear Weapons[9] is binding on the States parties at all times and in all circumstances and that all States parties should be held fully accountable with respect to strict compliance with their obligations under the Treaty, and calls upon all States parties to comply fully with all decisions, resolutions and commitments made at the 1995, 2000 and 2010 Review Conferences;

2.   *Also reiterates* the deep concern expressed by the 2010 Review Conference of the Parties to the Treaty on the Non-Proliferation of Nuclear Weapons at the catastrophic humanitarian consequences of any use of nuclear weapons, and the need for all States at all times to comply with applicable international law, including international humanitarian law;[3]

3.   *Acknowledges* the evidence presented at the Conferences on the Humanitarian Impact of Nuclear Weapons, and calls upon Member States, in their relevant decisions and actions, to give due prominence to the humanitarian imperatives that underpin nuclear disarmament and to the urgency of achieving this goal;

4.   *Recalls* the reaffirmation of the continued validity of the practical steps agreed to in the Final Document of the 2000 Review Conference of the Parties to the Treaty on the Non-Proliferation of Nuclear Weapons,[11] including the specific reaffirmation of the unequivocal undertaking of the nuclear-weapon States to accomplish the total elimination of their nuclear arsenals leading to nuclear disarmament, to which all States parties are committed under article VI of the Treaty, recalls the commitment of the nuclear-weapon States to accelerating concrete progress on the steps leading to nuclear disarmament, and calls upon the nuclear-weapon States to take all steps necessary to accelerate the fulfilment of their commitments;

5.   *Calls upon* the nuclear-weapon States to fulfil their commitment to undertaking further efforts to reduce and ultimately eliminate all types of nuclear weapons, deployed and non-deployed, including through unilateral, bilateral, regional and multilateral measures;

6.   *Urges* all States possessing nuclear weapons to decrease the operational readiness of nuclear-weapon systems in a verifiable and transparent manner with a view to ensuring that all nuclear weapons are removed from high alert status;

7.   *Encourages* the nuclear-weapon States to make concrete reductions in the role and significance of nuclear weapons in all military and security concepts, doctrines and policies, pending their total elimination;

---

[11] *2000 Review Conference of the Parties to the Treaty on the Non-Proliferation of Nuclear Weapons, Final Document*, vol. I (NPT/CONF.2000/28 (Parts I and II)), part I, section entitled "Article VI and eighth to twelfth preambular paragraphs", para. 15.

8.   *Encourages* all States that are part of regional alliances that include nuclear-weapon States to diminish the role of nuclear weapons in their collective security doctrines, pending their total elimination;

9.   *Underlines* the recognition by States parties to the Treaty on the Non-Proliferation of Nuclear Weapons of the legitimate interest of non-nuclear-weapon States in the constraining by the nuclear-weapon States of the development and qualitative improvement of nuclear weapons and their ending the development of advanced new types of nuclear weapons, and calls upon the nuclear-weapon States to take steps in this regard;

10.   *Notes with concern* recent policy statements by nuclear-weapon States relating to the modernization of their nuclear weapon programmes, which undermine their commitments to nuclear disarmament and increase the risk of the use of nuclear weapons and the potential for a new arms race;

11.   *Encourages* further steps by all nuclear-weapon States, in accordance with the previous obligations and commitments on nuclear disarmament, to ensure the irreversible removal of all fissile material designated by each nuclear-weapon State as no longer required for military purposes, and calls upon all States to support, within the context of the International Atomic Energy Agency, the development of appropriate nuclear disarmament verification capabilities and legally binding verification arrangements, thereby ensuring that such material remains permanently outside military programmes in a verifiable manner;

12.   *Calls upon* all States parties to the Treaty on the Non-Proliferation of Nuclear Weapons to work towards the full implementation of the resolution on the Middle East adopted at the 1995 Review and Extension Conference of the Parties to the Treaty on the Non-Proliferation of Nuclear Weapons,[6] which is inextricably linked to the indefinite extension of the Treaty, and expresses disappointment and deep concern at the lack of a substantive outcome of the 2015 Review Conference of the Parties to the Treaty on the Non-Proliferation of Nuclear Weapons, including on the process to establish a Middle East zone free of nuclear weapons and all other weapons of mass destruction as contained in the 1995 resolution on the Middle East, which remains valid until fully implemented;

13.   *Urges* the co-sponsors of the 1995 resolution on the Middle East to exert their utmost efforts with a view to ensuring the early establishment of a Middle East zone free of nuclear weapons and all other weapons of mass destruction as contained in the 1995 resolution on the Middle East, including through support for the convening of the conference on the establishment of such a zone;

14.   *Stresses* the fundamental role of the Treaty on the Non-Proliferation of Nuclear Weapons in achieving nuclear disarmament and nuclear non-proliferation, and looks forward to the third session of the Preparatory

Committee for the 2020 Review Conference of the Parties to the Treaty on the Non-Proliferation of Nuclear Weapons, to be held in New York from 29 April to 10 May 2019;

15.   *Calls upon* all States parties to spare no effort to achieve the universality of the Treaty on the Non-Proliferation of Nuclear Weapons, and in this regard urges India, Israel and Pakistan to accede to the Treaty as non-nuclear-weapon States promptly and without conditions, and to place all their nuclear facilities under International Atomic Energy Agency safeguards;

16.   *Notes with encouragement* the dialogue and discussions held with the Democratic People's Republic of Korea, including the recent inter-Korean summits, and the summit between the United States of America and the Democratic People's Republic of Korea, urges the Democratic People's Republic of Korea to fulfil its commitments, to abandon all nuclear weapons and existing nuclear programmes, to return, at an early date, to the Treaty on the Non-Proliferation of Nuclear Weapons and to adhere to its International Atomic Energy Agency safeguards agreement,[12] with a view to achieving the denuclearization of the Korean Peninsula in a peaceful manner, and reaffirms its firm support for the Six-Party Talks;

17.   *Urges* all States to work together to overcome obstacles within the international disarmament machinery that are inhibiting efforts to advance the cause of nuclear disarmament in a multilateral context, and once again urges the Conference on Disarmament to commence immediately substantive work that advances the agenda of nuclear disarmament, particularly through multilateral negotiations;

18.   *Urges* all States parties to the Treaty on the Non-Proliferation of Nuclear Weapons to fully implement without delay their obligations and commitments under the Treaty and as agreed to at the 1995, 2000 and 2010 Review Conferences;

19.   *Also urges* all State parties to the Treaty on the Non-Proliferation of Nuclear Weapons to move forward with urgency in implementing their article VI obligations in order to ensure the good standing of the Treaty and its review process;

20.   *Urges* the nuclear-weapon States to implement their nuclear disarmament obligations and commitments, both qualitative and quantitative, in a manner that enables the States parties to regularly monitor progress, including through a standard detailed reporting format, thereby enhancing confidence and trust not only among the nuclear-weapon States but also between the nuclear-weapon States and the non-nuclear-weapon States and contributing to nuclear disarmament;

---

[12] United Nations, *Treaty Series*, vol. 1677, No. 28986.

21. *Also urges* the nuclear-weapon States to include in their reports to be submitted during the 2020 review cycle of the Treaty on the Non-Proliferation of Nuclear Weapons concrete and detailed information concerning the implementation of their obligations and commitments on nuclear disarmament;

22. *Encourages* States parties to the Treaty on the Non-Proliferation of Nuclear Weapons to improve the measurability of the implementation of nuclear disarmament obligations and commitments, including through tools such as a set of benchmarks or similar criteria, in order to ensure and facilitate the objective evaluation of progress;[13]

23. *Urges* Member States to pursue multilateral negotiations without delay in good faith on effective measures for the achievement and maintenance of a nuclear-weapon-free world, in keeping with the spirit and purpose of General Assembly resolution 1 (I) and article VI of the Treaty on the Non-Proliferation of Nuclear Weapons;

24. *Calls upon* Member States to continue to support efforts to identify, elaborate, negotiate and implement further effective legally binding measures for nuclear disarmament, and welcomes in this regard the adoption on 7 July 2017 of the Treaty on the Prohibition of Nuclear Weapons;[5]

25. *Recommends* that measures be taken to increase awareness among civil society of the risks and catastrophic impact of any nuclear detonation, including through disarmament education;

26. *Decides* to include in the provisional agenda of its seventy-fourth session, under the item entitled "General and complete disarmament", the sub-item entitled "Towards a nuclear-weapon-free world: accelerating the implementation of nuclear disarmament commitments" and to review the implementation of the present resolution at that session.

Action by the General Assembly

Date: 5 December 2018
Vote: 139-32-17
139-1-33, p.p. 4
122-35-17, p.p. 12
132-2-41, o.p. 13
162-4-8, o.p. 15
122-36-15, o.p. 24

Meeting: 45th plenary meeting
Report: A/73/510

Sponsors

Austria, Brazil, Egypt, Ghana, Ireland, Mexico, Namibia, New Zealand, Samoa, **South Africa**

---

[13] See NPT/CONF.2020/PC.I/WP.13.

Co-sponsors

Costa Rica, Liechtenstein, Nigeria, Philippines, Seychelles, Thailand

Recorded vote

As a whole

In favour:

Afghanistan, Algeria, Angola, Antigua and Barbuda, Argentina, Austria, Azerbaijan, Bahamas, Bahrain, Bangladesh, Barbados, Belarus, Belize, Benin, Bhutan, Bolivia (Plurinational State of), Botswana, Brazil, Brunei Darussalam, Burkina Faso, Burundi, Cabo Verde, Cambodia, Cameroon, Central African Republic, Chile, Colombia, Comoros, Congo, Costa Rica, Côte d'Ivoire, Cuba, Cyprus, Democratic Republic of the Congo, Djibouti, Dominica, Dominican Republic, Ecuador, Egypt, El Salvador, Equatorial Guinea, Eritrea, Eswatini, Ethiopia, Fiji, Gabon, Gambia, Ghana, Grenada, Guatemala, Guinea, Guinea-Bissau, Guyana, Honduras, Indonesia, Iran (Islamic Republic of), Iraq, Ireland, Jamaica, Jordan, Kazakhstan, Kenya, Kuwait, Kyrgyzstan, Lao People's Democratic Republic, Lebanon, Lesotho, Liberia, Libya, Liechtenstein, Madagascar, Malawi, Malaysia, Maldives, Mali, Malta, Mauritania, Mauritius, Mexico, Mongolia, Morocco, Mozambique, Myanmar, Namibia, Nauru, Nepal, New Zealand, Nicaragua, Niger, Nigeria, Oman, Palau, Panama, Papua New Guinea, Paraguay, Peru, Philippines, Qatar, Republic of Moldova, Rwanda, Saint Kitts and Nevis, Saint Lucia, Saint Vincent and the Grenadines, Samoa, San Marino, Sao Tome and Principe, Saudi Arabia, Senegal, Seychelles, Sierra Leone, Singapore, Solomon Islands, South Africa, Sri Lanka, Sudan, Suriname, Sweden, Switzerland, Syrian Arab Republic, Tajikistan, Thailand, Timor-Leste, Togo, Tonga, Trinidad and Tobago, Tunisia, Turkmenistan, Tuvalu, Uganda, United Arab Emirates, United Republic of Tanzania, Uruguay, Uzbekistan, Vanuatu, Venezuela (Bolivarian Republic of), Viet Nam, Yemen, Zambia, Zimbabwe

Against:

Albania, Belgium, Bulgaria, China, Croatia, Czechia, Denmark, Estonia, France, Germany, Greece, Hungary, India, Israel, Italy, Latvia, Lithuania, Luxembourg, Monaco, Montenegro, Netherlands, Norway, Poland, Portugal, Romania, Russian Federation, Slovakia, Slovenia, Spain, Turkey, United Kingdom, United States

Abstaining:

Andorra, Armenia, Australia, Bosnia and Herzegovina, Canada, Democratic People's Republic of Korea, Finland, Georgia, Iceland, Japan, Marshall Islands, Micronesia (Federated States of), Pakistan, Republic of Korea, Serbia, the former Yugoslav Republic of Macedonia, Ukraine

Fourth preambular paragraph

In favour:

Algeria, Angola, Antigua and Barbuda, Argentina, Australia, Austria, Azerbaijan, Bahamas, Bahrain, Bangladesh, Barbados, Belarus, Belgium, Belize, Benin, Bhutan, Bolivia (Plurinational State of), Botswana, Brazil, Brunei Darussalam, Burkina Faso, Burundi, Cabo Verde, Cambodia, Canada, Chile, China, Colombia, Comoros, Costa Rica, Côte d'Ivoire, Cuba, Cyprus, Democratic People's Republic of Korea, Democratic Republic of the Congo, Djibouti, Dominican Republic, Ecuador, Egypt, El Salvador, Equatorial Guinea, Eritrea, Eswatini, Ethiopia, Fiji, Finland, Gambia, Ghana, Guatemala, Guinea, Guinea-Bissau, Guyana, Honduras, Iceland, India, Indonesia, Iraq, Ireland, Jamaica, Japan, Jordan, Kazakhstan, Kenya, Kuwait, Kyrgyzstan, Lao People's Democratic Republic, Lebanon, Lesotho, Liberia, Libya, Liechtenstein, Madagascar, Malawi, Malaysia, Maldives, Mali, Malta, Mauritania, Mauritius, Mexico, Mongolia, Morocco, Mozambique, Myanmar, Namibia, Nepal, Netherlands, New Zealand, Nicaragua, Niger, Nigeria, Norway, Oman, Pakistan, Panama, Papua New Guinea, Paraguay, Peru, Philippines, Qatar, Republic of Korea, Republic of Moldova, Saint Kitts and Nevis, Saint Lucia, Saint Vincent and the Grenadines, Samoa, San Marino, Sao Tome and Principe, Saudi Arabia, Senegal, Serbia, Seychelles, Sierra Leone, Singapore, Solomon Islands, South Africa, Sri Lanka, Sudan, Suriname, Sweden, Switzerland, Thailand, Timor-Leste, Togo, Trinidad and Tobago, Tunisia, Turkmenistan, Tuvalu, Uganda, United Arab Emirates, United Republic of Tanzania, Uruguay, Uzbekistan, Vanuatu, Venezuela (Bolivarian Republic of), Viet Nam, Yemen, Zambia, Zimbabwe

Against:

United States

Abstaining:

Albania, Andorra, Armenia, Bosnia and Herzegovina, Bulgaria, Croatia, Czechia, Denmark, Estonia, France, Georgia, Germany, Greece, Hungary, Israel, Italy, Latvia, Lithuania, Luxembourg, Monaco, Montenegro, Poland, Portugal, Romania, Russian Federation, Slovakia, Slovenia, Spain, Syrian Arab Republic, the former Yugoslav Republic of Macedonia, Turkey, Ukraine, United Kingdom

Twelfth preambular paragraph

In favour:

Algeria, Angola, Antigua and Barbuda, Argentina, Austria, Azerbaijan, Bahamas, Bahrain, Bangladesh, Barbados, Belize, Benin, Bhutan, Bolivia (Plurinational State of), Botswana, Brazil, Brunei Darussalam, Burkina Faso, Burundi, Cabo Verde, Cambodia, Chile, Colombia, Comoros,

Costa Rica, Côte d'Ivoire, Cuba, Cyprus, Democratic Republic of the Congo, Djibouti, Dominican Republic, Ecuador, Egypt, El Salvador, Equatorial Guinea, Eritrea, Eswatini, Ethiopia, Fiji, Gambia, Ghana, Guatemala, Guinea, Guinea-Bissau, Guyana, Honduras, Indonesia, Iran (Islamic Republic of), Iraq, Ireland, Jamaica, Jordan, Kazakhstan, Kenya, Kuwait, Lao People's Democratic Republic, Lebanon, Lesotho, Liberia, Libya, Liechtenstein, Madagascar, Malawi, Malaysia, Maldives, Mali, Malta, Mauritania, Mauritius, Mexico, Mongolia, Morocco, Mozambique, Myanmar, Namibia, Nepal, New Zealand, Nicaragua, Niger, Nigeria, Oman, Panama, Papua New Guinea, Paraguay, Peru, Philippines, Qatar, Republic of Moldova, Rwanda, Saint Kitts and Nevis, Saint Lucia, Saint Vincent and the Grenadines, Samoa, San Marino, Sao Tome and Principe, Saudi Arabia, Senegal, Sierra Leone, Singapore, Solomon Islands, South Africa, Sri Lanka, Sudan, Suriname, Thailand, Timor-Leste, Togo, Trinidad and Tobago, Tunisia, Turkmenistan, Tuvalu, Uganda, United Arab Emirates, United Republic of Tanzania, Uruguay, Uzbekistan, Vanuatu, Venezuela (Bolivarian Republic of), Viet Nam, Yemen, Zambia, Zimbabwe

Against:

Albania, Australia, Belgium, Bulgaria, Canada, China, Croatia, Czechia, Denmark, Estonia, France, Germany, Greece, Hungary, Iceland, Israel, Italy, Latvia, Lithuania, Luxembourg, Monaco, Montenegro, Netherlands, Norway, Poland, Portugal, Republic of Korea, Romania, Russian Federation, Slovakia, Slovenia, Spain, Turkey, United Kingdom, United States

Abstaining:

Andorra, Armenia, Belarus, Bosnia and Herzegovina, Democratic People's Republic of Korea, Finland, Georgia, India, Japan, Kyrgyzstan, Pakistan, Serbia, Sweden, Switzerland, Tajikistan, the former Yugoslav Republic of Macedonia, Ukraine

Operative paragraph 13

In favour:

Algeria, Angola, Antigua and Barbuda, Argentina, Austria, Azerbaijan, Bahamas, Bahrain, Bangladesh, Barbados, Belarus, Belize, Benin, Bhutan, Bolivia (Plurinational State of), Botswana, Brazil, Brunei Darussalam, Burkina Faso, Burundi, Cabo Verde, Cambodia, Chile, China, Colombia, Comoros, Costa Rica, Côte d'Ivoire, Cuba, Cyprus, Democratic People's Republic of Korea, Democratic Republic of the Congo, Djibouti, Dominican Republic, Ecuador, Egypt, El Salvador, Equatorial Guinea, Eritrea, Eswatini, Ethiopia, Fiji, Finland, Gambia, Ghana, Guatemala, Guinea, Guinea-Bissau, Guyana, Honduras, Indonesia, Iran (Islamic Republic of), Iraq, Ireland, Jamaica, Jordan,

Kazakhstan, Kenya, Kuwait, Kyrgyzstan, Lao People's Democratic Republic, Lebanon, Lesotho, Liberia, Libya, Liechtenstein, Madagascar, Malawi, Malaysia, Maldives, Mali, Malta, Mauritania, Mauritius, Mexico, Mongolia, Morocco, Mozambique, Myanmar, Namibia, Nepal, New Zealand, Nicaragua, Niger, Nigeria, Oman, Pakistan, Panama, Papua New Guinea, Paraguay, Peru, Philippines, Qatar, Republic of Moldova, Russian Federation, Rwanda, Saint Kitts and Nevis, Saint Lucia, Saint Vincent and the Grenadines, Samoa, San Marino, Sao Tome and Principe, Saudi Arabia, Seychelles, Sierra Leone, Singapore, Solomon Islands, South Africa, Sri Lanka, Sudan, Suriname, Sweden, Switzerland, Syrian Arab Republic, Tajikistan, Thailand, Timor-Leste, Togo, Trinidad and Tobago, Tunisia, Turkmenistan, Uganda, United Arab Emirates, United Republic of Tanzania, Uruguay, Uzbekistan, Vanuatu, Venezuela (Bolivarian Republic of), Viet Nam, Yemen, Zambia, Zimbabwe

Against:
Israel, United States

Abstaining:
Albania, Andorra, Armenia, Australia, Belgium, Bosnia and Herzegovina, Bulgaria, Canada, Croatia, Czechia, Denmark, Estonia, France, Georgia, Germany, Greece, Hungary, Iceland, India, Italy, Japan, Latvia, Lithuania, Luxembourg, Monaco, Montenegro, Netherlands, Norway, Poland, Portugal, Republic of Korea, Romania, Serbia, Slovakia, Slovenia, Spain, the former Yugoslav Republic of Macedonia, Turkey, Tuvalu, Ukraine, United Kingdom

Operative paragraph 15*

In favour:
Albania, Algeria, Andorra, Angola, Antigua and Barbuda, Argentina, Armenia, Australia, Austria, Azerbaijan, Bahamas, Bahrain, Bangladesh, Barbados, Belarus, Belgium, Belize, Benin, Bolivia (Plurinational State of), Bosnia and Herzegovina, Botswana, Brazil, Brunei Darussalam, Bulgaria, Burkina Faso, Burundi, Cabo Verde, Cambodia, Canada, Chile, China, Colombia, Comoros, Costa Rica, Côte d'Ivoire, Croatia, Cuba, Cyprus, Czechia, Democratic Republic of the Congo, Denmark, Djibouti, Dominican Republic, Ecuador, Egypt, El Salvador, Equatorial Guinea, Eritrea, Estonia, Eswatini, Ethiopia, Fiji, Finland, Gambia, Ghana, Greece, Guatemala, Guinea, Guinea-Bissau, Guyana, Honduras, Iceland, Indonesia, Iran (Islamic Republic of), Iraq, Ireland, Italy, Jamaica, Japan, Jordan, Kazakhstan, Kenya, Kuwait, Kyrgyzstan, Lao People's Democratic Republic, Latvia, Lebanon, Lesotho, Liberia, Libya,

---

* Subsequently, the delegation of Andorra informed the Secretariat that it had intended to abstain. The voting tally above does not reflect this information.

Liechtenstein, Lithuania, Luxembourg, Madagascar, Malawi, Malaysia, Maldives, Mali, Malta, Mauritania, Mexico, Mongolia, Montenegro, Morocco, Mozambique, Myanmar, Namibia, Nepal, Netherlands, New Zealand, Nicaragua, Niger, Nigeria, Norway, Oman, Panama, Papua New Guinea, Paraguay, Peru, Philippines, Poland, Portugal, Qatar, Republic of Korea, Republic of Moldova, Romania, Russian Federation, Rwanda, Saint Kitts and Nevis, Saint Lucia, Saint Vincent and the Grenadines, Samoa, San Marino, Sao Tome and Principe, Saudi Arabia, Senegal, Serbia, Seychelles, Sierra Leone, Singapore, Slovakia, Slovenia, Solomon Islands, South Africa, Spain, Sri Lanka, Sudan, Suriname, Sweden, Switzerland, Syrian Arab Republic, Tajikistan, Thailand, the former Yugoslav Republic of Macedonia, Timor-Leste, Togo, Trinidad and Tobago, Tunisia, Turkey, Turkmenistan, Tuvalu, Uganda, United Arab Emirates, United Republic of Tanzania, Uruguay, Uzbekistan, Vanuatu, Venezuela (Bolivarian Republic of), Viet Nam, Yemen, Zambia, Zimbabwe

Against:
India, Israel, Pakistan, United States

Abstaining:
Bhutan, France, Georgia, Germany, Hungary, Monaco, Ukraine, United Kingdom

Operative paragraph 24**

In favour:
Algeria, Angola, Antigua and Barbuda, Argentina, Austria, Azerbaijan, Bahamas, Bahrain, Bangladesh, Barbados, Belize, Benin, Bhutan, Bolivia (Plurinational State of), Botswana, Brazil, Brunei Darussalam, Burkina Faso, Burundi, Cabo Verde, Cambodia, Chile, Colombia, Comoros, Costa Rica, Côte d'Ivoire, Cuba, Cyprus, Democratic Republic of the Congo, Djibouti, Dominican Republic, Ecuador, Egypt, El Salvador, Equatorial Guinea, Eritrea, Eswatini, Ethiopia, Fiji, Gambia, Ghana, Guatemala, Guinea, Guinea-Bissau, Guyana, Honduras, Indonesia, Iran (Islamic Republic of), Iraq, Ireland, Jamaica, Jordan, Kazakhstan, Kenya, Kuwait, Lao People's Democratic Republic, Lebanon, Lesotho, Liberia, Libya, Liechtenstein, Madagascar, Malawi, Malaysia, Maldives, Mali, Malta, Mauritania, Mauritius, Mexico, Mongolia, Morocco, Mozambique, Myanmar, Namibia, Nepal, New Zealand, Nicaragua, Niger, Nigeria, Oman, Panama, Papua New Guinea, Paraguay, Peru, Philippines, Qatar, Republic of Moldova, Saint Kitts and Nevis, Saint Lucia, Saint Vincent and the Grenadines, Samoa, San Marino, Sao Tome and Principe, Saudi Arabia, Seychelles, Sierra Leone, Singapore, Solomon Islands,

---

** Subsequently, the delegation of Andorra informed the Secretariat that it had intended to abstain. The voting tally above does not reflect this information.

South Africa, Sri Lanka, Sudan, Suriname, Switzerland, Syrian Arab Republic, Thailand, Timor-Leste, Togo, Trinidad and Tobago, Tunisia, Turkmenistan, Tuvalu, Uganda, United Arab Emirates, United Republic of Tanzania, Uruguay, Vanuatu, Venezuela (Bolivarian Republic of), Viet Nam, Yemen, Zambia, Zimbabwe

Against:

Albania, Andorra, Australia, Belgium, Bulgaria, Canada, China, Croatia, Czechia, Denmark, Estonia, France, Germany, Greece, Hungary, Iceland, Israel, Italy, Latvia, Lithuania, Luxembourg, Monaco, Montenegro, Netherlands, Norway, Poland, Portugal, Republic of Korea, Romania, Russian Federation, Slovakia, Slovenia, Spain, Turkey, United Kingdom, United States

Abstaining:

Armenia, Belarus, Bosnia and Herzegovina, Democratic People's Republic of Korea, Finland, Georgia, India, Japan, Kyrgyzstan, Pakistan, Serbia, Sweden, the former Yugoslav Republic of Macedonia, Ukraine, Uzbekistan

Action by the First Committee

Date: 1 November 2018	Meeting:	26th meeting
Vote: 134-31-18	Draft resolution:	A/C.1/73/L.64
134-1-36, p.p. 4		
120-35-18, p.p. 12		
131-2-41, o.p. 13		
160-5-9, o.p. 15		
122-35-17, o.p. 24		

Agenda item 101

73/71   Fourth Conference of Nuclear-Weapon-Free Zones and Mongolia, 2020

Text

The General Assembly,

Recalling its resolutions 64/52 of 2 December 2009 and 69/66 of 2 December 2014 by which it convened the second and third Conferences of States Parties and Signatories to Treaties that Establish Nuclear-Weapon-Free Zones and Mongolia in 2010 and 2015, respectively,

Recognizing the right of any group of States to conclude regional treaties in order to ensure the total absence of nuclear weapons in their respective territories, as established by article VII of the Treaty on the Non-Proliferation of Nuclear Weapons,[1]

Recalling the provisions on nuclear-weapon-free zones of the Final Document of the Tenth Special Session of the General Assembly, the first special session devoted to disarmament,[2]

Welcoming the important contribution of the treaties of Tlatelolco,[3] Rarotonga,[4] Bangkok[5] and Pelindaba[6] and the Treaty on a Nuclear-Weapon-Free Zone in Central Asia, as well as the Antarctic Treaty,[7] to the achievement of the objectives of nuclear disarmament and nuclear non-proliferation, and towards freeing the southern hemisphere and adjacent areas covered by those treaties from nuclear weapons,

Recalling its resolution 71/43 of 5 December 2016 on Mongolia's international security and nuclear-weapon-free status,

Reaffirming the conviction that, pending the total elimination of nuclear weapons, the establishment and maintenance of nuclear-weapon-free zones enhances global and regional peace and security, strengthens the nuclear non-proliferation regime and contributes towards realizing the objectives of nuclear disarmament,

Urging States that have not yet established nuclear-weapon-free-zone treaties to accelerate efforts in this direction, particularly in the Middle East, through agreements freely arrived at among the States of the region concerned,

---

[1] United Nations, *Treaty Series*, vol. 729, No. 10485.
[2] Resolution S-10/2.
[3] United Nations, *Treaty Series*, vol. 634, No. 9068.
[4] *The United Nations Disarmament Yearbook*, vol. 10: 1985 (United Nations publication, Sales No. E.86.IX.7), appendix VII.
[5] United Nations, *Treaty Series*, vol. 1981, No. 33873.
[6] A/50/426, annex.
[7] United Nations, *Treaty Series*, vol. 402, No. 5778.

in accordance with the provisions of the Final Document of the first special session of the General Assembly devoted to disarmament and the principles adopted by the Disarmament Commission in 1999,[8]

Taking note of paragraph 232 of the Final Document of the Eighteenth Midterm Ministerial Meeting of the Movement of Non-Aligned Countries, held in Baku from 3 to 6 April 2018, in which the Ministers stated their belief that those nuclear-weapon-free zones were positive steps and important measures towards strengthening global nuclear disarmament and nuclear non-proliferation,

Recalling that States in regions in which there are nuclear-weapon-free zones are encouraged to ratify the respective treaties that establish said zones,

Recalling also that it is expected that the States to which the protocols to the treaties that establish nuclear-weapon-free zones are open for signature ratify them and constructively consult and cooperate to bring about the entry into force of the protocols,

Noting that, among other aspects, those protocols include the necessary security guarantees for the States belonging to nuclear-weapon-free zones,

Recognizing the progress made on increased collaboration within and between zones at the first, second and third Conferences of States Parties and Signatories to Treaties that Establish Nuclear-Weapon-Free Zones, held in Mexico City from 26 to 28 April 2005 and in New York on 30 April 2010 and 24 April 2015, respectively, at which States reaffirmed their need to cooperate in order to achieve their common objectives,

1.   *Decides* to convene the fourth Conference of Nuclear-Weapon-Free Zones and Mongolia as a one-day conference at United Nations Headquarters in New York on 24 April 2020;

2.   *Invites* all States Members and observer States of the United Nations that are States parties or signatories to the treaties that establish nuclear-weapon-free zones and Mongolia to participate in the Conference;

3.   *Invites* all States parties and signatories to the protocols to the treaties that establish nuclear-weapon-free zones to participate in the capacity of observers;

4.   *Encourages* all the other States Members and observer States of the United Nations to participate in the capacity of observers;

5.   *Decides* that the objective of the Conference will be to consider ways and means to enhance consultations and cooperation among nuclear-weapon-free zones and Mongolia, the treaty agencies and interested States, with the purpose of promoting coordination and convergence in the

---

[8] *Official Records of the General Assembly, Fifty-fourth Session, Supplement No. 42* (A/54/42), annex I, sect. C.

implementation of the provisions of the treaties and in strengthening the regime of nuclear disarmament and non-proliferation;

6. *Urges* the States parties and signatories to treaties that have established nuclear-weapon-free zones to develop activities of cooperation and coordination in order to promote their common objectives in the framework of the Conference;

7. *Welcomes* the offer by Mongolia to act as coordinator of the fourth Conference and to conduct preparatory meetings and informal consultations, including with relevant regional organizations, as may be necessary to prepare for the Conference and its rules of procedure and draft outcome document, beginning in early 2019;

8. *Requests* the Secretary-General to provide the support necessary to convene the fourth Conference of Nuclear-Weapon-Free Zones and Mongolia and to transmit the report of the fourth Conference to the Conference on Disarmament and the Disarmament Commission.

Action by the General Assembly

Date: 5 December 2018   Meeting: 45th plenary meeting
Vote: 179-0-5   Report: A/73/510

Sponsors

Argentina, **Brazil**, **Mongolia**

Co-sponsors

Indonesia, Jamaica, Kazakhstan, Mexico, Philippines, Thailand

Recorded vote

In favour:

Afghanistan, Albania, Algeria, Andorra, Angola, Antigua and Barbuda, Argentina, Armenia, Australia, Austria, Azerbaijan, Bahamas, Bahrain, Bangladesh, Barbados, Belarus, Belgium, Belize, Benin, Bhutan, Bolivia (Plurinational State of), Bosnia and Herzegovina, Botswana, Brazil, Brunei Darussalam, Bulgaria, Burkina Faso, Burundi, Cabo Verde, Cambodia, Cameroon, Canada, Central African Republic, Chile, China, Colombia, Comoros, Congo, Costa Rica, Côte d'Ivoire, Croatia, Cuba, Cyprus, Czechia, Democratic People's Republic of Korea, Democratic Republic of the Congo, Denmark, Djibouti, Dominica, Dominican Republic, Ecuador, Egypt, El Salvador, Equatorial Guinea, Eritrea, Estonia, Eswatini, Ethiopia, Fiji, Finland, Gabon, Gambia, Georgia, Germany, Ghana, Greece, Grenada, Guatemala, Guinea, Guinea-Bissau, Guyana, Haiti, Honduras, Hungary, Iceland, India, Indonesia, Iran (Islamic Republic of), Iraq, Ireland, Italy, Jamaica, Japan, Jordan, Kazakhstan, Kenya, Kuwait, Kyrgyzstan, Lao People's Democratic

Republic, Latvia, Lebanon, Lesotho, Liberia, Libya, Liechtenstein, Lithuania, Luxembourg, Madagascar, Malawi, Malaysia, Maldives, Mali, Malta, Marshall Islands, Mauritania, Mauritius, Mexico, Monaco, Mongolia, Montenegro, Morocco, Mozambique, Myanmar, Namibia, Nepal, Netherlands, New Zealand, Nicaragua, Niger, Nigeria, Norway, Oman, Pakistan, Panama, Papua New Guinea, Paraguay, Peru, Philippines, Poland, Portugal, Qatar, Republic of Korea, Republic of Moldova, Romania, Rwanda, Saint Kitts and Nevis, Saint Lucia, Saint Vincent and the Grenadines, Samoa, San Marino, Sao Tome and Principe, Saudi Arabia, Senegal, Serbia, Seychelles, Sierra Leone, Singapore, Slovakia, Slovenia, Solomon Islands, South Africa, Spain, Sri Lanka, Sudan, Suriname, Sweden, Switzerland, Syrian Arab Republic, Tajikistan, Thailand, the former Yugoslav Republic of Macedonia, Timor-Leste, Togo, Trinidad and Tobago, Tunisia, Turkey, Turkmenistan, Uganda, Ukraine, United Arab Emirates, United Republic of Tanzania, Uruguay, Uzbekistan, Vanuatu, Venezuela (Bolivarian Republic of), Viet Nam, Yemen, Zambia, Zimbabwe

Against:
None

Abstaining:
France, Israel, Russian Federation, United Kingdom, United States

Action by the First Committee

Date:	8 November 2018	Meeting:	30th meeting
Vote:	171-0-6	Draft resolution:	A/C.1/73/L.66

Agenda item 101 (aa)

73/72 Transparency and confidence-building measures in outer space activities

Text

The General Assembly,

Recalling its resolutions 60/66 of 8 December 2005, 61/75 of 6 December 2006, 62/43 of 5 December 2007, 63/68 of 2 December 2008, 64/49 of 2 December 2009, 65/68 of 8 December 2010, 68/50 of 5 December 2013, 69/38 of 2 December 2014, 70/53 of 7 December 2015, 71/42 of 5 December 2016, 71/90 of 6 December 2016 and 72/56 of 4 December 2017, as well as its decision 66/517 of 2 December 2011,

Recalling also the report of the Secretary-General of 15 October 1993 to the General Assembly at its forty-eighth session, the annex to which contains the study by governmental experts on the application of confidence-building measures in outer space,[1]

Reaffirming the right of all countries to explore and use outer space in accordance with international law,

Reaffirming also that preventing an arms race in outer space is in the interest of maintaining international peace and security and is an essential condition for the promotion and strengthening of international cooperation in the exploration and use of outer space for peaceful purposes,

Recalling, in this context, its resolutions 45/55 B of 4 December 1990 and 48/74 B of 16 December 1993, in which, inter alia, it recognized the need for increased transparency and confirmed the importance of confidence-building measures as a means of reinforcing the objective of preventing an arms race in outer space,

Noting the constructive debates that the Conference on Disarmament has held on this subject and the views expressed by Member States,

Noting also the introduction by China and the Russian Federation at the Conference on Disarmament of the draft treaty on prevention of the placement of weapons in outer space and of the threat or use of force against outer space objects,[2] and the submission of its updated version[3] in 2014,

Noting further that, since 2004, several States[4] have introduced a policy of not being the first State to place weapons in outer space,

---

[1] A/48/305 and A/48/305/Corr.1.

[2] See CD/1839.

[3] See CD/1985.

[4] Argentina, Armenia, Belarus, Bolivia (Plurinational State of), Brazil, Cuba, Ecuador, Guatemala, Indonesia, Kazakhstan, Kyrgyzstan, Nicaragua, Russian Federation, Sri Lanka, Suriname, Tajikistan, Uruguay, Venezuela (Bolivarian Republic of) and Viet Nam.

Welcoming the launch of discussions in the working group of the Disarmament Commission tasked with preparing recommendations relating to the practical implementation of transparency and confidence-building measures in outer space activities with the goal of preventing an arms race in outer space,

Noting the presentation by the European Union of a draft of a non-legally binding international code of conduct for outer space activities,

Recognizing that the work within the Committee on the Peaceful Uses of Outer Space, its Scientific and Technical Subcommittee and its Legal Subcommittee, including the promotion of the long-term sustainability of outer space activities, has a fundamental role to play in enhancing transparency and confidence-building among States and in ensuring that outer space is maintained for peaceful purposes,

Noting the contribution of Member States that have submitted to the Secretary-General concrete proposals on international outer space transparency and confidence-building measures pursuant to paragraph 1 of resolution 61/75, paragraph 2 of resolution 62/43, paragraph 2 of resolution 63/68 and paragraph 2 of resolution 64/49,

Welcoming the work done in 2012 and 2013 by the Group of Governmental Experts on Transparency and Confidence-building Measures in Outer Space Activities, which was convened by the Secretary-General, on the basis of equitable geographical distribution, to conduct a study on outer space transparency and confidence-building measures,

Noting the consideration of the report of the Group of Governmental Experts,[5] as well as views on the modalities of making practical use of the recommendations contained therein, as set out in the report of the Committee on its fifty-eighth session, held in 2015,[6] at which it found that the Committee had a fundamental role to play in enhancing transparency and confidence-building among States, as well as in ensuring that outer space is maintained for peaceful purposes,

Noting also that, in its report, the Group of Governmental Experts recognized the value of the work of the Committee on the Peaceful Uses of Outer Space in developing a set of voluntary, non-legally binding guidelines for the long-term sustainability of outer space activities, some of which could be considered as potential transparency and confidence-building measures, while others could enhance the safety of outer space activities and thereby provide the technical basis for the further implementation of additional transparency and confidence-building measures,

---

[5] A/68/189.

[6] *Official Records of the General Assembly, Seventieth Session, Supplement No. 20* (A/70/20).

Taking note of the special report by the Inter-Agency Meeting on Outer Space Activities (UN-Space) on the implementation of the report of the Group of Governmental Experts on Transparency and Confidence-building Measures in Outer Space Activities, and the recommendations contained therein, as submitted to the Committee at its fifty-ninth session, in 2016,[7]

Welcoming resolution 186 of 7 November 2014 of the International Telecommunication Union on strengthening the role of the Union with regard to transparency and confidence-building measures in outer space activities, adopted by the 2014 Plenipotentiary Conference of the Union, held in Busan, Republic of Korea, from 20 October to 7 November 2014,

1.   *Stresses* the importance of the report of the Group of Governmental Experts on Transparency and Confidence-building Measures in Outer Space Activities,[5] considered by the General Assembly on 5 December 2013;

2.   *Encourages* Member States to continue to review and implement, to the greatest extent practicable, the proposed transparency and confidence-building measures contained in the report, through the relevant national mechanisms, on a voluntary basis and in a manner consistent with the national interests of Member States;

3.   *Also encourages* Member States, in accordance with the recommendations contained in the report, with a view to promoting the practical implementation of transparency and confidence-building measures, to hold regular discussions in the Committee on the Peaceful Uses of Outer Space, the Disarmament Commission and the Conference on Disarmament on the prospects for their implementation;

4.   *Requests* the relevant entities and organizations of the United Nations system, to which, in accordance with its resolution 68/50, the report was circulated, to assist in effectively implementing the conclusions and recommendations contained therein, as appropriate;

5.   *Encourages* the relevant entities and organizations of the United Nations system to coordinate, as appropriate, on matters related to the recommendations contained in the report;

6.   *Welcomes* the joint ad hoc meetings of the First and Fourth Committees, held on 22 October 2015 and 12 October 2017, on possible challenges to space security and sustainability, convened in accordance with the report and its resolutions 69/38 and 71/90, and the substantive exchanges of opinions on various aspects of security in outer space that took place during the meetings;

---

[7] A/AC.105/1116.

7.   *Calls upon* Member States and the relevant entities and organizations of the United Nations system to support the implementation of the full range of conclusions and recommendations contained in the report;

8.   *Takes note* of the report of the Secretary-General on transparency and confidence-building measures in outer space activities in the United Nations system, which contains summaries of the submissions received from Member States giving their views on transparency and confidence-building measures in outer space activities;[8]

9.   *Invites* Member States to continue to submit, within the relevant forums, information on the specific unilateral, bilateral, regional and multilateral transparency and confidence-building measures in outer space activities implemented in accordance with the recommendations contained in the report of the Group of Governmental Experts;

10.   *Decides* to convene, within existing resources, a joint half-day panel discussion of the Disarmament and International Security Committee (First Committee) and the Special Political and Decolonization Committee (Fourth Committee) to address possible challenges to space security and sustainability, and to include in the provisional agenda of its seventy-fourth session, under the item entitled "General and complete disarmament", a sub-item entitled "Joint panel discussion of the First and Fourth Committees on possible challenges to space security and sustainability";

11.   *Also decides* to include in the provisional agenda of its seventy-fourth session, under the item entitled "General and complete disarmament", the sub-item entitled "Transparency and confidence-building measures in outer space activities".

Action by the General Assembly

Date: 5 December 2018   Meeting: 45th plenary meeting
Vote: 180-2-1   Report: A/73/510

Sponsors

China, Russian Federation

Co-sponsors

Armenia, Belarus, Bolivia (Plurinational State of), Cuba, Guinea, Kyrgyzstan, Mongolia, Myanmar, Namibia, Nicaragua, Suriname, Switzerland, Syrian Arab Republic, Uzbekistan, Venezuela (Bolivarian Republic of), Zimbabwe

---

[8] A/72/65 and A/72/65/Add.1.

Recorded vote

In favour:

Afghanistan, Albania, Algeria, Andorra, Angola, Antigua and Barbuda, Argentina, Armenia, Australia, Austria, Azerbaijan, Bahamas, Bahrain, Bangladesh, Barbados, Belarus, Belgium, Belize, Benin, Bhutan, Bolivia (Plurinational State of), Bosnia and Herzegovina, Botswana, Brazil, Brunei Darussalam, Bulgaria, Burkina Faso, Burundi, Cabo Verde, Cambodia, Canada, Central African Republic, Chile, China, Colombia, Comoros, Congo, Costa Rica, Côte d'Ivoire, Croatia, Cuba, Cyprus, Czechia, Democratic People's Republic of Korea, Democratic Republic of the Congo, Denmark, Djibouti, Dominica, Dominican Republic, Ecuador, Egypt, El Salvador, Equatorial Guinea, Eritrea, Estonia, Eswatini, Ethiopia, Fiji, Finland, France, Gabon, Gambia, Georgia, Germany, Ghana, Greece, Grenada, Guatemala, Guinea, Guinea-Bissau, Guyana, Honduras, Hungary, Iceland, India, Indonesia, Iran (Islamic Republic of), Iraq, Ireland, Italy, Jamaica, Japan, Jordan, Kazakhstan, Kenya, Kuwait, Kyrgyzstan, Lao People's Democratic Republic, Latvia, Lebanon, Lesotho, Liberia, Libya, Liechtenstein, Lithuania, Luxembourg, Madagascar, Malawi, Malaysia, Maldives, Mali, Malta, Mauritania, Mauritius, Mexico, Micronesia (Federated States of), Monaco, Mongolia, Montenegro, Morocco, Mozambique, Myanmar, Namibia, Nepal, Netherlands, New Zealand, Nicaragua, Niger, Nigeria, Norway, Oman, Pakistan, Panama, Papua New Guinea, Paraguay, Peru, Philippines, Poland, Portugal, Qatar, Republic of Korea, Republic of Moldova, Romania, Russian Federation, Rwanda, Saint Kitts and Nevis, Saint Lucia, Saint Vincent and the Grenadines, Samoa, San Marino, Sao Tome and Principe, Saudi Arabia, Senegal, Serbia, Seychelles, Sierra Leone, Singapore, Slovakia, Slovenia, Solomon Islands, South Africa, Spain, Sri Lanka, Sudan, Suriname, Sweden, Switzerland, Syrian Arab Republic, Tajikistan, Thailand, the former Yugoslav Republic of Macedonia, Timor-Leste, Togo, Trinidad and Tobago, Tunisia, Turkey, Tuvalu, Uganda, Ukraine, United Arab Emirates, United Kingdom, United Republic of Tanzania, Uruguay, Uzbekistan, Vanuatu, Venezuela (Bolivarian Republic of), Viet Nam, Yemen, Zambia, Zimbabwe

Against:

Israel, United States

Abstaining:

Palau

Action by the First Committee

Date: 5 November 2018 Meeting: 28th meeting
Vote: 176-2-2 Draft resolution: A/C.1/73/L.68/Rev.1

Agenda item 102 (a)

73/73   United Nations disarmament fellowship, training and advisory services

Text

The General Assembly,

Having considered the report of the Secretary-General,[1]

Recalling its decision, contained in paragraph 108 of the Final Document of the Tenth Special Session of the General Assembly, the first special session devoted to disarmament,[2] to establish a programme of fellowships on disarmament, as well as its decisions contained in annex IV to the Concluding Document of the Twelfth Special Session of the General Assembly, the second special session devoted to disarmament,[3] including its decision to continue the programme,

Noting that the programme continues to contribute significantly to developing greater awareness of the importance and benefits of disarmament and a better understanding of the concerns of the international community in the field of disarmament and security, as well as to enhancing the knowledge and skills of fellows, allowing them to participate more effectively in efforts in the field of disarmament at all levels,

Recognizing the need for Member States to take into account gender equality when nominating candidates to the programme,

Recalling all the resolutions on the matter since the thirty-seventh session of the General Assembly, in 1982, including resolution 50/71 A of 12 December 1995,

Believing that the forms of assistance available under the programme to Member States, in particular to developing countries, will enhance the capabilities of their officials to follow ongoing deliberations and negotiations on disarmament, both bilateral and multilateral,

1.   *Reaffirms* its decisions contained in annex IV to the Concluding Document of the Twelfth Special Session of the General Assembly[3] and the guidelines approved by the Assembly in its resolution 33/71 E of 14 December 1978;[4]

2.   *Notes with satisfaction* that the programme has trained a large number of officials from Member States throughout its 40 years of existence,

---

[1]   A/73/113.

[2]   Resolution S-10/2.

[3]   *Official Records of the General Assembly, Twelfth Special Session, Annexes*, agenda items 9–13, document A/S-12/32.

[4]   A/33/305.

many of whom hold positions of responsibility in the field of disarmament within their own Governments;

3. *Expresses its appreciation* to all Member States and organizations that have consistently supported the programme throughout the years, thereby contributing to its success, in particular to the European Union and to the Governments of China, Germany, Japan, Kazakhstan, the Republic of Korea and Switzerland for continuing extensive and highly educative study visits for the participants in the programme during 2017 and 2018;

4. *Expresses its appreciation* to the International Atomic Energy Agency, the Organisation for the Prohibition of Chemical Weapons, the Preparatory Commission for the Comprehensive Nuclear-Test-Ban Treaty Organization, the International Court of Justice, the Organization for Security and Cooperation in Europe and the Vienna Centre for Disarmament and Non-Proliferation for organizing specific study programmes in the field of disarmament in their respective areas of competence, thereby contributing to the objectives of the programme;

5. *Encourages* Member States to leverage the knowledge of the United Nations disarmament fellows as a useful resource on matters related to disarmament and international security;

6. *Commends* the Secretary-General for the diligence with which the programme has continued to be carried out;

7. *Requests* the Secretary-General to continue to implement annually the programme within existing resources and to report thereon to the General Assembly at its seventy-fifth session;

8. *Decides* to include in the provisional agenda of its seventy-fifth session, under the item entitled "Review and implementation of the Concluding Document of the Twelfth Special Session of the General Assembly", the sub-item entitled "United Nations disarmament fellowship, training and advisory services".

Action by the General Assembly

Date: 5 December 2018   Meeting: 45th plenary meeting
Vote: Adopted without a vote   Report: A/73/511

Sponsors

Albania, Algeria, Argentina, Australia, Austria, Belgium, Bulgaria, China, Colombia, Comoros, Croatia, Cuba, Cyprus, Czechia, Denmark, El Salvador, Estonia, Eswatini, Finland, France, Gambia, Germany, Ghana, Greece, Guatemala, Hungary, Iceland, Iran (Islamic Republic of), Ireland, Italy, Jamaica, Japan, Latvia, Lebanon, Lesotho, Lithuania, Luxembourg, Malta, Mongolia, Morocco, Myanmar, Namibia, Netherlands, **Nigeria**, Norway, Peru, Philippines, Poland, Portugal, Republic of Korea,

Romania, Serbia, Sierra Leone, Singapore, Slovakia, Slovenia, South Africa, Spain, Sudan, Sweden, Switzerland, Togo, Uganda

Co-sponsors

Burkina Faso, Eritrea, Guinea, Guinea-Bissau, Montenegro, Republic of Moldova, Thailand

Action by the First Committee

Date: 8 November 2018   Meeting: 31st meeting
Vote: Adopted without a vote   Draft resolution: A/C.1/73/L.41/Rev.1

Agenda item 102 (b)

73/74 Convention on the Prohibition of the Use of Nuclear Weapons

Text

The General Assembly,

Convinced that the use of nuclear weapons poses the most serious threat to the survival of humankind,

Bearing in mind the advisory opinion of the International Court of Justice of 8 July 1996 on the legality of the threat or use of nuclear weapons,[1]

Convinced that a multilateral, universal and binding agreement prohibiting the use or threat of use of nuclear weapons would contribute to the elimination of the nuclear threat and to the climate for negotiations leading to the ultimate elimination of nuclear weapons, thereby strengthening international peace and security,

Conscious that some steps have been taken by the Russian Federation and the United States of America towards a reduction of their nuclear weapons and that further steps – in all relevant formats – on nuclear arms control and disarmament can contribute to the improvement of the international climate and the goal of the complete elimination of nuclear weapons,

Recalling that in paragraph 58 of the Final Document of the Tenth Special Session of the General Assembly[2] it is stated that all States should actively participate in efforts to bring about conditions in international relations among States in which a code of peaceful conduct of nations in international affairs could be agreed upon and which would preclude the use or threat of use of nuclear weapons,

Reaffirming that any use of nuclear weapons would be a violation of the Charter of the United Nations and a crime against humanity, as declared in its resolutions 1653 (XVI) of 24 November 1961, 33/71 B of 14 December 1978, 34/83 G of 11 December 1979, 35/152 D of 12 December 1980 and 36/92 I of 9 December 1981,

Recognizing that a legally binding prohibition of the use of nuclear weapons is not contrary to but in fact contributes to international efforts for the achievement and maintenance of a world free of nuclear weapons,

Stressing that an international convention on the prohibition of the use of nuclear weapons would be an important step in a phased programme towards the complete elimination of nuclear weapons, with a specified framework of time,

---

[1] A/51/218, annex.
[2] Resolution S-10/2.

Noting with regret that the Conference on Disarmament, during its 2017 session, was unable to undertake negotiations on this subject as called for in General Assembly resolution 72/59 of 4 December 2017,

1.   *Reiterates its request* to the Conference on Disarmament to commence negotiations in order to reach agreement on an international convention prohibiting the use or threat of use of nuclear weapons under any circumstances;

2.   *Requests* the Conference on Disarmament to report to the General Assembly on the results of those negotiations.

Action by the General Assembly

Date: 5 December 2018   Meeting: 45th plenary meeting
Vote: 124-50-13   Report: A/73/511

Sponsors

Angola, Bhutan, Cuba, Honduras, **India**, Lao People's Democratic Republic, Myanmar, Nepal, Samoa, Viet Nam

Co-sponsors

Bangladesh, Central African Republic, Indonesia, Iran (Islamic Republic of), Kazakhstan, Maldives, Mauritius, Namibia, Seychelles, Sri Lanka

Recorded vote

In favour:

Algeria, Angola, Antigua and Barbuda, Argentina, Azerbaijan, Bahamas, Bahrain, Bangladesh, Barbados, Belize, Benin, Bhutan, Bolivia (Plurinational State of), Botswana, Brunei Darussalam, Burkina Faso, Burundi, Cabo Verde, Cambodia, Cameroon, Central African Republic, Chile, China, Colombia, Comoros, Congo, Costa Rica, Côte d'Ivoire, Cuba, Democratic People's Republic of Korea, Democratic Republic of the Congo, Djibouti, Dominica, Dominican Republic, Ecuador, Egypt, El Salvador, Equatorial Guinea, Eritrea, Eswatini, Ethiopia, Fiji, Gabon, Gambia, Ghana, Grenada, Guatemala, Guinea, Guinea-Bissau, Honduras, India, Indonesia, Iran (Islamic Republic of), Iraq, Jamaica, Jordan, Kazakhstan, Kenya, Kuwait, Lao People's Democratic Republic, Lebanon, Lesotho, Liberia, Libya, Madagascar, Malawi, Malaysia, Maldives, Mauritania, Mauritius, Mexico, Mongolia, Morocco, Mozambique, Myanmar, Namibia, Nauru, Nepal, Nicaragua, Niger, Nigeria, Oman, Pakistan, Palau, Panama, Papua New Guinea, Paraguay, Peru, Qatar, Saint Kitts and Nevis, Saint Lucia, Saint Vincent and the Grenadines, Samoa, Sao Tome and Principe, Saudi Arabia, Senegal, Seychelles, Sierra Leone, Singapore, Solomon Islands, South Africa, Sri Lanka, Sudan, Suriname, Syrian Arab Republic, Tajikistan, Timor-Leste,

Togo, Tonga, Trinidad and Tobago, Tunisia, Turkmenistan, Tuvalu, Uganda, United Arab Emirates, United Republic of Tanzania, Uruguay, Uzbekistan, Vanuatu, Venezuela (Bolivarian Republic of), Viet Nam, Yemen, Zambia, Zimbabwe

Against:

Albania, Andorra, Australia, Austria, Belgium, Bosnia and Herzegovina, Bulgaria, Canada, Croatia, Cyprus, Czechia, Denmark, Estonia, Finland, France, Georgia, Germany, Greece, Hungary, Iceland, Ireland, Israel, Italy, Latvia, Liechtenstein, Lithuania, Luxembourg, Malta, Micronesia (Federated States of), Monaco, Montenegro, Netherlands, New Zealand, Norway, Poland, Portugal, Republic of Korea, Republic of Moldova, Romania, San Marino, Slovakia, Slovenia, Spain, Sweden, Switzerland, the former Yugoslav Republic of Macedonia, Turkey, Ukraine, United Kingdom, United States

Abstaining:

Armenia, Belarus, Brazil, Guyana, Haiti, Japan, Mali, Marshall Islands, Philippines, Russian Federation, Rwanda, Serbia, Thailand

Action by the First Committee

Date: 1 November 2018   Meeting: 26th meeting
Vote: 120-50-15   Draft resolution: A/C.1/73/L.44

Agenda item 102 (c)

73/75 United Nations Regional Centre for Peace and Disarmament in Africa

Text

The General Assembly,

Mindful of the provisions of Article 11, paragraph 1, of the Charter of the United Nations, in which it is stipulated that a function of the General Assembly is to consider the general principles of cooperation in the maintenance of international peace and security, including the principles governing disarmament and arms limitation,

Recalling its resolutions 40/151 G of 16 December 1985, 41/60 D of 3 December 1986, 42/39 J of 30 November 1987 and 43/76 D of 7 December 1988 on the United Nations Regional Centre for Peace and Disarmament in Africa and its resolutions 46/36 F of 6 December 1991 and 47/52 G of 9 December 1992 on regional disarmament, including confidence-building measures,

Recalling also its subsequent resolutions on the Regional Centre, the most recent of which is resolution 72/60 of 4 December 2017,

Recalling further its resolution 71/56 of 5 December 2016, in which it recognized the role of women in disarmament, non-proliferation and arms control,

Reaffirming the role of the Regional Centre in promoting disarmament, peace and security at the regional level,

Welcoming the continuing and deepening cooperation between the Regional Centre, the African Union and African subregional organizations in the context of the adoption of Agenda 2063 by the Assembly of Heads of State and Government of the African Union, and in particular the objective of silencing the guns in Africa by 2020,

Welcoming also the work of the Regional Centre in support of the achievement of the Sustainable Development Goals,[1] in particular Goal 16 on peace, justice and strong institutions, and target 16.4, which addresses the reduction of illicit arms flows,

Recalling the decision taken by the Executive Council of the African Union at its eighth ordinary session, held in Khartoum from 16 to 21 January 2006,[2] in which the Council called upon member States to make voluntary contributions to the Regional Centre to maintain its operations,

---

[1] See resolution 70/1.
[2] A/60/693, annex II, decision EX.CL/Dec.263 (VIII).

Recalling also the call by the Secretary-General for continued financial and in-kind support from Member States, which would enable the Regional Centre to discharge its mandate in full and to respond more effectively to requests for assistance from African States,

1.   *Takes note* of the report of the Secretary-General;[3]

2.   *Commends* the United Nations Regional Centre for Peace and Disarmament in Africa for its sustained support to Member States in implementing disarmament, arms control and non-proliferation activities through seminars and conferences, capacity-building and training, policy and technical expertise, and information and advocacy at the regional and national levels;

3.   *Welcomes* the continental dimension of the activities of the Regional Centre in response to the evolving needs of African Member States and the region's new and emerging challenges in the areas of disarmament, peace and security, including maritime security;

4.   *Recalls* the undertaking by the Regional Centre to deepen its partnership with the African Union Commission in the context of the Joint United Nations-African Union Framework for Enhanced Partnership in Peace and Security, signed on 19 April 2017, as well as with African subregional organizations, and requests the Secretary-General to continue to facilitate close cooperation between the Regional Centre and the African Union, in particular in the areas of disarmament, peace and security;

5.   *Welcomes* the contribution of the Regional Centre to continental disarmament, peace and security, in particular its contribution to the implementation of Agenda 2063 adopted by the Assembly of Heads of State and Government of the African Union, the objective of silencing the guns in Africa and its master road map of practical steps to silence the guns in Africa by the year 2020, as well as its assistance to the African Commission on Nuclear Energy in its implementation of the African Nuclear-Weapon-Free Zone Treaty (Treaty of Pelindaba);[4]

6.   *Also welcomes* efforts by the Regional Centre to promote the role and representation of women in disarmament, non-proliferation and arms control activities;

7.   *Notes with appreciation* the tangible achievements of the Regional Centre and the impact of the assistance that it provides to African States to control small arms and light weapons through capacity-building for national commissions on small arms and light weapons, defence and security forces, and United Nations peacekeeping mission personnel, as well as the support that the Centre provided to States in preventing the diversion of such weapons,

---

[3]   A/73/151.
[4]   A/50/426, annex.

in particular to non-State armed groups and terrorist groups,[5] and also notes with appreciation the assistance provided by the Centre in the implementation of the Central African Convention for the Control of Small Arms and Light Weapons, Their Ammunition and All Parts and Components That Can Be Used for Their Manufacture, Repair and Assembly (Kinshasa Convention),[6] which entered into force on 8 March 2017, and its substantive support to the United Nations Standing Advisory Committee on Security Questions in Central Africa, in the implementation of the Economic Community of West African States Convention on Small Arms and Light Weapons, Their Ammunition and Other Related Materials and on security sector reform initiatives, and to East Africa on programmes to control brokering of small arms and light weapons, including the additional assistance provided by the Centre to African Member States in the implementation of Security Council resolution 1540 (2004) of 28 April 2004 and the Convention on the Prohibition of the Development, Production and Stockpiling of Bacteriological (Biological) and Toxin Weapons and on Their Destruction;[7]

8.   *Commends* the Regional Centre for the support and assistance that it provided to African States, upon request, on the Arms Trade Treaty,[8] including through the organization of subregional and regional seminars and workshops;

9.   *Urges* all States, as well as international, governmental and non-governmental organizations and foundations, to make voluntary contributions to enable the Regional Centre to carry out its programmes and activities and meet the needs of African States;

10.   *Urges*, in particular, States members of the African Union to make voluntary contributions to the trust fund for the United Nations Regional Centre for Peace and Disarmament in Africa, in conformity with the decision taken by the Executive Council of the African Union in Khartoum in January 2006;[2]

11.   *Requests* the Secretary-General to continue to provide the Regional Centre with the support necessary for greater achievements and results;

12.   *Also requests* the Secretary-General to report to the General Assembly at its seventy-fourth session on the implementation of the present resolution;

13.   *Decides* to include in the provisional agenda of its seventy-fourth session, under the item entitled "Review and implementation of the Concluding Document of the Twelfth Special Session of the General

---

[5] Security Council resolution 2370 (2017).
[6] See A/65/517-S/2010/534, annex.
[7] United Nations, *Treaty Series*, vol. 1015, No. 14860.
[8] See resolution 67/234 B.

Assembly", the sub-item entitled "United Nations Regional Centre for Peace and Disarmament in Africa".

Action by the General Assembly

Date: 5 December 2018	Meeting: 45th plenary meeting
Vote: Adopted without a vote	Report: A/73/511

Sponsors

Australia, Austria, Georgia, **Nigeria** (on behalf of the States Members of the United Nations that are members of the Group of African States)

Co-sponsors

Maldives

Action by the First Committee

Date: 8 November 2018	Meeting: 30th meeting
Vote: Adopted without a vote	Draft resolution: A/C.1/73/L.34

Agenda item 102 (d)

73/76   United Nations Regional Centre for Peace, Disarmament and Development in Latin America and the Caribbean

Text

The General Assembly,

Recalling its resolutions 41/60 J of 3 December 1986, 42/39 K of 30 November 1987 and 43/76 H of 7 December 1988 on the United Nations Regional Centre for Peace, Disarmament and Development in Latin America and the Caribbean, with headquarters in Lima,

Recalling also its resolution 72/61 of 4 December 2017 and all previous resolutions on the Regional Centre,

Recognizing that the Regional Centre has continued to provide substantive support for the implementation of regional and subregional initiatives and has intensified its contribution to the coordination of United Nations efforts towards peace and disarmament and for the promotion of economic and social development, and emphasizing the role of the Centre in providing support for the realization of the 2030 Agenda for Sustainable Development,[1]

Reaffirming the mandate of the Regional Centre to provide, on request, substantive support for the initiatives and other activities of the Member States of the region for the implementation of measures for peace and disarmament and for the promotion of economic and social development,

Taking note of the report of the Secretary-General,[2] and expressing its appreciation for the important assistance provided, upon request, by the Regional Centre to several countries in the region, including through capacity-building and technical assistance activities for the implementation of disarmament, non-proliferation and arms control instruments,

Welcoming the support provided by the Regional Centre to Member States in the implementation of disarmament and non-proliferation instruments,

Emphasizing the need for the Regional Centre to develop and strengthen its activities and programmes in a comprehensive and balanced manner, in accordance with its mandate and in line with the requests for assistance by Member States,

---

[1] Resolution 70/1.

[2] A/73/127.

Welcoming the ongoing support provided by the Regional Centre to Member States in the implementation of the Programme of Action to Prevent, Combat and Eradicate the Illicit Trade in Small Arms and Light Weapons in All Its Aspects,[3]

Welcoming also the assistance provided by the Regional Centre to some States, upon request, in the management and securing of national weapons stockpiles and in the identification and destruction of surplus, obsolete or seized weapons and ammunition, as declared by competent national authorities, in particular the establishment of a regional training centre in Port of Spain to manage weapons stockpiles,

Welcoming further the initiative of the Regional Centre to continue to conduct activities in line with efforts to promote the equitable representation of women in all decision-making processes with regard to matters related to disarmament, non-proliferation and arms control, as encouraged in its resolutions 65/69 of 8 December 2010 and subsequent resolutions, including resolution 71/56 of 5 December 2016,

Recalling the report of the Group of Governmental Experts on the relationship between disarmament and development,[4] referred to in General Assembly resolution 59/78 of 3 December 2004, which is of utmost interest with regard to the role that the Regional Centre plays in promoting the issue in the region in pursuit of its mandate to promote economic and social development related to peace and disarmament,

Noting that security, disarmament and development issues have always been recognized as significant topics in Latin America and the Caribbean, the first inhabited region in the world to be declared a nuclear-weapon-free zone,

Recognizing the cooperation between the Regional Centre and the Agency for the Prohibition of Nuclear Weapons in Latin America and the Caribbean on strengthening the nuclear-weapon-free zone established by the Treaty for the Prohibition of Nuclear Weapons in Latin America and the Caribbean (Treaty of Tlatelolco),[5] as well as its efforts in promoting peace and disarmament education,

Bearing in mind the important role of the Regional Centre in promoting confidence-building measures, arms control and limitation, disarmament and development at the regional level,

Recognizing the importance of information, research, education and training for peace, disarmament and development in order to achieve understanding and cooperation among States,

---

[3] *Report of the United Nations Conference on the Illicit Trade in Small Arms and Light Weapons in All Its Aspects, New York, 9–20 July 2001* (A/CONF.192/15), chap. IV, para. 24.

[4] See A/59/119.

[5] United Nations, *Treaty Series*, vol. 634, No. 9068.

1.   *Reiterates its strong support* for the role of the United Nations Regional Centre for Peace, Disarmament and Development in Latin America and the Caribbean in the promotion of activities of the United Nations at the regional and subregional levels to strengthen peace, disarmament, stability, security and development among its Member States;

2.   *Welcomes* the activities carried out in the past year by the Regional Centre, and requests the Centre to continue to take into account the proposals to be submitted by the countries of the region for the implementation of the mandate of the Centre in the areas of peace, disarmament and development and for the promotion of, inter alia, nuclear disarmament, the prevention, combating and eradication of the illicit trade in small arms and light weapons, ammunition and explosives, the non-proliferation of weapons of mass destruction, confidence-building measures, arms control and limitation, transparency and the reduction and prevention of armed violence at the regional and subregional levels;

3.   *Expresses its appreciation* for the political support provided by Member States, as well as for the financial contributions made by Member States and international governmental and non-governmental organizations, to strengthen the Regional Centre, its programme of activities and the implementation thereof, and encourages them to continue to make and to increase voluntary contributions;

4.   *Invites* all States of the region to continue to take part in the activities of the Regional Centre, proposing items for inclusion in its programme of activities and maximizing the potential of the Centre to meet the current challenges facing the international community with a view to fulfilling the aims of the Charter of the United Nations in the areas of peace, disarmament and development;

5.   *Recognizes* that the Regional Centre has an important role in the promotion and development of regional and subregional initiatives agreed upon by the countries of Latin America and the Caribbean in the field of weapons of mass destruction, in particular nuclear weapons, and conventional arms, including small arms and light weapons, in the relationship between disarmament and development, including the implementation of the Sustainable Development Goals,[1] in the promotion of the participation of women in this field and in strengthening voluntary confidence-building measures among the countries of the region;

6.   *Encourages* the Regional Centre to further develop activities in all countries of the region in the important areas of peace, disarmament and development and to provide, upon request and in accordance with its mandate, support to Member States of the region in the national implementation of relevant instruments, inter alia, the Programme of Action to Prevent, Combat and Eradicate the Illicit Trade in Small Arms and Light Weapons in All Its

Aspects[3] and the Arms Trade Treaty,[6] as well as in the implementation of the Caribbean 1540 programme on the non-proliferation of weapons of mass destruction;

7. *Requests* the Secretary-General to report to the General Assembly at its seventy-fourth session on the implementation of the present resolution;

8. *Decides* to include in the provisional agenda of its seventy-fourth session, under the item entitled "Review and implementation of the Concluding Document of the Twelfth Special Session of the General Assembly", the sub-item entitled "United Nations Regional Centre for Peace, Disarmament and Development in Latin America and the Caribbean".

Action by the General Assembly

Date: 5 December 2018 Meeting: 45th plenary meeting
Vote: Adopted without a vote Report: A/73/511

Sponsors

Peru (on behalf of the States Members of the United Nations that are members of the Group of Latin American and Caribbean States)

Action by the First Committee

Date: 8 November 2018 Meeting: 30th meeting
Vote: Adopted without a vote Draft resolution: A/C.1/73/L.56

---

[6] See resolution 67/234 B.

Agenda item 102 (e)

73/77 United Nations Regional Centre for Peace and Disarmament in Asia and the Pacific

Text

The General Assembly,

Recalling its resolutions 42/39 D of 30 November 1987 and 44/117 F of 15 December 1989, by which it established the United Nations Regional Centre for Peace and Disarmament in Asia and renamed it the United Nations Regional Centre for Peace and Disarmament in Asia and the Pacific, with headquarters in Kathmandu and with the mandate of providing, on request, substantive support for the initiatives and other activities mutually agreed upon by the Member States of the Asia-Pacific region for the implementation of measures for peace and disarmament, through appropriate utilization of available resources,

Welcoming the tenth anniversary of the physical operation of the Regional Centre from Kathmandu in accordance with General Assembly resolution 62/52 of 5 December 2007, and the youth-focused outreach activities undertaken in commemoration thereof,

Recalling the mandate of the Regional Centre to provide, on request, substantive support for the initiatives and other activities mutually agreed upon by the Member States of the Asia-Pacific region for the implementation of measures for peace and disarmament,

Taking note of the report of the Secretary-General,[1] and expressing its appreciation to the Regional Centre for its important work in promoting confidence-building measures through the organization of meetings, conferences and workshops in the region, including: national and subregional workshops on the control of small arms and light weapons; the sixteenth United Nations-Republic of Korea Joint Conference on Disarmament and Non-Proliferation Issues, held on Jeju Island, Republic of Korea, on 16 and 17 November 2017; the twenty-seventh United Nations Conference on Disarmament Issues, held in Hiroshima, Japan, on 29 and 30 November 2017; a technical and legal assistance project to assist the Philippines in the implementation of the Programme of Action to Prevent, Combat and Eradicate the Illicit Trade in Small Arms and Light Weapons in All Its Aspects[2] and to help to build capacity towards ratification of the Arms Trade Treaty;[3] and a joint project with the Organization for Security and Cooperation in Europe

---

[1] A/73/126.

[2] *Report of the United Nations Conference on the Illicit Trade in Small Arms and Light Weapons in All Its Aspects, New York, 9–20 July 2001* (A/CONF.192/15), chap. IV, para. 24.

[3] See resolution 67/234 B.

in support of regional implementation of Security Council resolution 1540 (2004) of 28 April 2004 in Central Asia and Mongolia,

Expressing appreciation for the timely execution by Nepal of its host country commitments for the physical operation of the Regional Centre,

Welcoming the work by the Regional Centre in support of the achievement of the Sustainable Development Goals,[4] in particular Goal 16 on peace, justice and strong institutions, as well as target 16.4, which addresses the reduction of illicit arms flows,

Welcoming also the efforts by the Regional Centre to promote the role and representation of women in disarmament, non-proliferation and arms control activities,

1.   *Expresses its satisfaction* at the activities carried out over the past year by the United Nations Regional Centre for Peace and Disarmament in Asia and the Pacific, and invites all States of the region to continue to support the activities of the Regional Centre, including by continuing to take part in them, where possible, and by proposing items for inclusion in the programme of activities of the Centre, in order to contribute to the implementation of measures for peace and disarmament;

2.   *Expresses its gratitude* to the Government of Nepal for its cooperation and financial support, which has enabled the Regional Centre to operate from Kathmandu;

3.   *Expresses its appreciation* to the Secretary-General and the Office for Disarmament Affairs of the Secretariat for providing the necessary support with a view to ensuring the smooth operation of the Regional Centre and to enabling the Centre to function effectively;

4.   *Appeals* to Member States, in particular those within the Asia-Pacific region, as well as to international governmental and non-governmental organizations and foundations, to make voluntary contributions, the only resources of the Regional Centre, to strengthen its programme of activities and the implementation thereof;

5.   *Reaffirms its strong support* for the role of the Regional Centre in the promotion of activities of the United Nations at the regional level to strengthen peace, stability and security among its Member States;

6.   *Underlines* the importance of the Kathmandu process for the development of the practice of region-wide security and disarmament dialogues;

7.   *Requests* the Secretary-General to report to the General Assembly at its seventy-fourth session on the implementation of the present resolution;

---

[4] See resolution 70/1.

8.   *Decides* to include in the provisional agenda of its seventy-fourth session, under the item entitled "Review and implementation of the Concluding Document of the Twelfth Special Session of the General Assembly", the sub-item entitled "United Nations Regional Centre for Peace and Disarmament in Asia and the Pacific".

Action by the General Assembly

Date: 5 December 2018   Meeting: 45th plenary meeting
Vote: Adopted without a vote   Report: A/73/511

Sponsors

Australia, Austria, China, Japan, Mongolia, Myanmar, **Nepal**, New Zealand, Philippines, Samoa, Viet Nam

Co-sponsors

Bangladesh, Bhutan, India, Indonesia, Malaysia, Maldives, Micronesia (Federated States of), Papua New Guinea, Republic of Korea, Singapore, Sri Lanka, Thailand

Action by the First Committee

Date: 8 November 2018   Meeting: 30th meeting
Vote: Adopted without a vote   Draft resolution: A/C.1/73/L.38

Agenda item 102 (f)

73/78   Regional confidence-building measures: activities of the United Nations Standing Advisory Committee on Security Questions in Central Africa

Text

The General Assembly,

Recalling its previous relevant resolutions, in particular resolution 72/63 of 4 December 2017,

Recalling also the guidelines for general and complete disarmament adopted at its tenth special session, the first special session devoted to disarmament,

Bearing in mind the establishment by the Secretary-General on 28 May 1992 of the United Nations Standing Advisory Committee on Security Questions in Central Africa, the purpose of which is to encourage arms limitation, disarmament, non-proliferation and development in the Central Africa subregion,

Recalling that the purpose of the Standing Advisory Committee is to conduct reconstruction and confidence-building activities in Central Africa among its member States, including through confidence-building and arms limitation measures,

Reaffirming the importance and relevance of the Standing Advisory Committee as an instrument of preventive diplomacy in the subregional architecture for the promotion of peace and security in Central Africa,

Bearing in mind the revitalization of the activities of the Standing Advisory Committee decided upon at the forty-fourth ministerial meeting of the Committee, held in Yaoundé from 29 May to 2 June 2017, with a view to enhancing its contribution to the achievement of the objectives of peace, security and development in Central Africa,

Noting the entry into force of the Central African Convention for the Control of Small Arms and Light Weapons, Their Ammunition and All Parts and Components That Can Be Used for Their Manufacture, Repair and Assembly (Kinshasa Convention) on 8 March 2017[1] and the third Conference of States Parties to the Arms Trade Treaty, held in Geneva from 11 to 15 September 2017,

Convinced that the resources released by disarmament, including regional disarmament, can be devoted to economic and social development

---

[1] See A/65/517-S/2010/534, annex.

and to the protection of the environment for the benefit of all peoples, in particular those of developing countries,

Welcoming the Libreville Declaration on the Adoption and Implementation of the Regional Strategy and Plan of Action for Combating Terrorism and the Trafficking in Small Arms and Light Weapons in Central Africa, adopted by the States members of the Standing Advisory Committee on 26 November 2015 at their forty-first ministerial meeting, held in Libreville from 23 to 27 November 2015,[2]

Welcoming also the adoption, at the forty-fourth ministerial meeting of the Standing Advisory Committee, of the plan of action and schedule for the implementation of the regional strategy under the auspices of the Economic Community of Central African States,

Considering the importance and effectiveness of confidence-building measures taken on the initiative and with the participation of all States concerned and taking into account the specific characteristics of each region, since such measures can contribute to regional stability and to international peace and security,

Convinced that development can be achieved only in a climate of peace, security and mutual confidence both within and among States,

Recalling the Brazzaville Declaration on Cooperation for Peace and Security in Central Africa,[3] the Bata Declaration for the Promotion of Lasting Democracy, Peace and Development in Central Africa[4] and the Yaoundé Declaration on Peace, Security and Stability in Central Africa,[5]

Bearing in mind resolutions 1196 (1998) and 1197 (1998), adopted by the Security Council on 16 and 18 September 1998, respectively, following its consideration of the report of the Secretary-General on the causes of conflict and the promotion of durable peace and sustainable development in Africa,[6]

Welcoming the successful conclusion of the Summit of Heads of State and Government on Maritime Safety and Security in the Gulf of Guinea, held in Yaoundé on 24 and 25 June 2013, the inauguration in Yaoundé, on 11 September 2014, of the Interregional Coordination Centre for Maritime Security in the Gulf of Guinea, the effective commencement of its activities with the installation of its statutory officials in Yaoundé on 22 February 2017, the inauguration of new offices of the Regional Centre for Maritime Security in Central Africa in Pointe Noire, Congo, on 20 October 2014, and the launch of the Multinational Maritime Coordination Centre in Cotonou, Benin, in March 2015, and also the conclusion of the African Union Extraordinary

---

[2] See A/70/682-S/2016/39, annex 3.
[3] A/50/474, annex I.
[4] A/53/258-S/1998/763, annex II, appendix I.
[5] A/53/868-S/1999/303, annex II.
[6] A/52/871-S/1998/318.

Summit of Heads of State and Government on Maritime Security and Safety and Development in Africa, held in Lomé on 15 October 2016,

Recalling its resolution 69/314 of 30 July 2015, the first such resolution on tackling illicit trafficking in wildlife, and also its resolutions 70/301 of 9 September 2016 and 71/326 of 11 September 2017, and welcoming the outcome of the high-level meetings on poaching and illicit wildlife trafficking, hosted by Gabon and Germany and held on the margins of the high-level segments of the sixty-eighth and sixty-ninth sessions of the General Assembly,

Emphasizing the need to strengthen the capacity for early warning, conflict prevention and peacekeeping in Africa, and taking note in this regard of the concrete conflict prevention initiatives facilitated by the Department of Political Affairs of the Secretariat,

Welcoming the close cooperation established between the United Nations Regional Office for Central Africa and the Economic Community of Central African States, as well as the signing of the framework of cooperation agreement between the two entities on 14 June 2016,

Bearing in mind the increased focus of the Standing Advisory Committee on human security questions, such as trafficking in persons, especially women and children, as an important consideration for subregional peace, stability and conflict prevention, and welcoming the adoption by the General Assembly at its seventy-second session of the political declaration on the implementation of the United Nations Global Plan of Action to Combat Trafficking in Persons[7] following the high-level meeting of the Assembly on the appraisal of the Global Plan of Action,

Expressing continued concern about the fragile situation in the Central African Republic and in the neighbouring countries affected, and noting the importance of promoting the political process through the implementation of the African Initiative for Peace and Reconciliation in the Central African Republic in order to make tangible progress, in particular with regard to the protection of civilians, disarmament, demobilization and reintegration of former combatants, and strengthening the authority of the State,

Taking note of the Kigali Declaration on the Situation in the Central African Republic,[8] highlighting the regional security implications of the situation in the Central African Republic, and reiterating the commitment of States members of the Standing Advisory Committee to supporting the implementation of the African Union road map for peace and reconciliation, including through financial contributions, and their cooperation to fight more effectively the risks of instability in the country,

---

[7] Resolution 72/1.
[8] A/73/224, annex I.

Taking note also of the Brazzaville Declaration on Confidence-Building Measures,[9] and expressing concern that the issue of mercenaries has become a major security concern, undermining trust and creating tensions among States members of the Standing Advisory Committee,

Expressing concern about the increasing impact of cross-border criminality, in particular the activities of the Lord's Resistance Army, the terrorist attacks by Boko Haram in the Lake Chad basin region and incidents of piracy in the Gulf of Guinea, and the issue of transhumance and its cross-border security implications on peace, security and development in Central Africa,

Welcoming the progress made by the States members of the Lake Chad Basin Commission and Benin in making the Multinational Joint Task Force operational in order to combat effectively the threat posed by the Boko Haram terrorist group to the Lake Chad basin region,

Welcoming also the adoption by the Lake Chad Basin Commission, with the support of the African Union, of the Regional Stabilization, Recovery and Resilience Strategy for Areas Affected by Boko Haram in the Lake Chad Basin Region in Abuja on 30 August 2018,

Bearing in mind Security Council resolution 2349 (2017) of 31 March 2017, in which the Council called for, inter alia, increased assistance to the countries of the region,

Considering the urgent need to prevent the possible movement of illicit weapons, mercenaries and combatants involved in conflicts in the Sahel and in neighbouring countries in the Central African subregion,

1.   *Reaffirms its support* for efforts aimed at promoting confidence-building measures at the regional and subregional levels in order to ease tensions and conflicts in Central Africa and to further sustainable peace, stability and development in the subregion;

2.   *Welcomes and encourages* the initiative of the States members of the United Nations Standing Advisory Committee on Security Questions in Central Africa to further develop collaboration and synergies with the Economic Community of Central African States, in particular the Commission for Defence and Security, including by means of closed meetings, with a view to promoting the implementation of the regional strategy for combating terrorism and the trafficking in small arms and light weapons in Central Africa adopted by the Committee;

3.   *Welcomes* the adoption by the Standing Advisory Committee of the Kigali Declaration on the Reform of the Council for Peace and Security in Central Africa,[10] and urges the States members of the Standing Advisory

---

[9]   Ibid., annex IV.
[10] Ibid., annex II.

Committee and the international community to provide technical and financial support to accelerate the reform of the Council;

4.   *Also welcomes* efforts under way by the Standing Advisory Committee and its secretariat to implement the communication strategy adopted at the forty-fifth ministerial meeting of the Committee, held in Kigali from 4 to 8 December 2017, and encourages Member States and other partners to support initiatives aimed at increasing the visibility of the Committee, including among the populations of the subregion, in cooperation with civil society;

5.   *Reaffirms* the importance of disarmament and arms control programmes in Central Africa carried out by the States of the subregion with the support of the United Nations, the African Union and other international partners;

6.   *Encourages* Member States to provide assistance to those States members of the Standing Advisory Committee that have ratified the Arms Trade Treaty,[11] and encourages those that have not yet done so to ratify the Treaty;

7.   *Encourages* States members of the Standing Advisory Committee and other interested States to provide financial support for the implementation of the Central African Convention for the Control of Small Arms and Light Weapons, Their Ammunition and All Parts and Components That Can Be Used for Their Manufacture, Repair and Assembly (Kinshasa Convention),[1] and encourages signatories that have not yet done so to ratify the Convention;

8.   *Welcomes* the holding of the first Conference of States Parties to the Central African Convention for the Control of Small Arms and Light Weapons, Their Ammunition and All Parts and Components That Can Be Used for Their Manufacture, Repair and Assembly, in Yaoundé from 11 to 13 June 2018, in accordance with article 34, paragraph 3, of the Kinshasa Convention;

9.   *Encourages* Member States to assist States parties to the Kinshasa Convention with coordination activities for the control of small arms and light weapons at the regional and national levels, including funding thereof, as expeditiously as possible;

10.   *Reaffirms its support* for the United Nations Global Counter-Terrorism Strategy[12] and its four pillars, which constitute an ongoing effort, and calls upon Member States, the United Nations and other appropriate international, regional and subregional organizations to step up their efforts to implement the Strategy in an integrated and balanced manner and in all aspects;

---

[11]   See resolution 67/234 B.
[12]   Resolution 60/288.

11.   *Urges* the States members of the Standing Advisory Committee to implement the Libreville Declaration on the Adoption and Implementation of the Regional Strategy and Plan of Action for Combating Terrorism and the Trafficking in Small Arms and Light Weapons in Central Africa,[2] and requests the United Nations Regional Office for Central Africa, the United Nations Regional Centre for Peace and Disarmament in Africa, the Security Council Committee established pursuant to resolution 1373 (2001) concerning counter-terrorism and the international community to support those measures;

12.   *Urges* the States members of the Economic Community of Central African States to implement the integrated strategy and plan of action for combating terrorism and the trafficking in small arms and light weapons in Central Africa, and requests the United Nations Regional Office for Central Africa to support the efforts of States members of the Economic Community of Central African States in this regard;

13.   *Welcomes* the joint summit of the Heads of State and Government of the Economic Community of West African States and the Economic Community of Central African States, in coordination with the African Union Commission, on peace, security, stability and the fight against terrorism and violent extremism, held in Lomé on 30 July 2018, and also welcomes the Lomé Declaration on Peace, Security, Stability and the Fight against Terrorism and Violent Extremism adopted at that summit;

14.   *Encourages* the Economic Community of Central African States and the Economic Community of West African States to work together towards the implementation of the Lomé Declaration;

15.   *Encourages* the States members of the Standing Advisory Committee to carry out the programmes of activities adopted at their ministerial meetings, and requests the United Nations Regional Office for Central Africa to continue to provide support;

16.   *Appeals* to the international community to support the efforts undertaken by the States concerned to implement disarmament, demobilization and reintegration programmes, and urges the States concerned to ensure that such programmes take into consideration the needs of women and children associated with former combatants;

17.   *Welcomes* the efforts of Cameroon and the Congo in providing assistance to the Interregional Coordination Centre for Maritime Security in the Gulf of Guinea and the Regional Centre for Maritime Security in Central Africa, respectively, and urges other member States to honour their financial commitments in order to ensure the predictable and sustainable operation of the two Centres;

18.   *Encourages* Member States to continue to implement the outcomes of the Summit of Heads of State and Government on Maritime Safety and Security in the Gulf of Guinea by operationalizing the Interregional

Coordination Centre for Maritime Security in the Gulf of Guinea and activities of the Regional Centre for Maritime Security in Central Africa, and also encourages the implementation of the Charter on Maritime Security and Safety and Development in Africa adopted at the African Union Extraordinary Summit of Heads of State and Government on Maritime Security and Safety and Development in Africa;

19. *Calls upon* Member States and subregional bodies to take immediate concerted action to counter the phenomenon of poaching and trafficking in wildlife and natural resources, including through the implementation of the provisions of its resolutions 69/314, 70/301 and 71/326;

20. *Welcomes* the determination of the Heads of State and Government of the Economic Community of Central African States and the Economic Community of West African States to initiate common policies and joint programmes on the management of transhumance, sustainable water resources and the modernization of agriculture and livestock farming, and to identify measures for the prevention and peaceful management of conflicts between herders and farmers, as contained in the Lomé Declaration;

21. *Expresses its full support* for the efforts of the Economic Community of Central African States, the African Union and the United Nations in the Central African Republic, and calls upon the international community to support these efforts;

22. *Encourages* the States members of the Standing Advisory Committee to pursue their discussions on concrete conflict prevention initiatives, and requests in this regard the assistance of the Secretary-General;

23. *Requests* the United Nations Regional Office for Central Africa, in collaboration with the United Nations Regional Centre for Peace and Disarmament in Africa, to facilitate the efforts undertaken by the States members of the Standing Advisory Committee, in particular for their execution of the Implementation Plan for the Kinshasa Convention;[13]

24. *Requests* the Secretary-General and the Office of the United Nations High Commissioner for Refugees, with the support of the international community, to continue to assist the countries of Central Africa in tackling the issues of refugees and displaced persons in their territories;

25. *Requests* the Secretary-General and the United Nations High Commissioner for Human Rights to continue to provide their full assistance for the proper functioning of the Subregional Centre for Human Rights and Democracy in Central Africa;

26. *Welcomes* the increased contributions made by several Member States to the trust fund of the United Nations Standing Advisory Committee

---

[13] See A/65/717-S/2011/53, annex.

on Security Questions in Central Africa, reminds the States members of the Standing Advisory Committee of the commitments that they undertook on the adoption of the Declaration on the Trust Fund of the United Nations Standing Advisory Committee on Security Questions in Central Africa on 8 May 2009[14] and the Bangui Declaration on 10 June 2016,[15] and invites those States members of the Committee that have not already done so to contribute to the trust fund;

27. *Urges* other Member States and intergovernmental and non-governmental organizations to support the activities of the Standing Advisory Committee effectively through voluntary contributions to the trust fund;

28. *Urges* the States members of the Standing Advisory Committee, in accordance with Security Council resolution 1325 (2000) of 31 October 2000, to strengthen the gender component of the various meetings of the Committee relating to disarmament and international security, in line with the Sao Tome Declaration on the Participation of Women in the Statutory Meetings of the United Nations Standing Advisory Committee on Security Questions in Central Africa, adopted on 1 December 2016,[16] in which States members were invited to increase the representation of women in delegations participating in the statutory meetings of the Committee;

29. *Expresses its satisfaction* to the Secretary-General for his support to the Standing Advisory Committee, expresses appreciation for the role played by the United Nations Regional Office for Central Africa, welcomes the strengthening of the Office, and strongly encourages the States members of the Standing Advisory Committee and international partners to support the work of the Office;

30. *Welcomes* the efforts of the Standing Advisory Committee towards addressing cross-border security threats in Central Africa, including activities of Boko Haram and the Lord's Resistance Army, and acts of piracy and armed robbery at sea in the Gulf of Guinea, the issue of transhumance and its cross-border security implications, as well as the fallout from the situation in the Central African Republic, and also welcomes the role of the United Nations Regional Office for Central Africa in coordinating those efforts, working closely with the Economic Community of Central African States, the African Union and all relevant regional and international partners;

31. *Expresses its satisfaction* to the Secretary-General for his support for the revitalization of the activities of the Standing Advisory Committee, and requests him to continue to provide the assistance needed to ensure the success of its regular biannual meetings;

---

[14] A/64/85-S/2009/288, annex I.

[15] A/71/293, annex I.

[16] A/72/363, annex II.

32. *Calls upon* the Secretary-General to submit to the General Assembly at its seventy-fourth session a report on the implementation of the present resolution;

33. *Decides* to include in the provisional agenda of its seventy-fourth session, under the item entitled "Review and implementation of the Concluding Document of the Twelfth Special Session of the General Assembly", the sub-item entitled "Regional confidence-building measures: activities of the United Nations Standing Advisory Committee on Security Questions in Central Africa".

Action by the General Assembly

Date: 5 December 2018   Meeting: 45th plenary meeting
Vote: Adopted without a vote   Report: A/73/511

Sponsors

Cameroon, **Congo** (on behalf of the States Members of the United Nations that are members of the Economic Community of Central African States)

Action by the First Committee

Date: 8 November 2018   Meeting: 30th meeting
Vote: Adopted without a vote   Draft resolution: A/C.1/73/L.69/Rev.1

Agenda item 102 (g)

73/79   United Nations Disarmament Information Programme

Text

The General Assembly,

Recalling its decision taken in 1982 at its twelfth special session, the second special session devoted to disarmament, by which the World Disarmament Campaign was launched,[1]

Bearing in mind its resolution 47/53 D of 9 December 1992, in which it decided, inter alia, that the World Disarmament Campaign should be known thereafter as the United Nations Disarmament Information Programme and the World Disarmament Campaign voluntary trust fund as the voluntary trust fund for the United Nations Disarmament Information Programme,

Recalling its resolutions 51/46 A of 10 December 1996, 53/78 E of 4 December 1998, 55/34 A of 20 November 2000, 57/90 of 22 November 2002, 59/103 of 3 December 2004, 61/95 of 6 December 2006, 63/81 of 2 December 2008, 65/81 of 8 December 2010, 67/67 of 3 December 2012, 69/71 of 2 December 2014 and 71/74 of 5 December 2016,

Welcoming the report of the Secretary-General,[2]

1.   *Commends* the Secretary-General for his efforts to make effective use of the limited resources available to him in disseminating, as widely as possible, information on arms control and disarmament to Governments, the media, non-governmental organizations, educational communities and research institutes and in carrying out a seminar and conference programme;

2.   *Stresses* the importance of the United Nations Disarmament Information Programme as a significant instrument in enabling all Member States to participate fully in the deliberations and negotiations on disarmament in the various United Nations bodies, in assisting them in complying with treaties, as required, and in contributing to agreed mechanisms for transparency;

3.   *Commends with satisfaction* the launch of *The United Nations Disarmament Yearbook* for 2016 and 2017, as well as its online editions, by the Office for Disarmament Affairs of the Secretariat;

4.   *Notes with appreciation* the cooperation of the Department of Public Information of the Secretariat and its information centres in pursuit of the objectives of the Programme;

---

[1] See *Official Records of the General Assembly, Twelfth Special Session, Plenary Meetings*, 1st meeting, paras. 110–111.

[2] A/73/120.

5. *Recommends* that the Programme continue to inform, educate and generate public understanding of the importance of multilateral action and support for it, including action by the United Nations and the Conference on Disarmament, in the field of arms control and disarmament, in a factual, balanced and objective manner, and that it focus its efforts:

(a) To continue to publish *The United Nations Disarmament Yearbook*, the flagship publication of the Office for Disarmament Affairs, in all official languages, as well as its *Occasional Papers, Study Series* and other ad hoc information materials in accordance with the current practice;

(b) To continue to update the disarmament website as a part of the United Nations website in as many official languages as feasible;

(c) To promote the use of the Programme as a means to provide information related to progress in the implementation of nuclear disarmament measures;

(d) To continue to intensify United Nations interaction with the public, principally non-governmental organizations and research institutes, to help to further an informed debate on topical issues of arms limitation, disarmament and security;

(e) To continue to organize discussions on topics of interest in the field of arms limitation and disarmament with a view to broadening understanding and facilitating an exchange of views and information among Member States and civil society;

6. *Recognizes* the importance of all support extended to the voluntary trust fund for the United Nations Disarmament Information Programme, and once again invites all Member States to make further contributions to the fund with a view to sustaining a strong outreach programme;

7. *Takes note* of the recommendations contained in the report of the Secretary-General on disarmament and non-proliferation education,[3] which reviews the implementation of the recommendations made in the 2002 study on disarmament and non-proliferation education;[4]

8. *Requests* the Secretary-General to submit to the General Assembly at its seventy-fifth session a report covering both the implementation of the activities of the Programme by the United Nations system during the previous two years and the activities of the Programme contemplated by the system for the following two years;

9. *Decides* to include in the provisional agenda of its seventy-fifth session, under the item entitled "Review and implementation of the Concluding Document of the Twelfth Special Session of the General

---

[3] A/73/119.
[4] A/57/124.

Assembly", the sub-item entitled "United Nations Disarmament Information Programme".

Action by the General Assembly

Date: 5 December 2018 Meeting: 45th plenary meeting
Vote: Adopted without a vote Report: A/73/511

Sponsors

Argentina, Australia, Austria, Canada, Costa Rica, Ecuador, Germany, Guatemala, **Mexico**, Peru, Portugal, Samoa, Spain, Thailand, Uruguay

Co-sponsors

Indonesia, Lebanon, Norway, Paraguay, Philippines

Action by the First Committee

Date: 8 November 2018 Meeting: 30th meeting
Vote: Adopted without a vote Draft resolution: A/C.1/73/L.45

Agenda item 102 (h)

73/80   United Nations regional centres for peace and disarmament

Text

The General Assembly,

Recalling its resolutions 60/83 of 8 December 2005, 61/90 of 6 December 2006, 62/50 of 5 December 2007, 63/76 of 2 December 2008, 64/58 of 2 December 2009, 65/78 of 8 December 2010, 66/53 of 2 December 2011, 67/63 of 3 December 2012, 68/57 of 5 December 2013, 69/70 of 2 December 2014, 70/61 of 7 December 2015, 71/80 of 5 December 2016 and 72/64 of 4 December 2017 regarding the maintenance and revitalization of the three United Nations regional centres for peace and disarmament,

Recalling also the reports of the Secretary-General on the United Nations Regional Centre for Peace and Disarmament in Africa,[1] the United Nations Regional Centre for Peace and Disarmament in Asia and the Pacific[2] and the United Nations Regional Centre for Peace, Disarmament and Development in Latin America and the Caribbean,[3]

Reaffirming its decision, taken in 1982 at its twelfth special session, to establish the United Nations Disarmament Information Programme, the purpose of which is to inform, educate and generate public understanding and support for the objectives of the United Nations in the field of arms control and disarmament,

Bearing in mind its resolutions 40/151 G of 16 December 1985, 41/60 J of 3 December 1986, 42/39 D of 30 November 1987 and 44/117 F of 15 December 1989 on the regional centres for peace and disarmament in Nepal, Peru and Togo,

Recalling that the thirtieth anniversary of the establishment by the General Assembly of the United Nations Regional Centre for Peace and Disarmament in Africa, the United Nations Regional Centre for Peace and Disarmament in Asia and the Pacific and the United Nations Regional Centre for Peace, Disarmament and Development in Latin America and the Caribbean was celebrated in 2016 and in 2017,

Recognizing that the changes that have taken place in the world have created new opportunities and posed new challenges for the pursuit of disarmament, and bearing in mind in this regard that the regional centres for peace and disarmament can contribute substantially to understanding and

---

[1]   A/73/151.

[2]   A/73/126.

[3]   A/73/127.

cooperation among States in each particular region in the areas of peace, disarmament and development,

Noting that, in paragraph 240 of the Final Document of the Eighteenth Midterm Ministerial Meeting of the Movement of Non-Aligned Countries, held in Baku from 3 to 6 April 2018, the Ministers emphasized the importance of United Nations activities at the regional level to increase the stability and security of its Member States, which could be promoted in a substantive manner by the maintenance and revitalization of the three regional centres for peace and disarmament,

1.   *Reiterates* the importance of United Nations activities at the regional level to advance disarmament and to increase the stability and security of its Member States, which could be promoted in a substantive manner by the maintenance and further strengthening of the three regional centres for peace and disarmament;

2.   *Commends* the three regional centres for peace and disarmament for their sustained support provided to Member States for over 30 years in implementing disarmament, arms control and non-proliferation activities through seminars and conferences, capacity-building and training, policy and technical expertise, and information and advocacy at the global, regional and national levels;

3.   *Reaffirms* that, in order to achieve positive results, it is useful for the three regional centres to carry out dissemination and educational programmes that promote regional peace and security and that are aimed at changing basic attitudes with respect to peace and security and disarmament so as to support the achievement of the purposes and principles of the United Nations;

4.   *Appeals* to Member States in each region that are able to do so, as well as to international governmental and non-governmental organizations and foundations, to make voluntary contributions to the regional centres in their respective regions in order to strengthen their activities and initiatives;

5.   *Emphasizes* the importance of the activities of the Regional Disarmament Branch of the Office for Disarmament Affairs of the Secretariat;

6.   *Requests* the Secretary-General to provide all support necessary, within existing resources, to the regional centres in carrying out their programmes of activities;

7.   *Decides* to include in the provisional agenda of its seventy-fourth session, under the item entitled "Review and implementation of the Concluding Document of the Twelfth Special Session of the General Assembly", the sub-item entitled "United Nations regional centres for peace and disarmament".

Action by the General Assembly

Date: 5 December 2018   Meeting: 45th plenary meeting
Vote: Adopted without a vote   Report: A/73/511

Sponsors

Indonesia (on behalf of the States Members of the United Nations that are members of the Movement of Non-Aligned Countries)

Action by the First Committee

Date: 8 November 2018   Meeting: 30th meeting
Vote: Adopted without a vote   Draft resolution: A/C.1/73/L.18

Agenda item 103 (a)

73/81   Report of the Conference on Disarmament

Text

The General Assembly,

Having considered the report of the Conference on Disarmament,[1]

Convinced that the Conference on Disarmament, as the single multilateral disarmament negotiating forum of the international community, has the primary role in substantive negotiations on priority questions of disarmament,

Recognizing the addresses of the Secretary-General of the United Nations, as well as those of Ministers for Foreign Affairs and other high-level officials in the Conference on Disarmament, and referring to their various expressions of support for and concern about the endeavours of the Conference and calls for the Conference to commence negotiations without delay to advance disarmament goals through the adoption of a balanced and comprehensive programme of work,

Recognizing also the need to conduct multilateral negotiations with the aim of reaching agreement on concrete issues, and emphasizing the importance of effective multilateralism in the context of the changing international climate,

Noting with renewed concern that, despite the intensive efforts by States members and Presidents of the Conference on Disarmament at its 2018 session to reach consensus on a programme of work on the basis of relevant proposals and suggestions, the Conference did not succeed in commencing its substantive work by means of negotiations, as called for by the General Assembly in its resolution 72/65 of 4 December 2017, or agree to a programme of work, although the Conference did hold substantive discussions in the framework of subsidiary bodies established for that purpose,

Recalling, in this respect, that the Conference on Disarmament has a number of priority issues for negotiation to achieve disarmament goals,

Welcoming the overwhelming call for greater flexibility with respect to implementing the substantive work of the Conference on Disarmament on the basis of a balanced and comprehensive programme of work,

Appreciating the continued cooperation among the States members of the Conference on Disarmament as well as among the successive Presidents of the Conference,

---

[1] *Official Records of the General Assembly, Seventy-third Session, Supplement No. 27* (A/73/27).

Noting with appreciation the significant contributions made at the 2018 session to promote substantive discussions on issues on the agenda, notably the work of the five subsidiary bodies established pursuant to the decision adopted on 16 February 2018,[2] and the adoption by the Conference on Disarmament of reports of four of the subsidiary bodies, and noting the discussions on the functioning of the Conference, as well as the discussions held on other issues that could also be relevant to the current international security environment,

Acknowledging the United Nations Institute for Disarmament Research, as a stand-alone, autonomous institution, and the contribution that its research makes,

Recognizing the importance of engagement between civil society and the Conference on Disarmament according to decisions taken by the Conference,

1. *Reaffirms* the role of the Conference on Disarmament as the single multilateral disarmament negotiating forum of the international community;

2. *Appreciates* the strong support expressed for the Conference on Disarmament at its 2018 session by Ministers for Foreign Affairs and other high-level officials, while also acknowledging their concern about its ongoing impasse, and takes into account their calls for greater flexibility with respect to commencing the substantive work of the Conference without further delay;

3. *Calls upon* the Conference on Disarmament to further intensify consultations and to explore possibilities for overcoming its ongoing deadlock of two decades by adopting and implementing a balanced and comprehensive programme of work at the earliest possible date during its 2019 session, bearing in mind the decision on the programme of work adopted by the Conference on 29 May 2009,[3] as well as other relevant present, past and future proposals;

4. *Takes note with appreciation* of the decision of the Conference on Disarmament on the establishment of subsidiary bodies on agenda items 1 to 4, and one on agenda items 5, 6 and 7,[2] which also considered emerging and other issues relevant to substantive work of the Conference, for the 2018 session, and welcomes the adoption by the Conference of substantive reports of four of the subsidiary bodies, as a basis for substantive work, including negotiations, at its 2019 session;

5. *Encourages* the current President of the Conference on Disarmament and the incoming President of the Conference to conduct consultations during the intersessional period and, if possible, to make recommendations, taking into account all relevant proposals, past, present and future, including those submitted as documents of the Conference, views

---

[2] Ibid., para. 13.
[3] Ibid., *Sixty-fourth Session, Supplement No. 27* (A/64/27), para. 18.

presented and discussions held, and to endeavour to keep the membership of the Conference informed, as appropriate, of their consultations;

6. *Requests* the current President of the Conference on Disarmament and successive Presidents to cooperate with the States members of the Conference in the effort to guide the Conference to the early commencement of its substantive work, including negotiations, at its 2019 session;

7. *Recognizes* the importance of continuing consultations in 2019 on the question of the expansion of the membership of the Conference on Disarmament;

8. *Requests* the Secretary-General to continue to ensure and to strengthen, if needed, the provision to the Conference on Disarmament of all necessary administrative, substantive and conference support services;

9. *Requests* the Conference on Disarmament to submit to the General Assembly at its seventy-fourth session a report on its work;

10. *Decides* to include in the provisional agenda of its seventy-fourth session, under the item entitled "Review of the implementation of the recommendations and decisions adopted by the General Assembly at its tenth special session", the sub-item entitled "Report of the Conference on Disarmament".

Action by the General Assembly

Date: 5 December 2018   Meeting: 45th plenary meeting
Vote: Adopted without a vote   Report: A/73/512

Sponsors

Turkey

Action by the First Committee

Date: 8 November 2018   Meeting: 30th meeting
Vote: Adopted without a vote   Draft resolution: A/C.1/73/L.40

Agenda item 103 (b)

73/82 Report of the Disarmament Commission

Text

The General Assembly,

Having considered the report of the Disarmament Commission,[1]

Recalling its resolutions 47/54 A of 9 December 1992, 47/54 G of 8 April 1993, 48/77 A of 16 December 1993, 49/77 A of 15 December 1994, 50/72 D of 12 December 1995, 51/47 B of 10 December 1996, 52/40 B of 9 December 1997, 53/79 A of 4 December 1998, 54/56 A of 1 December 1999, 55/35 C of 20 November 2000, 56/26 A of 29 November 2001, 57/95 of 22 November 2002, 58/67 of 8 December 2003, 59/105 of 3 December 2004, 60/91 of 8 December 2005, 61/98 of 6 December 2006, 62/54 of 5 December 2007, 63/83 of 2 December 2008, 64/65 of 2 December 2009, 65/86 of 8 December 2010, 66/60 of 2 December 2011, 67/71 of 3 December 2012, 68/63 of 5 December 2013, 69/77 of 2 December 2014, 70/68 of 7 December 2015, 71/82 of 5 December 2016 and 72/66 of 4 December 2017,

Considering the role that the Disarmament Commission has been called upon to play and the contribution that it should make in examining and submitting recommendations on various problems in the field of disarmament and in promoting the implementation of the relevant decisions adopted by the General Assembly at its tenth special session,

Recalling in particular General Assembly resolution 45/62 B of 4 December 1990, in which it noted with satisfaction the adoption by consensus of a set of "Ways and means to enhance the functioning of the Disarmament Commission",[2] Assembly decision 52/492 of 8 September 1998 concerning the efficient functioning of the Commission and Assembly resolution 61/98, which contains additional measures for improving the effectiveness of the methods of work of the Commission,

Reaffirming the mandate of the Disarmament Commission as the specialized, deliberative subsidiary body of the General Assembly that allows for in-depth deliberations on specific disarmament issues, leading to the submission of concrete recommendations on those issues, and recalling that the Commission shall make every effort to ensure that, insofar as possible, decisions on substantive issues be adopted by consensus, as set forth in paragraph 118 of the Final Document of the Tenth Special Session of the General Assembly,[3]

---

[1] *Official Records of the General Assembly, Seventy-third Session, Supplement No. 42* (A/73/42).
[2] Resolution 44/119 C, annex.
[3] Resolution S-10/2.

Emphasizing once again the important place of the Disarmament Commission within the United Nations multilateral disarmament machinery,

1. *Takes note* of the report of the Disarmament Commission;[1]

2. *Reaffirms* the importance of further enhancing the dialogue and cooperation among the First Committee, the Disarmament Commission and the Conference on Disarmament;

3. *Emphasizes* the need for a focused and results-oriented discussion of the items on the agenda of the Disarmament Commission;

4. *Requests* the Disarmament Commission to continue its work in accordance with its mandate, as set forth in paragraph 118 of the Final Document of the Tenth Special Session of the General Assembly,[3] and with paragraph 3 of Assembly resolution 37/78 H of 9 December 1982 and to that end to make every effort to achieve specific recommendations on the items on its agenda, taking into account the adopted "Ways and means to enhance the functioning of the Disarmament Commission";[2]

5. *Welcomes* the fact that, in accordance with General Assembly decision 52/492, at its 368th meeting, on 21 February 2018, the Disarmament Commission adopted the provisional agenda for its substantive session of 2018, and that the Commission decided that the agenda for its substantive session of 2018 should serve for the period 2018–2020;

6. *Recommends* that the Disarmament Commission continue its consideration of the following items at its substantive session of 2019:

(a) Recommendations for achieving the objective of nuclear disarmament and non-proliferation of nuclear weapons;

(b) Preparation of recommendations to promote the practical implementation of transparency and confidence-building measures in outer space activities with the goal of preventing an arms race in outer space, in accordance with the recommendations set out in the report of the Group of Governmental Experts on Transparency and Confidence-Building Measures in Outer Space Activities;[4]

7. *Notes* that the Disarmament Commission encourages the Chairs of its working groups to continue informal consultations during the intersessional period on the agenda item allocated to each of the groups;

8. *Encourages* the Disarmament Commission to invite, as appropriate, the United Nations Institute for Disarmament Research to prepare background papers on the items on its agenda and, if need be, other disarmament experts to present their views, as provided for in paragraph 3 (e) of resolution 61/98, upon the invitation of the Chair and with the prior approval of the Commission;

---

[4] A/68/189.

9.   *Requests* the Disarmament Commission to meet for a period not exceeding three weeks during 2019, namely from 8 to 29 April, and to submit a substantive report to the General Assembly at its seventy-fourth session, and stresses that the report of the Commission should contain a summary by the Chair of the proceedings to reflect different views or positions if no agreement can be reached on the specific agenda item deliberated on, as provided for in paragraph 3.4 of the adopted "Ways and means to enhance the functioning of the Disarmament Commission";

10.   *Requests* the Secretary-General to ensure full provision to the Disarmament Commission and its subsidiary bodies of interpretation and translation facilities in the official languages and to assign, as a matter of priority, all the resources and services necessary, including verbatim records, to that end, and also requests the Secretary-General to transmit to the Commission the annual report of the Conference on Disarmament on its 2018 session,[5] together with all the official records of the seventy-third session of the General Assembly relating to disarmament matters, and to render all assistance that the Commission may require for implementing the present resolution;

11.   *Invites* Member States to submit their views and proposals on the matter early enough to enable practical consultations among them prior to the beginning of the substantive session of 2019 of the Disarmament Commission, with a view to facilitating its constructive outcome, and in this regard encourages the Chair-designate, upon nomination, to commence consultations and preparations for the substantive session of 2019 in a timely manner;

12.   *Decides* to include in the provisional agenda of its seventy-fourth session, under the item entitled "Review of the implementation of the recommendations and decisions adopted by the General Assembly at its tenth special session", the sub-item entitled "Report of the Disarmament Commission".

Action by the General Assembly

Date: 5 December 2018   Meeting: 45th plenary meeting
Vote: Adopted without a vote   Report: A/73/512

Sponsors

Australia

Action by the First Committee

Date: 8 November 2018   Meeting: 30th meeting
Vote: Adopted without a vote   Draft resolution: A/C.1/73/L.36

---

[5] *Official Records of the General Assembly, Seventy-third Session, Supplement No. 27* (A/73/27).

Agenda item 104

73/83　The risk of nuclear proliferation in the Middle East

Text

The General Assembly,

Bearing in mind its relevant resolutions, the latest of which is resolution 72/67 of 4 December 2017,

Taking note of the relevant resolutions adopted by the General Conference of the International Atomic Energy Agency, the latest of which is resolution GC(62)/RES/12, adopted on 20 September 2018,

Cognizant that the proliferation of nuclear weapons in the region of the Middle East would pose a serious threat to international peace and security,

Mindful of the immediate need for placing all nuclear facilities in the region of the Middle East under full-scope safeguards of the Agency,

Recalling the decision on principles and objectives for nuclear non-proliferation and disarmament adopted by the 1995 Review and Extension Conference of the Parties to the Treaty on the Non-Proliferation of Nuclear Weapons on 11 May 1995,[1] in which the Conference urged universal adherence to the Treaty on the Non-Proliferation of Nuclear Weapons[2] as an urgent priority and called upon all States not yet parties to the Treaty to accede to it at the earliest date, particularly those States that operate unsafeguarded nuclear facilities,

Recognizing with satisfaction that, in the Final Document of the 2000 Review Conference of the Parties to the Treaty on the Non-Proliferation of Nuclear Weapons,[3] the Conference undertook to make determined efforts towards the achievement of the goal of universality of the Treaty, called upon those remaining States not parties to the Treaty to accede to it, thereby accepting an international legally binding commitment not to acquire nuclear weapons or nuclear explosive devices and to accept Agency safeguards on all their nuclear activities, and underlined the necessity of universal adherence to the Treaty and of strict compliance by all parties with their obligations under the Treaty,

Recalling the resolution on the Middle East adopted by the 1995 Review and Extension Conference of the Parties to the Treaty on 11 May 1995,[1] in

---

[1] See *1995 Review and Extension Conference of the Parties to the Treaty on the Non-Proliferation of Nuclear Weapons, Final Document, Part I* (NPT/CONF.1995/32 (Part I) and NPT/CONF.1995/32 (Part I)/Corr.2), annex.

[2] United Nations, *Treaty Series*, vol. 729, No. 10485.

[3] *2000 Review Conference of the Parties to the Treaty on the Non-Proliferation of Nuclear Weapons, Final Document*, vols. I–III (NPT/CONF.2000/28 (Parts I and II), NPT/CONF.2000/28 (Part III) and NPT/CONF.2000/28 (Part IV)).

which the Conference noted with concern the continued existence in the Middle East of unsafeguarded nuclear facilities, reaffirmed the importance of the early realization of universal adherence to the Treaty, and called upon all States in the Middle East that had not yet done so, without exception, to accede to the Treaty as soon as possible and to place all their nuclear facilities under full-scope Agency safeguards,

Acknowledging that, in the Final Document of the 2010 Review Conference of the Parties to the Treaty on the Non-Proliferation of Nuclear Weapons,[4] the Conference emphasized the importance of a process leading to full implementation of the 1995 resolution on the Middle East and decided, inter alia, that the Secretary-General of the United Nations and the co-sponsors of the 1995 resolution, in consultation with the States of the region, would convene a conference in 2012, to be attended by all States of the Middle East, on the establishment of a Middle East zone free of nuclear weapons and all other weapons of mass destruction, on the basis of arrangements freely arrived at by the States of the region, and with the full support and engagement of the nuclear-weapon States,

Expressing regret and concern that the conference was not convened in 2012 as mandated and that little progress has been achieved towards the implementation of the resolution on the Middle East adopted by the 1995 Review and Extension Conference of the Parties to the Treaty,

Noting, in this context, the relevant resolutions of the League of Arab States aiming at the establishment of a Middle East zone free of nuclear weapons and all other weapons of mass destruction,

Taking note with appreciation of the report of the Secretary-General,[5]

Recalling that Israel remains the only State in the Middle East that has not yet become a party to the Treaty,

Concerned about the threats posed by the proliferation of nuclear weapons to the security and stability of the Middle East region,

Stressing the importance of taking confidence-building measures, in particular the establishment of a nuclear-weapon-free zone in the Middle East, in order to enhance peace and security in the region and to consolidate the global non-proliferation regime,

Emphasizing the need for all parties directly concerned to seriously consider taking the practical and urgent steps required for the implementation of the proposal to establish a nuclear-weapon-free zone in the region of the Middle East in accordance with the relevant resolutions of the General Assembly and, as a means of promoting this objective, inviting the countries

---

[4] *2010 Review Conference of the Parties to the Treaty on the Non-Proliferation of Nuclear Weapons, Final Document*, vols. I–III (NPT/CONF.2010/50 (Vol. I), NPT/CONF.2010/50 (Vol. II) and NPT/CONF.2010/50 (Vol. III)).

[5] A/73/182 (Part II).

concerned to adhere to the Treaty and, pending the establishment of the zone, to agree to place all their nuclear activities under Agency safeguards,

Noting that 184 States have signed the Comprehensive Nuclear-Test-Ban Treaty,[6] including a number of States in the region,

1. *Recalls* the conclusions on the Middle East of the 2010 Review Conference of the Parties to the Treaty on the Non-Proliferation of Nuclear Weapons,[7] and calls for the speedy and full implementation of the commitments contained therein;

2. *Stresses* that the resolution on the Middle East adopted by the 1995 Review and Extension Conference of the Parties to the Treaty[1] is an essential element of the outcome of the 1995 Conference and of the basis on which the Treaty was indefinitely extended without a vote in 1995;

3. *Reiterates* that the resolution on the Middle East adopted by the 1995 Review and Extension Conference of the Parties to the Treaty remains valid until its goals and objectives are achieved;

4. *Calls for* immediate steps towards the full implementation of that resolution;

5. *Reaffirms* the importance of Israel's accession to the Treaty on the Non-Proliferation of Nuclear Weapons[2] and placement of all its nuclear facilities under comprehensive International Atomic Energy Agency safeguards, in realizing the goal of universal adherence to the Treaty in the Middle East;

6. *Calls upon* that State to accede to the Treaty without further delay, not to develop, produce, test or otherwise acquire nuclear weapons, to renounce possession of nuclear weapons and to place all its unsafeguarded nuclear facilities under full-scope Agency safeguards as an important confidence-building measure among all States of the region and as a step towards enhancing peace and security;

7. *Requests* the Secretary-General to report to the General Assembly at its seventy-fourth session on the implementation of the present resolution;

8. *Decides* to include in the provisional agenda of its seventy-fourth session the item entitled "The risk of nuclear proliferation in the Middle East".

Action by the General Assembly

Date: 5 December 2018	Meeting: 45th plenary meeting
Vote: 158-6-21	Report: A/73/513
168-3-4, p.p. 5	
167-3-4, p.p. 6	

---

[6] See resolution 50/245 and A/50/1027.

[7] *2010 Review Conference of the Parties to the Treaty on the Non-Proliferation of Nuclear Weapons, Final Document*, vol. I (NPT/CONF.2010/50 (Vol. I)), part I, *Conclusions and recommendations for follow-on actions*, sect. IV.

Sponsors

Algeria, Bahrain, Comoros, Djibouti, **Egypt** (on behalf of the States Members of the United Nations that are members of the League of Arab States), Iraq, Jordan, Kuwait, Lebanon, Libya, Mauritania, Morocco, Oman, Qatar, Saudi Arabia, Somalia, Sudan, Tunisia, United Arab Emirates, Yemen, State of Palestine

Recorded vote

As a whole

In favour:

Afghanistan, Albania, Algeria, Andorra, Angola, Antigua and Barbuda, Argentina, Armenia, Austria, Azerbaijan, Bahamas, Bahrain, Bangladesh, Barbados, Belarus, Belize, Benin, Bhutan, Bolivia (Plurinational State of), Bosnia and Herzegovina, Botswana, Brazil, Brunei Darussalam, Bulgaria, Burkina Faso, Burundi, Cabo Verde, Cambodia, Central African Republic, Chile, China, Colombia, Comoros, Congo, Costa Rica, Croatia, Cuba, Cyprus, Democratic People's Republic of Korea, Democratic Republic of the Congo, Djibouti, Dominica, Dominican Republic, Ecuador, Egypt, El Salvador, Equatorial Guinea, Eritrea, Estonia, Fiji, Finland, Gabon, Gambia, Ghana, Greece, Grenada, Guatemala, Guinea, Guinea-Bissau, Guyana, Honduras, Iceland, Indonesia, Iran (Islamic Republic of), Iraq, Ireland, Jamaica, Japan, Jordan, Kazakhstan, Kenya, Kuwait, Kyrgyzstan, Lao People's Democratic Republic, Latvia, Lebanon, Lesotho, Liberia, Libya, Liechtenstein, Madagascar, Malawi, Malaysia, Maldives, Mali, Malta, Mauritania, Mauritius, Mexico, Mongolia, Montenegro, Morocco, Mozambique, Myanmar, Namibia, Nauru, Nepal, New Zealand, Nicaragua, Niger, Nigeria, Norway, Oman, Pakistan, Papua New Guinea, Paraguay, Peru, Philippines, Portugal, Qatar, Republic of Korea, Republic of Moldova, Russian Federation, Saint Kitts and Nevis, Saint Lucia, Saint Vincent and the Grenadines, Samoa, San Marino, Sao Tome and Principe, Saudi Arabia, Senegal, Serbia, Seychelles, Sierra Leone, Singapore, Slovakia, Slovenia, Solomon Islands, South Africa, Spain, Sri Lanka, Sudan, Suriname, Sweden, Switzerland, Syrian Arab Republic, Tajikistan, Thailand, the former Yugoslav Republic of Macedonia, Timor-Leste, Togo, Trinidad and Tobago, Tunisia, Turkey, Turkmenistan, Tuvalu, Uganda, Ukraine, United Arab Emirates, United Republic of Tanzania, Uruguay, Uzbekistan, Vanuatu, Venezuela (Bolivarian Republic of), Viet Nam, Yemen, Zambia, Zimbabwe

Against:

Canada, Israel, Marshall Islands, Micronesia (Federated States of), Palau, United States

Abstaining:
Australia, Belgium, Cameroon, Côte d'Ivoire, Czechia, Denmark, Ethiopia, France, Georgia, Germany, Hungary, India, Italy, Lithuania, Luxembourg, Monaco, Netherlands, Panama, Poland, Romania, United Kingdom

Fifth preambular paragraph

In favour:
Afghanistan, Albania, Algeria, Andorra, Angola, Antigua and Barbuda, Argentina, Armenia, Australia, Austria, Azerbaijan, Bahamas, Bahrain, Bangladesh, Barbados, Belarus, Belgium, Belize, Benin, Bolivia (Plurinational State of), Bosnia and Herzegovina, Botswana, Brazil, Brunei Darussalam, Bulgaria, Burkina Faso, Burundi, Cabo Verde, Cambodia, Canada, Chile, China, Colombia, Comoros, Costa Rica, Côte d'Ivoire, Croatia, Cuba, Cyprus, Czechia, Democratic Republic of the Congo, Denmark, Djibouti, Dominican Republic, Ecuador, Egypt, El Salvador, Equatorial Guinea, Eritrea, Estonia, Eswatini, Ethiopia, Fiji, Finland, Gambia, Germany, Ghana, Greece, Guatemala, Guinea, Guinea-Bissau, Guyana, Honduras, Hungary, Iceland, Indonesia, Iran (Islamic Republic of), Iraq, Ireland, Italy, Jamaica, Japan, Jordan, Kazakhstan, Kenya, Kuwait, Kyrgyzstan, Lao People's Democratic Republic, Latvia, Lebanon, Lesotho, Liberia, Libya, Liechtenstein, Lithuania, Luxembourg, Madagascar, Malawi, Malaysia, Maldives, Mali, Malta, Mauritania, Mauritius, Mexico, Monaco, Mongolia, Montenegro, Morocco, Mozambique, Myanmar, Namibia, Nepal, Netherlands, New Zealand, Nicaragua, Niger, Nigeria, Norway, Oman, Panama, Papua New Guinea, Paraguay, Peru, Philippines, Poland, Portugal, Qatar, Republic of Korea, Republic of Moldova, Romania, Russian Federation, Saint Kitts and Nevis, Saint Lucia, Saint Vincent and the Grenadines, Samoa, San Marino, Sao Tome and Principe, Saudi Arabia, Senegal, Serbia, Seychelles, Sierra Leone, Singapore, Slovakia, Slovenia, Solomon Islands, South Africa, Spain, Sri Lanka, Sudan, Suriname, Sweden, Switzerland, Syrian Arab Republic, Tajikistan, Thailand, the former Yugoslav Republic of Macedonia, Timor-Leste, Togo, Trinidad and Tobago, Tunisia, Turkey, Turkmenistan, Tuvalu, Uganda, Ukraine, United Arab Emirates, United Kingdom, United Republic of Tanzania, Uruguay, Uzbekistan, Vanuatu, Venezuela (Bolivarian Republic of), Viet Nam, Yemen, Zambia, Zimbabwe

Against:
India, Israel, Pakistan

Abstaining:
Bhutan, France, Georgia, United States

Sixth preambular paragraph

In favour:

Afghanistan, Albania, Algeria, Andorra, Angola, Antigua and Barbuda, Argentina, Armenia, Australia, Austria, Azerbaijan, Bahamas, Bahrain, Bangladesh, Barbados, Belarus, Belgium, Belize, Benin, Bolivia (Plurinational State of), Bosnia and Herzegovina, Botswana, Brazil, Brunei Darussalam, Bulgaria, Burkina Faso, Burundi, Cabo Verde, Cambodia, Canada, Chile, China, Colombia, Comoros, Costa Rica, Côte d'Ivoire, Croatia, Cuba, Cyprus, Czechia, Democratic Republic of the Congo, Denmark, Djibouti, Dominican Republic, Ecuador, Egypt, El Salvador, Equatorial Guinea, Eritrea, Estonia, Ethiopia, Fiji, Finland, Gambia, Germany, Ghana, Greece, Guatemala, Guinea, Guinea-Bissau, Guyana, Honduras, Hungary, Iceland, Indonesia, Iran (Islamic Republic of), Iraq, Ireland, Italy, Jamaica, Japan, Jordan, Kazakhstan, Kenya, Kuwait, Kyrgyzstan, Lao People's Democratic Republic, Latvia, Lebanon, Lesotho, Liberia, Libya, Liechtenstein, Lithuania, Luxembourg, Madagascar, Malawi, Malaysia, Maldives, Mali, Malta, Mauritania, Mauritius, Mexico, Monaco, Mongolia, Montenegro, Morocco, Mozambique, Myanmar, Namibia, Nepal, Netherlands, New Zealand, Nicaragua, Niger, Nigeria, Norway, Oman, Panama, Papua New Guinea, Paraguay, Peru, Philippines, Poland, Portugal, Qatar, Republic of Korea, Republic of Moldova, Romania, Russian Federation, Saint Kitts and Nevis, Saint Lucia, Saint Vincent and the Grenadines, Samoa, San Marino, Sao Tome and Principe, Saudi Arabia, Senegal, Serbia, Seychelles, Sierra Leone, Singapore, Slovakia, Slovenia, Solomon Islands, South Africa, Spain, Sri Lanka, Sudan, Suriname, Sweden, Switzerland, Syrian Arab Republic, Tajikistan, Thailand, the former Yugoslav Republic of Macedonia, Timor-Leste, Togo, Trinidad and Tobago, Tunisia, Turkey, Turkmenistan, Tuvalu, Uganda, Ukraine, United Arab Emirates, United Kingdom, United Republic of Tanzania, Uruguay, Uzbekistan, Vanuatu, Venezuela (Bolivarian Republic of), Viet Nam, Yemen, Zambia, Zimbabwe

Against:

India, Israel, Pakistan

Abstaining:

Bhutan, France, Georgia, United States

Action by the First Committee

Date: 1 November 2018   Meeting: 26th meeting
Vote: 158-5-21   Draft resolution: A/C.1/73/L.2
      170-4-4, p.p. 5
      171-3-5, p.p. 6

Agenda item 105

73/84   Convention on Prohibitions or Restrictions on the Use of Certain Conventional Weapons Which May Be Deemed to Be Excessively Injurious or to Have Indiscriminate Effects

Text

The General Assembly,

Recalling its resolution 72/68 of 4 December 2017,

Recalling with satisfaction the adoption and entry into force of the Convention on Prohibitions or Restrictions on the Use of Certain Conventional Weapons Which May Be Deemed to Be Excessively Injurious or to Have Indiscriminate Effects[1] and its amended article 1,[2] the Protocol on Non-Detectable Fragments (Protocol I),[1] the Protocol on Prohibitions or Restrictions on the Use of Mines, Booby Traps and Other Devices (Protocol II)[1] and its amended version,[3] the Protocol on Prohibitions or Restrictions on the Use of Incendiary Weapons (Protocol III),[1] the Protocol on Blinding Laser Weapons (Protocol IV)[4] and the Protocol on Explosive Remnants of War (Protocol V),[5]

Recalling the results of the Fifth Review Conference of the High Contracting Parties to the Convention, held in Geneva from 12 to 16 December 2016,

Welcoming the results of the 2017 Meeting of the High Contracting Parties to the Convention, held in Geneva from 22 to 24 November 2017,

Welcoming also the results of the Nineteenth Annual Conference of the High Contracting Parties to Amended Protocol II, held in Geneva on 21 November 2017,

Welcoming further the results of the Eleventh Conference of the High Contracting Parties to Protocol V, held in Geneva on 20 November 2017,

Noting with satisfaction that the Meeting of the Group of Experts of the High Contracting Parties to Amended Protocol II, the Meeting of Experts of the High Contracting Parties to Protocol V and the two sessions of the Group of Governmental Experts related to emerging technologies in the area of lethal autonomous weapons systems of the High Contracting Parties to the Convention were held in 2018, and anticipating that the issue of non-payment

---

[1] United Nations, *Treaty Series*, vol. 1342, No. 22495.
[2] Ibid., vol. 2260, No. 22495.
[3] Ibid., vol. 2048, No. 22495.
[4] Ibid., vol. 2024, No. 22495.
[5] Ibid., vol. 2399, No. 22495.

will be addressed in order to deliver adequate and timely funding, enabling a positive financial situation that will allow meetings to be held next year,

Recalling the role played by the International Committee of the Red Cross in the elaboration of the Convention and the Protocols thereto, and welcoming the particular efforts of various international, non-governmental and other organizations in raising awareness of the humanitarian consequences of various categories of conventional weapons which may be deemed to be excessively injurious or to have indiscriminate effects,

Emphasizing the importance of the perspectives of women, men, boys and girls in considering the issues addressed by the Convention and its Protocols,

1. *Calls upon* all States that have not yet done so to take all measures to become parties, as soon as possible, to the Convention on Prohibitions or Restrictions on the Use of Certain Conventional Weapons Which May Be Deemed to Be Excessively Injurious or to Have Indiscriminate Effects[1] and the Protocols thereto, as amended, with a view to achieving the widest possible adherence to these instruments at an early date and so as to ultimately achieve their universality;

2. *Calls upon* all High Contracting Parties to the Convention that have not yet done so to express their consent to be bound by the Protocols to the Convention and the amendment extending the scope of the Convention and the Protocols thereto to include armed conflicts of a non-international character;

3. *Emphasizes* the importance of the universalization of the Protocol on Explosive Remnants of War (Protocol V);[5]

4. *Welcomes* additional ratifications and acceptances of or accessions to the Convention, as well as consents to be bound by the Protocols thereto;

5. *Acknowledges* the continued efforts of the Secretary-General, as depositary of the Convention and the Protocols thereto, and of the respective office holders of the conferences of the High Contracting Parties to the Convention, Protocol V and Amended Protocol II, on behalf of the High Contracting Parties, to achieve the goal of universality;

6. *Recalls* the following decisions by the Fifth Review Conference of the High Contracting Parties to the Convention:

(a) To establish an open-ended Group of Governmental Experts related to emerging technologies in the area of lethal autonomous weapons systems in the context of the objectives and purposes of the Convention, adhering to the agreed recommendations contained in document CCW/CONF.V/2, and to submit a report to the 2017 Meeting of the High Contracting Parties to the Convention consistent with those recommendations;

(b) To add to the agenda of the next Meeting of the High Contracting Parties in 2017 the item "Protocol III";

(c)   To add to the agenda of the next Meeting of the High Contracting Parties in 2017 the item "Mines other than anti-personnel mines";

(d)   To add to the agenda of the next Meeting of the High Contracting Parties in 2017 the item for informal discussion "Consideration of how developments in the field of science and technology relevant to the Convention may be addressed under the Convention";

(e)   To invite the Chair-elect to conduct consultations with a view to including on the agenda of the 2017 annual Meeting of the High Contracting Parties the item "Strengthening the respect for international humanitarian law and addressing, in the context and objectives of the Convention and its annexed Protocols, the challenges presented by the use of conventional weapons in armed conflicts and their impact on civilians, particularly in areas where there are concentrations of civilians";

(f)   To include on the agenda of the annual Meetings of the High Contracting Parties the item "Financial issues related to the Convention and its annexed Protocols" and to consider at the next such meeting efficiency and cost-saving measures and a report to be prepared by the Chair-elect;

(g)   To retain the practice of keeping summary records only for the final sessions of the future Review Conferences, the meetings of the High Contracting Parties to the Convention, and the Conferences of the High Contracting Parties to Amended Protocol II and Protocol V;

(h)   To continue the Sponsorship Programme;

7.   *Also recalls* the following decisions by the Meeting of the High Contracting Parties to the Convention in 2017:

(a)   To call for a 10-day meeting, to be held in Geneva in 2018, of the Group of Governmental Experts related to emerging technologies in the area of lethal autonomous weapons systems in the context of the objectives and purposes of the Convention;

(b)   To call for the universalization and full implementation of Protocol III on Prohibitions or Restrictions on the Use of Incendiary Weapons,[1] given the Protocol's importance, and to retain the agenda item "Protocol III";

(c)   To request the Chair-elect to hold an informal open consultation on how best to address the continuing differences of views on "Mines other than anti-personnel mines" and to report to the High Contracting Parties in 2018;

(d)   To place on the agenda of its next meeting the item "Emerging issues in the context of the objectives and purposes of the Convention" and to invite the High Contracting Parties to submit, no later than six weeks in advance of that meeting, working papers on issues they intend to raise;

(e)   To keep under regular review the implementation of the financial measures that were agreed upon, in the light of the report of the Chair, to improve the situation of the Convention;

(f)   To request the Chair-elect to identify and report to the High Contracting Parties in 2018 any further measures that could be considered to improve the stability of the Secretariat's support to the Convention;

8.   *Calls upon* all High Contracting Parties to ensure full and prompt compliance with their financial obligations under the Convention and its annexed Protocols;

9.   *Welcomes* the adoption by consensus of the financial measures by all High Contracting Parties at the Meeting of the High Contracting Parties in 2017 in response to the call to explore options to improve the financial situation and ways to ensure financial stability for the operation of the Convention and its annexed Protocols, and also welcomes the request to keep the measures under review in order to ensure the financial sustainability and the adequate and timely funding of the Convention;

10.   *Also welcomes* the commitment by the High Contracting Parties to continue to contribute to the further development of international humanitarian law, and, in this context, to keep under review both the development of new weapons and uses of weapons, which may have indiscriminate effects or cause unnecessary suffering;

11.   *Further welcomes* the commitment of the High Contracting Parties to Protocol V to the effective and efficient implementation of the Protocol and the implementation of the decisions of the First and Second Conferences of the High Contracting Parties to the Protocol establishing a comprehensive framework for the exchange of information and cooperation;

12.   *Notes* that, in conformity with article 8 of the Convention, conferences may be convened to examine amendments to the Convention or to any of the Protocols thereto, to examine additional protocols concerning other categories of conventional weapons not covered by existing Protocols or to review the scope and application of the Convention and the Protocols thereto and to examine any proposed amendments or additional protocols;

13.   *Also notes* the efforts of the Chair to find, as requested by the High Contracting Parties, a stable basis for the Implementation Support Unit within the Geneva Branch of the Office for Disarmament Affairs of the Secretariat, which was established following a decision by the 2009 Meeting of the High Contracting Parties to the Convention, and recalls the decision of the Meeting of the High Contracting Parties in 2017 requesting the Chair-elect to identify and report to the High Contracting Parties in 2018 any further measures that could be considered in order to improve the stability of the Secretariat's support to the Convention without prejudice to the outcome of the efforts of the 2018 Chair;

14.   *Underlines* the vital role of the full and equal participation of women in decision-making and implementation of the Convention;

15. *Requests* the Secretary-General to render the assistance necessary and to provide such services as may be required for the annual conferences and expert meetings of the High Contracting Parties to the Convention and of the High Contracting Parties to Amended Protocol II and Protocol V, as well as for any continuation of the work after the meetings;

16. *Also requests* the Secretary-General, in his capacity as depositary of the Convention and the Protocols thereto, to continue to inform the General Assembly periodically, by electronic means, of ratifications and acceptances of and accessions to the Convention, its amended article 1[2] and the Protocols;

17. *Decides* to include in the provisional agenda of its seventy-fourth session the item entitled "Convention on Prohibitions or Restrictions on the Use of Certain Conventional Weapons Which May Be Deemed to Be Excessively Injurious or to Have Indiscriminate Effects".

Action by the General Assembly

Date: 5 December 2018	Meeting: 45th plenary meeting
Vote: Adopted without a vote	Report: A/73/514

Sponsors

United Kingdom

Action by the First Committee

Date: 6 November 2018	Meeting: 29th meeting
Vote: Adopted without a vote	Draft resolution: A/C.1/73/L.67

Agenda item 106

73/85   Strengthening of security and cooperation in the Mediterranean region

Text

The General Assembly,

Recalling its previous resolutions on the subject, including resolution 72/69 of 4 December 2017,

Reaffirming the primary role of the Mediterranean countries in strengthening and promoting peace, security and cooperation in the Mediterranean region,

Welcoming the efforts deployed by the Euro-Mediterranean countries to strengthen their cooperation in combating terrorism, in particular through the adoption of the Euro-Mediterranean Code of Conduct on Countering Terrorism by the Euro-Mediterranean Summit, held in Barcelona, Spain, on 27 and 28 November 2005,

Bearing in mind all the previous declarations and commitments, as well as all the initiatives taken by the riparian countries at the recent summits, ministerial meetings and various forums concerning the question of the Mediterranean region,

Recalling, in this regard, the adoption on 13 July 2008 of the Joint Declaration of the Paris Summit for the Mediterranean, which launched a reinforced partnership, named the "Barcelona Process: Union for the Mediterranean", and the common political will to revive efforts to transform the Mediterranean into an area of peace, democracy, cooperation and prosperity,

Welcoming the entry into force of the African Nuclear-Weapon-Free Zone Treaty (Treaty of Pelindaba)[1] as a contribution to the strengthening of peace and security both regionally and internationally,

Recognizing the indivisible character of security in the Mediterranean and that the enhancement of cooperation among Mediterranean countries with a view to promoting the economic and social development of all peoples of the region will contribute significantly to stability, peace and security in the region,

Recognizing also the efforts made so far and the determination of the Mediterranean countries to intensify the process of dialogue and consultations with a view to resolving the problems existing in the Mediterranean region and to eliminating the causes of tension and the consequent threat to peace and security, as well as their growing awareness of the need for further joint

---

[1] A/50/426, annex.

efforts to strengthen economic, social, cultural and environmental cooperation in the region,

Recognizing further that prospects for closer Euro-Mediterranean cooperation in all spheres can be enhanced by positive developments worldwide, in particular in Europe, in the Maghreb and in the Middle East,

Reaffirming the responsibility of all States to contribute to the stability and prosperity of the Mediterranean region and their commitment to respecting the purposes and principles of the Charter of the United Nations as well as the provisions of the Declaration on Principles of International Law concerning Friendly Relations and Cooperation among States in accordance with the Charter of the United Nations,[2]

Noting the peace negotiations in the Middle East, which should be of a comprehensive nature and represent an appropriate framework for the peaceful settlement of contentious issues in the region,

Expressing concern at the persistent tension and continuing military activities in parts of the Mediterranean that hinder efforts to strengthen security and cooperation in the region,

Taking note of the report of the Secretary-General,[3]

1.   *Reaffirms* that security in the Mediterranean is closely linked to European security as well as to international peace and security;

2.   *Expresses its satisfaction* at the continuing efforts by Mediterranean countries to contribute actively to the elimination of all causes of tension in the region and to the promotion of just and lasting solutions to the persistent problems of the region through peaceful means, thus ensuring the withdrawal of foreign forces of occupation and respecting the sovereignty, independence and territorial integrity of all countries of the Mediterranean and the right of peoples to self-determination, and therefore calls for full adherence to the principles of non-interference, non-intervention, non-use of force or threat of use of force and the inadmissibility of the acquisition of territory by force, in accordance with the Charter and the relevant resolutions of the United Nations;

3.   *Commends* the Mediterranean countries for their efforts in meeting common challenges through coordinated overall responses, based on a spirit of multilateral partnership, towards the general objective of turning the Mediterranean basin into an area of dialogue, exchanges and cooperation, guaranteeing peace, stability and prosperity, encourages them to strengthen such efforts through, inter alia, a lasting multilateral and action-oriented cooperative dialogue among States of the region, and recognizes the role of the United Nations in promoting regional and international peace and security;

---

[2] Resolution 2625 (XXV), annex.
[3] A/73/94.

4.   *Recognizes* that the elimination of the economic and social disparities in levels of development and other obstacles, as well as respect and greater understanding among cultures in the Mediterranean area, will contribute to enhancing peace, security and cooperation among Mediterranean countries through the existing forums;

5.   *Calls upon* all States of the Mediterranean region that have not yet done so to adhere to all the multilaterally negotiated legal instruments in force related to the field of disarmament and non-proliferation, thus creating the conditions necessary for strengthening peace and cooperation in the region;

6.   *Encourages* all States of the region to favour the conditions necessary for strengthening the confidence-building measures among them by promoting genuine openness and transparency on all military matters, by participating, inter alia, in the United Nations Report on Military Expenditures and by providing accurate data and information to the United Nations Register of Conventional Arms;

7.   *Encourages* the Mediterranean countries to strengthen further their cooperation in combating terrorism in all its forms and manifestations, including the possible resort by terrorists to weapons of mass destruction, taking into account the relevant resolutions of the United Nations, and in combating international crime and illicit arms transfers and illicit drug production, consumption and trafficking, which pose a serious threat to peace, security and stability in the region and therefore to the improvement of the current political, economic and social situation and which jeopardize friendly relations among States, hinder the development of international cooperation and result in the destruction of human rights, fundamental freedoms and the democratic basis of pluralistic society;

8.   *Requests* the Secretary-General to submit to the General Assembly at its seventy-fourth session a report on means to strengthen security and cooperation in the Mediterranean region;

9.   *Decides* to include in the provisional agenda of its seventy-fourth session the item entitled "Strengthening of security and cooperation in the Mediterranean region".

Action by the General Assembly

Date: 5 December 2018   Meeting: 45th plenary meeting
Vote: 181-0-2   Report: A/73/515
     169-2-3, o.p. 2
     168-2-3, o.p. 5

Sponsors

Algeria, Angola, Austria, Central African Republic, Cyprus, Egypt, Georgia, Ghana, Greece, Ireland, Latvia, Libya, Malta, Mauritania,

Myanmar, Netherlands, Nigeria, Portugal, San Marino, Serbia, Sierra Leone, Sudan, Tunisia, United Kingdom, Zimbabwe

Co-sponsors

Andorra, Equatorial Guinea, Eritrea, Gambia, Guinea-Bissau, Jordan, Kazakhstan, Lebanon, Maldives, Montenegro, Morocco, Namibia, Romania, Saudi Arabia, Slovenia, Turkey, Zambia

Recorded vote

As a whole

In favour:

Afghanistan, Albania, Algeria, Andorra, Angola, Antigua and Barbuda, Argentina, Armenia, Australia, Austria, Azerbaijan, Bahamas, Bahrain, Bangladesh, Barbados, Belarus, Belgium, Belize, Benin, Bhutan, Bolivia (Plurinational State of), Bosnia and Herzegovina, Botswana, Brazil, Brunei Darussalam, Bulgaria, Burkina Faso, Burundi, Cabo Verde, Cambodia, Cameroon, Canada, Central African Republic, Chile, China, Colombia, Comoros, Congo, Costa Rica, Côte d'Ivoire, Croatia, Cuba, Cyprus, Czechia, Democratic People's Republic of Korea, Democratic Republic of the Congo, Denmark, Djibouti, Dominica, Dominican Republic, Ecuador, Egypt, El Salvador, Equatorial Guinea, Eritrea, Estonia, Eswatini, Ethiopia, Fiji, Finland, France, Gabon, Gambia, Georgia, Germany, Ghana, Greece, Grenada, Guatemala, Guinea, Guinea-Bissau, Guyana, Haiti, Honduras, Hungary, Iceland, India, Indonesia, Iraq, Ireland, Italy, Jamaica, Japan, Jordan, Kazakhstan, Kenya, Kuwait, Kyrgyzstan, Lao People's Democratic Republic, Latvia, Lebanon, Lesotho, Liberia, Libya, Liechtenstein, Lithuania, Luxembourg, Madagascar, Malawi, Malaysia, Maldives, Mali, Malta, Mauritania, Mauritius, Mexico, Monaco, Mongolia, Montenegro, Morocco, Mozambique, Myanmar, Namibia, Nepal, Netherlands, New Zealand, Nicaragua, Niger, Nigeria, Norway, Oman, Pakistan, Panama, Papua New Guinea, Paraguay, Peru, Philippines, Poland, Portugal, Qatar, Republic of Korea, Republic of Moldova, Romania, Russian Federation, Rwanda, Saint Kitts and Nevis, Saint Lucia, Saint Vincent and the Grenadines, Samoa, San Marino, Sao Tome and Principe, Saudi Arabia, Senegal, Serbia, Seychelles, Sierra Leone, Singapore, Slovakia, Slovenia, Solomon Islands, South Africa, Spain, Sri Lanka, Sudan, Suriname, Sweden, Switzerland, Syrian Arab Republic, Tajikistan, Thailand, the former Yugoslav Republic of Macedonia, Timor-Leste, Togo, Trinidad and Tobago, Tunisia, Turkey, Turkmenistan, Tuvalu, Uganda, Ukraine, United Arab Emirates, United Kingdom, United Republic of Tanzania, Uruguay, Uzbekistan, Vanuatu, Venezuela (Bolivarian Republic of), Viet Nam, Yemen, Zambia, Zimbabwe

Against:
    None
Abstaining:
    Israel, United States

Operative paragraph 2

In favour:
    Afghanistan, Albania, Algeria, Andorra, Angola, Antigua and Barbuda, Argentina, Armenia, Australia, Austria, Azerbaijan, Bahamas, Bahrain, Bangladesh, Barbados, Belarus, Belgium, Belize, Benin, Bhutan, Bolivia (Plurinational State of), Bosnia and Herzegovina, Botswana, Brazil, Brunei Darussalam, Bulgaria, Burkina Faso, Burundi, Cabo Verde, Cambodia, Canada, Chile, China, Colombia, Comoros, Costa Rica, Côte d'Ivoire, Croatia, Cuba, Cyprus, Czechia, Democratic People's Republic of Korea, Denmark, Djibouti, Dominican Republic, Ecuador, Egypt, El Salvador, Equatorial Guinea, Eritrea, Estonia, Eswatini, Ethiopia, Finland, France, Gambia, Georgia, Germany, Ghana, Greece, Guatemala, Guinea, Guinea-Bissau, Guyana, Honduras, Hungary, Iceland, India, Indonesia, Iran (Islamic Republic of), Iraq, Ireland, Italy, Jamaica, Japan, Jordan, Kazakhstan, Kenya, Kuwait, Lao People's Democratic Republic, Latvia, Lebanon, Lesotho, Liberia, Libya, Liechtenstein, Lithuania, Luxembourg, Madagascar, Malawi, Malaysia, Maldives, Mali, Malta, Mauritania, Mauritius, Mexico, Monaco, Mongolia, Montenegro, Morocco, Mozambique, Myanmar, Namibia, Nepal, Netherlands, New Zealand, Nicaragua, Niger, Nigeria, Norway, Oman, Pakistan, Panama, Papua New Guinea, Paraguay, Peru, Philippines, Poland, Portugal, Qatar, Republic of Korea, Republic of Moldova, Romania, Russian Federation, Saint Kitts and Nevis, Saint Lucia, Saint Vincent and the Grenadines, Samoa, San Marino, Sao Tome and Principe, Saudi Arabia, Senegal, Serbia, Seychelles, Sierra Leone, Singapore, Slovakia, Slovenia, Solomon Islands, South Africa, Spain, Sri Lanka, Sudan, Suriname, Sweden, Switzerland, Syrian Arab Republic, Tajikistan, Thailand, the former Yugoslav Republic of Macedonia, Timor-Leste, Trinidad and Tobago, Tunisia, Turkey, Turkmenistan, Uganda, Ukraine, United Arab Emirates, United Kingdom, United Republic of Tanzania, Uruguay, Uzbekistan, Vanuatu, Venezuela (Bolivarian Republic of), Viet Nam, Yemen, Zambia, Zimbabwe

Against:
    Israel, United States
Abstaining:
    Fiji, Togo, Tuvalu

Operative paragraph 5

In favour:

Afghanistan, Albania, Algeria, Andorra, Angola, Antigua and Barbuda, Argentina, Australia, Austria, Azerbaijan, Bahamas, Bahrain, Bangladesh, Barbados, Belarus, Belgium, Belize, Benin, Bhutan, Bolivia (Plurinational State of), Bosnia and Herzegovina, Botswana, Brazil, Brunei Darussalam, Bulgaria, Burkina Faso, Burundi, Cabo Verde, Cambodia, Canada, China, Colombia, Comoros, Costa Rica, Côte d'Ivoire, Croatia, Cuba, Cyprus, Czechia, Democratic People's Republic of Korea, Democratic Republic of the Congo, Denmark, Djibouti, Dominican Republic, Ecuador, Egypt, El Salvador, Equatorial Guinea, Eritrea, Estonia, Eswatini, Ethiopia, Finland, Gambia, Georgia, Germany, Ghana, Greece, Guatemala, Guinea, Guinea-Bissau, Guyana, Honduras, Hungary, Iceland, India, Indonesia, Iran (Islamic Republic of), Iraq, Ireland, Italy, Jamaica, Japan, Jordan, Kazakhstan, Kenya, Kuwait, Lao People's Democratic Republic, Latvia, Lebanon, Lesotho, Liberia, Libya, Liechtenstein, Lithuania, Luxembourg, Madagascar, Malawi, Malaysia, Maldives, Mali, Malta, Mauritania, Mauritius, Mexico, Mongolia, Montenegro, Morocco, Mozambique, Myanmar, Namibia, Nepal, Netherlands, New Zealand, Nicaragua, Niger, Nigeria, Norway, Oman, Pakistan, Panama, Papua New Guinea, Paraguay, Peru, Philippines, Poland, Portugal, Qatar, Republic of Korea, Republic of Moldova, Romania, Russian Federation, Rwanda, Saint Kitts and Nevis, Saint Lucia, Saint Vincent and the Grenadines, Samoa, San Marino, Sao Tome and Principe, Saudi Arabia, Senegal, Serbia, Seychelles, Sierra Leone, Singapore, Slovakia, Slovenia, Solomon Islands, South Africa, Spain, Sri Lanka, Sudan, Suriname, Sweden, Switzerland, Syrian Arab Republic, Tajikistan, Thailand, the former Yugoslav Republic of Macedonia, Timor-Leste, Togo, Trinidad and Tobago, Tunisia, Turkey, Turkmenistan, Uganda, Ukraine, United Arab Emirates, United Kingdom, United Republic of Tanzania, Uruguay, Uzbekistan, Vanuatu, Venezuela (Bolivarian Republic of), Viet Nam, Yemen, Zambia, Zimbabwe

Against:

Israel, United States

Abstaining:

Fiji, France, Tuvalu

Action by the First Committee

Date:	8 November 2018	Meeting:	30th meeting
Vote:	171-0-2	Draft resolution:	A/C.1/73/L.30
	166-2-1, o.p. 2		
	165-2-2, o.p. 5		

Agenda item 107

73/86   Comprehensive Nuclear-Test-Ban Treaty

Text

The General Assembly,

Reiterating that the cessation of nuclear-weapon test explosions or any other nuclear explosions constitutes an effective nuclear disarmament and non-proliferation measure, and convinced that this is a meaningful step in the realization of a systematic process for achieving nuclear disarmament,

Recalling that the Comprehensive Nuclear-Test-Ban Treaty, adopted by the General Assembly by its resolution 50/245 of 10 September 1996, was opened for signature on 24 September 1996,

Stressing that a universal and effectively verifiable Treaty constitutes a fundamental instrument in the field of nuclear disarmament and non-proliferation and will be a major contribution to international peace and security,

Stressing also the vital importance and urgency of achieving the entry into force of the Treaty, as noted also in Security Council resolution 2310 (2016) of 23 September 2016, and affirming its resolute determination, 22 years after the Treaty was opened for signature, to achieve its entry into force,

Encouraged by the signing of the Treaty by 184 States, including 41 of the 44 whose ratification is needed for its entry into force, and welcoming the ratification of the Treaty by 167 States, including 36 of the 44 whose ratification is needed for its entry into force, among which there are 3 nuclear-weapon States,

Recalling its resolution 72/70 of 4 December 2017,

Recalling also the adoption by consensus of the conclusions and recommendations for follow-on actions of the 2010 Review Conference of the Parties to the Treaty on the Non-Proliferation of Nuclear Weapons,[1] in which the Conference, inter alia, reaffirmed the vital importance of the entry into force of the Comprehensive Nuclear-Test-Ban Treaty as a core element of the international nuclear disarmament and non-proliferation regime and included specific actions to be taken in support of the entry into force of the Treaty,

Welcoming the Final Declaration adopted by the tenth Conference on Facilitating the Entry into Force of the Comprehensive Nuclear-Test-Ban Treaty, held in New York on 20 September 2017, convened pursuant to

---

[1] *2010 Review Conference of the Parties to the Treaty on the Non-Proliferation of Nuclear Weapons, Final Document*, vol. I (NPT/CONF.2010/50 (Vol. I)), part I, *Conclusions and recommendations for follow-on actions.*

article XIV of the Treaty, and recalling the Joint Ministerial Statement on the Comprehensive Nuclear-Test-Ban Treaty, adopted at the ministerial meeting held in New York on 27 September 2018,

Noting the conference of the Youth Group of the Preparatory Commission for the Comprehensive Nuclear-Test-Ban Treaty Organization, held in Moscow from 18 to 20 October 2017, and the "intergenerational dialogue", held in Astana from 28 August to 2 September 2018, which brought together members of the group of eminent persons established to support the article XIV process and members of the Youth Group to build and sustain momentum for the universalization and entry into force of the Treaty,

Welcoming continuing progress in the development of the Treaty's verification regime, which advances the Treaty's primary non-proliferation and disarmament objective, and the establishment of over 91 per cent of the stations planned for the International Monitoring System network,

Recognizing the civil and scientific benefits provided by the Treaty's global monitoring system,

1.   *Stresses* the vital importance and urgency of signature and ratification, without delay and without conditions, in order to achieve the earliest entry into force of the Comprehensive Nuclear-Test-Ban Treaty;[2]

2.   *Welcomes* the contributions by the signatory States to the work of the Preparatory Commission for the Comprehensive Nuclear-Test-Ban Treaty Organization, in particular its efforts to ensure that the verification regime of the Treaty will be capable of meeting the verification requirements of the Treaty upon its entry into force, in accordance with article IV of the Treaty, and encourages their continuation;

3.   *Underlines* the need to maintain momentum towards the completion of all elements of the verification regime;

4.   *Urges* all States not to carry out nuclear-weapon test explosions or any other nuclear explosions, to maintain their moratoriums in this regard and to refrain from acts that would defeat the object and purpose of the Treaty, while stressing that these measures do not have the same permanent and legally binding effect as the entry into force of the Treaty;

5.   *Condemns in the strongest terms* the six nuclear tests conducted by the Democratic People's Republic of Korea since 2006 in violation of relevant Security Council resolutions,[3] urges full compliance with the obligations under those resolutions, including that the Democratic People's Republic of Korea abandon its nuclear weapons programme and not conduct any further nuclear tests, notes with encouragement the statement of the Democratic

---

[2] See resolution 50/245 and A/50/1027.

[3] Including Security Council resolutions 1718 (2006), 1874 (2009), 2094 (2013), 2270 (2016), 2321 (2016) and 2375 (2017).

People's Republic of Korea concerning a moratorium on nuclear tests and efforts towards the dismantlement of the Punggye-ri nuclear test site, reaffirms its support for the complete, verifiable and irreversible denuclearization of the Korean Peninsula in a peaceful manner, including through the Six-Party Talks, and welcomes all efforts and dialogue to this end, including the recent inter-Korean summits and the summit between the United States of America and the Democratic People's Republic of Korea;

6. *Urges* all States that have not yet signed or ratified, or that have signed but not yet ratified, the Treaty, in particular those whose ratification is needed for its entry into force, to sign and ratify it as soon as possible and to accelerate their ratification processes with a view to ensuring their earliest successful conclusion;

7. *Welcomes*, since the adoption of its previous resolution on the subject, the ratification of the Treaty by Thailand and the signature of the Treaty by Tuvalu, since each ratification or signature is a significant step towards the entry into force of the Treaty;

8. *Encourages* further expressions from among the remaining States whose ratification is needed for the Treaty to enter into force of their intention to pursue and complete the ratification process;

9. *Urges* all States to remain seized of the issue at the highest political level and, where in a position to do so, to promote adherence to the Treaty through bilateral and joint outreach, seminars and other means;

10. *Decides* to include in the provisional agenda of its seventy-fourth session the item entitled "Comprehensive Nuclear-Test-Ban Treaty".

Action by the General Assembly

Date: 5 December 2018   Meeting: 45th plenary meeting
Vote: 183-1-4   Report: A/73/516
      167-0-11, p.p. 4
      172-0-7, p.p. 7

Sponsors

Albania, Argentina, Armenia, **Australia**, Austria, Belgium, Bosnia and Herzegovina, Bulgaria, Canada, Costa Rica, Croatia, Cyprus, Czechia, Denmark, Eritrea, Estonia, Finland, France, Georgia, Germany, Ghana, Greece, Honduras, Hungary, Iceland, Ireland, Italy, Japan, Kazakhstan, Lao People's Democratic Republic, Latvia, Liechtenstein, Lithuania, Luxembourg, Madagascar, Malawi, Malaysia, Malta, Mexico, Mongolia, Montenegro, Netherlands, New Zealand, Norway, Panama, Papua New Guinea, Paraguay, Philippines, Poland, Portugal, Romania, Samoa, San Marino, Senegal, Serbia, Slovakia, Slovenia, Spain, Sweden, Switzerland, Thailand, the former Yugoslav Republic of Macedonia, Turkey, United Kingdom, Uruguay, Zambia

Co-sponsors

Andorra, Burkina Faso, Colombia, Côte d'Ivoire, Dominican Republic, Guyana, Haiti, Iraq, Jamaica, Kyrgyzstan, Maldives, Micronesia (Federated States of), Monaco, Namibia, Republic of Korea, Republic of Moldova, Seychelles, Singapore, Sri Lanka, Trinidad and Tobago, Ukraine, United Arab Emirates

Recorded vote

As a whole

In favour:

Afghanistan, Albania, Algeria, Andorra, Angola, Antigua and Barbuda, Argentina, Armenia, Australia, Austria, Azerbaijan, Bahamas, Bahrain, Bangladesh, Barbados, Belarus, Belgium, Belize, Benin, Bhutan, Bolivia (Plurinational State of), Bosnia and Herzegovina, Botswana, Brazil, Brunei Darussalam, Bulgaria, Burkina Faso, Burundi, Cabo Verde, Cambodia, Cameroon, Canada, Central African Republic, Chile, China, Colombia, Comoros, Congo, Costa Rica, Côte d'Ivoire, Croatia, Cuba, Cyprus, Czechia, Democratic Republic of the Congo, Denmark, Djibouti, Dominica, Dominican Republic, Ecuador, Egypt, El Salvador, Equatorial Guinea, Eritrea, Estonia, Eswatini, Ethiopia, Fiji, Finland, France, Gabon, Gambia, Georgia, Germany, Ghana, Greece, Grenada, Guatemala, Guinea, Guinea-Bissau, Guyana, Haiti, Honduras, Hungary, Iceland, Indonesia, Iran (Islamic Republic of), Iraq, Ireland, Israel, Italy, Jamaica, Japan, Jordan, Kazakhstan, Kenya, Kuwait, Kyrgyzstan, Lao People's Democratic Republic, Latvia, Lebanon, Lesotho, Liberia, Libya, Liechtenstein, Lithuania, Luxembourg, Madagascar, Malawi, Malaysia, Maldives, Mali, Malta, Marshall Islands, Mauritania, Mexico, Micronesia (Federated States of), Monaco, Mongolia, Montenegro, Morocco, Mozambique, Myanmar, Namibia, Nepal, Netherlands, New Zealand, Nicaragua, Niger, Nigeria, Norway, Oman, Pakistan, Palau, Panama, Papua New Guinea, Paraguay, Peru, Philippines, Poland, Portugal, Qatar, Republic of Korea, Republic of Moldova, Romania, Russian Federation, Rwanda, Saint Kitts and Nevis, Saint Lucia, Saint Vincent and the Grenadines, Samoa, San Marino, Sao Tome and Principe, Saudi Arabia, Senegal, Serbia, Seychelles, Sierra Leone, Singapore, Slovakia, Slovenia, Solomon Islands, South Africa, Spain, Sri Lanka, Sudan, Suriname, Sweden, Switzerland, Tajikistan, Thailand, the former Yugoslav Republic of Macedonia, Timor-Leste, Togo, Tonga, Trinidad and Tobago, Tunisia, Turkey, Turkmenistan, Tuvalu, Uganda, Ukraine, United Arab Emirates, United Kingdom, United Republic of Tanzania, Uruguay, Uzbekistan, Vanuatu, Venezuela (Bolivarian Republic of), Viet Nam, Yemen, Zambia, Zimbabwe

Against:

Democratic People's Republic of Korea

Abstaining:

India, Mauritius, Syrian Arab Republic, United States

Fourth preambular paragraph

In favour:

Afghanistan, Albania, Algeria, Andorra, Angola, Antigua and Barbuda, Argentina, Armenia, Australia, Austria, Azerbaijan, Bahamas, Bahrain, Bangladesh, Barbados, Belarus, Belgium, Belize, Benin, Bhutan, Bosnia and Herzegovina, Botswana, Brunei Darussalam, Bulgaria, Burkina Faso, Burundi, Cabo Verde, Cambodia, Canada, Chile, China, Colombia, Comoros, Costa Rica, Côte d'Ivoire, Croatia, Cyprus, Czechia, Democratic Republic of the Congo, Denmark, Djibouti, Dominican Republic, Ecuador, El Salvador, Equatorial Guinea, Eritrea, Estonia, Eswatini, Ethiopia, Fiji, Finland, France, Gambia, Georgia, Germany, Ghana, Greece, Guatemala, Guinea, Guinea-Bissau, Guyana, Haiti, Honduras, Hungary, Iceland, Iraq, Ireland, Israel, Italy, Jamaica, Japan, Jordan, Kazakhstan, Kenya, Kuwait, Kyrgyzstan, Lao People's Democratic Republic, Latvia, Lebanon, Lesotho, Liberia, Libya, Liechtenstein, Lithuania, Luxembourg, Madagascar, Malawi, Malaysia, Maldives, Mali, Malta, Marshall Islands, Mauritania, Mexico, Micronesia (Federated States of), Monaco, Mongolia, Montenegro, Morocco, Mozambique, Myanmar, Namibia, Nepal, Netherlands, New Zealand, Niger, Nigeria, Norway, Oman, Pakistan, Panama, Papua New Guinea, Paraguay, Peru, Philippines, Poland, Portugal, Qatar, Republic of Korea, Republic of Moldova, Romania, Russian Federation, Saint Kitts and Nevis, Saint Lucia, Saint Vincent and the Grenadines, Samoa, San Marino, Sao Tome and Principe, Saudi Arabia, Senegal, Serbia, Seychelles, Sierra Leone, Singapore, Slovakia, Slovenia, Solomon Islands, South Africa, Spain, Sri Lanka, Sudan, Suriname, Sweden, Switzerland, Tajikistan, Thailand, the former Yugoslav Republic of Macedonia, Timor-Leste, Togo, Trinidad and Tobago, Tunisia, Turkey, Turkmenistan, Tuvalu, Uganda, Ukraine, United Arab Emirates, United Kingdom, United Republic of Tanzania, Uruguay, Uzbekistan, Vanuatu, Venezuela (Bolivarian Republic of), Viet Nam, Yemen, Zambia, Zimbabwe

Against:

None

Abstaining:

Bolivia (Plurinational State of), Brazil, Cuba, Egypt, India, Indonesia, Iran (Islamic Republic of), Mauritius, Nicaragua, Syrian Arab Republic, United States

Seventh preambular paragraph

In favour:

Afghanistan, Albania, Algeria, Andorra, Angola, Antigua and Barbuda, Argentina, Armenia, Australia, Austria, Azerbaijan, Bahamas, Bahrain, Bangladesh, Barbados, Belarus, Belgium, Belize, Benin, Bhutan, Bolivia (Plurinational State of), Bosnia and Herzegovina, Botswana, Brazil, Brunei Darussalam, Bulgaria, Burkina Faso, Burundi, Cabo Verde, Cambodia, Canada, Chile, China, Colombia, Comoros, Costa Rica, Côte d'Ivoire, Croatia, Cuba, Cyprus, Czechia, Democratic Republic of the Congo, Denmark, Djibouti, Dominican Republic, Ecuador, El Salvador, Equatorial Guinea, Eritrea, Estonia, Eswatini, Ethiopia, Fiji, Finland, France, Gambia, Georgia, Germany, Ghana, Greece, Guatemala, Guinea, Guinea-Bissau, Guyana, Haiti, Honduras, Hungary, Iceland, Indonesia, Iran (Islamic Republic of), Iraq, Ireland, Italy, Jamaica, Japan, Jordan, Kazakhstan, Kenya, Kuwait, Kyrgyzstan, Lao People's Democratic Republic, Latvia, Lebanon, Lesotho, Liberia, Libya, Liechtenstein, Lithuania, Luxembourg, Madagascar, Malawi, Malaysia, Maldives, Mali, Malta, Marshall Islands, Mauritania, Mexico, Micronesia (Federated States of), Monaco, Mongolia, Montenegro, Morocco, Mozambique, Myanmar, Namibia, Nepal, Netherlands, New Zealand, Nicaragua, Niger, Nigeria, Norway, Oman, Panama, Papua New Guinea, Paraguay, Peru, Philippines, Poland, Portugal, Qatar, Republic of Korea, Republic of Moldova, Romania, Russian Federation, Rwanda, Saint Kitts and Nevis, Saint Lucia, Saint Vincent and the Grenadines, Samoa, San Marino, Sao Tome and Principe, Saudi Arabia, Senegal, Serbia, Seychelles, Sierra Leone, Singapore, Slovakia, Slovenia, Solomon Islands, South Africa, Spain, Sri Lanka, Sudan, Suriname, Sweden, Switzerland, Tajikistan, Thailand, the former Yugoslav Republic of Macedonia, Timor-Leste, Togo, Trinidad and Tobago, Tunisia, Turkey, Turkmenistan, Tuvalu, Uganda, Ukraine, United Arab Emirates, United Kingdom, United Republic of Tanzania, Uruguay, Uzbekistan, Vanuatu, Venezuela (Bolivarian Republic of), Viet Nam, Yemen, Zambia, Zimbabwe

Against:

None

Abstaining:

Egypt, India, Israel, Mauritius, Pakistan, Syrian Arab Republic, United States

Action by the First Committee

Date:	1 November 2018	Meeting:	26th meeting
Vote:	181-1-4	Draft resolution:	A/C.1/73/L.26
	169-0-13, p.p. 4		
	170-0-9, p.p. 7		

Agenda item 108

73/87 Convention on the Prohibition of the Development, Production and Stockpiling of Bacteriological (Biological) and Toxin Weapons and on Their Destruction

Text

The General Assembly,

Recalling its previous resolutions relating to the complete and effective prohibition of bacteriological (biological) and toxin weapons and on their destruction,

Noting with satisfaction the increase in the number of ratifications of and accessions to the Convention on the Prohibition of the Development, Production and Stockpiling of Bacteriological (Biological) and Toxin Weapons and on Their Destruction,[1] and stressing at the same time that there is a continuing need to achieve its universalization,

Reaffirming its call upon all signatory States that have not yet ratified the Convention to do so without delay, and calling upon those States that have not signed the Convention to become parties thereto at the earliest possible date, thus contributing to the achievement of universal adherence to the Convention, which will facilitate its success,

Bearing in mind its call upon all States parties to the Convention to participate in the implementation of the recommendations of the review conferences of the parties to the Convention, including the exchange of information and data agreed to in the Final Declaration of the Third Review Conference of the Parties to the Convention on the Prohibition of the Development, Production and Stockpiling of Bacteriological (Biological) and Toxin Weapons and on Their Destruction, later amended by the Final Declaration of the Seventh Review Conference, and to provide such information and data in conformity with the standardized procedure to the Implementation Support Unit within the Office for Disarmament Affairs of the Secretariat on an annual basis and no later than 15 April,

Welcoming the reaffirmation made in the Final Declarations of the Fourth, Sixth, Seventh and Eighth Review Conferences that under all circumstances the use of bacteriological (biological) and toxin weapons and their development, production and stockpiling are effectively prohibited under article I of the Convention,

Recognizing the importance of ongoing efforts by States parties to enhance international cooperation, assistance and the fullest possible

---

[1] United Nations, *Treaty Series*, vol. 1015, No. 14860.

exchange of equipment, materials and scientific and technological information for the use of bacteriological (biological) agents and toxins for peaceful purposes, recognizing also that there still remain challenges to be overcome in order to enhance international cooperation, and recognizing further the value of building capacity through international cooperation as well as strengthening coordination and coherence of efforts of all relevant international organizations, in line with the Final Document of the Eighth Review Conference,[2]

Reaffirming the importance of national measures, in accordance with constitutional processes, in strengthening the implementation of the Convention by States parties, in line with the Final Document of the Eighth Review Conference,

Reaffirming also the importance of the review of developments in the field of science and technology related to the Convention,

Recalling previous intersessional processes carried out under the Convention,

Noting, in the decisions and recommendations of the Final Document, that the Eighth Review Conference decided that States parties would hold annual meetings and that the first such meeting would start on 4 December 2017, have a duration of up to five days and seek to make progress on issues of substance and process for the period before the next Review Conference, with a view to reaching consensus on an intersessional process,

Recalling the decision of the Eighth Review Conference that the Ninth Review Conference shall be held in Geneva not later than 2021,

1.   *Notes* the consensus outcome of and the decisions on all provisions of the Convention on the Prohibition of the Development, Production and Stockpiling of Bacteriological (Biological) and Toxin Weapons and on Their Destruction[1] reached at the Eighth Review Conference of the Parties to the Convention,[2] and calls upon States parties to the Convention to participate and actively engage in their continued implementation;

2.   *Notes with appreciation* that the meeting of States parties to the Convention, held in Geneva from 4 to 8 December 2017, was able to reach consensus on reaffirming previous intersessional programmes carried out during the period 2003–2015, on retaining the previous structure of annual meetings of States parties preceded by annual meetings of experts, and on reaffirming that the purpose of the intersessional programme was to discuss, and promote common understanding and effective action on, those issues identified for inclusion in the intersessional programme, and that the work of the intersessional period would be guided by the aim of strengthening the implementation of all articles of the Convention in order to better respond to current challenges;[3]

---

[2] BWC/CONF.VIII/4 and BWC/CONF.VIII/4/Corr.1.
[3] See BWC/MSP/2017/6.

3.   *Also notes with appreciation* that, in the light of the need to balance an ambition to improve the intersessional programme within the financial and human resources constraints facing States parties, 12 days were allocated to the intersessional programme each year from 2018 to 2020, that the meetings of experts for eight days would be held back to back and at least three months before the annual meetings of States parties of four days each, and that the meetings of experts would be open-ended and would consider the following topics: cooperation and assistance, with a particular focus on strengthening cooperation and assistance under article X (two days); review of developments in the field of science and technology related to the Convention (two days); strengthening national implementation (one day); assistance, response and preparedness (two days); and institutional strengthening of the Convention (one day);

4.   *Appreciates* the information and data on confidence-building measures provided by States parties to the Convention to date, and calls upon all States parties to participate in the exchange of information and data on confidence-building measures called for in the relevant decisions of the review conferences, and invites them to make use of the new platform for electronic submission, on a voluntary basis, without prejudice to their choice of methods for submission;

5.   *Notes* the decision of the Eighth Review Conference to continue and improve the database established by the Seventh Review Conference to facilitate requests for and offers of exchange of assistance and cooperation, and urges States parties to submit to the Implementation Support Unit, on a voluntary basis, requests for and offers of cooperation and assistance, including in terms of equipment, materials and scientific and technological information regarding the use of biological and toxin agents for peaceful purposes;

6.   *Encourages* States parties to provide, at least biannually, appropriate information on their implementation of article X of the Convention and to collaborate to offer assistance or training, upon request, as contained in specific proposals, in support of the legislative and other implementation measures of States parties needed to ensure their compliance with the Convention;

7.   *Notes* the decision of the Eighth Review Conference to renew the sponsorship programme established by the Seventh Review Conference in order to support and increase the participation of developing States parties in the annual meetings, welcomes the continued willingness among States parties to provide voluntary contributions, and calls upon States parties in a position to do so to offer voluntary contributions for the programme;

8.   *Also notes* the decision of the Eighth Review Conference to renew the mandate of the Implementation Support Unit agreed to at the Seventh Review Conference, mutatis mutandis, for the period from 2017 to 2021, and notes with appreciation the work of the Unit;

9.   *Notes with appreciation* the events organized by some States parties, regional organizations and the Office for Disarmament Affairs of the Secretariat for exchanges of views on the implementation of the Convention, and encourages States parties to continue to participate in such informal exchanges and discussions;

10.   *Requests* the Secretary-General to continue to render the necessary assistance to the depositary Governments of the Convention and to continue to provide such services as may be required for the conduct and the implementation of the decisions and recommendations of the review conferences;

11.   *Appreciates* that the meeting of States parties in Geneva in December 2017 considered financial matters under item 9 of its agenda, noted with concern the financial situation of the Convention on account of, inter alia, systemic issues with the current funding arrangements, as well as arrears in payment of assessed contributions, and requested the Chair of the 2018 meeting of States parties to prepare an information paper in consultation with the United Nations Office at Geneva, the Office for Disarmament Affairs of the Secretariat, the Implementation Support Unit and States parties on measures to address financial predictability and sustainability for the meetings agreed by States parties and for the Unit for review by States parties in 2018, and calls upon States parties to consider ways of addressing these serious issues as a matter of urgency, in line with paragraph 19 (f) of the report of the meeting of States parties;[3]

12.   *Decides* to include in the provisional agenda of its seventy-fourth session the item entitled "Convention on the Prohibition of the Development, Production and Stockpiling of Bacteriological (Biological) and Toxin Weapons and on Their Destruction".

Action by the General Assembly

Date: 5 December 2018	Meeting: 45th plenary meeting
Vote: Adopted without a vote	Report: A/73/517

Sponsors

Hungary

Action by the First Committee

Date: 5 November 2018	Meeting: 28th meeting
Vote: Adopted without a vote	Draft resolution: A/C.1/73/L.9

Agenda item 96

73/266 Advancing responsible State behaviour in cyberspace in the context of international security

Text

The General Assembly,

Recalling its resolutions 53/70 of 4 December 1998, 54/49 of 1 December 1999, 55/28 of 20 November 2000, 56/19 of 29 November 2001, 57/53 of 22 November 2002, 58/32 of 8 December 2003, 59/61 of 3 December 2004, 60/45 of 8 December 2005, 61/54 of 6 December 2006, 62/17 of 5 December 2007, 63/37 of 2 December 2008, 64/25 of 2 December 2009, 65/41 of 8 December 2010, 66/24 of 2 December 2011, 67/27 of 3 December 2012, 68/243 of 27 December 2013, 69/28 of 2 December 2014, 70/237 of 23 December 2015 and 71/28 of 5 December 2016, as well as its decision 72/512 of 4 December 2017,

Noting that considerable progress has been achieved in developing and applying the latest information technologies and means of telecommunication,

Affirming that it sees in this progress the broadest positive opportunities for the further development of civilization, the expansion of opportunities for cooperation for the common good of all States, the enhancement of the creative potential of humankind and additional improvements in the circulation of information in the global community,

Noting that the dissemination and use of information technologies and means affect the interests of the entire international community and that optimum effectiveness is enhanced by broad international cooperation,

Confirming that information and communications technologies are dual-use technologies and can be used for both legitimate and malicious purposes,

Stressing that it is in the interest of all States to promote the use of information and communications technologies for peaceful purposes and to prevent conflict arising from the use of information and communications technologies,

Expressing concern that these technologies and means can potentially be used for purposes that are inconsistent with the objectives of maintaining international stability and security and may adversely affect the integrity of the infrastructure of States, to the detriment of their security in both civil and military fields,

Underscoring the need for enhanced coordination and cooperation among States in combating the criminal misuse of information technologies,

Underlining the importance of respect for human rights and fundamental freedoms in the use of information and communications technologies,

Welcoming the effective work of the Group of Governmental Experts on Developments in the Field of Information and Telecommunications in the Context of International Security and the 2010,[1] 2013[2] and 2015[3] reports transmitted by the Secretary-General,

Stressing the importance of the assessments and recommendations contained in the reports of the Group of Governmental Experts,

Confirming the conclusions of the Group of Governmental Experts, in its 2013 and 2015 reports, that international law, and in particular the Charter of the United Nations, is applicable and essential to maintaining peace and stability and promoting an open, secure, stable, accessible and peaceful information and communications technology environment, that voluntary and non-binding norms, rules and principles of responsible behaviour of States in the use of information and communications technologies can reduce risks to international peace, security and stability, and that, given the unique attributes of such technologies, additional norms can be developed over time,

Confirming also the conclusions of the Group of Governmental Experts that voluntary confidence-building measures can promote trust and assurance among States and help to reduce the risk of conflict by increasing predictability and reducing misperception and thereby make an important contribution to addressing the concerns of States over the use of information and communications technologies by States and could be a significant step towards greater international security,

Confirming further the conclusions of the Group of Governmental Experts that providing assistance to build capacity in the area of information and communications technology security is also essential for international security, by improving the capacity of States for cooperation and collective action and promoting the use of such technologies for peaceful purposes,

Stressing that, while States have a primary responsibility for maintaining a secure and peaceful information and communications technology environment, effective international cooperation would benefit from identifying mechanisms for the participation, as appropriate, of the private sector, academia and civil society organizations,

1.   *Calls upon* Member States:

(a)   To be guided in their use of information and communications technologies by the 2010,[1] 2013[2] and 2015[3] reports of the Group of

---

[1] A/65/201.

[2] A/68/98.

[3] A/70/174.

Governmental Experts on Developments in the Field of Information and Telecommunications in the Context of International Security;

(b) To support the implementation of cooperative measures, as identified in the reports of the Group of Governmental Experts, to address the threats emerging in this field and ensure an open, interoperable, reliable and secure information and communications technology environment consistent with the need to preserve the free flow of information;

2. *Invites* all Member States, taking into account the assessments and recommendations contained in the reports of the Group of Governmental Experts, to continue to inform the Secretary-General of their views and assessments on the following questions:

(a) Efforts taken at the national level to strengthen information security and promote international cooperation in this field;

(b) The content of the concepts mentioned in the reports of the Group of Governmental Experts;

3. *Requests* the Secretary-General, with the assistance of a group of governmental experts, to be established in 2019 on the basis of equitable geographical distribution, proceeding from the assessments and recommendations contained in the above-mentioned reports, to continue to study, with a view to promoting common understandings and effective implementation, possible cooperative measures to address existing and potential threats in the sphere of information security, including norms, rules and principles of responsible behaviour of States, confidence-building measures and capacity-building, as well as how international law applies to the use of information and communications technologies by States, and to submit a report on the results of the study, including an annex containing national contributions of participating governmental experts on the subject of how international law applies to the use of information and communications technologies by States, to the General Assembly at its seventy-sixth session;

4. *Requests* the Office for Disarmament Affairs of the Secretariat, through existing resources and voluntary contributions, on behalf of the members of the group of governmental experts, to collaborate with relevant regional organizations, such as the African Union, the European Union, the Organization of American States, the Organization for Security and Cooperation in Europe and the Regional Forum of the Association of Southeast Asian Nations, to convene a series of consultations to share views on the issues within the mandate of the group in advance of its sessions;

5. *Requests* the Chair of the group of governmental experts to organize two two-day informal consultative meetings, open-ended so that all Member States can engage in interactive discussions and share their views, which the Chair shall convey to the group of governmental experts for consideration;

6.   *Decides* to include in the provisional agenda of its seventy-fourth session the item entitled "Developments in the field of information and telecommunications in the context of international security".

Action by the General Assembly

Date: 22 December 2018   Meeting: 65th plenary meeting
Vote: 138-12-16   Report: A/73/505

Sponsors

Australia, Austria, Belgium, Bulgaria, Canada, Croatia, Cyprus, Czechia, Denmark, Estonia, Finland, France, Georgia, Germany, Greece, Hungary, Ireland, Israel, Italy, Japan, Latvia, Lithuania, Luxembourg, Malawi, Malta, Netherlands, Poland, Portugal, Romania, Slovakia, Slovenia, Spain, Sweden, Ukraine, United Kingdom, **United States**

Co-sponsors

Albania, Chile, Democratic Republic of the Congo, Guinea, Iceland, Liechtenstein, Montenegro, New Zealand, Norway, Republic of Korea, Republic of Moldova, Samoa, Sierra Leone, the former Yugoslav Republic of Macedonia, Turkey

Recorded vote

In favour:

Afghanistan, Albania, Andorra, Argentina, Armenia, Australia, Austria, Azerbaijan, Bahamas, Bahrain, Bangladesh, Barbados, Belgium, Belize, Benin, Bhutan, Bosnia and Herzegovina, Brazil, Brunei Darussalam, Bulgaria, Burkina Faso, Canada, Chile, Colombia, Costa Rica, Croatia, Cyprus, Czechia, Denmark, Djibouti, Dominican Republic, Ecuador, El Salvador, Eritrea, Estonia, Ethiopia, Fiji, Finland, France, Georgia, Germany, Ghana, Greece, Grenada, Guatemala, Guinea, Guyana, Haiti, Honduras, Hungary, Iceland, India, Indonesia, Iraq, Ireland, Israel, Italy, Jamaica, Japan, Jordan, Kazakhstan, Kenya, Kuwait, Latvia, Lebanon, Lesotho, Liberia, Libya, Liechtenstein, Lithuania, Luxembourg, Madagascar, Malaysia, Maldives, Mali, Malta, Marshall Islands, Mauritania, Mauritius, Mexico, Micronesia (Federated States of), Monaco, Mongolia, Montenegro, Morocco, Nepal, Netherlands, New Zealand, Nigeria, Norway, Oman, Panama, Paraguay, Peru, Philippines, Poland, Portugal, Qatar, Republic of Korea, Republic of Moldova, Romania, Saint Kitts and Nevis, Saint Lucia, Saint Vincent and the Grenadines, San Marino, Sao Tome and Principe, Saudi Arabia, Serbia, Sierra Leone, Singapore, Slovakia, Slovenia, Solomon Islands, Somalia, South Africa, Spain, Sri Lanka, Sudan, Sweden, Switzerland, Tajikistan, Thailand, the former Yugoslav Republic of Macedonia, Timor-Leste, Togo, Trinidad and Tobago, Tunisia, Turkey, Ukraine, United Arab

Emirates, United Kingdom, United Republic of Tanzania, United States, Uruguay, Uzbekistan, Vanuatu, Viet Nam, Yemen

Against:

Bolivia (Plurinational State of), China, Comoros, Cuba, Democratic People's Republic of Korea, Egypt, Iran (Islamic Republic of), Nicaragua, Russian Federation, Syrian Arab Republic, Venezuela (Bolivarian Republic of), Zimbabwe

Abstaining:

Algeria, Belarus, Botswana, Cambodia, Cameroon, Côte d'Ivoire, Equatorial Guinea, Lao People's Democratic Republic, Malawi, Mozambique, Myanmar, Namibia, Pakistan, Palau, Papua New Guinea, Senegal

Action by the First Committee

Date: 8 November 2018	Meeting: 31st meeting
Vote: 139-11-18	Draft resolution: A/C.1/73/L.37

DECISIONS

Agenda item 95

73/511 Maintenance of international security — good-neighbourliness, stability and development in South-Eastern Europe

Text

The General Assembly decides to include in the provisional agenda of its seventy-fifth session the item entitled "Maintenance of international security — good-neighbourliness, stability and development in South-Eastern Europe".

Action by the General Assembly

Date: 5 December 2018　　Meeting: 45th plenary meeting
Vote: Adopted without a vote　Report: A/73/504

Sponsors

The former Yugoslav Republic of Macedonia

Action by the First Committee

Date: 8 November 2018　　Meeting: 30th meeting
Vote: Adopted without a vote　Draft decision: A/C.1/73/L.47

Agenda item 99 (c)

73/512 Further practical measures for the prevention of an arms race in outer space

Text

The General Assembly, recalling its resolution 72/250 of 24 December 2017 and other resolutions on this matter, decides:

(a) To welcome the commencement of the work of the United Nations Group of Governmental Experts tasked with considering and making recommendations on substantial elements of an international legally binding instrument on the prevention of an arms race in outer space, including, inter alia, on the prevention of the placement of weapons in outer space;

(b) To welcome the discussions in subsidiary body 3 of the Conference on Disarmament on the prevention of an arms race in outer space;

(c) To include in the provisional agenda of its seventy-fourth session, under the item entitled "Prevention of an arms race in outer space", the sub-item entitled "Further practical measures for the prevention of an arms race in outer space".

Action by the General Assembly

Date: 5 December 2018   Meeting: 45th plenary meeting
Vote: 128-3-48   Report: A/73/508

Sponsors

Algeria, Bolivia (Plurinational State of), Brazil, Burundi, **China**, Cuba, Egypt, Iran (Islamic Republic of), Kazakhstan, Lao People's Democratic Republic, Malawi, Myanmar, Namibia, Nicaragua, Nigeria, **Russian Federation**, South Africa, Suriname, Syrian Arab Republic, Uganda, Venezuela (Bolivarian Republic of), Zambia, Zimbabwe

Co-sponsors

Armenia, Belarus, Ecuador, Eritrea, Guinea, Indonesia, Kyrgyzstan, Seychelles, Sierra Leone, Tajikistan, Uzbekistan

Recorded vote

In favour:

Afghanistan, Algeria, Angola, Antigua and Barbuda, Argentina, Armenia, Azerbaijan, Bahamas, Bahrain, Bangladesh, Barbados, Belarus, Belize, Benin, Bhutan, Bolivia (Plurinational State of), Botswana, Brazil, Brunei Darussalam, Burkina Faso, Burundi, Cabo Verde, Cambodia, Central African Republic, Chile, China, Colombia, Comoros, Congo, Costa Rica, Côte d'Ivoire, Cuba, Democratic People's Republic of Korea,

Democratic Republic of the Congo, Djibouti, Dominican Republic, Ecuador, Egypt, El Salvador, Equatorial Guinea, Eritrea, Eswatini, Ethiopia, Fiji, Gambia, Ghana, Grenada, Guatemala, Guinea, Guinea-Bissau, Guyana, Honduras, India, Indonesia, Iran (Islamic Republic of), Iraq, Jamaica, Jordan, Kazakhstan, Kenya, Kuwait, Kyrgyzstan, Lao People's Democratic Republic, Lebanon, Lesotho, Liberia, Libya, Madagascar, Malawi, Malaysia, Maldives, Mali, Mauritania, Mauritius, Mexico, Mongolia, Morocco, Mozambique, Myanmar, Namibia, Nauru, Nepal, Nicaragua, Niger, Nigeria, Oman, Pakistan, Panama, Papua New Guinea, Paraguay, Peru, Philippines, Qatar, Russian Federation, Rwanda, Saint Lucia, Saint Vincent and the Grenadines, Samoa, Sao Tome and Principe, Saudi Arabia, Senegal, Serbia, Seychelles, Sierra Leone, Singapore, South Africa, South Sudan, Sri Lanka, Sudan, Suriname, Switzerland, Syrian Arab Republic, Tajikistan, Thailand, Togo, Trinidad and Tobago, Tunisia, Tuvalu, Uganda, United Arab Emirates, United Republic of Tanzania, Uruguay, Vanuatu, Venezuela (Bolivarian Republic of), Viet Nam, Yemen, Zambia, Zimbabwe

Against:

Israel, Ukraine, United States

Abstaining:

Albania, Andorra, Australia, Austria, Belgium, Bosnia and Herzegovina, Bulgaria, Cameroon, Canada, Croatia, Cyprus, Czechia, Denmark, Estonia, Finland, France, Georgia, Germany, Greece, Hungary, Iceland, Ireland, Italy, Japan, Latvia, Liechtenstein, Lithuania, Luxembourg, Malta, Monaco, Montenegro, Netherlands, New Zealand, Norway, Palau, Poland, Portugal, Republic of Korea, Republic of Moldova, Romania, San Marino, Slovakia, Slovenia, Spain, Sweden, the former Yugoslav Republic of Macedonia, Turkey, United Kingdom

Action by the First Committee

Date: 5 November 2018		Meeting:	28th meeting
Vote: 127-3-49		Draft decision:	A/C.1/73/L.50

Agenda item 101 (t)

73/513 Missiles

Text

The General Assembly, recalling its resolutions 54/54 F of 1 December 1999, 55/33 A of 20 November 2000, 56/24 B of 29 November 2001, 57/71 of 22 November 2002, 58/37 of 8 December 2003, 59/67 of 3 December 2004, 61/59 of 6 December 2006 and 63/55 of 2 December 2008 and its decisions 60/515 of 8 December 2005, 62/514 of 5 December 2007, 65/517 of 8 December 2010, 66/516 of 2 December 2011, 67/516 of 3 December 2012, 68/517 of 5 December 2013, 69/517 of 2 December 2014 and 71/516 of 5 December 2016, decides to include in the provisional agenda of its seventy-fifth session the item entitled "Missiles".

Action by the General Assembly

Date: 5 December 2018   Meeting: 45th plenary meeting
Vote: 174-2-7   Report: A/73/510

Sponsors

Egypt, Indonesia, **Iran (Islamic Republic of)**

Recorded vote

In favour:

Afghanistan, Albania, Algeria, Andorra, Angola, Antigua and Barbuda, Argentina, Armenia, Austria, Azerbaijan, Bahamas, Bahrain, Bangladesh, Barbados, Belarus, Belgium, Belize, Benin, Bhutan, Bolivia (Plurinational State of), Bosnia and Herzegovina, Botswana, Brazil, Brunei Darussalam, Bulgaria, Burkina Faso, Burundi, Cabo Verde, Cambodia, Cameroon, Canada, Central African Republic, Chile, China, Colombia, Comoros, Congo, Costa Rica, Côte d'Ivoire, Croatia, Cuba, Cyprus, Czechia, Democratic People's Republic of Korea, Democratic Republic of the Congo, Denmark, Djibouti, Dominica, Dominican Republic, Ecuador, Egypt, El Salvador, Equatorial Guinea, Eritrea, Estonia, Eswatini, Ethiopia, Finland, France, Gabon, Gambia, Georgia, Germany, Ghana, Greece, Grenada, Guatemala, Guinea, Guinea-Bissau, Guyana, Hungary, Iceland, India, Indonesia, Iran (Islamic Republic of), Iraq, Ireland, Italy, Jamaica, Jordan, Kazakhstan, Kenya, Kuwait, Kyrgyzstan, Lao People's Democratic Republic, Latvia, Lebanon, Lesotho, Liberia, Libya, Liechtenstein, Lithuania, Luxembourg, Madagascar, Malawi, Malaysia, Maldives, Mali, Malta, Mauritania, Mauritius, Mexico, Monaco, Mongolia, Montenegro, Morocco, Mozambique, Myanmar, Namibia, Nepal, Netherlands, New Zealand, Nicaragua, Niger, Nigeria, Norway, Oman, Pakistan, Panama,

Papua New Guinea, Paraguay, Peru, Philippines, Poland, Portugal, Qatar, Republic of Korea, Republic of Moldova, Romania, Russian Federation, Rwanda, Saint Kitts and Nevis, Saint Lucia, Saint Vincent and the Grenadines, Samoa, San Marino, Sao Tome and Principe, Saudi Arabia, Senegal, Serbia, Seychelles, Sierra Leone, Singapore, Slovakia, Slovenia, Solomon Islands, South Africa, Spain, Sri Lanka, Sudan, Suriname, Sweden, Switzerland, Syrian Arab Republic, Tajikistan, Thailand, the former Yugoslav Republic of Macedonia, Togo, Trinidad and Tobago, Tunisia, Turkey, Uganda, Ukraine, United Arab Emirates, United Kingdom, United Republic of Tanzania, Uruguay, Uzbekistan, Vanuatu, Venezuela (Bolivarian Republic of), Viet Nam, Yemen, Zambia, Zimbabwe

Against:
Israel, United States

Abstaining:
Australia, Fiji, Haiti, Honduras, Japan, Palau, Tonga

Action by the First Committee

Date: 1 November 2018   Meeting: 26th meeting
Vote: 166-2-9   Draft decision: A/C.1/73/L.10

Agenda item 101 (nn)

73/514 Nuclear disarmament verification

Text

The General Assembly, recalling its resolution 71/67 of 5 December 2016 and its decision 72/514 of 4 December 2017, and noting that the group of governmental experts on nuclear disarmament verification has commenced its work, decides to include in the provisional agenda of its seventy-fourth session, under the item entitled "General and complete disarmament", the sub-item entitled "Nuclear disarmament verification".

Action by the General Assembly

Date: 5 December 2018   Meeting: 45th plenary meeting
Vote: 181-0-2   Report: A/73/510

Sponsors

Chile, Finland, Mexico, Morocco, Netherlands, **Norway**, Switzerland, United Kingdom

Recorded vote

In favour:

Afghanistan, Albania, Algeria, Andorra, Angola, Antigua and Barbuda, Argentina, Armenia, Australia, Austria, Azerbaijan, Bahamas, Bahrain, Bangladesh, Barbados, Belarus, Belgium, Belize, Benin, Bhutan, Bolivia (Plurinational State of), Bosnia and Herzegovina, Botswana, Brazil, Brunei Darussalam, Bulgaria, Burkina Faso, Burundi, Cabo Verde, Cambodia, Canada, Central African Republic, Chile, China, Colombia, Comoros, Costa Rica, Côte d'Ivoire, Croatia, Cuba, Cyprus, Czechia, Democratic Republic of the Congo, Denmark, Djibouti, Dominica, Dominican Republic, Ecuador, Egypt, El Salvador, Equatorial Guinea, Eritrea, Estonia, Eswatini, Ethiopia, Fiji, Finland, France, Gabon, Gambia, Georgia, Germany, Ghana, Greece, Grenada, Guatemala, Guinea, Guinea-Bissau, Guyana, Haiti, Honduras, Hungary, Iceland, India, Indonesia, Iraq, Ireland, Israel, Italy, Jamaica, Japan, Jordan, Kazakhstan, Kenya, Kuwait, Kyrgyzstan, Lao People's Democratic Republic, Latvia, Lebanon, Lesotho, Liberia, Libya, Liechtenstein, Lithuania, Luxembourg, Madagascar, Malawi, Malaysia, Maldives, Mali, Malta, Marshall Islands, Mauritania, Mauritius, Mexico, Micronesia (Federated States of), Monaco, Mongolia, Montenegro, Morocco, Mozambique, Myanmar, Namibia, Nepal, Netherlands, New Zealand, Nicaragua, Niger, Nigeria, Norway, Oman, Pakistan, Palau, Panama, Papua New Guinea, Paraguay, Peru, Philippines, Poland, Portugal, Qatar, Republic of Korea, Republic of Moldova, Romania, Russian

Federation, Rwanda, Saint Kitts and Nevis, Saint Lucia, Saint Vincent and the Grenadines, Samoa, San Marino, Sao Tome and Principe, Saudi Arabia, Senegal, Serbia, Seychelles, Sierra Leone, Singapore, Slovakia, Slovenia, Solomon Islands, South Africa, Spain, Sri Lanka, Sudan, Suriname, Sweden, Switzerland, Tajikistan, Thailand, the former Yugoslav Republic of Macedonia, Timor-Leste, Togo, Trinidad and Tobago, Tunisia, Turkey, Tuvalu, Uganda, Ukraine, United Arab Emirates, United Kingdom, United Republic of Tanzania, United States, Uruguay, Uzbekistan, Vanuatu, Venezuela (Bolivarian Republic of), Viet Nam, Yemen, Zambia, Zimbabwe

Against:
    None

Abstaining:
    Iran (Islamic Republic of), Syrian Arab Republic

Action by the First Committee

Date:	1 November 2018	Meeting:	26th meeting
Vote:	177-0-3	Draft decision:	A/C.1/73/L.31

Agenda item 104

73/546 Convening a conference on the establishment of a Middle East zone free of nuclear weapons and other weapons of mass destruction

Text

The General Assembly decides:

(a)   To entrust to the Secretary-General the convening, no later than 2019 for a duration of one week at United Nations Headquarters, of a conference on the establishment of a Middle East zone free of nuclear weapons and other weapons of mass destruction, to which all States of the Middle East,[1] the three co-sponsors of the resolution on the Middle East adopted by the 1995 Review and Extension Conference of the Parties to the Treaty on the Non-Proliferation of Nuclear Weapons,[2] in the light of their responsibility for the implementation of that resolution, the other two nuclear-weapon States and the relevant international organizations shall be invited, provided that:

(i)   The conference shall take as its terms of reference the resolution on the Middle East adopted by the 1995 Review and Extension Conference;

(ii)   The conference shall aim at elaborating a legally binding treaty establishing a Middle East zone free of nuclear weapons and other weapons of mass destruction, on the basis of arrangements freely arrived at by the States of the region;

(b)   To affirm the special responsibility of the three co-sponsors of the resolution on the Middle East adopted by the 1995 Review and Extension Conference, as the depository States of the Treaty on the Non-Proliferation of Nuclear Weapons,[3] and to call upon them to fulfil their relevant obligations in accordance with the agreed outcomes of the 1995, 2000 and 2010 Review Conferences;

(c)   To request the International Atomic Energy Agency, the Organisation for the Prohibition of Chemical Weapons and the Biological Weapons Convention Implementation Support Unit to prepare the background documents necessary for the conference;

(d)   To request the Secretary-General to convene annual sessions of the conference for a duration of one week at United Nations Headquarters until the conference concludes the elaboration of a legally binding treaty

---

[1] See the report by the Director General of the International Atomic Energy Agency on the application of Agency safeguards in the Middle East (GOV/2018/38-GC(62)/6).

[2] See *1995 Review and Extension Conference of the Parties to the Treaty on the Non-Proliferation of Nuclear Weapons, Final Document, Part I* (NPT/CONF.1995/32 (Part I) and NPT/CONF.1995/32 (Part I)/Corr.2), annex.

[3] United Nations, *Treaty Series*, vol. 729, No. 10485.

establishing a Middle East zone free of nuclear weapons and other weapons of mass destruction;

(e) To also request the Secretary-General to report annually to the General Assembly on developments in this regard.

Action by the General Assembly

Date: 22 December 2018   Meeting: 65th plenary meeting
Vote: 88-4-75   Report: A/73/513

Sponsors

Algeria, Bahrain, Comoros, Djibouti, **Egypt** (on behalf of the States Members of the United Nations that are members of the League of Arab States), Iraq, Jordan, Kuwait, Lebanon, Libya, Mauritania, Morocco, Oman, Qatar, Saudi Arabia, Somalia, Sudan, Tunisia, United Arab Emirates, Yemen, State of Palestine

Recorded vote

In favour:

Afghanistan, Algeria, Azerbaijan, Bahrain, Bangladesh, Belarus, Belize, Benin, Bhutan, Bolivia (Plurinational State of), Botswana, Brunei Darussalam, Burkina Faso, Cabo Verde, Cambodia, Chile, China, Comoros, Costa Rica, Cuba, Democratic People's Republic of Korea, Djibouti, Dominican Republic, Ecuador, Egypt, El Salvador, Eritrea, Ghana, Guatemala, Guinea, Guyana, Indonesia, Iran (Islamic Republic of), Iraq, Jamaica, Jordan, Kazakhstan, Kenya, Kuwait, Kyrgyzstan, Lao People's Democratic Republic, Lebanon, Lesotho, Libya, Madagascar, Malaysia, Maldives, Mali, Mauritania, Mauritius, Mongolia, Morocco, Mozambique, Myanmar, Namibia, Nicaragua, Nigeria, Oman, Pakistan, Paraguay, Peru, Philippines, Qatar, Russian Federation, Saint Kitts and Nevis, Saint Lucia, Saint Vincent and the Grenadines, Saudi Arabia, Senegal, Singapore, Somalia, South Africa, Sri Lanka, Sudan, Syrian Arab Republic, Tajikistan, Thailand, Tonga, Trinidad and Tobago, Tunisia, Turkmenistan, United Arab Emirates, United Republic of Tanzania, Uzbekistan, Venezuela (Bolivarian Republic of), Viet Nam, Yemen, Zimbabwe

Against:

Israel, Liberia, Micronesia (Federated States of), United States

Abstaining:

Albania, Andorra, Argentina, Australia, Austria, Bahamas, Belgium, Bosnia and Herzegovina, Brazil, Bulgaria, Cameroon, Canada, Chad, Colombia, Côte d'Ivoire, Croatia, Cyprus, Czechia, Democratic Republic of the Congo, Denmark, Equatorial Guinea, Estonia, Ethiopia, Fiji, Finland, France, Georgia, Germany, Greece, Haiti, Honduras,

Hungary, Iceland, India, Ireland, Italy, Japan, Latvia, Liechtenstein, Lithuania, Luxembourg, Malawi, Malta, Mexico, Monaco, Montenegro, Nepal, Netherlands, New Zealand, Norway, Panama, Papua New Guinea, Poland, Portugal, Republic of Korea, Republic of Moldova, Romania, San Marino, Sao Tome and Principe, Serbia, Slovakia, Slovenia, Solomon Islands, Spain, Sweden, Switzerland, the former Yugoslav Republic of Macedonia, Timor-Leste, Togo, Turkey, Tuvalu, Ukraine, United Kingdom, Uruguay, Vanuatu

Action by the First Committee

Date:	1 November 2018	Meeting:	26th meeting
Vote:	103-3-71	Draft decision:	A/C.1/73/L.22/Rev.1

ANNEX

List of reports and notes of the Secretary-General

Agenda item 94	**African Nuclear-Weapon-Free Zone Treaty**
Agenda item 95	**Maintenance of international security — good-neighbourliness, stability and development in South-Eastern Europe**
Agenda item 96	**Developments in the field of information and telecommunications in the context of international security**
Agenda item 97	**Establishment of a nuclear-weapon-free zone in the region of the Middle East**
A/73/182 (Part I)	Establishment of a nuclear-weapon-free zone in the region of the Middle East: Report of the Secretary-General (Part I)
Agenda item 98	**Conclusion of effective international arrangements to assure non-nuclear-weapon States against the use or threat of use of nuclear weapons**
A/73/27	Report of the Conference on Disarmament (Suppl. No. 27)
Agenda item 99	**Prevention of an arms race in outer space**
(a)	*Prevention of an arms race in outer space*
A/73/27	Report of the Conference on Disarmament (Suppl. No. 27)
(b)	*No first placement of weapons in outer space*
(c)	*Further practical measures for the prevention of an arms race in outer space*
Agenda item 100	**Role of science and technology in the context of international security and disarmament**
A/73/177	Current developments in science and technology and their potential impact on international security and disarmament efforts: Report of the Secretary-General

Agenda item 101	**General and complete disarmament**
A/73/185	United Nations Register of Conventional Arms: Report of the Secretary-General
(a)	*Treaty banning the production of fissile material for nuclear weapons or other nuclear explosive devices*
A/73/159	Report of the high-level fissile material cut-off treaty expert preparatory group: Note by the Secretary-General
(b)	*Nuclear disarmament*
A/73/116	Nuclear disarmament; follow-up to the advisory opinion of the International Court of Justice on the legality of the threat or use of nuclear weapons; reducing nuclear danger: Report of the Secretary-General
(c)	*Notification of nuclear tests*
(d)	*Relationship between disarmament and development*
A/73/117	Relationship between disarmament and development: Report of the Secretary-General
(e)	*Regional disarmament*
(f)	*Conventional arms control at the regional and subregional levels*
A/73/114	Conventional arms control at the regional and subregional levels: Report of the Secretary-General
(g)	*Convening of the fourth special session of the General Assembly devoted to disarmament*
(h)	*Observance of environmental norms in the drafting and implementation of agreements on disarmament and arms control*
A/73/92	Observance of environmental norms in the drafting and implementation of agreements on disarmament and arms control: Report of the Secretary-General
(i)	*Follow-up to the advisory opinion of the International Court of Justice on the legality of the threat or use of nuclear weapons*

A/73/116	Nuclear disarmament; follow-up to the advisory opinion of the International Court of Justice on the legality of the threat or use of nuclear weapons; reducing nuclear danger: Report of the Secretary-General
(j)	*Consolidation of peace through practical disarmament measures*
A/73/168	The illicit trade in small arms and light weapons in all its aspects, assistance to States for curbing the illicit traffic in small arms and light weapons and collecting them, and consolidation of peace through practical disarmament measures: Report of the Secretary-General
(k)	*Implementation of the Convention on the Prohibition of the Development, Production, Stockpiling and Use of Chemical Weapons and on Their Destruction*
A/73/97	Cooperation between the United Nations and the Organization for the Prohibition of Chemical Weapons: Note by the Secretary-General
(l)	*Measures to uphold the authority of the 1925 Geneva Protocol*
A/73/91	Measures to uphold the authority of the 1925 Geneva Protocol: Report of the Secretary-General
(m)	*Implementation of the Convention on the Prohibition of the Use, Stockpiling, Production and Transfer of Antipersonnel Mines and on Their Destruction*
(n)	*Assistance to States for curbing the illicit traffic in small arms and light weapons and collecting them*
A/73/168	The illicit trade in small arms and light weapons in all its aspects, assistance to States for curbing the illicit traffic in small arms and light weapons and collecting them, and consolidation of peace through practical disarmament measures: Report of the Secretary-General
(o)	*Treaty on a Nuclear-Weapon-Free Zone in Central Asia*

(p)	*Reducing nuclear danger*
A/73/116	Nuclear disarmament; follow-up to the advisory opinion of the International Court of Justice on the legality of the threat or use of nuclear weapons; reducing nuclear danger: Report of the Secretary-General
(q)	*The illicit trade in small arms and light weapons in all its aspects*
A/73/168	The illicit trade in small arms and light weapons in all its aspects, assistance to States for curbing the illicit traffic in small arms and light weapons and collecting them, and consolidation of peace through practical disarmament measures: Report of the Secretary-General
(r)	*Towards a nuclear-weapon-free world: accelerating the implementation of nuclear disarmament commitments*
(s)	*Mongolia's international security and nuclear-weapon-free status*
A/73/202	Mongolia's international security and nuclear-weapon-free status: Report of the Secretary-General
(t)	*Missiles*
(u)	*Disarmament and non-proliferation education*
A/73/119	Disarmament and non-proliferation education: Report of the Secretary-General
(v)	*Promotion of multilateralism in the area of disarmament and non-proliferation*
A/73/95	Promotion of multilateralism in the area of disarmament and non-proliferation: Report of the Secretary-General
(w)	*Measures to prevent terrorists from acquiring weapons of mass destruction*
A/73/112	Measures to prevent terrorists from acquiring weapons of mass destruction: Report of the Secretary-General

(x)	*Confidence-building measures in the regional and subregional context*
A/73/96	Confidence-building measures in the regional and subregional context: Report of the Secretary-General
(y)	*The Hague Code of Conduct against Ballistic Missile Proliferation*
(z)	*Information on confidence-building measures in the field of conventional arms*
(aa)	*Transparency and confidence-building measures in outer space activities*
(bb)	*The Arms Trade Treaty*
(cc)	*Effects of the use of armaments and ammunitions containing depleted uranium*
A/73/99	Effects of the use of armaments and ammunitions containing depleted uranium: Report of the Secretary-General
(dd)	*Preventing the acquisition by terrorists of radioactive sources*
(ee)	*United action towards the total elimination of nuclear weapons*
(ff)	*Preventing and combating illicit brokering activities*
(gg)	*Women, disarmament, non-proliferation and arms control*
A/73/115	Women, disarmament, non-proliferation and arms control: Report of the Secretary-General
(hh)	*Follow-up to the 2013 high-level meeting of the General Assembly on nuclear disarmament*
A/73/122	Follow-up to the 2013 high-level meeting of the General Assembly on nuclear disarmament: Report of the Secretary-General
(ii)	*Countering the threat posed by improvised explosive devices*

A/73/156	Countering the threat posed by improvised explosive devices: Report of the Secretary-General
(jj)	*Humanitarian consequences of nuclear weapons*
(kk)	*Ethical imperatives for a nuclear-weapon-free world*
(ll)	*Implementation of the Convention on Cluster Munitions*
(mm)	*Universal Declaration on the Achievement of a Nuclear-Weapon-Free World*
A/73/118	Universal Declaration on the Achievement of a Nuclear-Weapon-Free World: Report of the Secretary-General
(nn)	*Nuclear disarmament verification*
(oo)	*Treaty on the Prohibition of Nuclear Weapons*
Agenda item 102	**Review and implementation of the Concluding Document of the Twelfth Special Session of the General Assembly**
(a)	*United Nations disarmament fellowship, training and advisory services*
A/73/113	United Nations disarmament fellowship, training and advisory services programme: Report of the Secretary-General
(b)	*Convention on the Prohibition of the Use of Nuclear Weapons*
A/73/27	Report of the Conference on Disarmament (Suppl. No. 27)
(c)	*United Nations Regional Centre for Peace and Disarmament in Africa*
A/73/151	United Nations Regional Centre for Peace and Disarmament in Africa: Report of the Secretary-General
(d)	*United Nations Regional Centre for Peace, Disarmament and Development in Latin America and the Caribbean*

A/73/127	United Nations Regional Centre for Peace, Disarmament and Development in Latin America and the Caribbean: Report of the Secretary-General
(e)	*United Nations Regional Centre for Peace and Disarmament in Asia and the Pacific*
A/73/126	United Nations Regional Centre for Peace and Disarmament in Asia and the Pacific: Report of the Secretary-General
(f)	*Regional confidence-building measures: activities of the United Nations Standing Advisory Committee on Security Questions in Central Africa*
A/73/224	Regional confidence-building measures: activities of the United Nations Standing Advisory Committee on Security Questions in Central Africa: Report of the Secretary-General
(g)	*United Nations Disarmament Information Programme*
A/73/120	United Nations Disarmament Information Programme: Report of the Secretary-General
Agenda item 103	**Review of the implementation of the recommendations and decisions adopted by the General Assembly at its tenth special session**
A/73/284	Thirty-fifth anniversary of the United Nations Institute for Disarmament Research: Report of the Secretary-General
A/73/256	Report of the Director of the United Nations Institute for Disarmament Research: Note by the Secretary-General
(a)	*Report of the Conference on Disarmament*
A/73/259	Work of the Advisory Board on Disarmament Matters: Report of the Secretary-General
A/73/27	Report of the Conference on Disarmament (Suppl. No. 27)
(b)	*Report of the Disarmament Commission*
A/73/42	Report of the Disarmament Commission for 2018 (Suppl. No. 42)

Agenda item 104	**The risk of nuclear proliferation in the Middle East**
A/73/182 (Part II)	Risk of nuclear proliferation in the Middle East: Report of the Secretary-General (Part II)
Agenda item 105	**Convention on Prohibitions or Restrictions on the Use of Certain Conventional Weapons Which May Be Deemed to Be Excessively Injurious or to Have Indiscriminate Effects**
Agenda item 106	**Strengthening of security and cooperation in the Mediterranean region**
A/73/94	Strengthening of security and cooperation in the Mediterranean region: Report of the Secretary-General
Agenda item 107	**Comprehensive Nuclear-Test-Ban Treaty**
Agenda item 108	**Convention on the Prohibition of the Development, Production and Stockpiling of Bacteriological (Biological) and Toxin Weapons and on Their Destruction**